the Complete Handbook of Novel Writing

Everything you need to know about creating & selling your work

THE EDITORS OF WRITER'S DIGEST

WRITER'S DIGEST
BOOKS

WritersDigest.*com*
Cincinnati, Ohio

For more resources for writers, visit www.writersdigest.com/books.

To receive a free weekly e-mail newsletter delivering tips and updates about writing and about Writer's Digest products, register directly at http://newsletters. fwpublications.com.

14 13 12 11 10   5 4 3 2 1

Distributed in Canada by Fraser Direct
100 Armstrong Avenue
Georgetown, Ontario, Canada L7G 5S4
Tel: (905) 877-4411

Distributed in the U.K. and Europe by David & Charles
Brunel House, Newton Abbot, Devon, TQ12 4PU, England
Tel: (+44) 1626-323200, Fax: (+44) 1626-323319
E-mail: postmaster@davidandcharles.co.uk

Distributed in Australia by Capricorn Link
P.O. Box 704, Windsor, NSW 2756 Australia
Tel: (02) 4577-3555

Library of Congress Cataloging-in-Publication Data
The complete handbook of novel writing / the editors of Writer's Digest Books.
-- 2nd ed.
    p. cm.
  ISBN 978-1-58297-958-8 (pbk. : alk. paper)
  1. Fiction--Authorship--Handbooks, manuals, etc. I. Writer's Digest Books
(Firm)
  PN3365.C65 2010
  808.3--dc22   2010014528

Designed by: Terri Woesner
Edited by: Melissa Hill
Production coordinated by: Mark Griffin

TABLE OF CONTENTS

Part One
THE ART AND CRAFT OF A STRONG NARRATIVE

Part Two
THE WRITING PROCESS

Part Three
EXPLORING NOVEL GENRES

Part Four

FINDING & CULTIVATING A MARKET FOR YOUR WORK

Part Five
INTERVIEWS WITH NOVELISTS

Part One

THE ART AND CRAFT OF A STRONG NARRATIVE

BEST-SELLING ADVICE: Inspiration & Ideas

"If you stuff yourself full of poems, essays, plays, stories, novels, films, comic strips, magazines, music, you automatically explode every morning like Old Faithful. I have never had a dry spell in my life, mainly because I feed myself well, to the point of bursting. I wake early and hear my morning voices leaping around in my head like jumping beans. I get out of bed quickly, to trap them before they escape." —Ray Bradbury

"Every idea is my last. I feel sure of it. So, I try to do the best with each as it comes and that's where my responsibility ends. But I just don't wait for ideas. I look for them. Constantly. And if I don't use the ideas that I find, they're going to quit showing up." —Peg Bracken

"Good writing is remembering detail. Most people want to forget. Don't forget things that were painful or embarrassing or silly. Turn them into a story that tells the truth." —Paula Danziger

"Don't put down too many roots in terms of a domicile. I have lived in four countries and I think my life as a writer and our family's life have been enriched by this. I think a writer has to experience new environments. There is that adage: No man can really succeed if he doesn't move away from where he was born. I believe it is particularly true for the writer." —Arthur Hailey

"A writer need not devour a whole sheep in order to know what mutton tastes like, but he must at least eat a chop. Unless he gets his facts right, his imagination will lead him into all kinds of nonsense, and the facts he is most likely to get right are the facts of his own experience." —W. Somerset Maugham

"Sit and quiet yourself. Luxuriate in a certain memory and the details will come. Let the images flow. You'll be amazed at what will come out on paper. I'm still learning what it is about the past that I want to write. I don't worry about it. It will emerge. It will insist on being told." —Frank McCourt

"My advice is not to wait to be struck by an idea. If you're a writer, you sit down and damn well decide to have an idea. That's the way to get an idea." —Andy Rooney

"I have never felt like I was creating anything. For me, writing is like walking through a desert and all at once, poking up through the hardpan, I see the top of a chimney. I know there's a house under there, and I'm pretty sure that I can dig it up if I want. That's how I feel. It's like the stories are already there. What they pay me for is the leap of faith that says: 'If I sit down and do this, everything will come out okay.'" —Stephen King

"As writers we live life twice, like a cow that eats its food once and then re-gurgitates it to chew and digest it again. We have a second chance at biting into our experience and examining it. ... This is our life and it's not going to last forever. There isn't time to talk about someday writing that short story or poem or novel. Slow down now, touch what is around you, and out of care and compassion for each moment and detail, put pen to paper and begin to write." —Natalie Goldberg

CHAPTER 1

TAMING THE BEAST

BY N.M. KELBY

After Truman Capote nearly destroyed himself writing his groundbreaking bestseller *In Cold Blood* in 1965, he was quoted as saying that his next book, a novel tentatively titled *Answered Prayers*, would be easy by comparison. "It's all in my head!"

And that was the problem. Capote was a perfectionist, and the novel in his head was an untamed beast. His standards were so impossibly high that when he died in 1984, he'd spent the better part of nineteen years writing, rewriting, missing deadlines, publishing excerpts, drinking himself into a frenzy—and never finishing the work.

What writer hasn't had a difficult time putting an idea into words—especially an idea for something as complex as a novel? I often have a million ideas bouncing around in my head like puppies at the pound. I want to write about themes of love, usually reckless love, and mystery. I want to be profound and funny, too. I want to take readers to places they've never imagined and make them feel things they haven't felt before. And, to top it all off, I want to make the words themselves do extraordinary things—to, for instance, evoke the precise sound of an ancient jazz quartet playing a Sunday brunch in the wrong end of the French Quarter.

Of course, I also want the resulting work to be a bestseller.

Sound familiar?

The desire to write The Great American Novel is like an overactive beast that needs obedience school. If you've ever had a dog, you know what I mean. Dogs are pack animals. You're supposed to be the leader. You're supposed to be in charge. If you're not, you're in trouble. Dogs will run wild unless you focus them with a calm, centered mind, an assertive hand, and a strong sense of purpose.

The same is true with your novel. Ideas often start with boundless energy, vying for your attention. But when you get them on the page, they don't always live up to how you thought they would be. A plot line feels contrived. An emotion falls flat. When this happens, you can easily feel defeated. You work and rework a paragraph or chapter, and it just doesn't feel like it's doing all the things you need it to do. When your ideas run wild, it's too easy for them to frustrate and eventually overwhelm you. And this is where many writers give up. But you shouldn't.

You just need to learn how to tame your beast.

ESTABLISH A CALM, CENTERED MIND

The television is blaring. Your loved one has no idea where the car keys are. Your neighbor is giving salsa lessons in his backyard. You live in a swirl of noise and confusion, so how are you supposed to be focused enough to cultivate a quiet place within you to write? Easy. Take out a rolled-up newspaper and whack your world on its hindquarters—not hard, but just enough to get everyone's attention, including your own. Nonexistent boundaries, unfocused expectations, and lack of routine are the writer's downfall. You need to be your own pack leader.

Make your workspace your sanctuary. Keep office hours. Close the door if you can. If you can't, put on earphones and listen to music. Writing is a meditation on life. You need to feel alone in the world so that you can be objective about it.

Don't ever panic. Keep in mind that even great writers like F. Scott Fitzgerald and Ernest Hemingway needed editing. You can always go back and fix what doesn't work. Nothing is perfect the first time out.

Don't despair. Some writing days are better than others. If you feel stuck, move on or just take a break and come back to it tomorrow. A night's sleep often makes a world of difference.

Don't place yourself in competitive situations while you're working on a book. Losing a "first-chapter" contest or workshopping a book-in-progress can lead to second-guessing. It's best to finish your draft before you ask for any critical evaluation. Sometimes when you're trying to progress through the early stages of a novel, writing groups can be like the blind leading the potentially sighted.

While working on your draft, don't buy the latest bestseller and try to figure out what it has that your book is missing. The best way to write a best-selling book is to write a book that you could give to anyone, including your mother-in-law and that salsa-dancing neighbor. Novels that really work are books that people can see their own hearts in. They're books that make people feel that you're writing about them. The best way to write such a genuine work is to write from an authentic part of yourself, rather than being distracted by what's selling and why.

Think of yourself as an athlete. Exercise. Eat right. If you're driving yourself crazy with work, stop and invite a friend to meet for coffee. Balance is key.

Don't be afraid to set your own pace and create your own work in a way that makes the most sense for you. Yes, your favorite author puts out a book a year, but you don't need to. You need to create a process that works for you and write your own work in your own time frame.

STUDY YOUR BREED

Just as you can't easily train a Chihuahua to retrieve ducks—it's just not in its nature—you can't write a book without thinking about what the reader demands from the genre. Every book, just like every breed, brings with it a certain set of natural expectations. Historical romance must address history. Mysteries must have some level of, well, mystery. Literary books are usually not plot-focused.

Understanding the "breed" of your book is the first step in bringing your novel to the page. Once you create a clearly defined set of expectations, you can train yourself to stay within them—and soon you'll be able to sit, roll over, and fetch with the best of them.

When Nancy Horan wrote the bestseller *Loving Frank*, a historically imagined novel about the tragic love affair of Frank Lloyd Wright and Mamah Borthwick Cheney, she chose a task with a rather large laundry list of expectations. She had to, first and foremost, create characters based on real people. In the case of Mamah, not much had been written about her, and only a few documents had been left behind. What was widely known was that Mamah was a great beauty who had left her young children and perfectly respectable husband for Frank—and who had done so in an era when those choices were especially taboo. Horan's challenge, then, was to make the woman sympathetic, while imagining the great pain and suffering Mamah's decision must have caused both herself and those around her. Horan's Mamah also had to have intellect and spirit so that she didn't seem like a mindless follower of the architect.

In effect, Horan had to crawl into Mamah's psyche and make it her own.

Of course, Frank also had to be handled with care. History has not always been kind to him. Biographers have depicted him as arrogant, vain, unreliable, and largely unschooled (because of his lack of structural training, many of his buildings are beautiful but flawed); he was not an easy subject to endear to modern readers. But Horan's instinct as a writer told her that the reader needed to see Wright as a man Mamah could fall in love with, needed to understand why she would leave her seemingly perfect life for a troubled (and married) man.

Then there were the historical considerations Horan had to take into account. She had to stay true to the era in every detail possible. In the early twentieth century, not only were affairs conducted via telegram rather than text message, but adultery was seen as a crime. What's more, Horan had to explain Wright's architecture and his aesthetic viewpoint in a way that was intelligent, fresh, simple, and yet not so simple as to bore those already knowledgeable about Wright's work.

All of these expectations for Horan's historical novel could have been outlined even before she wrote a word, showing her a clear path from idea to page.

So, you see, readers' expectations for your genre are a good place to start, and a general guideline that will help you throw out ideas that won't fit.

Once you've established your readers' expectations as a framework, you need to decide *how* to tell your story.

Consider *The Wonderful Wizard of Oz* and *Wicked: The Life and Times of the Wicked Witch of the West*. Both books are set in the same world. L. Frank Baum's hero in *The Wonderful Wizard of Oz* is Dorothy. Gregory Maguire's *Wicked* includes Dorothy's falling house as an unfortunate incident, but his hero is the witch. The book is sympathetic to her plight— and that changes everything.

While Baum's message is simple—"There's no place like home"— Maguire creates a complex tale with a complex message about the nature of good and evil. The two books couldn't be more different. And both have been wildly successful.

There's a myriad of ways to tell each and every tale; don't be afraid to make your story your own.

TRAIN YOUR FOCUS

Once you have your framework in place, you'll need to be ruthless. Everything in a story must work to tell the tale. Think of your novel like a TV news story. If the story is about a murder, you'll usually see a shot of where the murder took place or where the body was found, a photo of the victim, an interview with a witness who heard something or knew the victim, and a sound bite from the police officers investigating the story. The fact that the victim liked dogs wouldn't usually be included unless the barking of his dog alerted the neighbors, who then found the body. Every element works to tell the tale, and that should also be true for your novel.

You'll probably start out pursuing more ideas than you have room for in your story, but when it comes time to write, it's important to remember that you can't try to stuff things in just because you like them. For example, if you originally wanted to write about a chef, and you've spent three months researching culinary school, but suddenly this character no longer seems to fit into the framework of your science fiction thriller, you're going to have to cut him. It's painful, but it must be done.

Of course, if you did spend three months researching something, it's very difficult to toss that work away—so don't. Maybe you'll write half of your book and discover that it really does fit, but you just couldn't see it at first. Or maybe you'll discover that you'd really rather write about a chef, and so you create a new framework. Never throw anything away. I like to keep all my research in Moleskine notebooks that I carry around. I also glue postcards and business cards onto the pages. If I see a name that strikes my fancy, I'll jot it down. Sometimes photographs go in, too. When I'm finished, the notebook is crammed full of ideas—just like my head used to be. Some I can use now, some I save for later.

WALK YOUR INNER DOG

A calm, centered mind, "breed" wisdom, and the discipline to shape your focus—let's look at how this model works in the real world. Say you've just read an article about a sixteen-year-old boy who lived in a lifeboat in shark-infested waters for 227 days before he was rescued.

As soon as you read the story, you can imagine yourself living it. You can feel this boy's fear and begin to understand what it would take to survive all those days in open water. Perhaps you decide the idea has a *Robinson Crusoe* feeling to it. Like Daniel Defoe's book, it's an adventure—and so this becomes your model. You now know what "breed" of story you're working with.

Next you have to consider what the reader expects from an adventure story and what the facts of the situation are. Given the reality of a boy living at sea in a lifeboat, the novel, like *Crusoe*, must deal with overcoming great obstacles through hard work and patience. It also could be imagined that a boy adrift on a raft would begin to wonder about the nature of God, as he is certainly at odds with the whims of nature.

So when you sit down to write this story you could think of it as a reinvented version of *Crusoe*—unless you throw a 450-pound Bengal tiger in the mix. With a dangerous and hungry cat on board, you now have *Life of Pi,* Yann Martel's rumination on the nature of adventure, survival, faith, and truth. Martel took this simple story and added his unique take on it based on subjects he's interested in, such as faith and zoology. By being true to himself and his own vision of the world, he boldly created a fable that became an international bestseller.

While you write a book, it's art. When you're finished, it's business. Never confuse the two. Art encourages you to take risks, recreate reality, embrace adventure, and break all the rules—it makes you want to soar. Business is about sales, sales, and sales—and it makes you jumpy. You'll never tame your beast if you write while wondering how many books you can sell.

Don't worry about failing. Be fearless about taming your best ideas, and about tossing out those that don't fit your model. Choose paths that illuminate your own unique take on the world. Once you're in the habit of walking your inner dog, you never know where it might lead you.

FROM IDEA TO PAGE IN FOUR SIMPLE STEPS

Nothing is more exciting than the promise of a story in your head, but in order to get it on the page you need to figure out exactly what you need to do to make it work. You need to realistically outline and throw out what bogs readers down. You need to set up a game plan to hook your readers and keep them reading. Here are some simple steps to help you build the frame that you hang your story on.

Step 1. Always begin with your protagonist. The readers need to discover who the hero is and why they should root for him. Introduce your protagonist, either directly or indirectly, within the first 300 words.

Step 2. Establish time and place. Your readers should know exactly where they are. If they are wondering, they lose focus and may stop reading. They have to trust that you are in control of the story. Nobody likes to be left alone in the dark.

Step 3. Announce the stakes. Great prose will go a long way—about 2,500 words, more or less. After that, even the most literary readers want to know why they're reading. Just a simple sentence can do the trick. At the end of the first section of *The Things They Carried*, Tim O'Brien writes of the letters that Jimmy Cross received from a girl back home named Martha. He mentions that they're signed "Love, Martha," but acknowledges that using the word "love" is a custom and not anything more. At the end of this section, O'Brien writes, "Slowly, a bit distracted, he would get up and move among his men, checking the perimeter, then at full dark he would return to his hole and watch the night and wonder if Martha was a virgin."

Right there, the author lets us know what's *really* on the mind—and at the heart of the story—of this young man who is so very far away from home.

Step 4. Organize. Once you have your story structured around the beginning you've set in place, look at all the bits of writing you've done and all the notes you've taken and ask yourself one simple question: "Where the heck was I going with this?" If you don't know, or if where you're going now doesn't match where you were going when you set out, focus on better defining those areas before you go any further.

N.M. KELBY (nmkelby.com) is a critically acclaimed novelist and the author of *The Constant Art of Being a Writer: The Life, Art & Business of Fiction* and, most recently, the story collection *A Travel Guide for Reckless Hearts*. She is working on a film version of her novel *Whale Season* with Dwight Yoakam.

CHAPTER 2

MASTERING FICTION'S FIRST RULE

BY JACK M. BICKHAM

It's one of the first things a new fiction writer hears in the way of advice: "Show, don't tell." The advice is sound. But execution is sometimes something else. There's just an awful lot of confusion about this basic tactic of effective fiction.

Let's try to clear up some of it.

The phrase "Show, don't tell" is shorthand for this advice: "Don't lecture your reader; she won't believe you. Give her the story action, character thoughts, feelings, and sense impressions as the character would experience them in real life. Let her live the story for herself as she lives real life, by experience."

That's a mouthful, and it requires some explanation.

FROM FACTS TO FEELINGS

First, it may help to realize that most of your formal educational training and work experience have taught you to present information in a way that's inappropriate when writing fiction.

Most of our formal schooling emphasizes *telling*. We tell the teacher the facts we learned from our textbook reading—either in class recitation or in a written test. When we're assigned to write a term paper or report, we tell the facts from a logical, objective viewpoint—and probably try to keep our own personality entirely out of it. Later, in the business world, we are expected to find and analyze facts, then prepare reports or memoranda that are, again, designed to inform readers as factually and briefly as possible—by telling.

That's fine, in that world. But when you start to write fiction, you must turn the process upside down. Instead of keeping feelings out of the process and listing objective facts, you must be aware of feelings—your lead character's emotions and unique viewpoint on the story action—and then you must figure out how to make your readers experience the story world from that viewpoint and emotional stance. Instead of presenting facts and marshaling arguments in support of your position, as you do in the educational or business world, you must present the evidence and lead readers to form their own conclusions.

Thus, fiction convinces—if it does—in a way entirely different from our usual objective writing. Fiction can only involve and convince and excite readers if it lets them experience the story world the way they experience real life: by taking in stimuli and drawing their own conclusions. In real life, you don't walk outside in the morning and experience the start of the day with something internal like, "Cloud cover is thick. The temperature is 64 degrees, the humidity is 42 percent, traffic on the highway is heavy, it's late September, the postman is irritable today."

What you do do is walk outside and see with your eyes that it's gray and dim; you look up and see thick gray clouds; you feel the temperature with your skin ... and relax, or feel warm, or shiver. If you breathe deeply and the air feels thick to you, you may conclude it's humid. You hear the roar of cars nearby and conclude traffic is heavy on the highway. You see the postman coming up your driveway. Your eyes meet and you smile at him. His mouth turns down, his eyes squint, and he glares silently back at you. You conclude he is feeling grumpy.

So to convince your readers, you must make the experience of the story world as much like real life as you possibly can. You present evidence. You show; you don't tell.

That's what *show* means in the broadest sense. Your readers will only believe you—be transported into your story world and be enthralled—if you convey just as much information of all kinds through this process of making it a learning experience for them.

At the risk of being repetitious, let's state again that your readers will not believe dry, objective lectures. They will only believe the conclusions they form from the evidence you carefully select and present to them.

GET INTO VIEWPOINT—AND STAY THERE!

This process of showing, not telling, can be broken down into four essential steps. They are:

- Selection of, and adherence to, a single character's viewpoint
- Imagining the crucial sense or thought impressions that character is experiencing at any given moment
- Presenting those impressions as vividly and briefly as possible
- Giving those impressions to readers in a logical order

Getting into the viewpoint of your central story character—and staying there—helps enormously in showing instead of telling. If you're solidly in viewpoint, you won't be tempted to lecture readers because you will be revealing that character's experiences rather than reviewing some abstract, objectively written data. If you're well inside the viewpoint, for example, you can't dump a lot of author-intrusive factual information on readers because viewpoint characters, like real people, *experience* things rather than tell about them.

Further, adherence to viewpoint largely removes the temptation to tell readers stuff that's extraneous or unknowable to the viewpoint character. This is a useful limiting device for you. You simply cannot, for example, start telling what's over the next hill, or who might be walking up behind the character, or the precise temperature, or any of a million other details that *matter* to the character.

These details will not scatter all over time and space, either. They'll be imagined at every given moment. After all, we live our lives that way—moment by moment. Your character will experience sense impressions and everything else in the same way—briefly, often in a fragmentary manner, and very vividly because it's the real world he is experiencing. So you will be less tempted to launch into long prose lectures about the exact color of the tree or panoramic descriptions covering long periods of time. We just don't live like that!

Given the fact that your showing will therefore tend to be brief, you will find yourself working hard to boil down your wordage to make it as vivid and evocative as possible. You'll be very concrete and seldom abstract. You will not, for example, write a sentence that says, "He was a very tall man." That's an objective conclusion. You will instead write something closer to, "Even though he ducked as he entered the doorway, he cracked his head on the top. As he walked into the room, suddenly the eight-foot ceiling looked like someone had lowered it a foot." (Now readers will think, "Hey, this is a tall guy" and will *believe* it.)

Finally, in showing rather than telling, you will make sure that you give this evidence in a logical order, the order that readers will need to have a lifelike experience, yet at the same time understand what's going on.

Usually this means a chronological presentation. If someone knocks on your character's front door, for example, you simply can't start the next paragraph with dialogue, and then only later mention that, oh, by the way, it was Jim at the door, and his face was twisted in anger, and our viewpoint character was concerned and invited him in, and the two of them started to talk.

Instead, you'll take it a step at a time, logically, as you (and your readers) would experience it in real life: sound of knocking at the door; viewpoint character goes to the door and opens it, sees Jim standing out there, sees his angry scowl and clenched fists, asks, "Jim, what's wrong? Please come in—." Sits him down on the couch, notices his red-rimmed, sleepless eyes, feels more worried about him, and curious, and says, "Tell me what's happened and why you're here."

The only exception to the code of logical presentation can be found in those very rare instances when you want to show readers that your character is confused—that everything seems to be happening all at once, or the character's thoughts are badly muddled. Then you may jumble logicality to baffle readers for a few moments, thus convincing them of character confusion by making the readers experience such confusion.

(In 99 percent of the cases, however, logical presentation is required. The need for logical, lifelike order is so important that I wrote an entire chapter on it when I revised my book *Writing and Selling Your Novel.*)

DIVINING THE DOMINANT IMPRESSION

Of course, in all of this process you will most often be dealing with sense impressions. In working to improve your own sensitivity to vivid, suggestive sense impressions, it often helps to cultivate the habit of trying to identify, as you go through your normal everyday activities, the *dominant impression* you may be receiving at any given moment.

Consider, for example, the dominant impression you might experience turning your car around a curve in the road and suddenly having the setting sun directly on your windshield.

Or the dominant impression if you walked into an old cathedral in Europe at a quiet time, perhaps soon after a Catholic mass and benediction service.

Then imagine the dominant impression you receive when you walk into your local shopping mall.

Or the dominant impression of walking down a city street near a major repaving project.

Or the dominant impression when you walk into a bakery.

Very often, given the hierarchy of our senses, the source and quality of light is the first and dominant impression. In showing readers a room or office, for example, the brightness and source of the light often will be the first thing noticed in real life, and the first thing to be shown readers: Is it a large, dim, windowless room; a small black closet; a big office with sun-washed windows looking out onto the vast blue of the lake?

In other cases, however, the dominant impression may be dictated by the nature of the experience. Surely, in walking into an old cathedral, you would notice the vast space, perhaps dimness, perhaps vividly colored stained glass. But also high on the list to be "shown" would probably be the silence, the odor of incense, motes of dust in a stray shaft of sunlight.

Quite different from the mall. There the dominant impression might be the noise, or the crowds of people, or the ranks of glass display windows, or the garish neon, or the racket of canned music.

The major street work? Ear-shattering din of jackhammers. Roar of air compressors. Crash of debris being dumped into a truck. Smell of tar or asphalt. Of workmen's sweat or the foreman's acrid cigar.

Or consider the bakery. Oh, my, the smell of fresh-baked bread, and rows of glistening pastries in the cabinets. You might waste a half-page trying to tell your readers about walking into a bakery when all you need to do—to thrust readers into that experience—would be to "show" the sweet aroma of fresh-baked bread ... and maybe a touch of cinnamon in the warm air.

So every moment of showing may proceed from a different hierarchy of senses than the one that went before. Your ability to embed yourself deeply in your character's viewpoint and imagine that moment as vividly and truly as possible, starting with the dominant impression, will make your fiction convincing.

REVEALING CHARACTERS

The same general principle applies to showing your readers your other story characters. You can lecture readers endlessly about how nervous Joe may be, and how impatient, and how driven, and blah, blah, blah. But readers don't form impressions of real people from dull, objective character profiles, so why should they believe your manuscript if you do the same thing?

Again, you have to show—present the evidence—like this:

Joe walked jerkily into the office. The facial tic leaped under his left eye. He swooped onto the empty chair, drummed his fingers on the desktop, crossed and uncrossed his legs, and glared at Sally. "All right," he snapped. "I'm here. I don't have all day. Get to the point. I'm a busy man."

Now your readers will conclude from the evidence, "Hey, this is a nervous, impatient, driven man," and believe it because they were led to draw that conclusion for themselves.

Even the presentation of your viewpoint character's emotions can often be handled more convincingly through showing. It's always tempting to get inside the character and start analyzing—"Sally was so sad and depressed," for example, or "Sally felt the anger rise up in her so sharply that it shocked her." But in such cases, it's more compelling for readers if you find a way to show, something like:

> Suddenly she realized the sound in the room was her own sobbing. She felt tears on her cheeks. She raised a hand and it trembled before her eyes. *I could end it all*, she thought without warning.

Or:

> She began to shake. The words tumbling out of her mouth
> sounded horrible to her own ears—language she never used,
> viciousness. She didn't even recognize her own voice. Her hands
> formed claws and she struck out at him with her nails, raking
> bright, bloody tracks on his face.

These quick, crude examples may overdo it slightly. But they're exaggerated to make the point: Even internal character reactions should be shown far more often than given in a dull lecture.

WHEN TO "TELL"

So, to convince, we show rather than tell.

But are there ever times when telling is all right?

Of course there are. We tell when:

- The data are objective and absolutely essential to reader understanding.
- The factual information is so fascinating that it may "sell" the story. (This is very rare.)
- The point is quite minor and we can risk "cheating."
- Economy of words is vital at the moment.

Some "objective data" may be necessary in your story. For example, it may be important for readers to know that there has been violence in the neighborhood where your character lives, and readers should worry about it. Even after presenting evidence such as extra locks on the apartment doors, a patrol car going by outside, or scared looks on neighbors' faces, you might want simply to say that there had been two murders in the past week, or that Sally was scared and wanted to move, but couldn't afford it. A little such telling takes place in most stories.

Sometimes, too, in economically characterizing someone, it may be quite okay to slip in a bit of telling, as, "Jack was late, but Sally was not surprised. Jack made it a habit to be late. It was one way he proved to the world that he didn't give a hoot about anyone but himself."

In a novel, the presentation of factual data may be appealing as interesting information in its own right, as in the books of James Michener where the historical facts form part of the fascination for readers. If your story is of this type, designed to enthrall because it contains hard-won, truly interesting information that you believe will help sell the story, then you may tell quite a lot. (My novel *Twister* was such a case. It contains more straight, factual telling than anything else I have ever written. But such a "journalistic" approach is hard to handle and risky.)

If the point is very minor, it's also fine to tell—a little—once in a while. Perhaps it's as simple a statement, as "The weather was getting colder." Or "Marie looked grumpy." Or "In a city like Zenith, with its skyrocketing population of 256,000, up 50,000 in only the past five years … ."

These examples, in the purist's sense, constitute "cheating" a little. But they're done to get on with things. Readers will accept them if the point isn't critical to the story at the moment you slip them in.

Finally, let's admit that sometimes in a short story, you may simply be forced to tell because your total word limit doesn't allow you to present enough evidence to make the point convincingly. You may write a fine, lengthy paragraph showing David's depression, but when the story is done, you may find yourself a few hundred words too long. In such cases—if in your best judgment David's depression is not crucially important—you can get away with simply writing, "David slumped, appearing depressed, as he so often was during the long winters."

As a fiction writer, your goal is to immerse readers in your story world. That world must seem as much like the readers' real world as you can possibly make it. Readers experience your story world in a similar way: through evidence—sense impressions or whatever—that allow them to draw their own conclusions.

If you craft carefully in viewpoint and select your words well, you will show your readers not only the impressions, sights, sounds, and feelings you want them to believe, but will leave them feeling moved and satisfied.

Never lecture. Always strive to show.

JACK M. BICKHAM wrote more than eighty novels before his death in 1996. His books on writing include *Writing and Selling Your Novel* and two volumes in the Writer's Digest Books' Elements of Fiction Writing series—*Setting* and *Scene and Structure*.

CHAPTER 3
BEYOND BASIC BLUNDERS

BY JERRY B. JENKINS

MORNING-ROUTINE CLICHÉ

Clichés come in all shapes and sizes. There are just as many clichéd scenes as phrases and words. For instance, how may times have you seen a book begin with a main character being "rudely awakened" from a "sound sleep" by a "clanging" alarm clock? Have you written an opening like this yourself? Wondering where to start, you opt for first thing in the morning. Speaking of clichés, been there, done that. We all have. Don't ever do it again.

Compounding that cliché is having the "bleary-eyed" character drag himself from his bed, squinting against the intruding sunlight. And compounding *that* is telling the reader everything the character sees in the room. What comes next? He'll pass by or stand before a full-length mirror, and we'll get the full rundown of what the poor guy looks like.

Are you cringing? I've done the same kind of clichéd scene. Resolve to leave that whole morning-routine cliché to the millions of writers who'll follow in your footsteps.

I know you want me to suggest alternatives to those hackneyed constructs, but inventing fresh ways to start a story and describe a character is your job. If an early morning routine is endemic to your plot—say your character is wound tight and sleepless because of a crucial morning meeting—put him on the commuter train with an unsupervised child darting about. He doesn't know what she's doing amidst all the businesspeople, with their noses stuck in newspapers or laptop screens, but she points at him and says, "Don't you comb your hair?"

Mortal dread. Is it possible that, in his hurry to catch the last train that would get him to his job interview on time, our hero actually skipped a step in his personal routine? Now he has to find his reflection in the train window or the aluminum back of the seat in front of him. And then what does he do?

ANSWERING-THE-PHONE CLICHÉ

Another deadly cliché is how people answer the phone. This happens even in the movies or on stage. Be aware of yourself the next time your phone rings. It's such a common occurrence that we don't even think about it. But one thing you likely do *not* do is look up, startled. You don't turn and look at the phone. You know where it is; it's been there for years, and you've heard it ring before. You simply rise and go answer it.

If your character gets a phone call, resist the urge to have her look up, startled, then rise, cross the room, pick up the receiver and say,

"Hello?"

"Hi, Mary?"

"Yes."

"This is Jill."

"Hi, Jill. What's up?"

(Or if you're a mystery writer): "Hi, Jill. Is anything wrong?"

Enough already.

Here is another problematic phone scene, from an unpublished manuscript:

The tinny ring echoed through the dark house. The shiny white receiver waited on the stone countertop. Another outburst. Chester, handsome, dark-haired, and taller than normal, craned his neck to look at the ringing reminder of his loneliness. After the phone's third cry for attention, Chester stood up and strode purposefully toward the kitchen. His long legs were encased in brown corduroys, which swished in the silence as he moved toward the phone. Ring four. He knew the machine would click on if he didn't move quickly. He plucked the receiver delicately from the cradle with his bronzed hand and said in warm, resonant tones, "Hello. Chester here."

"Hi, Chester. It's Mary."

You get the idea. Here's my version:

Late that night, Mary phoned.

Give your readers credit. If you tell them Mary phoned Chester, they can assume he heard the ring, stood, moved to the phone, picked it up, and introduced himself. You'd be amazed at how many manuscripts are cluttered with such details.

Even in a period piece where the baking of a cake from scratch is an engrossing trip down memory lane, the good writer gives readers credit for thinking. While she may outline all the steps the heroine goes through to make the cake, she'll avoid having her rise and stride to the kitchen or even pull open the oven door—unless there's something about that oven door novel enough to include. If the character has to use a towel to lift the iron lid, fine. But if she does that, we know she had to stand and walk first.

SKIP THE RECITALS OF ORDINARY LIFE

We all get dressed, walk out to the car, open the door, slide in, turn the key, and back out of the driveway. If your character backs into the garbage truck, that's a story. Just say it:

That morning, as Bill backed out of the driveway, his mind was on the tongue-lashing he had endured the day before from his boss. Only when he heard the ugly crunch and scrape and his head snapped back did he realize he had not bothered to check his rearview mirror. He had plowed into a garbage truck that looked half as big as his house.

DON'T SPELL IT OUT

One of the clichés of conversation is feeling the need to explain more than once what's going on, as if the reader can't figure it out on his own. I actually read a novel in which, when a character said something quirky like "promptly, punctually, and prissily" (which was actually funny and fit the personality), the author felt the need to add, "he said alliteratively."

Other writers have a character respond to a diatribe from another with "Yep," or "Nope," or a shrug. Perfect. I love to learn about personalities this way. The character is a man of few words. But too often, the author intrudes, adding, "he said, eschewing small talk."

If you create a character who backs into a conversation with tentative phrases like, "Oh, I was just wondering," or, "I don't know how to say this, but if I, well, let me say it this way," we get it. We understand this is a timid, nervous person, afraid of saying something wrong, sensitive to others' feelings. Avoid the temptation to explain. Don't follow that with, "she began nervously, unsure how to broach the subject."

Maybe the responder to that speaker says, "Is there a question in there somewhere? What *are* you saying?" That tells us all we need to know. You don't have to explain with, "the insensitive jerk said."

PASS ON THE PREACHINESS

If your whole reason for writing is to pontificate on, for example, the dangers of certain habits or lifestyles, you risk sounding preachy. I see this problem in many manuscripts: all talk, straw men, plots contrived to prove a point but little that grabs and subtly persuades the reader. If your theme is the danger of alcoholism, simply tell a story in which an alcoholic suffers because of his bad decisions and give the reader credit. If your story is powerful enough, your theme will come through.

As you might imagine, preachiness is the bane of too much writing today (especially in the inspirational market). We're trying to make the same kinds of points, naturally, that preachers do. But preachers are *supposed* to preach. It's what they do. No one complains that his preacher is too preachy. That would be like saying a ballerina is too dancey.

For some reason, however, preachiness on paper offends the reader's sensibilities. If you're like me, you like to be given some credit as a reader and thinker. Even as a child, when I heard the story of the boy who cried wolf, I got it. I didn't need someone saying, "So you see, Jerry, if you lie often enough, no one will take you seriously when you're telling the truth." That's the beauty of morality tales: They make their own points.

Preachiness doesn't need to be as obvious as stopping the story to say, "And so, dear reader, as you travel down life's highway, remember ... ."

Sometimes obvious point-making comes when the writer of a first-person piece tries to shift gears without engaging the clutch and writes, "That was the day I learned that if that little girl could be so brave in the face of that kind of danger, I could certainly face the uncertainty of ... ."

A rule of thumb? The Golden Rule. Put yourself in the skin of your reader. Read your piece to yourself and imagine how you'd feel at the end of it. Does the story or nonfiction article make its own point? Has the writer (in this case, you) added a sermonette to the end? When in doubt, cut it out.

SETTING THE SCENE

Because of the proliferation of all sorts of visual media these days, it's more important than ever that novelists write with the eye in mind. Fortunately, just as in the days of radio, what can be produced in the theater of the mind (in our case, the reader's mind) is infinitely more creative than what a filmmaker can put on the screen.

Be visual in your approach. People buy tickets to the movies or subscribe to cable channels hoping to see something they've never seen before. A good novel can provide the same, only—because of the theater of the mind—millions of readers can see your story a million different ways.

Although I'm encouraging you to be visual, I eschew too much description. I loved it when great potboiler writer John D. MacDonald described a character simply as "knuckly." A purist might have demanded hair length and color; eye size, shape, and color; height; weight; build; gait. Not me. "Knuckly" gave me all I needed to picture the man. And if I saw him thinner, taller, older than you did, so much the better. MacDonald offered a suggestion that allowed his readers to populate their own scenes.

I recall an editor asking me to expound on my "oily geek" computer techie in one of my books in the Left Behind series. I argued: (1) he was an orbital character, and while I didn't want him to be a cliché from central casting, neither did I feel the need to give him more characteristics than he deserved, and (2) he was there to serve a purpose, not to take over the scene, and certainly not to take over the book.

The editor countered, "But the reader will want to see him, and you haven't told us enough. Like, I see him in his twenties, plump, pale, with longish, greasy hair and thick glasses."

What could I say? "Eureka! You just proved my point! All I wrote was that he was an oily geek, and look what you brought to the table." Every reader has his own personal vision of a computer techie, so why not let each mental creation have its fifteen seconds of fame on the theater screen of the mind?

COINCIDENCES

In real life, I love coincidences. I'm fascinated by them. In fiction, more than one in each novel is too many, and even the one has to be handled well. (In comedies, sure, coincidences are fun and expected. How many times in *Seinfeld* do the characters run into the same people they tangled with early in the story?)

Say you invent a yarn about two people who marry, come to hate each other, and get divorced. Years pass, and each fails at yet another marriage. Available again, they run into each other thousands of miles from home at a bazaar in Turkey. *Bizarre* is more like it. People won't buy it. If the couple reconnected at their high school reunion, that would be plausible, or if they both chickened out of that event at the same time and ran into each other at a fast food place nearby, that would be an interesting, more believable coincidence.

So you see, dear reader ... oops. Okay, I'm going to give you some credit for getting the point.

JERRY B. JENKINS is the author of more than 175 books, including the Left Behind series. He owns Jenkins Entertainment (jenkins-entertainment. com), a filmmaking company in Los Angeles, and the Christian Writers Guild (ChristianWritersGuild.com), which trains writers.

CHAPTER 4

FIRE UP YOUR FICTION

BY DONALD MAASS

Many fiction manuscripts submitted to my literary agency feel lackluster. Much genre fiction feels tired. Many mainstream and literary novels also strike me as stale. Even when well written, too often manuscripts fail to engage and excite me.

What is missing when a manuscript hugs the wall and refuses to dance? Originality is not the key. It can't be, otherwise no wounded detective would ever have a chance and every new vampire series would be dead on arrival. Even over-published clichés can sometimes break out and sell big. The same is true of look-alike mainstream and literary fiction.

The issue, then, is not whether a story has a cool new premise. Whether hiking a well-worn trail or blazing uncharted wilderness, when a manuscript succeeds it is invariably fired by inspiration. Passion comes through on the page.

How does that passion get there? Here are some exercises to apply to your novel-in-progress. They are designed to dig up what matters in your story and infuse it in your manuscript in effective—but not obvious—ways.

FIND THE UNCOMMON IN COMMON EXPERIENCE

To get passion into your story, do it through your characters. What angers you can anger them. What lifts them up will inspire us in turn. Even ordinary people can be poets, prophets, and saints. That's true in life, so why not in your fiction?

Here is an exercise designed to discover and utilize what is universal in the experience of your characters, especially when they are regular folk like you and me.

Write down what comes to mind when you read the prompts below.

1. Is your story realistic? Are your characters ordinary people?

2. What in the world of your story makes you angry? What are we not seeing? What is the most important question? What puzzle has no answer? What is dangerous in this world? What causes pain?

3. Where in the world of your story is there unexpected grace? What is beautiful? Who is an unrecognized hero? What needs to be saved?

4. Give your feelings to a character. Who can stand for something? Who can turn the plot's main problem into a cause?

5. Create a situation in which this character must defend, explain, or justify his actions. How is the plot's main problem larger than it looks? Why does it matter to us all?

6. Find places in your manuscript to incorporate the emotions, opinions, and ideas generated in the prompts above.

FIND THE COMMON IN UNCOMMON EXPERIENCE

What if your protagonist is already a genuine hero? If your hero or heroine is an above-average, courageous, principled, and unstoppable doer of good, you may believe that you don't have a problem. Cheering will begin automatically, right?

Wrong. Perfect heroes and heroines are unrealistic. Readers know that. They will not strongly bond with such characters. To connect, they need to feel that such paragons are real.

That is also true for the world of your story. The rarefied stratosphere of national politics, international intrigue, or any other out-of-the-ordinary milieu will not draw readers in unless there they find some way to relate to it.

The following are steps you can take to humanize your hero and make the exotic world of your story real for us ordinary mortals.

1. Is your story about uncommon events? Are your characters out of the ordinary?

2. Find for your hero a failing that is human, a universal frustration, a humbling setback, or any experience that everyone has had. Add this early in the manuscript.

3. What in the world of the story is timelessly true? What cannot be changed? How is basic human nature exhibited? What is the same today as one hundred years ago, and will be the same one hundred years ahead?

4. What does your protagonist do the same way as everyone? What is his lucky charm? Give this character a motto. What did she learn from her mom or dad?

5. Create a situation in which your exceptional protagonist is in over his head, feels unprepared, is simply lost, or in any other way must admit to himself that he's not perfect.

6. Find places in your manuscript to incorporate the results of the steps above.

DEVELOP THE MORAL OF THE STORY

What if your novel already has a driving message? Suppose its purpose is in some way to wake us up? That's great, but your message will harden your readers' hearts if you lecture or preach. To avoid that, let your story itself be your lesson. The teacher is your central plot problem. The students? Those are your characters.

Here are ways to use those elements to get across your point.

1. Is there a moral or lesson in your story?

2. When does your protagonist realize she got something wrong?

3. Who in the story can, at the end, see things in a completely different way?

4. At the end, how is your hero or heroine better off?

5. At the end, what does your hero or heroine regret?

6. Who, in the midst of the story, is certain there is no solution, nor is there any way to fully comprehend the problem?

7. Why is the problem good, timely, universal, or fated?

8. Find places in your manuscript to incorporate the results of the questions above.

BUILD THE FIRE IN FICTION

Did you ever get lost in the middle of writing a manuscript? Have you ever wondered, deep in revisions, if your story holds together or any longer makes sense? Have you ever lost steam?

Steal from life. That's what it's for, isn't it? How often, when something bad happened to you, did you think to yourself, *at least this will be good material for a story some day?*

Well, now's your chance. What has happened to you, its details and specifics, are tools with which you can make every scene personal and powerful. Use the following prompts whenever you are stuck, or if inspiration simply is low.

1. Choose any scene that seems weak or wandering. Who is the point-of-view character?

2. Identify whatever this character feels most strongly in this scene. Fury? Futility? Betrayal? Hope? Joy? Arousal? Shame? Grief? Pride? Self-loathing? Security?

3. Recall your own life. What was the time when you most strongly felt the emotion you identified in the last step?

4. Detail your own experience: When precisely did this happen? Who was there? What was around you? What do you remember best about the moment? What would you most like to forget? What was the quality of the light? What exactly was said? What were the smallest and largest things that were done?

5. In this experience from your life, what twisted the knife or put the icing on the cake? It would have stirred this feeling anyway, but what really provoked it was ... what?

6. What did you think to yourself as the importance of this experience struck you?

7. Give the details of your experience to your character, right now, in this very scene.

DONALD MAASS is a the president of Donald Maass Literary Agency. He is the author of *The Fire in Fiction: Passion, Purpose and Techniques to Make Your Novel Great* from which this chapter is excerpted.

CHAPTER 5
WHY REAL-LIFE STORIES OFTEN DON'T MAKE GOOD FICTION

BY ALYCE MILLER

How many times have you been inspired to turn a true story (amusing anecdote, tragic episode, personal experience) into fiction? Or after hearing a particularly good story, one that moved you to laughter or close to tears, you've thought, "Wow! Now that would make a good piece of fiction"?

Why is it that after transcribing the story to paper, you discover it has failed miserably on the page? Worse, readers and editors conspire to tell you the story is boring (nothing happens), improbable, predictable, or even unrealistic. How can real stories seem unrealistic? Don't most fiction writers borrow material from real life for their stories?

The answer is yes, but fiction writers draw on many other sources as well. Often what appears in works of fiction is a combination of "true stories," imagination, and invention. This is what distinguishes fiction from much nonfiction.

Probably six of the biggest pitfalls in writing directly from true life are as follows:

1. Writing stories from which you have either too much or too little distance. With too much distance, you may not know enough to flesh out the story beyond anecdote; with too little distance, your familiarity may get in your way as you assume your reader will automatically feel the same way you do about the material.

2. Relying on and allowing the "real-life" plot to drive the story toward "the way it really happened," rather than exploring alternate routes.

3. Neglecting character development; assuming that because you think a real-life person is funny or tragic, your reader will, too.

4. Wanting to stay in control and explain why everything happened the way it did; overlooking the wonderful possibilities of ambiguity, irony, and understatement.

5. Straitjacketing the writing itself because you know exactly where the story is going.

6. Failing to include essential details that convince and give texture. Again, relying on your own emotional response to a real-life situation, rather than to the careful detail and development that move the story machinery.

INVENTING ANOTHER KIND OF TRUTH

It's helpful to remember that one of the shifts that marks so much contemporary fiction is from "what the writer already knows and wants to impart" to "what the writer discovers." Contemporary fiction typically resists demonstration and instruction, and leans more toward exploration and open-endedness. Readers of contemporary fiction expect to play a very different role from their nineteenth-century counterparts.

Writers who get stuck in transcribing real-life stories cheat themselves and their readers of the potential for mutual discovery.

My creative writing students frequently express frustration with their flawed attempts to transform real life to fiction. A student in an adult fiction class I recently taught dismissed all critiques of weak moments in her stories with this rationalization: "But that's the way it really happened. It's the truth." Her readers' responses were, "But you haven't convinced us."

What my student forgot is that fiction is, as the adage tells us, a means of transforming, not simply transcribing, life. "Truth" is always prismatic. Fiction, by its very nature, alters and falsifies. The fictive dream offers the illusion of truth. It is very different from factual reportage.

Certainly, fiction writers often borrow ideas from real life, but they also mix and blend real-life events, characters, and images with what they invent and imagine. Often, writers may start with a snippet of conversation or an interesting image from real life and work from there, allowing each idea to choose the next. Fiction writers must always be open to possibility. Perhaps in real life the main characters of your story live in southern California, but if you know little or nothing about southern California and the landscape and culture of southern California are not essential to the story, you might consider choosing a setting you are more familiar with. Readers can tell when you're stretching thin what little you do know.

Sculpting real-life events and characters is a given in fiction. Remember, you're not a journalist concerned with the exact recording of "facts." Fiction writers are inventors of another kind of truth.

EXAMINING THE TRUTH

Another student of mine recently wrote a long, involved love story based on an emotional experience that really happened to him. The story failed on many levels.

It opened with the accidental reunion of two high school sweethearts in a small western town that they just happened to find themselves in. The woman now worked as a waitress in a bar where the man had coincidentally stopped to gamble. We are told in the second paragraph that the woman had jilted the man eighteen years before, and the man was still nursing a broken heart. By page 3, the couple had slipped off to a motel and fallen into bed together. In the afterglow of sexual ecstasy, they realized they had never stopped being in love. By page 5, they were living together. The woman had a young daughter, by another lover, named Valentine. The little girl immediately became attached to the male protagonist, no questions asked. The three lived in perfect familial harmony for a year until the final pages when the man realized he simply could not make a commitment. We never knew why, since up until that point everything seemed to be going along swimmingly. The story ended with the departing man promising the little girl he would send her a card every year on her birthday, which fell on Valentine's Day.

So how did the story fail?

First, coincidence (in this case, the accidental meeting) is always difficult to pull off in fiction. Handled carelessly, it comes across as a trick, or even laziness on the part of the author (the way the line, "And then I woke up," does). The coincidence in the student's story, even though true, rightly struck the readers as "hokey." But because it "really happened," the student was reluctant to part with that detail.

Since the coincidence was not essential to the story, the student might have considered other possibilities that would have helped the character development. Example: What might happen if the man deliberately came looking for the woman? What if he had been seeking revenge? What if he was happily married to someone else? What factors in her present life might have prompted him to seek out the old girlfriend? What if the reunion took place in their old home town, which the woman had never left, making it logical for the two to be in the same place simultaneously? What if the man didn't recognize the woman right away, or vice versa? What if she had come looking for him?

A second problem: The student relied on the weight of his own emotional attachment to the situation, rather than character development, to convince the reader to care about the two characters. He assumed the readers would automatically accept the man's passion for the woman. What he forgot is that the real-life subject matter was not loaded for his readers in the same way it was for him.

Third, his choice of perspective through a thinly disguised version of himself as the male protagonist allowed him no opportunity to play with point-of-view possibilities. Writing "himself" restricted him. The issue of distance arises here. Perhaps because he felt so emotionally linked to the situation, he found it impossible to write with a certain necessary detachment that might have led him to a more fully realized character. As a result, he ended up with a shamelessly bland protagonist whose motives were vague and whose actions seemed unfathomable. Hard to feel sympathy for such a character!

Fourth, the dialogue between the two lovers showed none of the tension or irony that this strained situation would ostensibly produce. The student stuck pretty much to "real-life small talk," which may have been true to life but is rarely of interest. Fictionalized dialogue *simulates* real-life dialogue, but must be carefully selected for the way in which it serves the story. A line like, "What a nice house you have" could work if it was, say, ironic, for example, if we knew the woman lived in a rundown trailer. But the student's dialogue consistently mirrored the action ("Would you like some lemonade?" she asked, handing him a pitcher) and revealed nothing about the characters' feelings or true motives. When in conflict or crisis, people often don't say what they really mean and this can be used to great advantage by writers in developing tension. Many times actions speak louder than any words. For example, how would the reader have read the same scene if the woman offered the man lemonade and her hands were trembling? Or she poured him a glass of lemonade without asking him if he wanted any? Or she gave him a glass of lemonade while she drank beer? Or she gave him lemonade that was too sour?

Fifth, the student failed to develop the dynamics inherent in the main conflict between the two characters. After all, the man had been jilted by the woman. What must he be feeling? How would he behave? When he jumped in bed with her, were his motives mixed? The setup offered tremendous potential for the subtle expression of complex dynamics, but the story as the student wrote it lacked any of the tension suggested organically by the circumstances.

Finally, the student relied on a cliché at the end as a stand-in for the complexity of the man's sadness at leaving the little girl named Valentine. Even though in real life the child's birthday fell on Valentine's Day and her name was Valentine, the device felt corny. Readers objected that the story had descended unforgivably into bathos. How to get away from that? The student might have reconsidered whether the Valentine's Day detail was crucial to the story and discovered he was using it as an easy stand-in for more complex dynamics yet to be explored. Or he might have set out to discover what would happen if the little girl were not so likable. Or what if she weren't six (as she was in "real life"), but ten or fourteen? What if she had been omitted entirely from the story?

AVOIDING THE CLICHÉS OF LIFE

Writers must be attentive to the clichés that real life serves up and either make something of them (freshen them, challenge them, work against them) or abandon them altogether.

Speaking of clichés, the love story is by its very nature already a cliché. How to work against that? Consider a piece as poignant and disturbing as Chekov's "The Lady With the Dog" or Lawrence's "Horse Dealer's Daughter." Both are love stories. But both leave the reader uneasy by resisting what is expected and challenging the reader to think beyond the narrative lines of "boy meets and gets girl."

Another problem with translating directly from real life is that it is only infrequently punctuated by trouble that is interesting. A happy family reunion in which all the relatives are thrilled to see one another, true as it may be, is boring to read about because nothing happens. It lacks the critical elements essential to fiction: conflict or crisis. A conflict or crisis can be as subtle as the boy narrator's thwarted romantic quest in Joyce's short story "Araby," or as shocking as the murderous jealous rage of Tolstoy's protagonist in "The Kreutzer Sonata."

At the other end of the spectrum, remember that real life can be stranger than fiction. "Trouble" in real life may be far too complicated or unbelievable to translate directly into fiction. It may need condensing and distilling in order to make it work. Again, the very strangeness of real life may be a stumbling block unless the writer can work in the details that convince, or push the strangeness to new levels.

I have often wrestled with the challenges of fictionalizing the complexities of real people and events. For example, I tried to write about a woman I know who has been kidnapped, raped, and beaten; who has had seven abortions and three children, all by different men; who has struggled with alcohol and drug abuse; who finally shot to death her abusive common-law husband and spent four years in prison, where she was impregnated by a guard. When she gave birth in the prison hospital, her family had only a couple of days to make arrangements to get the baby out. After the woman's release from prison, she dated an ex-prisoner who, at age fourteen, had bludgeoned his grandparents to death. Shortly thereafter, she slept repeatedly with her one sister's husband, also an ex-convict.

She had a second sister who was an alcoholic and lived with a string of abusive men.

All of the these facts are drawn from real life, yet their very volume proved distracting. I discovered that the undiluted, untransformed truth was far too complicated and implausible to work as fiction. I realized I would have to stretch my readers' credibility too far and run the risk of disrupting the fictive illusion. I might easily be accused of contrivance or soap-opera camp.

When working from complicated real-life stories, you might consider simplifying and concentrating on one event, allowing the story to blossom from that point. Discover what it is that interests you most. For example, I might have chosen to focus on the moment when the woman's baby was born in the prison hospital. Or the moment when she had to hand the child over to her alcoholic sister. Or I might have focused on the hours leading up to her sister's discovery of the adultery.

Some of the other real-life events might work as texture, woven into the background fabric. By narrowing the overwhelming number of explosive facts about this woman's life, I would be more likely to develop the story with depth and not rely on a barrage of sensational events to pump up emotion. And I could have made use of some of the other details through implication and understatement.

Remember that writing fiction is a selection process. Writers sift through a vast array of experiences (real, imagined, and borrowed) and choose the details that serve the story. Real life has no such filters. It comes in gusts and storms.

Fiction, like life, is not static or fixed. Writing is an act of discovery in an infinite field of possibility. Telling a story exactly as it happened may put a stranglehold on the sheer delight and pace of invention. Don't suffocate the life out of interesting stories. Allow them to breathe and grow.

SOME THINGS TO REMEMBER

Real life is only one source for your story ideas. Combine what you observe in real life with what you invent and imagine. Keep a writer's notebook. Collect ideas.

Truth is often stranger than fiction. Create composites of people and events by finding their "essence." Simplify without flattening. Say more through less. Allow implication and nuance, not volume, to create texture and depth.

Real life happens a day at a time. A hundred years can pass in a fictional sentence. An hour can be elongated to last an entire novel. Time in fiction is often collapsed or prolonged. It does not adhere to the neat little increments of real life. Condense or skip over periods of time that have little bearing on your story.

Complexities and contradictions of human beings must usually be refined in fiction without reducing characters to attributes. Consider what is most interesting about the characters you're working with. Resist the urge to overexplain, a habit with tellers of real-life stories. Allow your curiosity to roam freely. Allow real-life characters to be transformed. Don't hold any real-life detail too precious. Be ruthless. If it's not working, abandon it.

Try starting with the kernel of a real-life story. The best way to enter a story is through your own curiosity. In real life, you know Aunt Carol wept at Grandma's funeral because she was sad. But your curiosity might suggest that maybe Aunt Carol's tears signified something other than sadness. What if she was actually elated Grandma died and her tears are tears of joy? Or she's crying out of guilt because her last words to Grandma were cruel? Or perhaps her tears have nothing to do with Grandma at all, but with the unexpected presence of her ex-lover at the funeral.

If you've conveniently entered the story from your real-life point of view, try telling the story through another character's eyes. Explore different "I" narrators. Explore the use of third person (both limited and omniscient). Notice how a change in point of view allows the thinly disguised version of yourself to become someone else?

Finally, don't get stuck in real life. Keep your fictive possibilities open! Real life is only part of the story.

ALYCE MILLER is the author of three books of fiction, and more than 200 stories, essays, and poems. Her latest book, *Water*, won the Mary McCarthy Prize for Short Fiction.

BEST-SELLING ADVICE: Plot & Structure

"To me, everything in a novel comes down to people making choices. You must figure out in advance what those choices are going to be." —Marion Zimmer Bradley

"The problem for me is finding my own plots. They take a long time. ... I like to have it happen, just like in our own lives. We don't always know where they're going, and if we make formal decisions on a given night, if we sit down and put a list of things we're going to do on a piece of paper, they almost never work out right." —Norman Mailer

"I make a very tight outline of everything I write before I write it. ... By writing an outline you really are writing in a way, because you're creating the structure of what you're going to do. Once I really know what I'm going to write, I don't find the actual writing takes all that long." —Tom Wolfe

"For a book to really work, form and function must go hand in hand, just like with buildings, as any decent architect will tell you." —Tracy Chevalier

"Transitions are critically important. I want the reader to turn the page without thinking she's turning the page. It must flow seamlessly." —Janet Evanovich

"Sometimes one can overanalyze, and I try not to do that. To a great degree, much of the structure has got to come naturally out of the writing. I think if you try to preordain, you're going to stifle yourself. You've got a general idea, but the rest has to come naturally out of the writing, the narrative, the character, and the situation." —Robert Ludlum

"There is no finer form of fiction than the mystery. It has structure, a story line, and a sense of place and pace. It is the one genre where the reader and the writer are pitted against each other. Readers don't want to guess the ending, but they don't want to be so baffled that it annoys them. ... The research you do is crucial. In mystery fiction, you have to tell the truth. You can't fool the reader and expect to get away with it." —Sue Grafton

"Too many writers think that all you need to do is write well—but that's only part of what a good book is. Above all, a good book tells a good story. Focus on the story first. Ask yourself, 'Will other people find this story so interesting that they will tell others about it?' Remember: A best-selling book usually follows a simple rule, 'It's a wonderful story, wonderfully told'; not, 'It's a wonderfully told story.'" —Nicholas Sparks

"We're past the age of heroes and hero kings. If we can't make up stories about ordinary people, who can we make them up about? ... Most of our lives are basically mundane and dull, and it's up to the writer to find ways to make them interesting." —John Updike

CHAPTER 6
THE PHILOSOPHY OF PLOT

BY JAMES N. FREY

Fiction writers come up with some interesting metaphors when speaking of plot. Some say the plot is the highway and the characters are the automobiles. Others talk about stories that are "plot-driven," as if the plot were neither the highway nor the automobile, but the chauffeur. Others seem to have plot phobia and say they never plot. Still others turn up their noses at the very notion, as if there's something artificial, fraudulent, contrived.

Metaphors aside, readers and critics also say strange things about plot. They'll say a work of fiction is "*tightly* plotted," or "*strongly* or *weakly* plotted," or that a story "has too much plot," as if plot were the sort of spice that requires just the right amount. How much is too much?

It's said that some plots stink, and that others are tortured, feeble, confused, boring, or trite.

Fiction writers sometimes speak of character and plot as if they were in opposition to each other. They'll say that they think of their stories as being "70 percent character and 30 percent plot." But how can that be, when a plot is really nothing more than a recap of what the characters do? If the characters do nothing, if they're just sitting there being characters, there isn't a plot at all.

Talking about plot in the abstract, separated from character, is rather like talking about the *pretty* separated from the *maid*. A plot, of course, is not *only* a recap of what characters do. If it were, then a recap of my day thus far would be a plot:

I got up. I read the *San Francisco Chronicle* while the water boiled for coffee. I kissed my wife good-bye as she hurried off to work. I ate a bowl of bran cereal. I did twenty minutes on my exercise bike while I watched part of a tape of *Damn the Defiant!* I took a shower. I wrote a little on "The Philosophy of Plot." I met a friend for lunch. We both had vegetarian lasagna.

This isn't a plot because the actions of the characters have no significance. What gives significance to actions is taking them toward the resolution of some kind of predicament the character is facing. The predicaments fictional characters might face are infinite in their variety, from trying to light a lifesaving fire with just a few matches, to finding who killed Roger Axelrod, to coming to terms with some inner devil such as self-hatred, loneliness, or the silence of the gods.

All plotted works of fiction are not born equal. Some are intended to be more entertainments, and others are intended to be serious works of art that attempt to shed some light on the insanity of the human condition—or to point out that there is no light to shed and we might as well stop whining about it. But, in all of these stories, the plot is what the characters do in overcoming obstacles in a progression toward a resolution.

ENTERTAINING PLOTS

In entertainments, the characters tend to face problems that most flesh-and-blood people would never encounter. In an entertainment, a character might find a dead body in the trunk of his car, or be caught in an intergalactic war on Zorgon, or be skewered with Cupid's arrow.

Entertainment plots are largely determined by the conventions of the genre. A detective must unmask a killer. A detective must care who killed Roger Axelrod. In a Western, the heroic marshal can't decide to retire to the Bahamas. In a romance, the heroine doesn't decide to give up on the guy and become a nun.

Furthermore, the characters are engaged in accomplishing specific and concrete goals. The intrepid detective pursues the goal of unmasking the murderer, no matter how many knocks on the head she receives. What the characters do—those actions that constitute the plot—are somewhat predictable. The surprises, the originality, the creativity, come in the way in which the goals are accomplished. When James Bond sets out to stop Dr. No from incinerating all the major metropolitan centers of the world with his diamond laser in the sky, the reader knows what the outcome will be; it's the clever and inventive way the demise of Dr. No is accomplished that matters.

A fiction writer plotting entertainments, then, is charged with finding a *mission* for each of the major characters, both heroes and villains, making their motives believable, and seeing to it that they carry out their mission in clever, determined, and resourceful ways. The mission might be to fall in love, to commit a murder, to steal some jewels—virtually anything that'll result in the appropriate actions.

The opposing missions of the various characters create the plot. The best writers of entertainments think of fresh and original ways for these missions to be carried out. Plot, then, for the author of an entertainment, is a matter of playing a game of chess with an alter ego, always asking what clever and resourceful, surprising, yet believable thing this character will do next. And then asking how the character's antagonists will react. In the end there's often a climactic duel—James Bond dumps Dr. No in a fish tank full of sharks, or the like. Something deliciously, poetically just.

PLOTTING THE SERIOUS WORK

Melodramatic derring-do is not remotely related to the plot of a serious work of fiction. In serious fiction, what matters is character development. Take, for example, *Zorba the Greek*, the story of the free-spirited Zorba, who lives for wine, women, and song, and converts his "Boss," the narrator of the story, a rather uptight bookworm, to a life of passion. In *Zorba the Greek*, the Boss's bookworminess is the predicament he's in—he's so trapped he cannot give free rein to his passions. The plot of *Zorba the Greek* is the progress toward the resolution of that predicament, which is the Boss's development.

In *The Red Badge of Courage*, the hero, Henry Fleming, is at first a coward in battle. That is his predicament. He must find his courage. That's *his* development.

It has been eighty-four days since he caught a fish, and the other fishermen have started thinking Santiago, the hero of Hemingway's *The Old Man and the Sea*, is finished. On the eighty-fifth day, Santiago rows out into the deepest part of the Gulf Stream. He's not only after a fish, he's after the reclaiming of his manhood. He succeeds, and that's his development.

In a detective story, the hero often has no development. Hercule Poirot is pretty much the same from beginning to end of a particular novel; he merely changes in the way he perceives things. Popular action heroes such as James Bond, Dirk Pitt, or Captain Kirk don't develop much either; they're pretty much the same beginning to end, from book to book. But in a more serious work of dramatic fiction, the characters do change, often profoundly.

Scrooge in *A Christmas Carol* turns from unrepentant miser to generous celebrant; Charlie Allnut in *The African Queen* changes from a drunken sot to a responsible husband. Fred C. Dobbs in B. Traven's *The Treasure of the Sierra Madre* is changed from a rather likable, down-and-out tramp to a greedy paranoiac by his lust for gold.

Well-plotted, serious dramatic fiction is transformational by its very nature. The vicarious experience of this transformation is the most important reason people read serious fiction. A plot isn't just a matter of one thing happening after another; it's the progress toward the resolution of a predicament that transforms the character.

Plotting is further complicated by the problem of time.

Say we invent a protagonist, Fred Fix, for a story called "Guess What Happened at the 7-Eleven?" Here's the plot:

> Fred goes to work late one morning and his boss fires him. Because he's fired, he falls into despair. He drinks. He drags himself home at 3:30 the next morning. His wife is frantic. What will they do without money? She weeps bitterly, threatens to leave him. Fred decides to rob a 7-Eleven. ...

This story follows a *plot line*. In a plot line, everything that happens leads directly to the next. Such plots are often considered to be *tightly woven*. This is a very powerful way to tell a story because, as the story gains momentum, the tensions are not dissipated through gaps in time. Each event folds into the next.

Most entertainments—romances, thrillers, detective stories, Hollywood films—as well as many classics (*The Red Badge of Courage*, *The*

Old Man and the Sea, *Native Son*, *Of Mice and Men*, and hundreds more) are plot line stories.

But others are not, such as *Moby-Dick*, which covers many months and has a story line. In a story line, the events of the story are not causally related to one another but, rather, are part of the same chain of events that are progressing toward resolution.

Les Miserables is told in a story line covering decades. So are *Gone With the Wind*, *The Autobiography of Miss Jane Pittman*, and *Moll Flanders*. In a story line, the character development may be greater because the characters are not only changing as a result of the actions they're taking, but they're growing older as well. A story line is more difficult to handle because the emotions of the characters tend to evaporate over time between the events of the plot. It's difficult to believe, for example, that the flames of passion can still burn after twenty years.

It is possible to combine a story line and plot line in the same work. Usually the story line comes first, serving as a background to the plot line, but not always. In *Zorba the Greek*, for example, the first 90 percent or so of the story that takes place on Crete has a tightly woven plot line. The last chapter, the remaining 10 percent or so, relates Zorba's life of many years after he leaves Crete. The plot line becomes a story line.

OVERCOMING PLOT PROBLEMS

At one time or another, all writers—beginners and seasoned professionals, big talents and bad hacks—seem to have problems plotting. The most common problem is that the characters refuse to do what the author has planned for them. Whatever the author does to straighten this out, whatever action she pushes the characters to take, just doesn't seem right. The old sheriff won't strap on his gun as he's supposed to. The heroine won't go up to the hero's loft to see his etchings. The knight in shining armor won't enter the cave and do battle with the dragon.

This problem occurs because the author often identifies too strongly with the protagonist. The author is thinking of how the author would handle the problem, not how the character would handle the problem. The author is plotting her own story, not the character's story.

Frequently, however, characters lie dead on the page not because the author is pushing them to do what is not in them, but because they aren't well orchestrated. Plot arises out of opposing forces—forces that come out of the characters. One of the reasons *Leave It to Beaver* is the butt of so many jokes is that the characters, especially Mr. and Mrs. Cleaver, are badly orchestrated. Mr. and Mrs. Cleaver share the same values, opinions, hopes, and dreams. They're both perfect embodiments of their sterile, suburban, middle-class background. Since they're identical in every way, they're never in conflict with one another. Their bland sameness is stultifying. It's only the obnoxious sociopathic Eddie Haskell who rescues the TV series from the pit of total boredom.

All good plots come from well-orchestrated characters pitted against one another in a conflict of wills. The "Boss" and Zorba, Santiago and the marlin, Scrooge and Bob Cratchit are all well-orchestrated pairs, which by their natures will push the plot forward toward resolution.

If *The African Queen* had focused on *two* old sots in that rickety old boat, it would have been nothing more than a bug-infested adventure yarn. But when the uptight, straitlaced, Bible-thumping Rose is pitted against the old sot Charlie Allnut, you have fireworks in every line.

If, at the earliest stages of a work, the author creates the characters as strikingly different from one another as possible, plotting problems will be minimized. Say you're writing about a streetwise kid. Why not have him hide out from the law in a retirement home? Maybe you want to write about a high-powered woman lawyer in her forties. Why not have her fall in love with a twenty-six-year-old ski bum? That's good orchestration.

When you start with well-orchestrated characters, the plot often begins to unfold automatically. Once the characters are pitted against one another, the author needs only to present the predicament to send the characters on their mission. It is in working through the mission that the plot comes alive.

If what the characters do is true to their motivations and personalities and in keeping with their mission, the plot that emerges will not be artificial, fraudulent, or contrived, tortured, feeble, or weak. It will be tight and true to the characters and will have no falsity in it. Creating the plot from a set of well-orchestrated characters is one of the truly creative aspects of the fiction writer's craft. It is an art in itself, the practice of which is one of the great joys of writing.

JAMES N. FREY's nonfiction works include *How to Write a Damn Good Novel, How to Write a Damn Good Novel II: Advanced Techniques, The Key: How to Write Damn Good Fiction Using the Power of Myth,* and *How to Write a Damn Good Mystery: A Practical Step-by-Step Guide From Inspiration to Finished Manuscript.* He is an award-winning playwright and the author of nine novels, including *The Long Way To Die,* which was nominated for an Edgar Award by the Mystery Writers of America, and *Winter of the Wolves,* a Literary Guild Selection.

CHAPTER 7
THE PLOT THICKENS

BY MONICA WOOD

Every good story needs a complication. We learn this fiction-writing fundamental in courses and workshops, by reading a lot or, most painfully, through our own abandoned story drafts. After writing twenty pages about a harmonious family picnic, say, or a well-received rock concert, we discover that a story without a complication flounders, no matter how lovely the prose. A story needs a point of departure, a place from which the character can discover something, transform himself, realize a truth, reject a truth, right a wrong, make a mistake, come to terms.

This point of departure is the story's complication. The dog must get lost. The father must have a heart attack. The sound equipment must break down. The rock star's boyfriend must show up in a rage. A good complication engages the reader, gets the story going, and forms the beginning of a dramatic arc that will lead eventually to the story's conclusion.

Despite being a story's most critical structural element, the complication is often misunderstood, even by writers versed in the fundamentals of storytelling. Armed with the knowledge that a complication is necessary to good fiction, many of us make the mistake of thinking that if an event is exciting enough—an earthquake, a hurricane, a nine-car pileup on the interstate—it constitutes a good complication. This assumption is reasonable enough, but not necessarily true.

COMPLICATION VS. SITUATION

Let's say you're writing a story about a lowly clerk laboring at a nine-to-five job at the Internal Revenue Service. All you have so far is a vague idea of this character: You picture his rumpled shirt, his dirty eyeglasses, his old shoes. You place him in a secondhand Pontiac driving home from work. In other words, you have created a setup: a regular Joe in a dull job heading home. Now what? Something must happen. Enter the nine-car pileup on the interstate. The lowly IRS clerk pulls his car over and gets out. People are screaming, a baby is crying, doors are slamming, engine fires are breaking out; every few minutes our clerk cringes at the squealing brakes of other cars trying to avoid collision.

This is a pretty exciting predicament, filled with sounds and textures and high drama. The story is cooking on all four burners now. The nine-car pileup is a stroke of genius, a textbook complication, right? Wrong. You have made the very common early draft error of mistaking a situation for a complication.

It's often hard to determine, especially in early drafts, whether or not a story has a bona fide complication. Remember this: A complication must either illuminate, thwart, or alter what the character wants. A good complication puts emotional pressure on a character, prompting that character not only to act, but to *act with purpose*. If the circumstance does none of these things, it's not a complication at all—it's a situation. This situation, or setup, might be interesting or even astonishing, but it gives the story no point of departure. The character has no compelling motivation to act any differently from anyone else in the same circumstances. We learn nothing about him that we don't already know in general. Putting a character in a situation without adding a complication is like putting him on a hamster wheel—he might run fast, but he gets nowhere, and neither does your story.

Let's go back to the IRS clerk. As the story stands, he can respond in one of two ways to the so-called complication you have put in his way. He can sit in his car and wait till the cops clear the accident scene, or he can get out and start helping people. If he sits in his car feeling bad about himself, there isn't much more you can do with him. If he starts saving people and feels good about himself, the story might be a tad more interesting, but still won't go far. We won't learn much about him because he's not acting—he's reacting. He has nothing at stake, nothing to make this terrible accident anything more than a terrible accident.

He might pull some people from a burning back seat or give CPR to a kid on the road, but he's still on the hamster wheel.

Good complications are connected to character—they usually stir some kind of desire or regret, conscious or unconscious, in the character. How can you complicate this situation—a clerk coming upon a pileup—by connecting it to desire or regret within the character? What if the clerk had lost a son in an accidental drowning on a father-son fishing trip? Suddenly this new accident becomes more personal, and the clerk must act with purpose. He has a motivation that's bigger than that of an ordinary bystander helping at the scene. He tries to save as many people as he can, seeking to make up for not having saved his son. The drowning, not the interstate accident, is the complication in this story. The clerk now has something at stake. He must act upon that stake, and his actions illuminate both his desire (to resurrect his son) and his regret (that he could not save his son from drowning).

Now the story has a point of departure: We can learn all about the clerk's inner life by watching him act out the scenario he wishes he could have acted out when his son was in jeopardy. Certain sounds, voices, and faces can recall to him all the tragic aspects of that fateful fishing trip. Upon the stage of this traffic accident, this character can replay the most important event of his life and reveal to us who he is.

Let's apply a different complication to the same situation. What if the clerk recognizes one of the burning cars as belonging to his worst enemy, a supervisor who cooked the books and then blamed him, resulting in his demotion? When he gets to the car, he finds his enemy's wife and kids trapped inside. The wife and kids, not the accident itself, are the story's complication. Again, the complication personalizes the situation: The clerk can save the wife and kids and use the rescue as his trump card, perhaps a way to get his old job back. It illuminates the character's desire for one-upmanship.

Or maybe you decide on a complication that offers the clerk an opportunity for personal redemption. The wife and kids force him to admit that his enemy is a human being with human connections. In this case, the complication thwarts the character's desire to make his enemy suffer.

In both the drowning example and the wife-and-kids example, the complication provides the story with a point of departure—a way to discover what makes this character tick. Paradoxically, it's often the more subtle, internal elements that complicate a story. The larger predicaments become the stage on which these internal complications are played out.

TELLING THE DIFFERENCE

How do you tell the difference between a true complication and a mere situation? Experience helps. Try the following examples, asking yourself if each contains a complication that offers a point of departure, or merely a situation that places the character on a hamster wheel. In each example, I have included what the character wants.

1. Ralph's beloved wife is terminally ill. The complication is that she asks him to write her will. (What Ralph wants is to avoid facing the rest of his life alone.)

2. After eight years, a runaway teenager, now a young woman, returns to her parents' house. The complication is that her parents have moved and another family now lives there. (What the runaway wants is to be part of her family again.)

Of these examples, only the second meets the requirements of a complication. In the first, Ralph can write the will, feel sad about it, have a quiet moment with his wife, and that's about it. It's a situation fraught with sadness and maybe even a bit of tension, but it contains no point of departure. But what if the wife includes instructions for her funeral, which she envisions as a block party with a rock band playing "Stairway to Heaven"? This leaves shy Ralph with quite a burden—to contact his neighbors, find a band, and so on—and a vibrant, comical stage on which to play out his impending grief. If what Ralph wants is to avoid facing his life alone, the complication has the potential to illuminate this desire, or alter it, by forcing him into contact with other people.

In the second example, the new homeowners create an instant dilemma for the runaway. She can either search for her parents or try to insinuate herself into the family that's living in her parents' house.

The new family is indeed a complication, for it forces the character to act. If what she wants is to be part of a family, this complication can either thwart (her parents have moved away), alter (she decides against finding them, preferring the new family), or illuminate (she'll take any family, not necessarily the one she lost) her desire.

RAISING THE STAKES

Now that we have two examples that contain complications, let's determine whether they are good complications. As we saw in the opening example of the IRS clerk, a good complication should raise the stakes for the character. Do the preceding examples meet that criterion?

1. If Ralph is asked to write his wife's will, he has a stake in the sense that the will reminds him of his wife's imminent death. But a story about a man writing his wife's will provides no opportunity for the stakes to change. By adding a good complication (the eccentric terms of the will), we raise the stakes for Ralph. Suddenly he has to face not only death, but also life (hiring a band, meeting the neighbors), which he is even more frightened of.

2. The runaway teen who finds a new family in her old house is a good example of a complication. The stakes rise instantly for this character because the complication reverses her position. Instead of playing the prodigal daughter, she has been thrust into the position of searcher, which is the very position she put her parents in eight years ago.

THICKENING THE PLOT

So far, so good. Both complications raise the stakes for the character. But a good complication should also open pathways to a further complication. Let's test our examples:

1. The eccentric terms of the will open not only one path to Ralph, but several. He could find a band to hire and discover a whole new world of music and youth; he could meet a neighbor on the block who turns out to be an acquaintance from

high school; he could discover unknown facts about his wife through the neighbors.

2. The missing parents is a complication that also opens up several paths. The runaway could sit down with the new homeowners and work her way in, trying to turn strangers into substitute parents; she could discover things about her parents by conducting a search—maybe they went broke trying to find her or had another baby to replace her.

A well-chosen complication should give you choices. Juggling choices for your characters is what makes writing fun, after all. If you discover that you're struggling more than you ought to with a draft, perhaps you've run out of interesting choices, or have given yourself too few choices to begin with. Go back to the complication, fatten it up, and start over.

SUSTAINING DRAMATIC TENSION

Besides raising the stakes and thickening the plot, a complication should create and sustain dramatic tension throughout the story. Do our examples pass the "dramatic tension" test?

1. The eccentric terms of the will could create conflict between Ralph and his wife. As Ralph tries to complete the tasks before him, each offers Ralph new drama and new possibilities for discovering something (either good or bad) about his wife or himself—in short, more tension.

2. A runaway returning to a set of strangers is dramatic all by itself. The tension can be sustained or increased depending on the reaction of the new homeowners. Perhaps they try to help the runaway more than she wants; maybe the runaway realizes that the new homeowners have themselves lost a child and see her as a miraculous replacement; or the tension could increase as the runaway conducts her search and discovers unwanted or shocking information about her parents.

THE STORY'S WEIGHT

As you can see, your story's complication serves a variety of functions. Even if it fulfills these functions adequately, however, the complication still may not be strong enough to hold up the weight of the story. You have to take a hard look at the complication and decide whether it can carry the number of pages you're planning.

For example, a simple complication—a man loses his job—might carry a very short story of four to eight pages. For a longer story—up to twelve pages—the complication should be more complex: A man loses his job, so his wife kicks him out of the house. For a still longer story, we need a complication that can lead further: A man loses his job, gets kicked out of the house, and, in a fit of despair and nostalgia, goes searching for his long-lost high school sweetheart. This kind of complication can hold up twenty-five or thirty pages for it can lead almost anywhere: The sweetheart can turn out to be dead, or a prostitute, or a CEO in a company owned by the one that just fired him. The wife can chase after her husband once she sees what he's up to, or she can serve him with divorce papers. The choices are many—and the more choices, the more pages the story can credibly sustain.

INTERNAL AND EXTERNAL COMPLICATIONS

Complications can spring from internal factors, from things within your character, or from external developments. The IRS clerk, for example, has an internal complication—the memory of his son. The runaway's complication—the parents having moved away—is an external one, an event that has happened outside of her, something she discovers.

Internal complications usually lead to reflection rather than action. Reflective stories are usually short, partly because internal change goes more quickly on the page and partly because reflective stories can try the reader's patience after about ten pages.

External complications typically require more room to play themselves out. The runaway's complication, for instance, demands a lot of action on the part of the character—she must undergo a search, moving from scene to scene as she comes closer to a resolution about her parents' disappearance.

Sometimes it pays to hedge your bets, balancing an internal complication (or a very simple one) with an exciting or unusual situation. In the case of the IRS clerk, the complication is deeply internal, but the situation in which the complication appears—the interstate pileup—is full of action.

Experience will show you how far to take a complication, and how to use it to advance the story, explore character, and engage the reader. The trick is making sure that the complication you have created is a real one in the first place, and provides the hinge on which your story swings open. That's when fiction takes off and when complication turns into fascination for your readers.

MONICA WOOD is the author of the novels *Any Bitter Thing, My Only Story, Secret Language,* and a book of connected short stories titled *Ernie's Ark.* She is also the author of *Pocket Muse: Ideas and Inspirations for Writing, Pocket Muse 2: Endless Inspiration for Writers, Description,* from the Writer's Digest Elements of Fiction series, and several guides to contemporary literature in the high school classroom.

CHAPTER 8

WHAT I STOLE FROM THE MOVIES

BY LES STANDIFORD

Every genre of writing has its essential structural element: poems accrete line by line; nonfiction moves paragraph by paragraph; stories and novels grow scene by scene. That last idea is an important realization for fiction writers, but not necessarily an easy one to make.

For me, the discovery was something of an accident, born of a midlife career detour that took me out of the classroom, where I'd been teaching writing for more than a decade, to Los Angeles, where I became a student again—specifically, a screenwriting fellow at the American Film Institute. I learned plenty about writing for film at AFI, but, as I like to tell my own students nowadays, the most valuable lessons I learned there had to do with the writing of fiction. And particularly the kind of fiction intended to engage the attention of an audience. I was still trying to place my first novel when I began to study screenwriting; a dozen years later, I've published seven, and I credit a large part of this success to techniques I stole from Hollywood.

A SCENIC DISCOVERY

The fiction I wrote before my foray westward was typical. Like most other novelists, I made use of the five basic modes of fictional discourse when writing a story: dialogue (*"I love you," she said softly*), action (*She reached across the rumpled sheets to touch the back of his neck*), description (*The motel's clanky air conditioning unit coughed and throbbed in response*), thought (*She wondered for a moment if he'd even heard her*), and exposition (*She'd been in Key Largo for a year now, drawn to the tropics from Detroit by the prospect of meeting a more exciting type of man).*

One of the sad truths I faced as I began writing for the screen was that I could no longer take refuge in exposition or thought, there being no opportunity to use those modes in dramatic writing (with the possible exception of the soliloquy or the voice-over, neither technique being much in filmic vogue these days). Difficult as it was to be deprived of 40 percent of the fiction writer's bag of tricks, I accepted soon enough that anything I wanted to convey about my film characters and story would have to be conveyed dramatically, through description, dialogue, and action alone.

Ultimately, the process brought me to a new appreciation of scene—that dramatic unit of action that features a character or characters speaking/acting/interacting and is delineated by a shift in time or place, or the entrance or exit of a character. The more scenes I wrote for film, the more that style began to creep into my fiction as well. Yet I discovered that far from losing power as a fiction writer, I seemed to be gaining it instead. And I was discovering an entirely new way of propelling my stories forward.

DIRTY HARRY MEETS McDONALD'S

Let me show you what I discovered.

Assume that as scriptwriters, we've already established a MAN in his thirties pulling into the parking lot of a fast-food restaurant late at night and parking his jalopy toward the back.

In the next scene, we see the employee's entrance door swinging inward with a BANG, our less-than-enthusiastic guy from the jalopy now slogging down the hallway past a locker room, snatching a white coat and paper hat from a hook and moving on into the bowels of the place until he reaches the nook where the take-out station is housed. Our guy notes the time on a wall clock—midnight straight up. He shoos a pimply KID off the stool there, sits down with a sigh. He shrugs his way into the coat, dons the ridiculous hat, adjusts the microphone used to communicate with the customers outside. He notes the pimply kid is watching him. He gives the kid an appraising glance, but there's not much to see. He turns away, closes his eyes for a moment, a pianist about to begin, a diver about to dive. He lets out his breath, opens his eyes, reaches into his coat, withdraws a Dirty-Harry-sized revolver that he clunks down on a shelf just beneath the take-out window. He reaches into another pocket, withdraws a half pint of something, takes a healthy swig. "They didn't say the new security man was gonna be a boozer," the kid says, as our guy slips his bottle back. Our guy thinks about it. "It steadies one's nerves under such tense circumstances," he says mildly, and bangs the flashing red intercom button with the flat of his hand. When we cut outside to a sleek low-rider with heavily smoked windows idling throatily, ominously, by the ordering station, we've moved on to the next scene.

Our scene is a short one, about a page long, amounting to about 1 percent of the typical, one hundred-minute-long contemporary film. If this scene were to stick in our hypothetical film—and said film were to actually be produced and end up costing, let's say, $30 million to make (and that's on the conservative side for a major studio production these days)—then that one-page scene proposed by the writer could be conceived of—in a strange way, admittedly—as a suggestion that someone actually spend about $300,000 to bring that figment of imagination into filmic life.

Let's put it another way: The writer would in fact be suggesting that this one-page scene is worth a cool three hundred grand.

Now, even though it costs a fiction writer virtually nothing to stage a scene on the page, it's my contention that there would be a heck of a lot more effective fiction being written if we all approached the work as if it did. We've all heard the advice: "Use every word you need, but not a single word more." The analogy to the film writer's world gives that principle of economy a brand new shade of meaning. And while dollars have little to do with it, the fiction writer should be asking the same question any capable film producer would ask: "Is this scene truly necessary?" It is the kind of thinking that, put into practice, results in a story with a sense of energy and direction, no handicap so far as editors and readers are concerned.

MAKING IT WORTH $300,000

Even without much context, the hypothetical scene above suggests its own reason for being. We are presented with a "security man" whose job it is to protect a burger franchise from the threat of late-night robbers. He's something of a burnout case, but not so far gone that he can't appreciate the tawdriness of his condition. And while he may not be a superhero on the face of it, he clearly poses more of a barrier to thieves than anyone else around. Finally, his very appearance sets up something of an experiment in anticipation for the audience. What would happen if this character had to use that formidable-looking weapon he's just plunked down?

A good scene will do at least one of three things just alluded to:

- enrich character
- provide necessary information to the audience
- move the plot forward

The best scenes do all three. Then there are those scenes that have wormed their way into the story because they have some sweet-sounding sentences (loving description of how those fast-food burgers sizzle and pop on the grill), or provide a glimpse of compelling but extraneous character (the pimply kid's girlfriend who has dropped by to show off her newly pierced tongue, only to leave as our security man enters), or repeat what we have already seen (our security man stops off to buy his half pint on the way to work, making a show of buying a cheap brand of whiskey). These scenes do none of the above and will simply have to go.

Such decisions are easily made in the world where pages are valued at $300,000 and up.

But the priceless principle of economy in fiction should be applied just as rigorously. Long gone are the days when editors had time to pare down mountainous manuscripts to expose the lean, mean stories embedded therein. Modern readers, bombarded by a million requests for their attention, have been conditioned to expect fiction that embeds the Bard's injunction: "More matter, less art."

Thinking in terms of a dramatic scene also makes it more likely that the writer will avoid that age-old bugaboo of the "passive protagonist," that sad sack of a main character who doesn't do much of anything but think or remember or sometimes—kicking and screaming all the way—react to circumstances. While it may be true that most of us, especially us writers, spend our real lives observing, reacting, mulling, and remembering, the most interesting fictional characters are those who get themselves into real jams by doing things.

Never open your story with a character thinking, I advise my students. As a further precaution, don't put a character in a room alone—create a friend, a bystander, a genie, for God's sake, *any* sentient creature with whom your main character can converse, perhaps argue or, better yet, engage in some action. If a person is out and doing, it's more likely that something interesting might happen to him. Shut up in a room with only his thoughts for company ... well, that way lies fictional disaster.

ONE ALL-BEEF SCENE—HOLD THE EXPO

As I've suggested, all scenes can enrich the characters, provide information, and advance the plot without calling on the least dramatic of the five fictional modes: thought and exposition. Were I to convert our Burgerama scene to fiction, I would surely expand it, noting details of our security man's dress (nothing remarkable, except for the surprisingly good shoes, or maybe a dinged-up but once-expensive watch), his specific brand of whiskey (Early Times? Jack Black? Wild Turkey?), the sights and sounds and smells of the backside of this burger emporium (ah, the grease, the disinfectant, the doomsday clang of that Dumpster). I might possibly extend the moment of meeting and conversation between the security man and pimply kid, but I doubt that I would change the scene's essentially dramatic nature. There's an inherent suspense in revealing our security man's mission in stages. He is transformed bit by bit from just another schlub piling out of his jalopy to an unlikely employee of the restaurant to a potential agent of justice in one short page.

Were I to allow my readers access to our guy's thoughts as he pulled in the lot (*Exley groaned inwardly as he contemplated the long night of surveillance ahead*), or allude to it directly through exposition as he walks down the hall toward his post at the take-out window (*Exley hadn't wanted this evening's assignment, but his superiors at Acme Security had been adamant*), I would lose something of the suspense I refer to and further vitiate the proceeding by "giving" readers information as opposed to allowing readers to participate in the process of discovery. (This is one of the principal reasons for that time-honored plea of the writing teacher: "Show me, don't tell me.")

Maybe it's because we as writers are alone so often, are so attuned to listening to the run of our thoughts, that we find it more natural to write down the thoughts rather than the deeds of our characters. But speaking as a teacher who has spent some twenty years slogging through manuscripts where thoughts and exposition pile up as thick as the aftermath of a California mudslide, I can attest to the power of the evocative detail, gesture, or fragment of speech. There's much that's implied in our security man's glance, or in his simple response to the kid's criticism of his drinking: "It steadies one's nerves under such tense circumstances."

JUST ONE SCENE AFTER ANOTHER

By structuring the Burgerama scene in the way that we have, we mirror the way stories as a whole are most profitably structured with a beginning, middle, and end, each scene or event linked and leading into the next. This linking reminds readers (as well as the writer) that this enterprise is going somewhere. "Ending" the scene decisively also guards against the tendency to drift along, and requires some hard thought about what will happen next.

This naturally prods the writer to imagine a subsequent event that will be in some way more interesting than what has been experienced to date. Who is in that mysterious, rumbling low-rider outside? And what will our security man do if it's who we think it might be? (By the way, Aristotle referred to this phenomenon as "rising action" and promulgated its value for literature long before the advent of wide screens and Dolby surround sound.)

Working scene by scene, the writer finds it easier to move the story along and to jump over extraneous material. If an angry husband throws up his hands in the midst of an argument with his wife and stomps toward the door of his apartment, announcing that he's going out for a drink, there's no need to follow him out the door and down the hall, into the stairwell, down to the street, into his car, and so on. We can simply end the first scene with the slamming of the apartment door and begin the next as our husband signals Charley the bartender for another beer. Readers can easily follow the jump and, once again, be grateful for the author's sense of economy.

Just how much can be skipped? That question gets into larger issues of plot, but let's leave it at this: Skip as much as possible. Get into a scene as late as possible and get out as quickly as you can. Most of today's readers have had considerable exposure to film and are accustomed to making significant jumps. Were we to cut from our security man's post in the bowels of Burgerama to a basement room somewhere and close in on the image of gloved hands jacking a round into the chamber of a shotgun, most viewers—and readers—would understand the connection.

All that's necessary is for readers to see or sense an inexorable flow, a linkage of events, one to the next. The classic illustration is given by E.M. Forster in *Aspects of the Novel*, where he distinguishes between the discontinuous events of a story. (The king died. And then the queen died) and the interconnected events of a plot (The king died. And then the queen died of grief).

There are vast differences between scripts and stories, of course. Few fiction writers would want to give up the opportunity to explore how the minds of their characters work, or to set aside the opportunity to provide necessary background exposition in a succinct fashion.

But even those modes can be enlivened by considering the lessons of artful scene writing: Make those thoughts vivid (*Exley tried to imagine the pimply kid kissing his girlfriend—would her tongue stud get hung up in his braces?*) and be sure any exposition is equally engaging (*Exley had worked the Burgerama stakeout for a month last year, downing all the burgers, fries, and shakes he wanted. He'd gone from a thirty-three waist to a thirty-six and used up two week's salary changing his wardrobe).*

SCENE SETTERS

"Steal from everybody," one of my early writing teachers told me. "Take help wherever you can find it." I'm not sure he had Hollywood in mind, but the advice stayed with me anyway.

To help it stay with you, get in the habit of asking yourself a few questions about your scene:

- Is this scene necessary, or am I keeping it around simply because I spent all that time and effort writing it?
- What exactly does it add in terms of character development, necessary information, or plot movement?
- How much of the scene's work can be done by the most dramatic modes of fiction: dialogue, action, and description?
- Have I given my scene its own beginning, middle, and end?
- Is there a place for a background element that might enrich the proceedings?
- Have I gotten in quickly and gotten out as soon as possible?
- What should or would happen next?

Asking yourself these questions at the end, or the beginning, of a day's work will inevitably result in more vivid, energetic, and compelling fiction. I stole the idea from the movies. You can, too.

LES STANDIFORD is director of the Creative Writing Program at Florida International University in Miami. The recipient of the Frank O'Connor Award for Short Fiction and fellowships in fiction from the NEA and the Florida Arts Council, he has published numerous articles and stories. His novels include *Spill*, *Done Deal*, *Raw Deal*, and *Deal to Die For.*

CHAPTER 9
GETTING YOUR ACT(S) TOGETHER

BY RIDLEY PEARSON

There are conventions, structures, and forms to writing fiction that help you hold all the pieces together and transform an idea into a story. The form called the three-act structure, handed down to us from the ancient Greeks, is one that's proven successful for thousands of years.

The study of the three-act structure has been ongoing since it evolved from the mythic adventures that have long been part of classical education, but Christopher Vogler put it into accessible terms. Each writer defines the three-act structure in his own way. Fiction is a fluid art form. But I highly recommend any writer pick up a copy of Vogler's *The Writer's Journey* before writing another word.

We dream our dreams in a basic structure, and the Ancient Greeks followed this structure in their myths. To write fiction in the structure in which we dream gives the reader a level of familiarity that makes stories meaningful and accessible.

The three acts are known by various titles and their ingredients referred to in various ways: Beginning, Middle, End; Opening, Development, Conclusion; The Decision to Act, The Action, The Consequences of the Action.

Following this form, or at least being aware of its long-proven success, will help you get a handle on what's working and what's not in your stories.

In starting an outline, I like to think up four or five big moments that will occur in the story. These are turning points, or darkest moments.

From here, I bridge to connect these scenes, adding several smaller turning points to connect the dots.

My technique is a holdover from scriptwriting. I card these scenes and hang them on the wall. But regardless of how you start the massive job of assembling the character(s) and story lines in your novel, in the end, the story should be structured in three acts.

ACT 1—THE CHALLENGE

This first act establishes action, characters, and what's at stake. Our protagonist, or lead character, faces something new—something that requires his participation. A journey. A quest. He must decide to accept the challenge. Vogler talks about the Hero leaving the "Ordinary World" and stresses that the early part of the story shows the Ordinary World in order to later distinguish the "Special World." I think of it in terms of set-up. You want to establish your character(s) in the real world; to set up the world where your character(s) exist. The reader needs a reference point, and somewhere early in the story is your chance to show the protagonist in his everyday life. That way, when we see the challenge that's the central conflict of the story, we'll start at the level ground from which the protagonist must climb the mountain. By seeing the mountain more clearly, this also allows us to identify the antagonist. By inference, we learn not only who our protagonist is, but also what he's made of, or at least the level of threat the antagonist presents.

In the first act, we learn what's at stake for the protagonist—what he has to lose, and therefore we begin to imagine what he might gain.

Vogler refers to the early element of Act 1 as the "Call to Adventure." The Hero is presented with a problem, challenge, or adventure that he must solve or complete. In a detective mystery, it's the first crime. In a story of revenge, it's a wrong to be righted. In a romance, it's an early encounter with a future love interest.

Story is character. Act 1 shows the reader the boundaries that the protagonist must operate within. This includes phobias, fears, limitations, and other flaws. They may be physical or mental; real or imagined; age-based or gender-based. Show your character as human. Show his flaws and his vulnerability because this is the character mountain he must climb while he follows his call to adventure. The protagonist is often reluctant to accept the challenge. He's facing his biggest fears and is in no hurry to jump into the fray. The characters face internal conflicts (character issues) just as they face external conflicts (the challenge of the story). Act 1 is where all of this is brought to the page.

He can still turn back at this point. You see the internal and external conflicts, and the reader is rooting for him to go for it. But before he does, he may need to be pushed.

Vogler writes of the mentor, the sage, the Obi-Wan character who's consulted and is the catalyst for the Hero to make the commitment to the Adventure. The mentor prepares the protagonist for the challenge. Think: The Good Witch explains about the Wizard and the Emerald City and then delivers the ruby slippers to Dorothy.

Consulting a mentor also gives the writer a chance to show, not tell, the reader about the protagonist. The mentor verbalizes the fears the protagonist must face; he can tell us or show us something about the protagonist by remembering something from the past. The mentor is therefore a vehicle to the backstory (and as the writer you must know the character's backstory, whether or not you choose to ever share it with the reader). The mentor is a great tool for exposition about the emotional depth of the protagonist and what events may be responsible for his greatest fears.

The end of Act 1 throws the protagonist into the decision to accept the challenge. This is the first big moment. This could be a first-hand confrontation with the evil—personified or not—and by taking a stand or simply by not running away from the challenge, the decision is made.

Here the protagonist overcomes the concerns, accepts the complications, passes the tests and, with an awareness that it's dangerous, decides to take on this challenge.

The conflict is now fully realized; it's no longer just talk. The protagonist's decision to move forward is seen by the reader as a defining moment; it forms a lasting impression of character in the reader's mind. We get our first really good look at what kind of person this is—and we like him.

Vogler calls it crossing the first threshold. The Hero faces the consequences of accepting the Call to Adventure. The story takes off. The Hero takes action. Think: Dorothy heads out onto the Yellow Brick Road.

ACT 2—ACTION

Act 2 involves development of story and character and the darkest moment. Action heats up. Challenges complicate. Characters expand. The protagonist has accepted the challenge, and he must come to face that challenge and move forward to survive.

Vogler defines the start of the second act as a series of tests, a time to confirm allies and enemies. The Hero learns the rules of this Special World. Vogler points out that surprisingly often, saloons and bars offer the necessary backdrop (think *Star Wars*), settings that allow exposition of both the new world and the various characters involved.

Complications make the pursuit (of truth, of love, of a treasure or individual) more difficult than expected. In a detective story or mystery, there might be more murders discovered at this stage. Whatever the case, the level of confusion for the protagonist and the reader increases.

In romance, relationships entangle and nothing is as it seemed. Preparation is needed to face one's fears and one's mortal enemy. This next phase isn't to be taken lightly.

It's during this preparation that there's a reflective moment where lovers or fellow protagonists share backstory and further inform us of who they are. This is the "sitting around the fire" moment—and it precedes entering the dark place.

Vogler talks about the Hero standing at the mouth of the cave. Plans must be made before he enters. When he finally crosses that line and enters the inmost cave, he crosses a second threshold, or another big moment. Very often the ordeal takes place, literally, in a cave or dark underground place. (In my novel *The Art of Deception*, I used a little-known subterranean space under Seattle.) Stories are rich with these locations for the obvious reference to Hell. The Hero faces the ordeal and appears to die. The reader is depressed by the apparent loss of the Hero, only to be overjoyed when he resurfaces. Having survived and beaten the dragon, he grabs the sword (the treasure, truth, knowledge, or relationship) and leaves the inmost cave.

This darkest moment is when everything goes to ruin, and we fear for the protagonist's life (or relationship or whatever's at stake). The airplane is out of fuel, and the parachutes turn out to be twenty years old and made of rotting cloth, for example. But the protagonist prevails, surviving when we thought he was doomed. He puts the challenge behind him. Or so we think. This is the beauty of the end of the second act: What feels like a finale is in fact a setup to the third and final act.

The second act is a balance of action, story development, and interiorizing the characters. We're not going to have time to resolve everything in the third act without it feeling forced. This is a place first-time novelists make mistakes. Near the end of the second act is a good time to resolve subplots, or at least move them along so you can resolve them quickly in the third act. Red herrings in mysteries need to be exposed and/or new developments need to arise that eliminate many of them as well as many of the earlier complications. We clear the reader's mind to focus on the protagonist getting home safely with the treasure in hand. We're not going to want to stop and explain things in the third act, so now's the time to get stuff out of the way. You can use dialogue to do this, letting one character explain or show something to another character that, in turn, informs the reader that we don't need to think about that (person, place, or thing) any longer.

ACT 3—THE CONSEQUENCES

Now it's time for the unexpected to give rise to a final threat that brings closure. The third act is where the chase hits full stride. It begins with the unexpected and ends with the long anticipated. This is where winning at the end of Act 2 turns out to be only a minor victory, and the threat the protagonist overcame turns out to be not the only one he'll have to overcome. This is also the act for the big twist; shock value pays off. The character, having achieved new heights, must remain on or above those heights; there's no return, no lessening of strength in this act—the character has hit his stride and now, if anything, must run even faster. If we spent the first two acts making our protagonist flawed, vulnerable, and human, here's where he overachieves and becomes superhuman. Dorothy will kill the witch. Luke will slay Lord Vader.

The opening of Act 3 typically involves a chase. Vogler explains that the Hero is pursued on the road back by the same forces he disturbed by Seizing the Sword. The Hero elects to return to the Ordinary World from which he came; the Special World must be left behind. Challenges, dangers, and more tests still lie ahead.

Act 3 provides for the big twist. What we thought was true turns out to be false. The elusive truth finally takes hold, and we realize we've been wrong all along. This propels the protagonist to a final threat.

The final threat is the "dead" guy jumping in from stage left, not dead at all. This is the guy pulling himself out of the river and dragging himself to shore to attack the protagonist one final time. It's the lover coming back to mend the wounds, only to see the protagonist with a new lover.

The protagonist, having learned something (about himself or others) at the conclusion of Act 2 can now reap the benefit of that knowledge and prevail one final time. In doing so, he's a changed man. He's made it. It's over. He can return, with no desire to be somewhere else or someone else. He's whole again.

Vogler writes that the story is meaningless if the Hero returns without what he calls the elixir. This is a truth, an antidote, a treasure, a lesson. Dorothy realizes there's no place like home. Someone graduates from college, or training camp or boot camp. There's a truth gained, and it's worth all he's gone through.

This is the payoff. All that's been accomplished, all that's been learned. Not only has he gained the external treasure, but he's also cemented a character change in the protagonist that will affect him in a positive way and allow for healing, or a better relationship, or stability. We celebrate with the protagonist that this has all been worth it.

The end often shows the reuniting with someone from whom the protagonist separated at the start of the story: This could be an idea, a belief system, or a person. The protagonist, and the reader along with him, is made whole. Ordinary life can continue again.

There's no simple formula for fiction. But there's a centuries-proven form to good storytelling that follows this three-act structure. All of these conventions are there to be fooled with—there's no right way. In my novel *Cut and Run*, I started the book in Act 2 by weaving the elements of Act 1 into a story that was already moving at the pace of an Act 2. The result is a fast read, but it was no simple task to construct the story this way.

The three-act form is there because it works. Name a film or book you think rises above others, and chances are, if you go back and study it, the story line will fit into this form. We often think of the start of a story as a blank page—nothing there but our idea. But it's not true. With the three-act structure, we have a massive foundation to support, sustain and maintain our stories.

RIDLEY PEARSON is a nationally best-selling author of more than twenty-five crime fiction novels. In 2008–2009 he served as a visiting professor in the College of International Language and Literature at Fudan University, Shanghai, China where he taught Mythic Three Act Structure in Contemporary Fiction.

CHAPTER 10
NAILING THE CONCLUSION

BY MICHAEL ORLOFSKY

There is a paradox about the beginnings of short stories that is helpful when writing their endings: The opening of a story is both its strongest and weakest place. Strongest because it must hook reader interest; weakest because every following line enriches or deepens the narrative.

There is no such paradox about endings: Each of these must be the strongest point in its story. In its subtlety, the ending will give reason for pause and reflection; in its magnificence, the ending will prompt cheering readers to splinter the author's door from its hinges, to lay hands on him and carry him through the streets on their shoulders.

Because of stakes such as these, I find that many beginning writers become unnerved by endings. More than once I've written *Don't bail out!* on one of my student's manuscript when the ending seemed too easy, vague, matter of fact, bombastic, or, ironically, conclusive.

When beginning writers fail to grasp their *story's sense of ending*, it's often because they haven't fully grasped the *sense of story*. The old chestnut remains true: In the end, the protagonist should be changed by the plot or have been faced with the opportunity to change.

A RHETORIC OF ENDINGS

What is an ending supposed to do? On a basic level, of course, it simply concludes the plot. Homer said it all, and he's a good place to start. For all the richness of *The Iliad*, Homer finishes the epic quite plainly with the line: "So they performed the funeral rites of Hektor, tamer of horses." The burial of the Trojan hero is handled simply yet powerfully, but the function of the scene is to bring the plot to a close. Period. The end.

The end is just the beginning, on the other hand, for characters in the contemporary story, and *this* paradox is responsible for the often-criticized blandness or ambiguity of many modern endings. As the sense of helplessness, desperation, and cynicism in our century has evolved—and as the Act of the Hero has devolved from crossing the Rubicon to waking up one morning as a cockroach—acts of individuality have become mute and tentative.

In light of this modern condition, the so-called "resolution" at the end of the modern short story often resolves little. Novels need resolutions because of the reader's need to tie up loose ends. A story, on the other hand, *is* a loose end, which often simply *exposes* the subtle and sometimes enigmatic shifts in a character's attitude or outlook. The old-fashioned Aristotelian terms for these shifts in attitude and outlook are *reversal* and *recognition*, and they are as valid today as ever.

Reversal is a change of situation—Aristotle would have identified it as a 180-degree change in fortune, as when Oedipus falls from king of Thebes to blind beggar. In modern fiction, however, the concept of reversal is more important than the *degree* of reversal. For example, at the end of a story, a couple can be shown falling from love to not quite love.

Recognition goes hand in hand with reversal. It happens when the protagonist *realizes* his reversal, realizes the consequences of his choice, or at least lingers on the cusp of realization. Aristotle stresses that reversal and recognition must satisfy the moral sense.

Moral sense is not synonymous with a happy or even righteous ending, however; many endings are unhappy, and life is often unjust. Rather, it is the sense that something humanly important has been at stake in the story: integrity, love, hope, humility, courage, or their opposites.

One of my professors at the Iowa Writers Workshop, Jim McPherson, says one of the major problems of much modern fiction is the lack of a sense of ending. He observes that these endings tend to be static—displaying neither choice nor the struggle of the soul.

Yet, choice and struggle are important, McPherson says, "*if* you believe in fiction as serving a moral purpose." Serious stuff, and the Pulitzer Prize winner was a serious teacher.

Endings should suggest this seriousness. Serious fiction has *always* served a moral purpose because, after all, what is character except a collection of values?

TYPES OF ENDINGS

Every ending should be unique and, ideally, the author should say things that have never been said before. There are several types of endings that are enduring, however, and their sheer popularity over the centuries shows that they are, somehow, inherently satisfying to readers. Here are six of them.

Dead Men Tell No Tales

Death is how all our personal stories will end. But the first *don't* I tell my writing classes is this: Don't kill off characters. Death at the end of a story is valid for two effects—shock or sentimentality—and neither makes for a satisfying ending (except, *maybe*, in thrillers or romances). Killing off characters is a cheap way to achieve closure, and perhaps what bothers me most when students resort to this tactic is my sense of their casualness about violence and death.

Several years ago, a student turned in a story about a couple who responds to a newspaper ad for a crossbow. They drive to the home of another couple selling the weapon. After nine pages of development, in which the foursome are seen in a kind of story of manners, the visiting husband suddenly shoots the seller in the head with one of the crossbow bolts. The visitors leave, deciding they don't want the crossbow after all—because the draw weight was too low.

Whoa! The ending wasn't supported by the plot or characterizations. There was no argument, no suggestion that the visitors were homicidal, no motivation. I told the student to rewrite the end. Well, the rascal revised the story, but in addition to killing the seller, the husband now went into the kitchen and killed the seller's wife. Nice and neat shock value, but the student invalidated his nine pages of character development.

The struggle is life, not death. No student has yet persuaded me that a character killed in a story deserves a point of view. Dead men tell no tales.

At the end of *For Whom the Bell Tolls*, Hemingway shows Robert Jordan alive, alone, badly injured, and facing a troop of Franco's cavalry. Hemingway's ending? "He could feel his heart beating against the pine needle floor of the forest." The resonance of the line—kinesthetically and emotionally—is great.

Recognition

Little turns off a mature and sensitive reader more quickly and more intransigently than being told what to think. Yet, beginning fiction writers do this all the time. This is what I mean by endings that are too conclusive. In all likelihood, this is a symptom of a story told more for its message than its drama.

These stories are about an *idea* rather than about a *character* struggling with an idea. The dialogue sounds like philosophical debate; the exposition reads like a set of instructions.

A student once submitted a story about a college student who works her way through four years of school dancing in a strip joint. The woman has been grinding away at the club to the tune of five hundred dollars a night, but as graduation nears, she's faced with the dilemma of staying with the fast money or teaching junior high.

The author provided this ending: "A tough decision lay ahead, but [she] knew she would make the right choice. She had achieved her goals and surpassed them, and even though she had compromised herself with her job, she had every reason to be proud of herself."

There's not much room for reflection here, is there? I understand students' interest in idea and theme because they come to my writing class primed with two, three, or four years of university training in text analysis. I constantly remind them to think like writers, not like literary critics: It's not what an ending means that's important, but how it means. *How* has the author achieved suspense, irony, or empathy?

The best endings never conclude or close; they open. They always keep the synapses firing between the story's pages and the reader's imagination.

The ending of James Joyce's "Araby" is an example of an author's skillful use of theme in combination with a character's dilemma. In the story, the young protagonist finally arrives late at a bazaar he has been waiting anxiously to attend. Many of the stalls already have closed, and the lights in the hall are dimming: "Gazing up into the darkness I saw myself as a creature driven and derided by vanity; and my eyes burned with anguish and anger."

Framing With Repetition

One of the most effective ways to produce closure is by framing the narrative. In fiction, well-handled repetition creates richness and resonance—like two parallel mirrors reflecting endlessly.

Imagery often is repeated during periods of emotional crisis; an example would be that of the rain in Hemingway's *A Farewell to Arms*. But any element of writing—dialogue, setting, characterization, even a word—can be repeated for resonance. Dante ends *Inferno*, *Purgatorio*, and *Paradiso* with the same word: *stars*. Carson McCullers introduces and ends "The Ballad of the Sad Café" with the same sentence: "You might as well go down to the Forks Falls highway and listen to the chain gang."

In addition to providing thematic or tonal completeness, framing also serves the structural function of physically closing the narrative. It satisfies the reader's esthetic need for pattern.

Surprise or Revelation

Unveiling a surprise—an unexpected twist in plot or character behavior—may be the oldest tactic for ending a story. It plays on the reader's natural penchant for suspense and delight in revelation.

In contemporary fiction, however, the surprise ending has fallen out of favor. For the highly literate and informed reader, there are few surprises left. Assassinations, drive-by shootings, and other cruel twists of fate are in the headlines every day.

Writers sometimes slap a surprise ending on a story for shock value. For instance, a husband trying to talk his wife into fellatio while driving along the Lake Pontchartrain Causeway when their pickup suddenly swerves into the guardrail and catapults over the water. The end. "But it happens in real life," students say, rallying to defend the story. But real life doesn't always make good fiction.

Surprise endings work best when they evoke irony, anguish, pity, or wonder at human capacity.

Journeys

Another traditional tactic for ending a story is showing the character setting out, or deciding to set out, on a journey. Leave-takings are emotionally charged situations, and the writer can use this built-in emotion to his advantage.

Leave-taking also satisfies one of the basic requirements of the ending: Things can never be the same. A character can escape the plot by embarking on a journey, but the author should never bail out of a difficult story through an "escape" route.

Journeys abound in fiction. Remember the end of *Huckleberry Finn* in which Huck wraps up the plot and then decides to light out for the Territory because he doesn't want Aunt Sally to "sivilize" him?

Lighting out for the Territory—whether it's a physical place on a map or a metaphysical place in the soul—is an American archetype.

In "Barn Burning," for example, William Faulkner describes a boy's escaping a mean and vicious home life:

> He got up. He was a little stiff, but walking would cure that ... .
> He went on down the hill, toward the dark woods within which
> the liquid silver voices of the birds called unceasing—the rapid
> and urgent beating ... heart of the late spring night. He did not
> look back.

Another advantage of a journey is that it leaves the narrative open for a sequel.

Responding to the Theme

All endings respond to the story's theme to one extent or another: sometimes as a whisper, sometimes as a roar. The tactic works best, however, when emotional and intellectual power are balanced.

Of the many ways to end a story, responding to the theme takes the most skill. Too little emphasis, and the ending will seem flat or vague; too much, and it will sound contrived, with the added consequence that the story may appear told for the sake of meaning rather than for drama.

The tradition goes back (at least) to the Greek tragedies of the fifth century b.c., when the chorus's final speech would reveal the play's moral. In a modern story that ends with a response to theme, the author also steps forward to comment on matters in the narrative.

Either the authorial voice makes the declaration, or the thoughts or words of a character do. At the end of D.H. Lawrence's "Odour of Chrysanthemums," a wife has just finished washing and shrouding her husband, who was killed in a mine accident:

> Then with peace sunk heavy on her heart, she went about making tidy the kitchen. She knew she submitted to life, which was her immediate master. But from death, her ultimate master, she winced with fear and shame.

Sometimes the author addresses theme by asking questions about a character or situation—but as often as not, the questions go unanswered. At the end of "Goodbye, My Brother," John Cheever asks, "Oh, what can you do with a man like that?" He responds with lovely imagery and this final line: "Diana and Helen ... . I saw that they were naked, unshy, beautiful, and full of grace, and I watched the naked women walk out of the sea."

METHODS FOR WRITING ENDINGS

You've got the idea, the opening, the characters, the plot, even the climax. But you don't know how to end the story. Here are a few tactics to discover the meaningful ending hidden in every good story.

Freewriting

Perhaps the most basic approach to finding an ending is to discover it through writing. The author just writes until his intuition tells him that *this* ganglia of sentences is right.

The advantage to this approach is that it frees the author to explore plot and character. The disadvantage is that the author may write *ad infinitum* without discovering a satisfying climax.

In such a case, the author may have to go through a process of elimination to get to the heart of the matter. These are the questions to ask: Who is the story really about? What is really at stake?

Remembering the average length of a short story—twenty double-spaced typed pages—while writing is a good check and balance. With that built-in limit, the subconscious will often act as a natural editor.

In her hard but truthful way, Flannery O'Connor writes in *Mystery and Manners*: "[If you] start with a real personality, a real character, then something is bound to happen; and you don't have to know what before you begin. In fact, it may be better if you don't know what before you begin. You ought to be able to discover something from your stories. If you don't, probably *nobody* else will [my italics]."

Writing Back From the Climax

An opposite approach to fast-and-loose freewriting is deciding on the climax first and then developing a plot to reach it.

The disadvantage of writing to a preconceived ending is that plots and characters are notorious for having wills of their own—and they often want to take the story in directions other than the ones planned by the author. These directions may, in fact, be the better alternative, but the writer may be resistant to following them.

John Gardner writes that most well-made stories are built by working backward from the climax "since in the final draft, we can be sure, the writer will have introduced whatever preparation his ending needs."

The key element Gardner introduces is *revision*. I suspect many students believe that a story should drop whole from their heads through some sort of parthenogenesis, like Athena dropping from

Zeus's brow—in full armor, beautiful, immortal. Gardner tells young writers to reread their drafts critically at least a hundred times. In the process, they can add passages that will help readers understand the endings.

Save the Best for Last

Every writer has had the experience of creating exquisite prose, rich imagery, or snappy dialogue. Often the experience extends to sketches or scene-length material. Many writers call these passages "gifts" because they come almost effortlessly and invariably are *right*.

Sometimes the material is so strong that it should be saved for an ending. That's how Richard Bausch explains the ending of his story, "The Fireman's Wife," collected in *The Best American Short Stories 1990:* "During the writing of it, I came upon the last line somewhere just after the middle. I circled the line and went on writing, knowing it was the end, and that I hadn't earned it yet."

Here's the line Bausch saved for his ending:

> As she closes the door, something in the flow of her own mind appalls her, and she stops, stands in the dim hallway, frozen in a kind of wonder: she had been thinking in an abstract way, almost idly, as though it had nothing at all to do with her, about how people will go to such lengths leaving a room—wishing not to disturb, not to awaken, a loved one.

It's helpful to remember those notes that drift across your consciousness while writing. I jot them down at the bottom of the page I'm on. Too often I've postponed noting an image or snatch of dialogue, and it vanished before I could think twice about it.

CHOOSING THE RIGHT ENDING

How do you know which ending is right? An experienced author knows just as a bird knows when it's time to head south for the winter: There's a certain slant of light, a certain tingling in the spine. Inexperienced writers will learn, too, but it takes time.

Broadly speaking, there are three types of stories: those told for plot (action, adventure, mystery), those exploring an idea (religious, romance, historical, experimental), and those concerned with character (slice-of-life, psychological profile, autobiographical fiction, "literary" stories).

Decide on your story's most important quality: plot, idea, or character. All stories will be a mixture, of course, but one of these elements always outweighs the others.

A story leaning heavily on plotting, a murder mystery for example, has to end with a surprise or revelation—some element of the plot. The reader's anticipation and excitement must be satisfied—the culprit must make a fatal mistake, or the missing clue must surface, exposing the killer.

A story exploring an idea should ultimately come to terms with that idea by addressing the theme. Readers want to feel in the company of an author who has thought deeply about his subject. Readers hate to be left hanging and, in the end, their natural impulse is to applaud, so make it easy for them to do that. In a story about love triumphing over adversity, for example, readers should be shown (not told) the triumph.

Stories focusing on character are really focusing on personality, the psyche, the soul. Endings that work best for examinations of character often come right out of life: *dialogue* that gives the character pause to reflect; a repeated *image* that has assumed significance for the protagonist; a *journey* of escape or—better yet—a journey of challenge.

Once you know what you're creating, start freewriting or, if you already have a climax in mind, building the plot around the epiphany. If you're confident of your sense of story—if your character has changed as a result of a difficult decision, choice, or moral struggle—then the perfect ending should flow naturally from the events that have preceded it.

Just one final word of advice: Don't bump your head on the door frame as cheering crowds carry you from the house.

MICHAEL ORLOFSKY is a professor at Troy University in Alabama where he teaches writing and literature. He's a graduate of the Iowa Writers Workshop and has taught short fiction at the Iowa Summer Writing Festival.

CHAPTER 11
WHY SETTING MATTERS

BY LISA LENARD-COOK

Does it matter where your story unfolds? Not only is the answer yes, it's true in far more ways than you may have previously considered. It matters, for example, if you want to use your setting to help reveal your characters and plot. Think about what Hogwarts reveals about Harry Potter and his friends and their story, what Africa reveals about *The Poisonwood Bible*'s multiple narrators and their stories, even what a largely unnamed suburbia reveals for Rick Moody's or Ann Beattie's characters and plots. And it also matters if you want to make an immediate connection with your reader, immersing her at once in your story's particular universe.

In fact, the term *setting* encompasses far more than the place a story unfolds; it establishes a story's mood, feeling, and historical era. In addition, setting is tied to a story's point of view—so much so that until point of view has been firmly established, the setting can't really be distinctly rendered. Of course, while the term *point of view* refers only to sight, the strongest settings are created by using all of the senses (even—or especially—the sixth).

Last but not least, your story's setting offers it—and you, its author—credence, by way of its veracity. In other words, the truer your setting is, the more believable the fictional world you invite your reader to enter.

SETTING AS STORY

When creating a vivid palette, it's important to choose details that are right for your particular story. Here, for example, is Scout Finch in the opening pages of Harper Lee's classic *To Kill a Mockingbird*:

> Maycomb was an old town, but it was a tired old town when
> I first knew it. In rainy weather the streets turned to red slop;

grass grew on the sidewalks, the courthouse sagged in the square. Somehow, it was hotter, then: a black dog suffered on a summer's day; bony mules hitched to Hoover carts flicked flies in the sweltering shade of the live oaks on the square. Men's stiff collars wilted by nine in the morning. Ladies bathed before noon, after their three-o'clock naps, and by nightfall were like soft teacakes with frostings of sweat and sweet talcum.

In this brief paragraph, Lee sets the stage for all that follows by employing the classic (dare I use the word?) formula for setting: accuracy, originality, and the telling detail.

Let's look at each of these three items individually. First, accuracy: The particularity of the details Lee chooses lends the novel a credence that feels "true" to the reader. Second, originality: Look at how Lee describes the rainy streets: They "turned to red slop." Or, the verb she chooses to describe the men's "stiff collars": They "wilted by nine in morning." More striking, however, are the details themselves, which in their distinct originality show us not only the heat but how this specific heat affects the people (and, in this case, the animals) in this town; for example, those ladies who "by nightfall were like soft teacakes with frostings of sweat and sweet talcum."

This is an especially perfect detail because it not only describes the ladies and the town but also shows us something else about the town at the same time—that this is the kind of place where such teacakes might be served. In fact, the best details will always relate to the greater whole, or, to put it another way, they'll belong in a particular story. If Lee had used, say, Saharan desert imagery to describe her Maycomb, not only would the reader be confused, the author wouldn't have fulfilled the secondary purpose of using setting to reveal character and plot. But because Lee uses details that belong in this story, this paragraph moves far beyond the usual visual description. We feel the sagging courthouse, smell the mules flicking flies, and can almost taste those ladies like soft teacakes.

Finally, in addition to drawing us a vivid portrait of this sleepy southern town, this marvelous paragraph tells us some important things about its narrator. First, she's a reminiscent narrator. We are clued in to this because of phrases such as "when I first knew it" and "it was hotter, then."

A reminiscent narrator will have the advantage of hindsight when looking back at her story, as the now-grown Scout does. Secondly, we learn that our narrator is curious, that she notices things and then reports them. This will become more and more important as the story unfolds.

SETTING AS MOOD

As surely as the weather, setting creates a story's mood. The first paragraph of *To Kill a Mockingbird* lets us know this novel will be full of slow, hot days, during which even the slightest of movements will take some effort. A different story, however, will begin with a different setting, as does Raymond Chandler's first novel, *The Big Sleep*:

> It was about eleven o'clock in the morning, mid-October, with the sun not shining and a look of hard wet rain in the clearness of the foothills. I was wearing my powder-blue suit, with dark blue shirt, tie, and display handkerchief, black brogues, black wool socks with dark blue clocks on them. I was neat, clean, shaved, and sober, and I didn't care who knew it. I was everything the well-dressed private detective ought to be. I was calling on four million dollars.

"Now, wait!" you might be saying. "That's a whole lot about what he's wearing and only one bit of setting!" I'm using Chandler as an example largely because of that objection. Chandler, like most seasoned writers, mixes all his fictive techniques together. So while it may seem like we're getting Marlowe's wardrobe of the day, we're also getting the time (11 A.M., mid-October); the weather; Marlowe's voice, character, and point of view; and the setting (Marlowe's "calling on four million dollars"). It tells us everything we need to know about where we are.

Of course, in the next paragraph, we get a lot more detail on what "four million dollars" looks like. The paragraph begins, "The main hallway of the Sternwood place was two stories high," and continues on to describe a stained-glass panel over the entrance doors in great detail before moving on to the outdoors visible at the back of the hall. Here, too, Chandler can't help but give us voice, character, and point of view: "Beyond the garage were some decorative trees trimmed as carefully as poodle dogs."

I can see those trees; can you? In fact, I can picture everything about the Sternwood place, just from the details Chandler provides. This is because we see it through Marlowe's cynical eyes and hear his jaded voice telling us what he sees. In this way, the contrast between his internal and external environments sets the mood. The best telling detail acquires a sort of guilt by association, in this case, the "hard wet rain" of an L.A. October and the voice of a "well-dressed private detective."

SETTING AS MYSTERY

Even if you're not writing a mystery, you can establish questions in a reader's mind via your setting. Here's a brief example from my short story "Wild Horses."

> Neighbors watched for her little pickup along the county road. Sometimes Althea would pull over, or not pull over, and stop. Janet Kendall once found her sitting on her tailgate in the middle of the road just over a rise, had slammed on her brakes and skidded to a dusty halt just short of the rear bumper.

This section appears fairly early in the story, and, while it's clear from the outset that something's not quite right with Althea, we don't yet know what's wrong with her. This brief scene, which further establishes the story's southwest Colorado milieu, at the same time adds to the reader's curiosity about what's wrong with Althea.

SETTING AS COMFORT ZONE

Still another way of using setting to convey mood is by creating a sense of comfort. This can go two ways, of course. Consider just about anything written by Stephen King, who lulls the reader into a false sense of security by the very everydayness of his opening settings. Or, read the opening of *To Kill a Mockingbird*, which practically rocks us to sleep with its familiar, slow, hot summer afternoon.

SETTING AS TIME PERIOD

Still another thing both Lee and Chandler are doing via their chosen details is establishing the historical period, Lee with her powdered ladies and Chandler with his dressed-to-the-nines private investigator. Details in settings are like clues, and the astute reader will learn more about a fiction's time period from the right details than from a tidy header that reads, "Los Angeles, California, 1939."

Here's an example from Judith Freeman's *Red Water*:

> We landed at the port of Boston and traveled across country by train, in boxcars fitted out with special seats, reaching Iowa City on July 5th. With the help of the Perpetual Emigrating Fund, which advanced us much-needed money for our journey, we were able to secure a place with the Willy Handcart Company, and although it was late in the year to begin the crossing of the plains, our party was anxious to set out, for nothing less than Zion awaited us in the mountains to the west.

Notice how this selection establishes voice (via its nineteenth-century phrasings) and mood (anticipation, fear, and longing), as well as its historical period. In fact, the voice is part of what clues us in to the time period. Contemporary settings are similarly immediately recognizable to a reader, as in this brief aside from Carol Shields's novel *Unless*:

> Emma Allen sent me an e-mail from Newfoundland yesterday. She and her daughter and her widowed daughter-in-law were off to a health spa for the weekend, she wrote ...

Just as the fact that Freeman's narrator must take a train across the country alerts us to a nineteenth-century America, Shields's e-mail and health spa let us know we're in our own time and milieu.

One last thing to be aware of as you use setting to create a time: As you likely learned in high school, you need to beware of anachronisms in your story. Nothing pulls a reader out of your story's world faster than having a character check his wristwatch before they were invented or having a letter arrive by Pony Express after its demise.

SETTING AS VIEWPOINT

The final key to making a setting vivid is to see it through one intense point of view. After all, if you want to make an immediate connection with your reader, you'll want to immerse him at once in your story's particular universe. It's easy to see the difference between these two settings, the first from George Eliot's *Adam Bede* and the second from Shields's *Unless*:

1. It is a very fine old place, of red brick, softened by a pale powdery lichen, which has dispersed itself with happy irregularity, so as to bring the red brick into terms of friendly companionship with the limestone ornaments surrounding the three gables, the windows and the door-place ...

2. On a December morning I went walking hand in hand with Tom in the Orangetown cemetery. ... The cold weather had broken, and the tops of the old limestone monuments, sun-plucked in their neat rows, were shiny with melting snow.

In the first example, Eliot reports the setting as if it were a gift from author to reader. Notice the vague adjectival clauses ("very fine"; "happy irregularity") and the lackluster verbs ("is"; "has"). Now compare this with the second brief example, from the vivid point of view of first-person narrator Reta Winters. Notice how we're looking at one thing, rows of gravestones, from one point of view. Even the limestone in the second selection appears clearer to the reader. Shields was a masterful writer (as was Eliot in her day), one who understood how the right verb (in this case, "sun-plucked") could do the work of three tired adjectives. But the lesson here goes further: When we see a setting through only one set of eyes, whether via first or third person, we see it far more clearly than we will when we view it from a distant omniscient point of view. Even when you're working in omniscient point of view, render physical detail through one character's eyes, and your reader will see your settings far more vividly.

The next time you're creating a setting, don't settle for the tried and trite. Make your setting work for you and for your story.

 LISA LENARD-COOK is a PEN-short-listed novelist.

CHAPTER 12
LOCATION, LOCATION, LOCATION: DEPICTING CHARACTER THROUGH PLACE

BY RICHARD RUSSO

My first novel, *Mohawk*, as it was eventually published, was a kind of ensemble novel that had a dozen or so important characters and employed numerous points of view. Put all the stories together and you had at their center a portrait of a place, a small fictional town in upstate New York, and in the center of that town a dive called the Mohawk Grill.

The town and the grill proved so compelling, at least to me, that I set another novel there. But you may be surprised to learn that the first completed draft of the novel that was published as *Mohawk* was set in Tucson, Arizona, where I happened to be living when I wrote it. The book was about an elderly woman named Anne Grouse, who began the book bitter and ended up more bitter still—not an emotional trajectory I particularly recommend, though it describes a fair number of contemporary novels.

Beyond these few facts, I don't really remember much about this early draft. I gave it to a friend and mentor, who read it and told me what I suspected and maybe even knew but certainly didn't want to hear. He explained that the book wasn't very good, that being in the company of a bitter person in a long work of fiction isn't much more fun than being in the company of a bitter person in real life. Also, my writing betrayed a tourist's knowledge of the Southwest, where I had spent the last six years in a study carrel at the University of Arizona library. On the slender plus side, my friend noted that Anne was a much more interesting person when she was younger, when she still had hopes and dreams and hadn't managed to mess up her life. About the only scenes that really lived were set in the upstate New York town where Anne was raised—one in a glove shop where Anne's father worked and the other at a down-at-the-heels amusement park on the lake.

Also, he told me, the minor characters were far more interesting than the major ones.

Well, this brutal honesty pretty much squared with my own sense of the book. The minor characters—mere functionaries, I'd thought—were people who grew out of the place and the necessity of the place. The glove shop where Anne's father worked was the one my grandfather had spent his entire adult life toiling in, and the dying amusement park, along its shabby midway, was where both my mother in the 1930s and I in the 1950s had learned to dream among the fluttering lights and the rigged games of chance. I was no tourist on that midway, but there was a problem: I wanted to be a tourist there. I'd left my hometown of Gloversville, New York, when I was eighteen, enrolled in a university twice the size of that town, and by the end of my first week there, learned my first lesson: that I'd do well to hide where I was from. For the next ten years, first as an undergraduate, then as a graduate student, I walked backward, erasing my tracks with that wonderful switch we call education. I learned how to read carefully and talk to smart people and work from the outside in when confronted at a table with more than one fork. In becoming a writer, I had intended to make use of these lessons I'd learned and for this reason, I was not pleased to learn that the only things I'd managed to bring to life in my first novel were the things I'd hoped—Judas that I was—to deny.

DISCOVERING YOUR PLACE

Intellectually, of course, I already knew that place *was* character. That's Intro Fiction 101. I could illustrate the point with numerous examples from my reading. I knew that London was a character in Dickens, and that it spawned Mr. Micawber, and Crook, and Scrooge. And I could tell what happened to Dickens when he ventured too far from the place that gave him the majority of his people. There's only one reason people read and teach *Hard Times* (the only Dickens novel not set, at least partly, in London) when the rest of the Dickens canon is available: It's short. And there were plenty of contemporary examples. I could see Larry McMurtry's characters growing directly out of the west Texas soil, and its windswept small towns, and then saw what happened when he tried to set a novel in Las Vegas. I'm sure McMurtry spent serious time in Vegas, and not in a study carrel either, but still.

Yes, I knew that place was character, but I knew it without, somehow, believing it. Otherwise, how to explain the sense of wonder I felt in the rewriting, the reimagining, of the book I eventually published as *Mohawk*? How else to explain the surprise I felt when, having created the Mohawk Grill from the memory of the half-dozen greasy spoons I frequented with my father, I discovered enough vivid characters to occupy every stool at the Formica counter?

INTERIOR PLACE

There's a distinction that's often made in discussions of place—that is, the difference between interior and exterior setting. Interior setting has come to mean, basically, an indoor place. The setting of *The Glass Menagerie* is primarily an interior one—Amanda Wingfield's apartment. We never leave it, never venture out of doors. We're told the action takes place in St. Louis, but it could be any city. Usually the play is staged in such a way that we glimpse an urban view from the windows of the Wingfield apartment—close brick walls and dark fire escapes and neighboring windows with tattered shades. The Wingfield apartment also has a fire escape, where Tom retreats to smoke, but the play makes clear that the fire escape is an illusion. There's no real escape for the characters, and none for viewers while we watch.

Most beginning writers do a pretty good job of interior setting because they understand that the objects people own comment on them—at times, even define them. Anyone who needs convincing might take a look at Mary Gordon's "The Important Houses," included in *The Best American Short Stories 1993*. In the back matter of the book, Gordon admits that the story isn't really a story at all, but rather an excerpt from a long memoir that happens to read like fiction, despite its lack of anything like plot or chronology or scene. What's amazing is that we get a marvelous sense of character despite the fact that we never meet any of the people, either directly or dramatically, who live in the houses she describes. The very contents of the grandmother's house offers us a portrait of the woman who owns it—honorable, harsh, judgmental, daunting, repressed, dark. The narrator describes the house:

> ... every object in her house belonged to the Old World. Nothing was easy; everything required maintenance of a complicated and specialized sort .... Each object's rightness of placement made me feel honored to be among them.

The other important house is the residence of the narrator's aunt, whose husband owns a liquor store:

> The house was full of new or newish objects: the plastic holders for playing cards, like shells or fans, the nut dishes in the shape of peanuts, the corn dishes in the shape of ears of corn, the hair dryer like a rocket, the make-up mirror framed by light bulbs, the bottles of nail polish, the ice bucket, the cocktail shaker, the deep freeze.

Though an apprentice writer's descriptions may not be as lush as Gordon's, even beginners understand and accept the basic principles of interior setting—that a person who owns an ice bucket and cocktail shaker is different from someone who owns a claw-footed tub for bathing.

EXTERIOR PLACE

The relationship between character and exterior setting is more mysterious. We don't own a landscape, a street, a neighborhood, or a river in the same sense that we own a cocktail shaker or a claw-footed tub. Nor can they be said to own us, in the way Thoreau meant when he observed in *Walden* that the things we own can own us in return. True, exterior landscapes can "run through us," in the sense that the river runs through the two brothers in Norman Maclean's memoir. But because the relationship is more tenuous, less sharply defined, it is more likely to be ignored, either in whole or in part, by apprentice writers. I'm forever asking my undergraduates very literal-minded questions about their stories, and the thinly veiled irritation with which these questions are often answered is suggestive.

Where does this story take place? I'll ask innocently, especially when it doesn't seem to have taken place anywhere. Well, I'll be told, it's really more about the people. In a story with a vague urban setting, I'll ask, Which city are we in here? It doesn't really matter, I'll be informed. Well, okay, but I need to know.

In fact, the need to know is not universally conceded. There are examples of great works of literature where the external setting is not specified, the city is not named, the landscape more symbolic or moral than real. My more sophisticated students will dredge up the ghost of Kafka. Where is the penal colony? We don't know. We don't need to know. Okay, I concede the point, but only after sharing an anecdote and some speculative theorizing.

Some years ago, I was making small talk with an influential New York editor, and I asked him what books he was excited to be bringing out on his spring list. He named and described half a dozen. I don't remember any of the books he wanted to recommend, but I do remember the way he talked about them. The first thing he'd say about each one was where it took place, a fact I remarked upon because it's often the way I begin talking about books I like and the way people often begin talking about my own books. I hadn't really given the matter much thought beyond the fairly obvious fact that the "where" of a book is an easy starting place, certainly easier to describe than the "who." But for this editor, it went much deeper, and it turned out my small talk had opened, or reopened, a vein. All the books he published and wanted to publish, he informed me, were ones with a strong sense of place. He said he had little faith in the vision of writers who didn't see clearly and vividly the world their characters inhabited. His most powerful need as a reader, he claimed, was to feel oriented. We agreed that we could do that anywhere—on a street in Calcutta, in the middle of an Iowa cornfield, on a boat in the ocean (that is to say, one place was probably as good as another)—but we couldn't feel oriented if we were nowhere or anywhere.

We discovered, too, that we had similar habits. We often didn't read very far into books that were set in places we'd never been before putting the book down long enough to consult an atlas. And we also agreed that we didn't care whether the place in question was fictional or real; we still wanted to know where it was located geographically. We'd both consulted maps of Minnesota to locate Jon Hassler's Staggerford, and I explained that my Mohawk was located north of the New York State Thruway in the foothills of the Adirondacks.

UNIVERSALITY IN A SMALL TOWN

With some graduate student writers I've taught, the prejudice against rich, detailed, vivid exterior settings was also rooted in the fear that the more specific the setting, the more regional and less "universal" the story's appeal. Nobody wants to be labeled a regional writer. At one point in his career, McMurtry announced his intention to leave Texas and never return in his fiction. He had his reasons, among them, I suspect, a desire to be more a citizen of the world than of Texas. If so, who can blame him?

But a moment's reflection will suggest the truth of the matter, and that is that there's no reason to fear the regional label. The American writer of the twentieth century who is the most universal in his concerns is probably William Faulkner, who is also the most regional, having seldom strayed imaginatively outside a single county. The real fear of being labeled regional—in the sense of, say, Hamlin Garland or Sarah Orne Jewett—is its unstated implication. These writers weren't more regional than Mark Twain and Faulkner; they, I believe, were less talented, less visionary, less true. It's this kinship with them that we fear, and it's not a fear that's rooted in geography. Writers have to recognize and accept an essential artistic paradox—that the more specific and individual things become, the more universal they feel.

The clearest expression of this that I can share with you is in the form of the two most consistent compliments from people who have read my work. "Boy, you really know those small upstate New York towns," they tell me. Often they explain how they know I know. "Hell, I've lived up there all my life," they say. Or, "I've got relatives in Utica and we visit them every year. It's like visiting a Richard Russo novel up there." The second group of people pay me what appears to be on the surface a contradictory compliment. "I thought that was my hometown you were writing about," they'll say about my Mohawk or North Bath, then they'll tell me about their hometown in Georgia or Oregon. Even in England I get this. My advice? Don't try to resolve the paradox of things that are vividly differentiated seeming more universal and familiar as a result. There's neither mathematical nor scientific logic to this. Just take advantage of it.

DESTINY IN A PLACE

In the end, the only compelling reason to pay more attention to place, to exterior setting, is the belief, the faith, that place and its people are intertwined, that place is character, and that to know the rhythms, the textures, the feel of a place is to know more deeply and truly its people. Such faith is not easy to come by or to sustain in this historical period.

Most people, in any historical period, seem able to focus on only one or two ideas at a time. In the matter of human destiny, an issue of some concern to fiction writers, the question of how people become what they become, why they do what they do, has been settled. In our time, the two great determiners of destiny are race and gender. It was not always this way, of course. There was a time in the not-too-distant past when social class was thought to have been a determining factor in human destiny. Remember the great proletarian novels of the thirties and forties? They seem dated now, in part because the idea of seeing human destiny as determined by class seems not to have survived the second World War and the GI Bill—this despite the fact that in the last two decades, the gap between the haves and have-nots has widened.

For my mother and many others of her generation, the issue is time. Since his death, my mother and I have spent many hours talking about my grandfather, a man who played a central role in our lives. Her devotion to his memory requires fierce loyalty, which in turn makes it difficult for her to admit her father's frailties. When she's able to do so, it's always with the same proviso. "Well," she says, "I guess he was a product of his time." She never lets it go at that either. She fixes me with a motherly gaze. We're *all* products of our time, she reminds me.

The truth, of course, is that we're products of a lot of things—race, gender, sexual orientation, time, genetics, and chance among them—and we're under no obligation to rank these larger forces. What's interesting to me is that just about the only people I know who seem to believe that place is crucial to human destiny and the formation of human personality are fiction writers. Admittedly, I intuit this from their work, but I think it's true.

Take Annie Proulx. *The Shipping News* is, at one level, the story of a man who manages to conquer a gesture. Her protagonist, Quoyle, has a huge jutting chin, courtesy of his Newfoundland genes, and we find him at the beginning of the book self-consciously covering his chin with his hand. Returning to Newfoundland, he finds a place where his movements, clumsy and awkward in New York, feel natural and graceful, a place where he can live without apology, without undue self-consciousness.

Ivan Doig seems to believe in place as a determiner of behavior. Like many western novelists, he suggests that the physical landscape of the West is responsible, at least in part, for philosophical, emotional, political, and spiritual differences between East Coast and West Coast mentalities. Danish author Peter Hoeg is also a believer. No work of fiction I've read in recent years is so dominated by a sense of place, where landscapes, interior and exterior, loom so powerfully over character, as in *Smilla's Sense of Snow*. Race, gender, and social class are also powerful forces in the novel, but in the end, it is literally Smilla's sense of snow—of the properties of snow, as well as her ability to navigate in a blizzard that is both physical and moral—that saves her, that provides her with the answers she's been looking for from the beginning.

WHERE HAVE ALL THE PLACES GONE?

Running contrary to such wisdom is our entire cultural climate, which minimizes the importance of place. Witness all those IBM commercials advertising "Solutions for a small planet." In these ads, we listen to people in other cultures speaking in foreign languages. Only the clever running subtitles reveal that the people are talking about their computers, their computer needs, which, it turns out, are the same as ours. We all yearn for more megabytes; it doesn't matter where we live. This message—it is a small world, it doesn't matter much where you are—is being reinforced by both perception and reality. As James Howard Kunstler points out in *The*

Geography of Nowhere, the interstate system of highways that allows us to travel five hundred miles a day in about half the time it would have taken thirty years ago has also had the unintended effect of making it seem, when we get to our final destination, that we haven't really gone any-where. The exit where we get off the interstate is a dead ringer for the one where we got on, their being fifteen hundred miles apart notwithstand-ing. Interstate travel (even more than air travel, I suspect) also suggests that the places we bypass aren't worth pausing at, a conclusion difficult to reconcile with the growing sameness of our major destinations.

A few years ago, I was invited to attend the Nashville Book Fair. I'd driven through, or rather around, Nashville many times, but I'd never stopped, never visited. I was put up in the Hilton, which was a lot like other Hiltons I'd stayed at, except you could get grits. The cable televi-sion offerings were identical to those offered by our local cable company in Maine, including the Nashville Network. The first of the conference sessions I attended was one on contemporary Southern writing. Several writers I'd long admired tried to identify what made Southern writing southern and to offer suggestions for how to preserve it. I have to say it was one of the stranger discussions I've ever listened to, and not just because I was a Yankee. There was little talk of landscape, or the rhythms of daily life, or architecture, or occupations. Members of the audience wanted to discuss the scent of magnolias and the redness of the earth, and a couple of members of the panel nervously admitted to having re-located to places like Massachusetts.

I came away with the distinct impression that even to articulate people who cared about it, our sense of place and what place means is rapidly eroding and that even our vocabulary for discussing place may be gone with the wind. One of the ideas I kept hoping would crop up was the question of how writers should handle the Wal-Mart sameness that is creeping into our cultural life, regardless of where we happen to be located. If what made Southern fiction distinctly Southern was being subtly eroded, couldn't the same be said for the notion of place in general? There may be a Burger King in every small town in America, but does that mean they should be similarly ubiquitous in our fiction?

I am of two minds on this subject. Personally, I avoid Burger Kings in fiction as I do in life, and for the same reasons. To me, they are neither nourishing nor enjoyable. I am suspicious of the fact that all you have to do is name such places and the reader is located, a kind of cultural shorthand. I prefer places that require and reward lots of description, and my own novels are strewn with the kinds of establishments that are poised on the brink of extinction. This may explain why I'm occasionally accused of harboring a nostalgic view of America. It's true that I become more curmudgeonly every year, and what's needed may be younger eyes. I still remember chortling with glee while reading the Sam Hodges novel of the new South, *B-Four*. Several of the scenes are set in a local IHOP, where the pancake syrup containers are so stuck to the lazy Susans that grown men have all they can do to liberate them.

The simple truth may be that there's no place in the world, and no object either, that can't be brought dancing to life when seen by the right eyes. Whether or not Burger Kings deserve a prominent place in our literature is less the issue than whether place itself, which is under siege both in reality and in metaphor, can be rescued from the endangered species list of important concepts.

ADVICE

If I have convinced you that place is an important resource for fiction writers, consider the following practical tips on how to handle place in your fiction.

1. Describe Selectively

The relative importance of place to any given story is independent of the amount of description given it. The best examples I can think of are John Cheever's Shady Hill stories. They are, in my opinion, the best stories in the Cheever canon. I've read and reread them and taught many of them. When one of my students wanted to write a critical essay on the importance of setting in fiction, I suggested the Shady Hill stories, picturing the vivid sense of life's rhythms that Cheever had created through what I remembered as lush descriptions.

The problem was that when my student read those stories herself, she found very little description. She couldn't, she told me, find a single sustained passage of description in any of them. Preposterous. "You've read 'O Youth and Beauty!'?" I asked her. " 'The Housebreaker of Shady Hill?' " She had. Closely. Which forced me to go back to the stories myself and, of course, she was right. There were very few descriptive details, and those were woven so skillfully into the stories' drama, in such seemingly subordinate ways, that they were difficult to extract, like molars in the back of the mouth, unseen but with the deepest roots imaginable. What kind of furniture does Cash Bentley hurtle in his friends' living rooms before his wife shoots him in midair? What's the architecture of the houses that Johnny Hake burgles? I'd had the impression that such information was offered in these stories. The deep sense of place that emerges from the Shady Hill stories has more to do with life's rhythms, where things are in relation to other things, whether the characters can walk there and how long that will take, whether they'll drive or take the train. We won't be told that the cocktail shaker is pure silver; we'll be told that it's sweating in the lazy Sunday midmorning sun. Rendering such passive details active makes us insiders, not tourists. We become giddy, well-heeled drinkers trying to banish hangovers, not sober, anthropological observers of curious behavior.

2. See Clearly From the Start

Something to guard against: My own experience of writing, which may be different from yours, is that even when I acknowledge the importance of the physical world, even when I make mental notes and scribble reminders, I still have to guard against the temptation to believe that I'll be able to add onto a scene later, and flesh it out after I've attended to other matters. If the scene is talky (too reliant on dialogue) or if it's too interior (too reliant on a character's thoughts at the expense of the physical world), I'm often tempted to let it go, move on to the next scene, promising to return later with a bucketful of descriptive details.

I know I'm not alone in this. When I complain to my students that their scenes are vague, that the dialogue seems to be coming out of thin air, as if the scene were wired in such a way that we had to choose between the audio and the video, they frequently tell me not to worry, that they'll go back and add the details of the physical world later. What they want to know is whether the characters are doing and saying the right things. Such an attitude not only ranks the various tasks of the fiction writer, subordinating the objective world, but it suggests something about the process that I've never found to be true. When I'm writing badly, I'm almost always in a kind of fast-forward, taking shorthand notes on what the characters are doing and saying. The edges of the picture are fuzzy and blurred by speed. Later, when I realize the scene isn't working, when I go back and try to "fill in the details," I find that the details I fill in often invalidate what the characters have said and done. Better and more efficient to slow down and see clearly to begin with. If character can grow out of place, as I've suggested, it follows that place cannot be the thing that's "grafted on" late in the process.

3. Create Distance

My own experience has been that the place I'm living is probably not the place I'm writing about. Now that I've lived in Maine for several years, I'm often asked by people who consider me a Maine writer by virtue of my address when I'll be writing a novel set in Maine. They don't realize what they're probably asking is when I plan to leave the state. The simple truth of the matter is, I've never written effectively about any place I was currently residing in. I not only need to leave but actually need to have been gone for some time for my imagination to kick in, to begin the process of necessary tempering knowledge.

It may be different for you, but the ability to look out my window and see what I'm describing in a story is not an advantage. If what I'm describing is really there, I'm too respectful of and dependent upon the senses, and the thing described, as a result, will often not have the inner life I want it to have. I'd rather make a mistake, get something physically wrong, put the button on the wrong side of the sleeve, than be dictated to by literal reality, than place intuition and imagination in a straitjacket. Maybe this is just a feeble justification for the many things I get wrong as a result, but I don't think so.

4. Use Research Selectively

Just as the importance and vividness of place is independent of the amount of description given it, there is also no direct correlation between the vividness of your setting and comprehensive, factual knowledge. Granted, throughout this essay, I've been insisting on the essential relationship between place and character, but I'm not particularly advocating Micheneresque research. An intimate understanding of place can lead to character breakthroughs, but that's not the same as to say that encyclopedic knowledge of the facts of place will yield interesting characters.

Often, the exact opposite will happen. Too much knowledge of the literal can stifle the metaphorical. Many bestsellers give the impression of having been written by tourists for tourists, and such books, for all their insistence upon location, somehow locate me in a world that's halfway between a library and a good travel agency. The difference between the places in these novels and the places in reality is the difference between the place itself and the picture of it on a color brochure.

A PRODUCT OF PLACE

Finally, even those among you who are convinced by the argument I've been articulating about the importance of place and the link between place and character, may not end up as place-oriented in your fiction as I am in mine. The writers I've discussed above are, as I'm sure you've noticed, like-minded. If I'd chosen different writers to draw examples from, my conclusions might have been different.

I can only give you my sense of how profoundly important place has been to my own life and my life as an artist. If I were black or gay or a woman, chances are my life as a person and as an artist would have been shaped more dramatically by race or gender or sexual orientation. But insofar as I'm a "product" of anything, to borrow my mother's term, I feel I'm a product of place, of places. And, insofar as my fiction has been a product of anything, since the moment I realized that my first novel could not be set in Arizona, it has been a product of places that have, in turn, offered up people by the dozens.

Some years ago, at an East Coast writers residency, C.J. Hribal, Michael Martone, and I were referred to by some as "the corn boys," the result, I suppose, of our teaching in Midwestern universities. It was odd for me to be referred to this way and I tried to conceal my annoyance lest it be considered geographical snobbery. I don't, believe me, consider the small, shabby town in upstate New York where I grew up to be superior to other places, and if I'd grown up in Iowa, I doubt I would have minded much being referred to as a "corn boy." I simply felt mislabeled, and therefore misunderstood, in much the same way I feel now when I'm referred to as a "Maine writer."

I may not be "the product" of upstate New York either, but the link is there and I feel it profoundly. How else would I explain the strange dreams I'm subject to for days before I visit my remaining relatives in my hometown? How would I explain the irrational fears that descend upon me when I return, primary among them the fear that I will be killed in an auto accident during one of these quick visits? This was my grandfather's fear for me. We lived one house down from one of the worse intersections in town, where local drivers routinely ignored a stop sign in plain view, bashing into each other and narrowly missing small children who were crossing the intersection on errands to the corner market. My grandfather feared I'd be run down in sight of the front porch before I could make my mark on the world, and now, forty years later, I have inherited his fear.

How else would I explain the fact that when I pass by the open door of the worst dive in town, I sense that the empty barstool farthest from the light is really mine, that it's being saved for me, that perhaps in some alternate universe I'm already occupying it, that when the phone rings, I no longer even have to remind the bartender that I'm not there. What these irrational fears have in common is the sense that this place has a claim on me, a claim that may be presented at any time, a claim that seems less perilous to acknowledge than to ignore.

 RICHARD RUSSO is the author of *Bridge of Sighs*, *The Whore's Child and Other Stories*, *Straight Man*, *Nobody's Fool*, *Mohawk*, and *The Risk Pool*. He is the recipient of the 2002 Pulitzer Prize for *Empire Falls*.

BEST-SELLING ADVICE: Characters

"People do not spring forth out of the blue, fully formed—they become themselves slowly, day by day, starting from babyhood. They are the result of both environment and heredity, and your fictional characters, in order to be believable, must be also." —Lois Duncan

"A genuine creation should have character as well as be one; should have central heating, so to say, as well as exterior lighting." —James Hilton

"The character on the page determines the prose—its music, its rhythms, the range and limit of its vocabulary—yet, at the outset at least, I determine the character. It usually happens that the fictitious character, once released, acquires a life and will of his or her own, so the prose, too, acquires its own inexplicable fluidity. This is one of the reasons I write: to 'hear' a voice not quite my own, yet summoned forth by way of my own." —Joyce Carol Oates

"I said the hell with Plot. I'm going to write stories about people that interest me, the way I see them. I'm sick of formula. I'm sick of Hero, Heroine, Heavy. I'm sick of neat, tidy, emasculated emotions, with every little puppet jerking through the paces of what ought to be and not what is. I'm sick of Characters. I'm going to write about men and women, all classes, types and conditions, within the limits of my own capabilities. People with faults, with nasty tempers, with weaknesses and loves and hates and fears and gripes against each other. People I can believe in because I know and understand them. People who aren't like anybody else's characters because they are themselves, like 'em or don't. ... And all of a sudden I began to sell." —Leigh Brackett

"When I was a Hollywood press agent, I learned how the Hollywood casting system worked. There was a roster of actors who were always perfect as doctors or lawyers or laborers, and the directors just picked the types they needed and stuffed them into film after film. I do the same [with my characters], book after book." —Richard Condon

"When you are dealing with the blackest side of the human soul, you have to have someone who has performed heroically to balance that out. You have to have a hero." —Ann Rule

"The writer must always leave room for the characters to grow and change. If you move your characters from plot point to plot point, like painting by the numbers, they often remain stick figures. They will never take on a life of their own. The most exciting thing is when you find a character doing something surprising or unplanned. Like a character saying to me: 'Hey, Richard, you may think I work for you, but I don't. I'm my own person.' " —Richard North Patterson

"Writers shouldn't fall in love with characters so much that they lose sight of what they're trying to accomplish. The idea is to write a whole story, a whole book. A writer has to be able to look at that story and see whether or not a character works, whether or not a character needs further definition." —Stephen Coonts

CHAPTER 13

CHARACTER STUDY

BY ALICE HOFFMAN

It's often said that all characters in a dream are pieces of the dreamer's consciousness; the dreamer is every character in her own dreams, including the cat and the dog. It's also true that every character in a writer's fiction is a piece of that writer's consciousness. Fully imagined characters—that is to say, characters that aren't based on real people—are drawn from our own subconscious. We should know these people deeply because in some way, whether a character is a mass murderer or a nun, we are them.

In concentrating on what's inside a character at the deepest level, there's often a story within the story about the character—one the reader may never know, but one that the writer must always know. A character's interior trauma or past experience is the core around which everything else is built. By writing so closely to a character's spirit, the process of writing needs to be free enough to allow the writer to enter into another person's consciousness. In a way, this is the greatest accomplishment for a writer in building character: When it's possible to "think inside someone else's head," we know we've succeeded in breathing life into a fictional person. Once this happens, we can stand back. The character can control his fate.

There are teachers who may tell you to write about what you know and to write about people you've seen, met, eavesdropped on, or sat down at a table with for a family dinner. But if a writer knows the inner truth of an emotional experience, he can write about it in every setting. As fiction writers, we can be inside the experience of every situation and every character. A woman doesn't have to be a man to write about one, even in the first person, and vice versa. The art of being a writer of fiction, as opposed to nonfiction or memoir, is to be yourself and yet have the ability to "imagine" yourself in another's circumstances. My mentor, Albert Guerard, always told his students that a writer didn't have to experience something to write about it; he only had to be able to imagine it. And I'd add that we also have to be able to feel it.

My method of character building is from the inside out—not necessarily the color of eyes and hair, the height and weight, but rather, how does a person sleep at night? What does he fear? Does he run from lightning or rush toward it?

One of the best devices in terms of imagining characters in an ongoing project such as a novel, which can take months or years to write, is to live inside the characters—to take them with you into the outside world, to experience real life in, say, a Starbucks or an airport, both as yourself and as your character. This means thinking about your character's reactions while you react as yourself. As fiction writers we split ourselves into parts: The self and the characters we write about all abide within us. At times, during the process of writing, it's possible to experience the disintegration of the self. This is the ecstasy of writing and of art, of losing oneself in the process of creating.

The moment when you know that your characters are fully alive is when they begin to make their own choices; this happened to me with my novel *Seventh Heaven*. In outline after outline, list after list, my character Nora Silk was planning to get involved with a police officer. But one day she did the oddest thing—she fell in love with someone completely unexpected. I tried to rewrite her into doing what I willed, what I wanted, but Nora Silk now had a mind of her own. I should have known she'd do as she pleased from the moment she entered my novel, driving fast and taking directions from no one.

> Nora Silk was trying to keep up with the moving van, but every time she stepped down hard on the gas and hit sixty-five miles an hour the Volkswagen shimmied for no reason at all. Nora had to hold tight to the steering wheel whenever the tires edged into the fast lane. She looked past the heat waves and concentrated on driving until she heard the pop of the cigarette lighter.

My first experience with the intensity of writing characters that seemed real was when I finished my first novel, *Property Of.* Fittingly, I dreamed about a ceremony in which my characters were leaving me, and I awoke in tears. It's a loss to finish with a character you've put so much time and energy into, and, of course, so much of yourself. But like dreams, there's an endless supply of characters waiting to be created and named.

ALICE HOFFMAN has published eighteen novels, two books of short fiction, and eight books for children and young adults. Her novel *Here on Earth* was an Oprah Book Club pick in 1998. Her novels have received mention as notable books of the year by *The New York Times*, *Entertainment Weekly*, *The Los Angeles Times*, *Library Journal*, and *People*.

CHAPTER 14

FOUR-DIMENSIONAL CHARACTERS

BY STEPHANIE KAY BENDEL

The difference between a good story and a great one is often
the depth to which the author examines the characters who people
the pages. Beginning writers are sometimes bewildered when they are
told their characters need more development or that they haven't really allowed the reader to "know" these people. In my teaching I have
discovered that a good way to make sure your characters are fully developed is to think of them as four-dimensional persons.

FIRST DIMENSION—THE PHOTOGRAPH

First-dimension characteristics are those you would observe looking
at a photograph of a person. Such qualities include height; weight; age;
coloring; body type; distinguishing physical traits such as scars, tat-
toos, or unusual proportions (for example, a man might have a large
head or very long fingers); type and style of clothing—I'm sure you can
think of many more. They help us form an impression of the person.
More importantly, they give us concrete characteristics to visualize.
All the writer can present to the reader is words on paper. The trick is
to present words that will create pictures in the reader's mind. At all
times you ought to be giving your reader something to look at—and
not only to look at, but to remember. Accordingly, the first-dimension
traits you select for your characters ought to be those things that are
most memorable.

The single biggest problem in presenting the reader with first-
dimension characteristics is that the traits themselves are static. It

is tempting to simply stop the action of the story and tell the reader what your hero looks like:

> Roland was short and stout with a receding hairline. His eyes were blue. He wore a light gray suit that was wrinkled. He entered the newsroom and, after pausing a moment, spotted the city editor's desk.

Vague, isn't it? You can't form a clear image of Roland. It's like looking at an Identi-Kit picture the police use to obtain a sketch of someone they're looking for. The author is putting together a bunch of generic pieces and trying to give us a picture of a real live person. That may be the best the police can do, but writers can do better. Let's get rid of those inactive verbs and see whether we can describe those static traits—blue-eyed, rumpled, short, stout, and balding—in some sort of action.

> When Roland entered the room, he ran his fingers across the top of his head and arranged the few remaining strands of hair there. Then he stood on his tiptoes, his blue eyes searching for the city editor's desk. He spotted it and made a cursory effort to smooth the wrinkles where his light gray suit strained across his ample stomach.

That's a little better. We've presented a couple of first-dimensional traits without stopping the story action. The reader has the experience of seeing Roland *do* something, even if it's only to arrange his hair and smooth his clothing.

Limitations of Viewpoint

The first-dimension traits you select to show the reader are limited by the point of view from which you tell the story. For example, if we were writing the above scene from Roland's point of view, we wouldn't say:

> Then I stood on my tiptoes, my blue eyes searching for the city editor's desk.

Roland would hardly be thinking about the fact that his eyes are blue, so why would he mention it here? If we want the reader to know the color of his eyes, we have to figure out a way to show that to them from Roland's point of view.

But we still have no idea what kind of person Roland is, what he's feeling, or why he's here. To answer those questions, we need to look into other dimensions of his character.

SECOND DIMENSION—THE VIDEOTAPE

Think of second-dimension traits as those you could observe by watching a videotape of a person. These characteristics are primarily ones of descriptive action, such as "lumbers," "ambles" or "strolls," which might show the way a person moves across a room. Now we can hear the character's voice, tone, pitch, accent, sentence structure, vocabulary, pace of speech, and so on. If she sits down, we can see whether she lowers herself gracefully onto the chair or plops onto it.

Just as we draw conclusions about a person when we look at a still photo, we draw more conclusions when we can observe that person in action.

> Julie hurried into the lab and rooted through the reports on the latest test results. She spread the sheets out on the Formica counter and studied them one by one, frowning. Occasionally she made a note to herself on the small pad she carried in the pocket of her lab coat. When she'd finished, she went through the sheets again and double-checked her notes. Then she gathered the papers, put them in order, and replaced them in the filing cabinet. She automatically straightened the row of beakers on the shelf above the counter and glanced around the lab before turning off the lights and locking the door.

In this paragraph, all we have done is watch *what* Julie is doing and how she does it. She isn't saying anything, and we can't read her thoughts. However, we can easily infer a lot about the kind of person Julie is simply by observing her closely. She's organized (carries a pad in her pocket and takes notes), thorough (double-checks the notes), and neat (straightens the beakers, puts things away). We have the impression that she doesn't waste time and would certainly spot something wrong.

Limitations of Viewpoint

Second-dimension characteristics are not as limited by a change in viewpoint as are first-dimensional traits. If you reread the description of Julie's visit to the lab and imagine rewriting it in her viewpoint, the transition is very simple. In fact, except for deleting the word "frowning," everything else could stay as it is, simply substituting "I" for "Julie" or "she" and "me" and "my" for "her."

Second-dimension traits help the reader bridge the transition from what a person *looks* like to what a person *is* like. To discover more, we must move on to the third dimension.

THIRD DIMENSION—THE STAGE PLAY

Third-dimension traits are those revealed when you watch people interacting or reacting to circumstances, as you do in a play. Here you get some sense of a character's intelligence; sensitivity level (e.g., tactful, unaware, empathetic, uncaring); social type (e.g., extrovert, introvert, leader, follower, loner, negotiator, organizer, diplomat); the level of responsibility generally assumed; ethical, political, and religious outlook; dependency level; and educational background.

Third-dimension traits are often easily displayed in dialogue, particularly when two or more characters are in conflict. For example:

> Bud slumped into the easy chair and covered his face with his hands. "I don't know how you can disappoint me like this!"
>
> "Pop, I don't want to disappoint you. Can't you see how important this is to me? Look at me, please!"
>
> The man put his hands in his lap and stared at them for a moment. "All these years," he said sadly, "I worked so you could have something—a future. Something I never had." He made a fist and shook it at the boy. "How can you throw it away?"
>
> "I'm not throwing it away," Matt murmured. "It's your business, and you'll still have it. It's not like it's going anywhere."
>
> "That's right! It's not going anywhere! How can it? I can't keep working fifteen hours a day, seven days a week, selling furniture. I'm not young anymore!"

Matt spread his hands in a gesture of helplessness. "You don't have to keep it up if you don't want to, Pop. You could sell the business. It must be worth quite a bit."

"Sell it? You cut out an old man's heart! You expect me to sell what I have spent my life building? I suppose you think then that I should give you the money so that you can do whatever nonsense it is you want."

"Write music, Pop. I want to write beautiful music. And you don't have to give me any money. I'll work, wait tables, pump gas, sweep floors—whatever it takes so I can go to school in Milson."

"Bah! Writing pretty songs! What kind of a man does that?"

"Pop, please!" The boy's voice cracked.

Bud stood and looked his son in the eye. "Let's get this straight," he said. "Either you go to work for me this fall, or I have no son." And before Matt could reply, he turned and walked out of the room.

Notice that there is no physical description of either character in this section, and there are only a couple of gestures presented. The author is letting the content of the dialogue show what the characters—and their relationship—are like.

Bud can't see that his son is different from him. He doesn't understand why Matt doesn't want what he wants. He knows no other way to interpret the boy's behavior except as ingratitude. He's trying desperately to hold on to his control over the boy, and when all else fails, he threatens.

Matt, on the other hand, clearly wants his father's approval—or at least acceptance—of his chosen profession. Another young man might have gotten angry at his father's heavy-handed attempt to make him feel guilty. Matt, however, keeps trying to be reasonable. From his willingness to support himself in school, we see how strongly he feels about pursuing a musical career. We have a pretty good idea what his decision will be, and we know how much pain will come with it.

Habitual Behavior as a Third-Dimension Trait

Sometimes repeated behaviors, rather than the content of dialogue, can be used to show the reader third-dimension aspects of a character's personality. For example, if Alice consistently removes her husband's coffee cup from the dinner table before he's through with it, this behavior may be showing us a controlling personality, excessive preoccupation, or impatience, depending on what else is going on in the story.

Another example: If Gerald interrupts everyone, it may indicate he is an overly aggressive, controlling person, or someone who cannot tolerate disagreement, either because of a rigid personality or a fear of being proven wrong. In either case, we will chalk him up as being extremely insensitive.

Another important thing to remember is that third-dimension traits are the *public persona* of that individual. They delineate how most people perceive a character most of the time. These traits are *observable*. However, they may or may not be consistent with the inner person—that is the *private persona*, or fourth-dimension characteristics.

FOURTH DIMENSION— PARTICIPATORY THEATER

Fourth-dimension traits are found in the same list as third-dimension traits, but there are two differences. The first is that fourth-dimension traits deal strictly with the *private persona*, that is, the person stripped of pretense and deception. As in participatory theater, where the audience enters into the play, the reader must enter the character's mind or discover its inner workings to explore fourth-dimension traits.

For example, Ellen is a staunch supporter of her boss's policies. She defends and praises Ms. Conklin every chance she gets. But if we were able to listen to some of Ellen's thoughts, we'd discover she can't stand Ms. Conklin. She knows that many of Conklin's decisions are bad for the business in the long run, but she can't bring herself to speak up or even confide in anyone, for fear the word will get back to her boss and she'll be fired.

Those people who work with Ellen can only observe Ellen in three dimensions and would be astounded to know what is going on in her mind.

They think they know her—that she's just as arrogant and misdirected as Ms. Conklin. They don't like her.

We know quite a different person. We see that Ellen is smart enough to see the error of her boss's ways, but too much of a wimp to stand up and take a risk. We don't like her either, but for different reasons.

Answer the Question, "Why?"

There is a second important aspect to fourth-dimension traits: In order to come to the deepest understanding of the person, the author must answer the question, "Why?" Two people may behave in exactly the same way for very different reasons, and unless you understand their motives, you cannot really know them.

Let's look at two seemingly similar characters: Mabel and Agnes each live alone; they both keep all their curtains drawn, use very low-wattage bulbs in their lamps, and avoid people. Neither goes outdoors much. If that were all we knew about the two of them, we might conclude their personalities are exactly alike. But suppose we learn Mabel has a medical condition that makes her susceptible to infection and her eyes painfully sensitive to light, and Agnes has been paranoid for years and is afraid that if she opens the curtains or goes outdoors, "they" will watch her. Now we realize there is very little similarity in their personalities. In the first three dimensions, these women could be twins; it is only in the fourth dimension—when we look at the inner workings of their minds—that we understand how different they are.

Likewise, two people may find themselves in exactly the same circumstances and react completely differently because they have different personalities. Thus, it is possible to explore the fourth dimensions of their characters by contrasting their behavior in similar situations.

For example: Neil and Kevin both grew up in families who spent every summer on Cape Cod, and both had wonderful experiences there. Now in middle age, Neil continues to return to the Cape every summer and enjoys reliving the memories of those summers. Kevin, on the other hand, spends every summer visiting a different country and hasn't been back to the Cape in years. He will tell you that the Cape is a wonderful spot, but the summers he spent there merely whetted his appetite to see the rest of the world.

Does This Person Have a Secret?

Another way to pursue fourth-dimension traits is to ask yourself, "What is there about this character that no one else knows, and how can I reveal that information to the reader?" Let's go back to our character, Ellen. We still don't know why she's so afraid of losing her job. Suppose we listen in on her thoughts a little longer and discover that she's a single mother who has a young daughter with an incurable medical condition that requires constant expensive treatment. If Ellen loses her job, she loses her medical coverage, and she knows that no one else will insure her little girl. Without insurance, there is no way she can get her child the treatment she needs. Now we see her toadying behavior in a different light. We realize how hard it must be to bite her tongue or even justify Ms. Conklin's actions when she disagrees with her boss, and if we write the story well, Ellen may become a quiet heroine instead of being an unlikeable woman.

How do you let your readers know why your character is behaving in a certain way? One obvious course is to get into the character's head and let the reader hear her thoughts, as we did with Ellen. But what if you need to tell the story from a point of view that does not allow you to get into the character's mind? Then you must help the reader infer from the behavior and speech of the character what is going on inside her head. Remembering that a person may speak or act deceptively, you need to present this material in circumstances where she is not likely to be doing so. For example, if in a moment of desperation, Ellen discloses her dilemma to a lifelong friend, her words will have the ring of truth, especially if they explain her previous behavior.

Examine the Character's Fantasies

Sometimes a person doesn't consciously know why he behaves the way he does. How, then, can the author show the reader what is going on without intruding on the story? A good way is to explore the character's fantasies. Remember Bud, the father who disowned his son because he wanted to study music? What could make a man behave this way? Let's see:

> Bud watched Gwenna walk away from him; her trim hips still
> wiggled in that fascinating way—sexy but not cheap. Definitely

not cheap. If he closed his eyes just a little, she still looked like she did in high school, fresh-faced and lush. She should have been *his* girl. Would have been—if only he'd had a little more time to show her how clever he was. But Charlie Blasing had moved in too quickly.

Blasing was an idiot—a goddamn idiot—and lucky as hell. Everything he touched turned into money. On top of that, Charlie had two brothers and they'd both gone into business with him and helped him become such a success.

Bud clenched his fists. It was so unfair. All these years he'd had to struggle alone. And now, just when Matt was old enough to be a real help to him, the kid wanted to go away—to study *music*, for Pete's sake! How was *that* going to help him sell furniture?

Now we begin to see how Bud's mind works. He fantasizes compensating for losing Gwenna by becoming a success like Charlie, but he doesn't give Charlie any credit for business acumen. He thinks it was just luck and the help of others that got Charlie where he is. Likewise, Bud takes no personal blame for his own lack of success. If he never becomes rich, it will be because his son wouldn't help him. It is clear, too, that Matt has no chance of changing his father's mind. Our story is beginning to take on tragic overtones.

In order to continue our story, we'll need to look into Matt's deepest thoughts and discover how he'll respond to his father's ultimatum and what his reasoning is—that is, we need to examine the fourth dimension of Matt's personality.

In order to create well-rounded, living individuals in your fiction, you need to show the reader aspects of all four dimensions of their personalities. If you follow this practice, your stories will be rich and your characters memorable.

STEPHANIE KAY BENDEL is a freelance writer who lives in Boulder, Colorado. She has taught writing for eighteen years and is the author of *Making Crime Pay: A Practical Guide to Mystery Writing* and the mystery *Scream Away* (under the name Andrea Harris).

CHAPTER 15
SEVEN TOOLS FOR TALK

BY JAMES SCOTT BELL

My neighbor John loves to work on his hot rod. He's an automotive whiz and tells me he can hear when something is not quite right with the engine. He doesn't hesitate to pop the hood, grab his bag of tools, and start to tinker. He'll keep at it until the engine sounds just the way he wants it to.

That's not a bad way to think about dialogue. We can usually sense when it needs work. What fiction writers often lack, however, is a defined set of tools they can put to use on problem areas.

So here's a set—my seven favorite dialogue tools. Stick them in your writer's toolbox for those times you need to pop the hood and tinker with your characters' words.

1. LET IT FLOW

When you write the first draft of a scene, let the dialogue flow. Pour it out like cheap champagne. You'll make it sparkle later, but first you must get it down on paper. This technique will allow you to come up with lines you never would have thought of if you tried to get it right the first time.

In fact, you can often come up with a dynamic scene by writing the dialogue first. Record what your characters are arguing about, stewing over, revealing. Write it all as fast as you can. As you do, pay no attention to attributions (who said what). Just write the lines.

Once you get these on the page, you will have a good idea what the scene is all about. And it may be something different than you anticipated. Good! You are cooking. Now you can go back and write the narrative that goes with the scene, and the normal speaker attributions and tags.

I have found this technique to be a wonderful cure for writer's fatigue. I do my best writing in the morning, but if I haven't done my quota by the evening (when I'm usually tired), I'll just write some dialogue. Fast and furious. It flows and gets me into a scene.

With the juices pumping, I find I'll often write more than my quota. And even if I don't use all the dialogue I write, the better I get at it.

2. ACT IT OUT

Before going into writing, I spent some time in New York pounding the boards as an actor. While there, I took an acting class, which included improvisation. Another member of the class was a Pulitzer Prize-winning playwright. When I asked him what he was doing there, he said improvisational work was a tremendous exercise for learning to write dialogue.

I found this to be true. But you don't have to wait to join a class. You can improvise just as easily by doing a Woody Allen.

Remember the courtroom scene in Allen's movie *Bananas*? Allen is representing himself at the trial. He takes the witness stand and begins to cross-examine, asking a question, running into the witness box for the answer, then jumping out again to ask another question.

I am suggesting you do the same thing (in the privacy of your own home, of course). Make up a scene between two characters in conflict. Then start an argument. Go back and forth, changing the actual physical location. Allow a slight pause as you switch, giving yourself time to come up with a response in each character's voice.

Another twist on this technique: Do a scene between two well-known actors. Use the entire history of movies and television. Pit Lucille Ball against Bela Lugosi, or have Oprah Winfrey argue with Bette Davis. Only you play all the parts. Let yourself go.

And if your local community college offers an improvisation course, give it a try. You might just meet a Pulitzer Prize winner.

3. SIDESTEP THE OBVIOUS

One of the most common mistakes new writers make with dialogue is creating a simple back and forth exchange. Each line responds directly to the previous line, often repeating a word or phrase (an "echo"). It looks something like this:

"Hello, Mary."

> "Hi, Sylvia."
>
> "My, that's a wonderful outfit you're wearing."
>
> "Outfit? You mean this old thing?"
>
> "Old thing! It looks practically new."
>
> "It's not new, but thank you for saying so."

This sort of dialogue is "on the nose." There are no surprises, and the reader drifts along with little interest. While some direct response is fine, your dialogue will be stronger if you sidestep the obvious:

> "Hello, Mary."
>
> "Sylvia. I didn't see you."
>
> "My, that's a wonderful outfit you're wearing."
>
> "I need a drink."

I don't know what is going on in this scene since I've only written four lines of dialogue. But this exchange is immediately more interesting and suggestive of currents beneath the surface than the first example. I might even find the seeds of an entire story here.

You can also sidestep with a question:

> "Hello, Mary."
>
> "Sylvia. I didn't see you."
>
> "My that's a wonderful outfit you're wearing."
>
> "Where is he, Sylvia?"

Hmm. Who is "he"? And why should Sylvia know? (Go ahead and find out for yourself if you want to.) The point is there are innumerable directions in which the sidestep technique can go. Experiment to find a path that works best for you. Look at a section of your dialogue and change some direct responses into off-center ripostes. Like the old magic trick ads used to say, "You'll be pleased and amazed."

4. CULTIVATE SILENCE

A powerful variation on the sidestep is silence. It is often the best choice, no matter what words you might come up with. Hemingway was a master at this. Consider this excerpt from his short story, "Hills Like White Elephants." A man and a woman are having a drink at a train station in Spain. The man speaks:

> "Should we have another drink?"

"All right."

The warm wind blew the bead curtain against the table.

"The beer's nice and cool," the man said.

"It's lovely," the girl said.

"It's really an awfully simple operation, Jig," the man said. "It's not really an operation at all."

The girl looked at the ground the table legs rested on.

"I know you wouldn't mind it, Jig. It's really not anything. It's just to let the air in."

The girl did not say anything.

In this story, the man is trying to convince the girl to have an abortion (a word that does not appear anywhere in the text). Her silence is reaction enough.

By using sidestep, silence, and action, Hemingway gets the point across. He uses the same technique in the famous exchange between mother and son in the story "Soldier's Home":

"God has some work for every one to do," his mother said. "There can't be no idle hands in His Kingdom."

"I'm not in His Kingdom," Krebs said.

"We are all of us in His Kingdom."

Krebs felt embarrassed and resentful as always.

"I've worried about you so much, Harold," his mother went on. "I know the temptations you must have been exposed to. I know how weak men are. I know what your own dear grandfather, my own father, told us about the Civil War and I have prayed for you. I pray for you all day long, Harold."

Krebs looked at the bacon fat hardening on the plate.

Silence and bacon fat hardening. We don't need anything else to catch the mood of the scene. What are your characters feeling while exchanging dialogue? Try expressing it with the sound of silence.

5. POLISH A GEM

We've all had those moments when we wake up and have the perfect response in a conversation that took place the night before. Wouldn't we all like to have those bon mots at a moment's notice?

Your characters can. That's part of the fun of being a fiction writer. I have a somewhat arbitrary rule—one gem per quarter. Divide your novel into fourths. When you polish your dialogue, find those opportunities in each quarter to polish a gem.

And how do you do that? Like the diamond cutter. You take what is rough and tap at it until it is perfect. In the movie *The Godfather*, Moe Greene is angry that a young Michael Corleone is telling him what to do. He might have said, "I made my bones when you were in high school!" Instead, screenwriter Mario Puzo penned, "I made my bones when you were going out with cheerleaders!" (In his novel, Puzo wrote something a little racier). The point is you can take almost any line and find a more sparkling alternative.

Just remember to use these gems sparingly. The perfect comeback grows tiresome if it happens all the time.

6. EMPLOY CONFRONTATION

Many writers struggle with exposition in their novels. Often they heap it on in large chunks of straight narrative. Backstory—what happens before the novel opens—is especially troublesome. How can we give the essentials and avoid a mere information drop?

Use dialogue. First, create a tension-filled scene, usually between two characters. Get them arguing, confronting each other. Then you can have the information appear in the natural course of things. Here is the clunky way to do it:

> John Davenport was a doctor fleeing from a terrible past. He had been drummed out of the profession for bungling an operation while he was drunk.

Instead, place this backstory in a scene where John is confronted by a patient who is aware of the doctor's past:

> "I know who you are," Charles said.
> "You know nothing," John said.
> "You're that doctor."
> "If you don't mind I—"
> "From Hopkins. You killed a woman because you were soused. Yeah, that's it."

And so forth. This is a much underused method, but it not only gives weight to your dialogue, it increases the pace of your story.

7. DROP WORDS

This is a favorite technique of dialogue master Elmore Leonard. By excising a single word here and there, he creates a feeling of verisimilitude in his dialogue. It sounds like real speech, though it is really nothing of the sort. All of Leonard's dialogue contributes, laserlike, to characterization and story.

Here's a standard exchange:

"Your dog was killed?

"Yes, run over by a car."

"What did you call it?"

"It was a she. I called her Tuffy."

This is the way Elmore Leonard did it in *Out of Sight*:

"Your dog was killed?"

"Got run over by a car."

"What did you call it?"

"Was a she, name Tuffy."

It sounds so natural, yet is lean and meaningful. Notice it is all a matter of a few words dropped, leaving the feeling of real speech.

As with any technique, you can always overdo it. Pick your spots and your characters with careful precision and focus. Your dialogue will thank you for it later.

Using tools is fun when you know what to do with them, and see results. I guess that's why John, my neighbor, is always whistling when he works on his car. You'll see results in your fiction—and have fun, too—by using these tools to make your dialogue sound just right.

Start tinkering.

JAMES SCOTT BELL (www.jamesscottbell.com) is a best-selling novelist and popular writing teacher. His books for the Write Great Fiction series, *Plot & Structure* and *Revision & Self-Editing*, have become standards of the fiction craft.

CHAPTER 16
THE BEST POV FOR YOUR STORY

BY NANCY KRESS

Because we lack telepathy, we humans are imprisoned in our own skulls. As Joseph Conrad wrote, "We live, as we dream, alone"—at least alone within our heads. The only thoughts, plans, dreams, and feelings we can directly experience are our own. It's because this one-viewpoint reality is hard-wired in us that fiction is so fascinating. It lets us experience the world from inside someone else's head.

This is the definition of point of view: whose eyes we view the action through, whose head we're inside of, whose feelings we experience as that character feels them. As such, your choice of point-of-view character or characters is critical to your story. It will determine what you tell, how you tell it and, often, even what the action means.

PROTAGONIST VS. POV CHARACTER

The protagonist of your story is the "star," the person we're most interested in, the one with the engaging action. Usually, but not inevitably, your protagonist will also be a POV character. Thus we see the events of John Grisham's best-selling *The King of Torts* through the eyes of its protagonist, Clay Carter, who is both the star and a POV character.

However, you can obtain some interesting effects by having your POV character be someone other than the protagonist. Two classics that do this are F. Scott Fitzgerald's *The Great Gatsby* and W. Somerset Maugham's *The Moon and Sixpence*.

Gatsby is told through the eyes of Nick Carraway, who is involved in the main action only peripherally, mostly as a standby friend and go-between. The real protagonists are the illicit lovers, Jay Gatsby and Daisy Buchanan, particularly Gatsby.

Maugham goes further yet. The protagonist of *The Moon and Sixpence* is Charles Strickland, who abandons his middle-class London existence to travel to the South Seas and become a painter. The unnamed narrator of the novel, the sole POV character, knows Strickland only slightly, as the friend of a friend. The narrator has several casual encounters with Strickland, but at no time does the narrator ever affect Strickland's life or Strickland affect the narrator's. Much of Strickland's later life is told to the narrator by other people, after the artist is dead.

The disadvantages of this convoluted structure are obvious: It lacks immediacy. Everything important that Strickland does, or that is done to him, occurs offstage. The narrator is told about events later, and he tells us about them. Maugham sacrifices a great deal of drama this way. So why did he do it?

Because separating your POV character from your protagonist also confers certain advantages:

- The POV character can continue the story after the protagonist dies, which both Strickland and Gatsby do during their respective novels. Maugham's POV character traces the fates of Strickland's widow, children, and paintings.

- The protagonist can be portrayed as much more secretive if he is not also a POV character. No one learns about Gatsby's real past until he is dead, and it's revealed that he has invented for himself a much more glamorous background than his actual one. Had Gatsby been a POV character, we readers would have known that from the very beginning, because we would have been "inside his head." Protagonists who are not also POV characters can preserve their mysteries. As Maugham's narrator says, "I felt that Strickland had kept his secrets to the grave."

- The POV character can make observations that would never in a million years occur to the protagonist. Carraway comes to see Buchanan as a careless lightweight and Gatsby as a touching idealist, views neither character (nor anyone else in the book) would have shared.

The first questions you should ask yourself about your use of POV are: *Will my protagonist and POV character(s) be the same? If not, do I have good reason for the split? Will I gain more than I lose?*

Once you know whether or not your protagonist will be a POV character, the next step is to determine who else will occupy that critical role.

POV CHARACTER SELECTION

It's a good idea, before you write anything at all, to consider all the choices for POV characters. The first choice to come to mind may not be the best pick.

Consider, for instance, Harper Lee's *To Kill a Mockingbird*, which takes place in pre–World War II Alabama. The main plotline concerns the framing of a black man, Tom Robinson, for the beating of a white woman, a crime he did not commit. His lawyer is the respected Atticus Finch, father of two children. Finch forces the identification of the true assailant, the victim's father, who then attempts revenge by attacking Finch's kids.

Lee could have told her story from any of these points of view. Instead, she embedded her main plot in a coming-of-age story and made her first-person narrator Finch's eight-year-old daughter, Scout. As a result, she ended up with a far different story than she would have if the POV character had been Atticus Finch, Robinson, or the true assailant. A better story? A worse one? No one can say; we haven't read any such alternate versions.

But certainly Scout is an effective choice. She meets the general criteria you should consider when choosing your POV character:

- **Who will be hurt by the action?** Someone strongly affected emotionally usually makes the best POV character (although Maugham, as we have seen, chose to sacrifice emotional immediacy for other goals). Scout is the victim of attempted murder by the disgruntled woman-beater and thus is in danger. Pick for your POV character someone with a strong stake in the outcome, including pain if the outcome will be negative. This criteria, incidentally, is why detective novels often work very hard to create a personal connection between the murderer and the detective. It raises the pain possibilities, which in turn increases narrative tension.

- **Who can be present at the climax?** In *To Kill a Mockingbird*, Scout is there. So is Nick Carraway in *The Great Gatsby*. Your POV character should be, too, or else we'll have to be told secondhand about the most important event of your story, thus distancing us from the action.

- **Who gets most of the good scenes?** We want to be present at those, too. Scout sneaks into the courtroom to witness her father's defense of Tom Robinson.

- **Who will provide an interesting outlook on the story?** Scout brings to Lee's novel an innocent, fresh view of racism that no adult could. Carraway similarly views the action of *The Great Gatsby* from a more idealistic, simpler vantage point than do its other characters, who are mostly New York sophisticates. What kind of observations about life do you want to make in your novel? Who is fit to make them? Do you want that character as your "eyes" and "heart"?

- **Whose head are you most interested in inhabiting during this story?** Don't underestimate this criterion; it really is key.

DIFFERENT EYES, DIFFERENT STORY

You may think you already know who your POV character will be. Perhaps you're right. But take a few moments to imagine what your story might be like if you were to choose differently.

Let us suppose, for instance, that you are writing a novel about the abduction of a child. Major characters are the father, the mother, the child, the abductor, a suspicious-but-innocent neighbor, and the lead detective on the case. The child will be recovered, but the family will never be the same again. There are at least six potential novels here, all vastly different.

- If the mother or father (or both) is your viewpoint, you will likely find yourself writing a novel of anguish (which might very well be what you want). These are good points of view if, for instance, the couple will eventually divorce, unable to incorporate the strain into an already fragile marriage. Perhaps one of them has an extramarital affair after the abduction. Perhaps one mounts an independent investigation. Perhaps one hires someone to murder the neighbor, who is then revealed—to the characters and to the reader—to be innocent.

- If the child is the POV character, you have a novel of bewilderment, fear, maybe rescue or escape. You will, of course, lose all scenes of the investigation and of parental interaction, because the kid won't see them. But you'll gain a lot of scenes between the abductor and abducted.

- If the neighbor is the POV character, you will have a novel of injustice. This could be quite interesting; stories of people wrongly accused always make for strong reader identification. Everyone loves to cheer on an innocent underdog.

- If the abductor is the POV character, you probably have a novel of either evil or madness. What is his motivation? Do you want to explore that? If so, he's your man.

- If the police officer or FBI agent is the POV character, you have a mystery novel. What's this character's stake in the conflict, beyond professional competence? Do you want to focus on how an investigation looks from the inside?

None of these POV choices is inherently better or worse than any other. It all depends on which suits the version of the story you want to tell. But if you don't at least consider points of view other than the one that first occurs to you, you may be cutting yourself off from some very exciting possibilities.

Who among your assembled cast might be an interesting POV character with a more original outlook on the plot than your first choice? If you were not the writer but the reader, whose viewpoint might tell the most satisfying story?

CASTS OF THOUSANDS

How many points of view are you allowed? There is no one answer. A rule of thumb is: Have as few points of view as you can get away with and still tell the story you want to tell.

The reason for this is the aforementioned entrapment in our own skulls. We're used to experiencing reality from one POV. Each time you switch from one fictional viewpoint to another, the reader must make a mental adjustment. If there are too many of these, the story feels increasingly fragmented and unreal.

On the other hand (there is always "another hand" in writing fiction), you may gain more than you lose. If you want to show how a romance feels to both parties, you need two points of view. If one character simply cannot be present at every important scene you need to present, you need more than one POV. You may need three, or even more, especially for a complicated or epic plot.

Figure out the fewest number of points of view you can have and still cover all major scenes and internal dialogues that your story requires. The point is to lessen the demands on the reader as much as possible so he can concentrate on the story and its implications, rather than being distracted by trying to remember what that eighth POV character was doing the last time we saw her, which was two hundred pages ago. Be aware that it can take a while to cycle through eight points of view and do justice to each one, and that too many points of view can be hard on the reader.

Then choose the best way to tell that reader your story.

 NANCY KRESS is the author of many short stories and books, including *Dynamic Characters* and *Beginnings, Middles & Ends*.

CHAPTER 17

EMOTION: FICTION'S CONNECTING LINK

BY KATHY JACOBSON

Without emotion, fiction becomes flat and boring. With it, you hook your readers, pull them in, hold them to the end, *and* make them eager for your next story or novel. So let's look at how you can enrich your writing by increasing the emotional level.

First of all, consider emotion as a triangle. One side represents the emotion of the author (your enthusiasm for the story), the second represents the emotions of the characters (how they interpret and respond to the events of the story), and the third represents the emotion of the readers (how closely they will identify with the characters). Your challenge is to make each side of the triangle strong enough to ensure the book doesn't collapse on itself (fail to interest an editor).

YOUR ENTHUSIASM

Do you love the genre you've picked? Are you an avid fan? You must have passion for the type of novel or story you plan to write or your work will lack excitement. The subject matter must fill you with enthusiasm, or the task of putting words on paper will soon become drudgery.

Love your work, love your story, love your characters, love the challenge of creating a book. Even when things don't go well, or you get a rejection, or your critique group discovers holes in your plot, remember that you write for the joy of it.

Also, don't be afraid of your own emotions. In the course of living, you've experienced hate, love, joy, anger, success, disappointment, fulfillment, and heartache. Strip away any inhibitors and screens you've developed to protect yourself from those who don't understand you, and let your feelings pour out on the page.

THE CHARACTER'S EMOTIONS

Stories are about people. They tell the stories of the characters that fill them. They describe who the characters are, where they go, what they do, who they encounter. But most important, stories portray *why* characters behave in certain ways, and the *why* always arises from emotion.

Suppose your character gets shoved while walking down the sidewalk. Will he beg pardon, swear but hurry on, shove back, or pull a knife? His reaction will come from his unique emotional state, whether he's frightened, harassed, or angry, or whether he views himself as a victim or a fighter. Obviously, the better you know your characters, the more surely you'll give them the right emotional reaction.

Unlike real life, where human beings often act irrationally, story people must behave with a certain consistency. You can't have your young heroine be naïve one moment and seductive the next. If she's shy and innocent, she'll be horrified by violence and profanity. On the other hand, if she's streetwise and cynical, she won't be looking at the world through rose-colored glasses. Her behavior will be believable because it will match her emotional reactions.

READER IDENTIFICATION

Readers like books to carry them into the unknown. They like characters who are unusual, who open new arenas for them, who introduce them to situations they might never personally experience. This means that as writers, we have unlimited opportunities to explore new worlds. But we must also give readers something they can relate to, something that will form a bridge between the familiar and the unknown. Emotion will *always* create such a bridge.

WHEN THE TRIANGLE DOESN'T WORK

Okay, so you're passionate about your story, your character's emotions are well motivated, and you believe any reader who picks up your book will be entranced by it. Then you give your manuscript to a friend (or your spouse or your mother) who returns it with an enthusiastic, "What a nice little story." Or worse, "Well, you know I don't really like romances, but this one seemed okay." Or more obtuse, "You really made me see the setting." Or you might be lucky enough to have a reader with guts enough to say, "You've got some good stuff here, but something's missing. I just don't know what it is."

When this happens, it is most often the second part of the triangle—the character's emotional response—that you'll need to shore up. So let's see how you can build your character's emotions into a strong connecting link between you, the writer, and your reader.

CONVEYING THE CHARACTER'S EMOTIONS

Your first challenge is deciding what the character feels. If you were to identify the character's primary driving emotion, what word would you use? Is he angry, eager, curious, hurt, happy, depressed? Try to find *one* adjective that best fits his emotional state, then identify how that one emotion defines his character.

If he's angry, how does he express that anger? Does he wear it like armor to deflect all attackers (real or imaginary)? Does he keep it locked tightly inside, like a bomb ready to explode? Or does he use it as a weapon, coldly and with firm purpose to get what he wants?

If he's eager, does this make him confident, aggressive, responsive to others, indifferent to roadblocks?

If he's hurt, does he keep a running total of insults and slights, letting them become the entire focus of his life? Or is he hunting for a cure, moving from psychiatrists to self-help books to love relationships to drugs, always looking for something outside of himself to solve his problem?

As you can see, the primary driving emotion gives you a cornerstone, and developing an emotional profile becomes your foundation. Once you have this foundation firmly in your mind, build the emotional framework by considering the following:

1. Identify Your Character's Worst Fault

To help you pinpoint the characteristic that will serve you best in looking for such a weakness, look to the end of your story. What insecurity, blind spot, failing, or fear will propel your character into the final crisis or black moment? He'll need to be working from some expectation or agenda that keeps him from resolving his problem until circumstances force him into it. What inner failing drives that expectation or agenda? What keeps him from making the choices that would have prevented the crisis?

Depending on the type of story you're writing, you may have to present the worst fault in a way that keeps the character likeable. For instance, in a romance, you can't allow your heroine to come across as a whiner or have your hero still needing to prove himself to his father. But don't short-change your characters by choosing tepid weaknesses. Remember, the harder the struggle, the more emotion you can build.

2. Recognize Your Character's Greatest Strength

What sets your character apart from the crowd? What inner emotional resource does your hero have that he can call on or discover to help him conquer in the end? Again, look to the final crisis of the story and consider what it will take for him to win. Just as you've given your character a fault to propel him into the black moment, give him a positive trait that will provide him with the power to overcome both his opponent and his own weaknesses.

3. Give Your Characters Specific, Urgent Goals

What the characters want must be strong enough to drive them to get it against all complications, all adversity, any danger, and often in spite of their better judgment. Does your character want anything that intensely?

Don't skimp. Make the goals important. Make them believable, and make sure they'll have emotional impact for the reader. If the character's long-range goal is to find happiness or inner peace, you'll have to give him a dramatic, difficult history that will infuse the goal with power through contrast.

No matter how important the goal is, it has to be urgent in order to have emotional force. Put pressure on the character's ability to achieve the goal. Make it a race—against time, an enemy, his own mental stability, financial security, danger, another's choices—to keep the tension high.

4. Consider How Your Character Will React in Various Situations

Is he likely to become insecure or belligerent when threatened? How does he react to generosity? When he's angry, does he erupt or hold it in? How can you tell if he's bored? Excited? Frustrated? Annoyed? What mannerisms does he adopt? What physical manifestations will his body exhibit?

Make sure his reactions are consistent. The reader will believe a character who trembles with anger, fidgets when bored, and cries for victims *if* you've shown that he wears his emotions on his sleeve. If he's built an emotional shell around himself so his eyes never fill with tears and he never raises his voice, we can believe he'd kill the man who raped his daughter *if* you show that by holding his emotions in, they've reached fever pitch.

5. Give the Character an Inner Conflict

Why is the character insecure, unhappy, angry, afraid, or frustrated? What motivates him to act? Will he fight or flee? Why? Can you force him into a situation (the conflict of your story) in which he must act against his true nature? If he's a fighter, what would it take to make him run? If he'd normally take flight, what circumstances would make him stand his ground?

6. Integrate Your Character Well

Since good fiction depends on good conflict, you want to build conflict wherever possible. But even when your fighter must flee, you have to make him self-consistent. You have to motivate the conflicts within your character as well as without, so make sure his goals reflect his personality and his strengths don't preclude his weaknesses. Make him as complex as you want, but be sure his personality reflects his background and motivations.

CONNECTING WITH THE READER

Once you know how the character will react, you have to present the emotions behind the reactions in a way that makes the reader feel what the character feels. You can do this in a number of ways, and showing is better than telling.

Some verbs always tell and never show, especially any form of *to be* or *to feel*. For example, if you write, *Mark was bitter*, or *Mark felt bitter*, you're telling. If you write, *Mark crumpled the letter from his father, vowing never to return home again*, you've given him two specific actions that show his emotion and help the reader *feel* Mark's bitterness.

Use verbs that connote emotion rather than merely describe action. For instance, strode, paced, ambled, marched, strolled, and tromped are all better than walked. In order, they convey purpose, anxiety, contentment, anger, leisure, and duty, while walked only shows movement.

Use adjectives that indicate the character's emotional interpretation. A room can be dingy, sterile, homey, oppressive, crowded, busy, inviting, silent, tacky, impressive, or intimidating, depending on who's looking at it. Be sure to choose adjectives that reflect the character's view and not your own, since the emotional bridge you want to build is between the *character* and the reader.

WATCH YOUR POINT OF VIEW

Recognize that the character is a stronger narrator than the author. Any time you start describing the action rather than letting the character experience it, you're distancing the character from the reader. This will cost you both immediacy and emotion. Look at this example in which an omniscient narrator describes Mark's situation:

> Mark's father had always ordered him around, and this letter was just another good example. Mark read it again and again, and bitterness grew acrid inside him. The daughter of one of his dad's old cronies would be visiting next week, and Mark was instructed to come home and meet her. Crumpling the letter, he decided the time had come to make a break.

Now look at it from Mark's point of view:

> Mark crumpled his father's letter and lobbed it into the garbage can. After two years, the old man still didn't get it. Mark made his own decisions now. He chose his own girlfriends. He sure as hell didn't rush home to meet the daughter of one of his dad's old cronies.

The Complete Handbook of Novel Writing

Can you see the difference in these two examples? Although both are well written, one pulls the reader tighter into the character's point of view and, therefore, his emotional state. Where the first describes the emotion, the second lets the character experience it.

APPLY THE EMOTIONAL FILTER

Everything in your story will have greater impact if you have your character interpret it emotionally. Involve the five senses to give your writing strong sensory texture, then make sure you convey your character's emotional assessment of what she experiences. For example, on assignment for the Star System Regulatory Agency, Lily lands on a planet she's never visited before. She's going to notice the color of the sky, the bleakness of the landscape, the odor of the air, and the flavor of the water, but her impressions are going to be more important than the details in drawing your reader into the scene. Let's see a simple description first:

> Lily stepped through the Theta Gate and took in the scene before her. Humanoids from a dozen planets mingled with multi-pods, avians, and the local Zerips. Pink clouds floated across the red sky. The air had a distinctly chlorine odor, and a few leafless trees lined the main route into the city.

Now let's run the scene through Lily's emotional filter and see how much richer it becomes:

> Lily stepped through the Theta Gate and wrinkled her nose in distaste. Humanoids from a dozen planets mingled with multi-pods, avians, and the local Zerips, but only the Zerips looked at home under the hideous red sky. She tried to filter enough oxygen out of the chlorine-heavy air to satisfy her lungs, but gave up after a few breaths. The air mix wouldn't kill her, although it didn't seem to do much for the few leafless trees that lined the main route into the city.

As a rule of thumb, if your character doesn't care enough about what she sees, hears, tastes, touches, and smells to give some emotional assessment to it, the reader won't care either. And this applies to everything—action, dialogue, description, and other characters. Here's an example of an exchange between two characters:

> Angie watched Hugh stride between the rows of computer terminals. He didn't glance at any of the data operators, but kept his eyes fixed on her. When he reached her desk, he smiled.
>
> "We brought Williams in last night," he said.
>
> She pressed her palms flat against her thighs. "Did he confess?"
>
> "Not in so many words." Hugh lifted his hand and examined his nails. When he spoke again, his eyes were serious. "He said Charlotte Mason was having an affair with Johnny Keno."
>
> Angie let the information sink in.

We have dialogue and action, but no emotion. We don't know Angie's opinion of Hugh, or his of her. We have no hint of whether she's glad or sorry to hear the news about Williams, or what effect the information about Charlotte has on her. To give your work more potency, run it through your focal character's emotional filter. Keep the reader constantly connected to the character by giving the character opinions and judgments. Let's look at the previous exchange again, this time with Angie's emotional filter in place:

> With her heart beating double time, Angie watched Hugh stride between the rows of computer terminals. Until yesterday, just being in his presence had sent her heart racing. Today, she feared what he would tell her.
>
> He didn't glance at any of the data operators, but kept his eyes fixed on her. When he reached her desk, he smiled. "We brought Williams in last night."
>
> Max Williams knew everything, but how much would he tell? Angie cleared her throat, hoping no trace of her fear would show in her voice. "Did he confess?"
>
> "Not in so many words." Hugh lifted his hand to examine his nails and let the suspense build.
>
> Suddenly she saw his hand in the whole sordid affair. He'd seduced her for what he could get from her, and now he toyed with

her like a cat who'd cornered a mouse. She pressed her palms flat on her thighs to keep from wringing her hands together.

When Hugh spoke again, his eyes were hard. "He said Charlotte Mason was having an affair with Johnny Keno."

The words flowed through Angie's mind and pooled near her heart like congealing tar. So Charlotte had been in on it all along.

Notice in the second version that Angie interprets her own reactions for the reader and conveys hints on Hugh's agenda. Since you don't want to go into Hugh's mind while in Angie's point of view, she has to transmit his behavior. Since she can't know what's going on in his head, she has to interpret it based on her on assumptions, which means we see him through her emotional filter.

OPINIONS AND JUDGMENTS

The emotional filter is always subjective. It presents your focal character's view of your story world, the situation, the other characters, and the conflicts. By attaching his opinions to his observations and having him make judgments on everyone else's behavior, he not only becomes a stronger character, but your reader will form a stronger emotional bond with him.

Every once in a while, you may find yourself writing a scene through the eyes of your villain or some other unsympathetic character. Be sure to make his filter true to him. Present his warped view in the living color of his hang-ups and destructive agenda. If you do this well, the reader will love reading about him because he will be so compellingly *un*likeable.

If you find it difficult to include the subtleties of an emotional filter while writing your first draft, don't self-edit during the creative process. Write your dialogue or your action and add opinions and judgments on the second or third time through. Invest heavily where you have the most control (your own effort and emotion), and reap the benefits when the reader connects emotionally to your characters and loves your story.

KATHY JACOBSON is the author of *A Novel Approach: Blending Emotion and Structure to Create a Salable Novel*. She has also written novels for Harlequin, including *The Sheriff With the Wyoming Size Heart*.

CHAPTER 18
SENSE & SENSUALITY

BY JANET FITCH

Our lives at the millennium in advanced Western culture are the most senses-deprived of any on earth. Biologically and psychologically, the human organism was designed for intense experience in a richly sensual world. But we find ourselves in a senses-depleted world, a world limited largely to visuals, and ersatz ones at that.

Our senses aren't mere perceptions. We're not robots. The senses act upon us; they stimulate us in countless ways. We are the instrument the music is played on, not merely the listener to what's being played.

Think how sensually paltry our lives have become at the end of the twentieth century, compared with the world inhabited by our ancestors, or even of our "less privileged" brothers and sisters in other regions of the world still rich in uncensored sights, sounds, smells, textures, tastes.

As creatures of our time and place in Western civilization, we're cut off from the full spectrum of life by our very affluence, by our control of our physical environment. The most primitive senses especially—touch and smell—have been relegated to tiny islands of experience, as opposed to the range of these stimuli when we were open to the vagaries of physical reality.

Take touch. We wear shoes, clothes; our homes are weather-proofed. Our environments are "smoothed" for us. We don't work manually, we don't live among livestock and seasons. As small children, we're told to "look but don't touch." In our culture, sight is "good" but touch is "bad." Stop touching yourself. Don't handle your food. Keep your hands to yourself.

Smell is also "bad." Our culture deodorizes life. We don't cook things for hours so the smoke and the scent won't clog the interior. Our wools don't smell of lanolin. We live in cities, we don't smell the earth warming in spring, we don't appreciate the variations of body odor, even traditional strong-smelling foods. We avoid the least "stink."

The millennial reader is starving for sensual information. He wants the world back. And this is what good writing gives us—a rich, "full spectrum" sensual experience. Appealing to the five senses is the feature that will always set writing apart from the visual media. A good writer will tell us what the world smells like, what the textures are, what the sounds are, what the light looks like, what the weather is.

In sensual writing, the reader doesn't simply watch a character; he enter the character's body. If the character is cold, the reader is cold. If she's hungry, the readers experience her hunger. Sensual writing satisfies the reader's need to be in the flesh of a story, experiencing a richness of life that has often been robbed from his daily environment.

How do you describe a sense impression? How hot is hot? How sharp is sharp? How blue is the sky? What is the taste of a peach in summer? How would you describe a sunset to a blind man, the mockingbird's song to the deaf?

ANGLING FOR DESCRIPTION

You can get a certain distance with literal descriptions, but the truth is, most sense impressions cannot be directly described. So how do you achieve this necessary sensual writing? The first clue is to come in at an angle, obliquely, the way you approach all things evanescent. The quality of *synesthesia*—using one sense to describe another—comes to our aid in a big way.

Wine reviews provide excellent examples. Ever notice the things that critics taste in a glass of wine? Baritone notes, grass, daisies, butterscotch. A blonde wine. Sunshine. They find a wine crisp, or strawlike, or oaken or flaxen or young. Sprightly (Does that mean that it's going to bound off into the distance?) or sharp (Does this mean that they're going to stick themselves on the Chardonnay? That they're going to need a tetanus shot?).

What these critics are doing is using the other senses—textures, smells, sounds, and visuals—to describe a taste, something very difficult to describe. A review might start with the literal—"tastes like apples" or "tastes tart"—but this is an area quickly exhausted. So synesthesia is brought into play. From there it's a short leap to the fiction writer's best tool—fantasy.

Back to the wine review example. After pursuing the literal, move into synesthesia—the chocolatey, oaken, baritone notes of the cabernet, the rich brocade of its velvets. But that's not the end. As a fiction writer, go one step further. Think through the thing itself and travel to its point of origin, the soil where it grew, the small village, the hands that picked the grapes, the time of year, the time of day, and emerge with a whole secondary series of sensual information. You drink the wine and go through it to Burgundy, where you stick your hands in the soil and raise them to your nose, you talk to your French grandfather Jean Luc as you have lunch on the red-and-white checked tablecloth during the harvest season.

For fiction writers, the senses are not only a window onto external reality, but also the gateway into the inner realms.

Exercise 1

Try this exercise to reach through a sense into fantasy. Take a food, preferably something strong enough to "reach through" into the imagination. (I've found the more processed and denatured, or desensualized, the item, the more difficult it is to "reach through.") Describe the taste first in literal terms. Then describe it synesthesially. Finally, move into the imagination. Take your time. See if you can reach through the taste into a complete scene, a time of year, a time of day, a place and people as you stretch out from your sense data.

I recommend you keep all these sense exercises in a three-ring binder, organized by category ("touch," "smell") for reference. You'll be surprised how useable this information will prove to be in your fiction writing.

Exercise 2

Practice this exercise using various fragrances. Try writing about simple scents, rather than perfumes, which already have implied moods and narratives. Sample essential oils, spices, herbs, even common household substances such as bleach, vinegar, or ammonia. (Don't sniff straight from the bottle, whether it's cologne or something toxic like bleach or ammonia!

Do as chemists do: Hold the open bottle away from your face and then waft the scent toward you with your hand.) Use your impressions to give your characters distinct scents, bringing another dimension of the sensual world into play.

A tool I regularly use is a "scent organ." At a garage sale, I found a box with ten small bottles that had once been used for ginseng. I put a wad of cotton in each one, and went to a local purveyor of body products and essential oils and paid them five bucks to give me a few drops of ten different fragrances in those vials. I took great care to select scents that were most evocative for me. Hawaiian pikake (my mother's perfume was pikake when I was a child), almond, rose, eucalyptus. Bitter California orange that smells like my old neighborhood here in L.A. where people didn't pick the fruit, just left it to rot on the trees. Whenever I open that vial, I am fifteen.

MAKING SENSE OF MEMORY

Nothing stimulates memory like sense data. Memory lies coiled within us like a magician's trick handkerchief, and a simple smell or taste can pluck the tiniest corner and pull out the world. When playing with sense exercises, watch for memories as they begin to emerge. Remember, Proust started with that little madeleine dipped in tea.

As you read over your sense exercises, you'll notice something readers have always instinctively known. The most interesting smells/colors/sounds are those that are not strictly speaking sense impressions at all, but instead, memories and fantasies, purely psychological matters.

Think of baby powder. You can describe it literally: sweet, chalky, talcy, dusty, sneezy. You can do synesthesias: smells pastel, smells tender. Then move to the psychological element. Take an attitude on that smell: insipid, cloying, stultifying, like diaper rash, airless. Try a different attitude: sad, lost, vulnerable, hopeless, eradicable. This is the Heisenberg aspect of description—a sense impression can be colored by the observer's take on that information, so that the description can reveal character as well as define the exterior experience.

Finally, move utterly into the realm of memory and fantasy, working to the associations of that smell: It smells like children, like bath time, like rabbits, bubble bath, lullabies, soft towels, the bluebirds over the dressing table, my mother's face, powder on my father's suit, bare bottoms of grandchildren, my own early motherhood, how tired I was, the fourteen diaper changes a day, my insecurity and fears, marital problems with the new father who wasn't used to being second banana. I imagine throwing the powder at him and how it fountains through the air.

The smell is merely the stimulus. Describe the stimulus, and then move to the psychological component.

THE INTENSITY OF TOUCH

The sense of touch is the most vivid and direct source of information about the world. It is also the most neglected, the most taboo. Touch is pain and pleasure, the most intense source of direct stimuli.

Keep a running list of vocabulary to describe aspects of touch, texture, and shape. You'll use it over and over again. Start by listing dichotomies: Hard/soft, smooth/rough, straight/curved, hot/cold, wet/dry, heavy/light, give or no give.

Exercise 3

Amass items that are texturally interesting: sand, a rock, a hammer, a feather duster, a piece of lace, a baseball, a sponge, a wooden spoon, a rubber duck, a nylon stocking, a stuffed animal, gravel, marbles. With your eyes closed, pick up one and really feel it. Experience it, finding the words to describe the sensations, both literally and synesthesially. Notice details, referring and adding to the list of texture words above. Exhaust the physical. The purpose of this exercise is to train your ability to write literal description.

Touch is an activity as well as a sensation. We can enjoy the fine sponginess of a piece of steel wool with our fingertips, or we can scrub it up and down the insides of our arms for a very different sensation. A strip of leather can be soft and pliable to the fingers, but if someone whips us with it .... So touch is a gesture as well as the thing touched. It is also the impact of an object on the skin, the largest organ of the body.

Exercise 4

This exercise illustrates touch as a springboard to fantasy/memory. Take a piece of fabric. Close your eyes and feel it. Feel it with your hands, with your arms, across the back of your neck, under your feet, behind your knees, across your chest. Press it to your cheek, your lips. Ask yourself, what is this cloth? A piece of scratchy wool might end up being a school uniform; a piece of velvet might be a theater chair or your grandmother's couch. Take an attitude. What's happening here? Be a character who is touching this cloth. Who are you? Where are you?

As you develop your awareness of the senses, you will find yourself collecting a vivid sensual vocabulary. As you read and write, you may note that the richest, most vivid words are those that use more than one of the senses at a time. For example, a yellow sky—how many senses does that appeal to? One—the visual. However, a lemon sky refers to color, taste, smell, and even texture. Four senses implied in a single word. Or take a brassy blonde—brass implies a sound, a color, and a texture, even a taste (if you've ever licked brass, you know what I mean). That's four senses. In this way, the synesthetic layering effect adds depth and dimensionality to your sensual world on the page.

WHAT AREN'T YOU HEARING?

Our world is a chaos of noise. In fact, we even use sound—music—to drown out the ambient sound as a way to control our environment, just as we use deodorant to cut us off from smell, and air conditioning and heating to alter our tactile environment.

But as writers, we want to pay attention to this neglected sound so when characters pause in dialogue, or when they are alone, they hear something in the silences.

Exercise 5

Take ten minutes and just listen. List what you hear. Record this ambient sound at various times of day, in various places, keeping this data for your sense notebook. Note over time the audible difference between summer and winter (summer is louder because the windows are usually open). Note the difference between morning ambient sound and that at 3 A.M.

Many writers are fond of playing music and writing to it, using it to control mood. As an exercise, I find I get more out of unfamiliar music, or music I don't like, more than old favorites. If you hate polka, try playing polka and see what kind of a reaction you can get out of it!

LOOK TO THE LIGHT

What can I teach you about seeing? As writers, we need to begin to see richly, the way a painter or photographer sees. We need to analyze what we see.

The first lesson of the visual is that all seeing is seeing light. We need to be continually conscious that what we see is the effect of how light strikes objects within our visual range. Think of how Rembrandt sculpted his light. Instead of writing about what things look like, try writing about the light and how the light strikes the objects.

A good way to expose yourself to the vocabulary of light is to read books on art. For example, water words describe light: it pours, it washes, it splashes, it soaks, it plays. Light is a painter, a sculptor: it strokes, it daubs, it rubs, it burnishes. Light does things to objects, so its verbs are quite active. Examination of light in describing a scene will eliminate once and for all the static descriptions because there can always be something active in a scene, if only the light itself.

Exercise 6

To write effectively about light, you must develop vocabulary to describe how light affects what you see. Light a candle in a room and "paint" what you see. Describe the angle at which the light falls. Note precisely what is illuminated and what is left in shadow. What is the quality of the light? What direction is the light coming from? What is the color of the light?

I've only touched on the coastline of the vast continent of sense exploration. I urge you to don your pith helmet and explore the interior, and use what you bring back in everything you write. If you learn to properly play your own instrument, your own five senses, you will be able to move another finely tuned instrument—your reader.

JANET FITCH is the author of *White Oleander* and *Paint It Black*. Her short fiction has appeared in *Black Warrior Review*, *Rain City Review*, and other journals.

CHAPTER 19
KILLER-DILLER DETAILS BRING FICTION TO LIFE

BY DONNA LEVIN

There's an expression, "God is in the details," and it applies to nothing more than it does to the writing of fiction. To that and to the art of telling good lies. And what is fiction but the telling of lies?

Well, not exactly, but fiction writing and lying do have something in common. (Picasso said, "Art is a lie that lets us see the truth.") In both cases you are making something up and trying to make someone believe it. Even when you write about something that "really happened" in your personal life, in fiction you will find that making the reader believe it is one of your chief tasks.

Now, I mean "believe" in a specialized sense. A reader picks up a book in a store knowing it's fiction, or fictionalized. But when the reader actually buys the book, he's in effect saying to the author, "I'm going to give you a chance to tell me a story that I can at least pretend is real for the duration of the book." Providing the details is how you make your reader into a believer. It's how you put your reader into the action.

As a writer, you should know that if you really want the reader to believe he's reading about an African safari, you'd better describe the long purple tongues of the giraffes. You must learn that giraffes have purple tongues, or imagine they do, or remember that detail from your real-life safari or trip to the zoo. The purple tongue of the giraffe lets us see the giraffe.

A detail doesn't need to be real in the conventional sense in order to have power. Science fiction and horror writers know very well the power of invented, but authentic, details.

One of the most compelling aspects of Anne Rice's *Interview With the Vampire* is that Rice really makes you believe that vampires exist, and she does so by the exquisite detailing of the way they live (or, we might say, unlive) and function. She casually dismisses any familiar Hollywood notions or even any traditional ones that don't suit her. "Forget that," she says, "this is the way it is." And then she follows her own rules with a steely consistency.

In the same way, the science fiction writer has to let us know that the South Forkorian qebor eats yodels and that yodels eat mordons in order to establish the food chain on the planet Zen.

When writing historical fiction, you must weave in as many of the factual details as you can. But sometimes you will be called upon to fill gaps that history has left. Your inventions—whether they are to surmise the way that the Huns celebrated wedding ceremonies or to recreate dialogue spoken by Charlemagne—will also make history seem real.

QUALITY, NOT QUANTITY

When it comes to details, more is not necessarily better. The number of details you need to describe a person or to dramatize an event is a result of several factors. The first is your writing style. Some writers like to give the reader just enough of the bare facts to keep from getting lost. Others like to write lavish descriptions of every crinoline.

Both the amount and type of details you include will also be a function of the genre you're writing in. The readers of a Judith Krantz-style "sex and shopping" novel will be looking for lots of brand names, especially of designer clothes. A sword-and-sorcery novel will require you to authenticate the magic by inventing the details of how it works. A police procedural requires the details of how evidence is collected, suspects interviewed, and bodies autopsied.

Another factor in gauging the amount of details you need is to ask how familiar or unfamiliar the situation you're writing about is. The more unfamiliar, the more details you'll need to give. For example, I had a student who was writing about a mythical colony of semihumans who lived underground. She needed to describe their underground life in fairly thorough detail. By contrast, a book about modern life may require fewer details because we already know what a McDonald's looks like and how fast the average car can drive.

That doesn't mean you should eliminate all the details about contemporary life. It's the job of literary writers in particular to let us see commonplace occurrences as if for the first time—and they can often do that by their careful choice of details. The novelist Sue Miller has a gift for it. In *The Good Mother*, she describes a laundromat: "The long row of gleaming yellow washers sat silent, lids up, open-mouthed." Elsewhere: "I liked the laundromat—the way it smelled, the rhythmic slosh of the machines, the ticking of buttons, zippers, in the dryers ... ." There's more, but not much, because we've all seen laundromats. But by honing in on a few details, Miller brings this ordinary setting to life.

Whether your style and genre dictate that you shovel or sprinkle on the details, it's still important to choose well, to make your details earn their living by revealing much in a few words. One well-chosen detail can do the work of twenty banal ones. And when they do, I call them "killer-diller details."

SPECIFIC DETAILS

Sometimes you can turn a banal detail into a killer-diller one by being specific. Don't say the man was wearing a suit—tell us it was double-breasted chalkstripe.

Challenge yourself to see just how specific you can get. "A red scarf" might be adequate, but how about a vermilion, crimson, or raspberry one? You might get away with "a stylish car," but a 1996 Mercedes 450SL in aubergine will tell us more about the person behind the wheel.

Metaphors and similes can help make your details more specific, too. In both cases, the writer is taking a person and comparing him to something else that isn't there.

If you write, "her face was as expressionless as a hard-boiled egg," the image of the woman's face lodges much more solidly in our minds than if you write, "Her face was blank." The latter, a familiar idiom, passes through the reader's consciousness without leaving a footprint.

Anne Tyler, in *Dinner at the Homesick Restaurant*, writes of "a spindly, starved cat with a tail as matted as a worn-out bottle-brush." Forever and ever I can perfectly see that cat's tail.

BEYOND BLUE-EYED BLONDES

Killer-diller details are not the obvious ones. Say your character is walking into a kitchen. Most kitchens have stoves and refrigerators and to tell us that this kitchen does, too, isn't telling us much. In the name of being specific, you might tell us that the kitchen has a restaurant-style oven with a six-burner range top, or an avocado side-opening General Electric refrigerator, and you'd be telling us more. But you might also try to zero in on what's in this kitchen that is not in the usual kitchen. A bowl of strawberries from the owner's own garden. A child's artwork on the refrigerator (and what does the artwork depict?). A manual Smith-Corona typewriter on the Formica table.

When describing people, beginning writers usually check off hair and eye color. "She was a redhead with green eyes." Then, if they have any energy left, they may get into general physique and cite the character's age.

I had a student once whose character descriptions were so formulaic that I suspected her of having created a format in her computer for them. "The thirty-six-year-old brunette mother of two was five-five." "The twenty-five-year-old blonde beauty was five-foot-eight."

I had a devil of a time breaking her of this habit, which to her seemed efficient, since it covered a character's vital statistics in a few words. When I first encouraged her to vary the description, she came up with, "At six-four, the hulky forty-year-old had gray hair and blue eyes."

It's true that in real life we often appraise the people we meet casually. If you tried to remember what the waitress at the coffee shop this morning looked like, you might come up with hair color and approximate height, if that. If you're not "into" houses, you might not remember much about your neighbor's living room beyond the color of the couch and wing chair.

But paradoxically, in order to make your reader believe in your fiction, it has to be more intense than real life. Documenting only the obvious facts about a character or an environment isn't enough. Sure, we often want to know what a character's hair and eye color are, her age and height. But we also need to know what it is about this character, or this couch, or this bowling ball, that is unlike any other person, couch, or bowling ball in the universe. We want to see the one loose button on a man's shirt. The graffiti scratched in the wood (and perhaps what it says). The Band-Aids on the fingertips of a nail-biter.

DETAILS AS INFORMATION

The facts of how things work are important details. When Tom Wolfe wrote *The Bonfire of the Vanities*, he made us believe that Sherman Mc-Coy was a bond trader by carefully detailing just how bonds are traded, giving us information that only a bond trader (or someone who had done thorough research) would know.

If you ever saw Billy Crystal and Danny DeVito in the movie *Throw Momma From the Train*, you know what I'm talking about from its opposite. Billy Crystal is a teacher of fiction writing (there should be more movies about teachers of fiction), and in an early scene in the film, one of his students has written a story about men on a submarine. She reads with great energy. " 'Dive! Dive!' yelled the captain through the thing. So the man who makes it dive pressed a button or something and it dove. And the enemy was foiled again."

Billy Crystal tactfully points out, "When you write a novel that takes place on a submarine, it's a good idea to know the name of the instrument that the captain speaks through." Knowing the names of the various equipment on a submarine is a necessary starting point. The slang expression that Navy personnel use under stress would be a killer-diller detail.

HOW THE PART BECOMES THE WHOLE

In a novel by Ken Kulhken, *The Angel Gang*, an old man, Leo, receives a beating at the hands of some thugs. At one point, the author describes how the thugs cut a slit in Leo's eyelid. When Leo closes his eyes, he can see through his eyelid. The image is horrific, but also very specific and concise. The one detail stands in for the whole beating.

That doesn't necessarily mean that you then eliminate all the rest of the description of that beating. As we've discussed, the exact number of details and the amount of description you include is a function of your style, the genre, and the content. But always be on the lookout for the killer-diller details that can encapsulate a person, environment, or incident.

In Barbara Kingsolver's novel *Animal Dreams*, the narrator describes how her sister Hallie was so honest that, "I'd seen her tape dimes to broken parking meters." This killer-diller detail becomes the whole person for a moment, allowing us to imagine how she'd act in a hundred different situations. That doesn't mean that we don't want or need to know more about Hallie—of course we do, and the more important she is to the book as a whole, the more we'll want to know. Kingsolver in fact gives us many more killer-diller details to describe her.

AN EXERCISE FOR DETAIL-SPOTTING

There's a technique for training yourself to produce these killer-diller details. Around dinnertime or later (if you're a night person), take ten minutes to note the five most interesting things you observed that day. Make this a rigid habit for at least a month.

Now, when I say write down what you observed, I don't mean the weighty insights you had while watching the clerk bag your groceries. I mean the most specific, and sometimes offbeat, details that you see (or hear, or taste, or smell, or touch). I'm talking about details you might miss if you weren't paying attention. How *does* the clerk bag the groceries? Did he have any unusual physical features? Did he ask you a too-personal question that made you uncomfortable?

Maybe while walking up and down the aisles at the store, you noticed that someone had stuck a package of linguine on top of the canned pineapple. Maybe you overheard a pair of twins fighting over who would get to ride in the cart. Those kind of details are hardly earth-shattering. But they're real and not immediately obvious, the way that writing, "It was a big, crowded grocery store with Muzak playing," *would* be obvious—and banal. As you learn to add these types of details judiciously to your scenes, they, too, will become more real.

Here are some things I observed in the past couple of days:

- Two women were talking in Vietnamese, peppering their speech with "Wow!" and "Okay."

- The bus driver wore a royal blue-purple cable knit sweater that washed out her pale skin and white-blond eyebrows.

- My wedding ring tapping on the banister as I went down the stairs.

- An old man wearing a cardigan that used to be a woman's; the giveaway was that the buttons were backward.

- A man with a belt-length black beard and a parrot on a leash.

- At the deli, there was a woman wearing the jumpsuit of an American Airlines mechanic. Her name patch said, "Cupcake."

Remember as you practice observing that it's not a contest to see what offbeat or dramatic occurrences you can witness. (No extra points for going to a hospital emergency room.) Nor is the goal to come up with details that you can actually use in your novel or story, although you may do that in the process. Rather, the point is to become more aware of what's going on around you. The point is to learn to mine even familiar surroundings for what's specific and unique about them. Then use those details in your writing to go beyond blue-eyed blondes, a description that probably fits 15 percent of the population.

Observing and recording your observations are also helpful exercises to get you back into a writing routine when you've been away for a while, or when you're feeling stuck. But the greatest value lies in how your observations will translate, over time, to an improved ability to invent precise, informative, unpredictable details—in other words, killer-diller details that make the reader take notice.

And that's no lie.

 DONNA LEVIN is the author of *Get That Novel Started!* and *Get That Novel Written!*, from which this article was adapted.

CHAPTER 20
THE FIFTY-PAGE DASH

BY DAVID KING

When I asked an agent recently how she decided whether or not to take on a manuscript, she told me she asked for the first fifty pages and read the first sentence. If she liked the first sentence, she read the second. If she liked that one, she read the third, and so on. If she reached the end of the first fifty pages without putting the manuscript down, she signed it up.

Granted, most readers are willing to read your second sentence even if the first one isn't brilliant, but the agent's answer shows the importance of "hook." If you don't grab your readers within, say, your first fifty pages, you won't have them at all. So if you've been gleaning compliments from your writers' group and getting good responses to your query letters, but your first fifty pages keep coming back with polite rejections, then you may have a good story that doesn't get started soon enough. If so, it's time to go back to the beginning and start looking for trouble.

STARTING THE REAL STORY

Since at least the time of Shakespeare, storytellers have known that leading with a good noisy fight or a ghost was a great way to get the attention of the guys in the cheap seats. Many of my clients open their manuscripts with loud, attention-grabbing scenes. But many of them *became* clients partly because they failed to follow their attention grabber with the actual story. Sometimes that tense, exciting scene at the beginning of chapter one doesn't connect to the real plot until chapter ten.

One recent client opened her story with an army nurse's first day in the blood and mayhem of a field hospital in Vietnam. Unfortunately, the novel was less about the nurse's Vietnam experiences than how those experiences affected her later marriage and motherhood, and we didn't even meet her future husband for another 150 pages. The author solved the problem by opening the next draft with the ex-nurse going into labor for the first time and experiencing a flashback that leaves her huddled under her hospital bed. The maternity ward is less exciting than the field hospital, but the new opening focused less on Vietnam itself and more on how Vietnam affected the nurse, which is where the true story was.

Remember, you want to do more than get your readers' attention in your first fifty pages—you want to draw readers into the story. These opening pages are where you first create the tension that will drive your readers through to the climax. So if you've already opened with an attention-grabbing scene, check back to make sure it also raises the questions that your ending resolves and that the next few scenes enlarge on these questions. If you simply get your readers' attention without doing anything with it, they're bound to resent you and are unlikely to keep reading.

Also, make sure you've made things tough for your main character by the end of your first fifty pages. Your opening scenes may eventually have an impact on the main character, but until the character is actually in trouble, your story hasn't really started.

I recently worked on a medical thriller that opened with a "code"— a team of doctors battling to save a patient, with arcane medications administered in a rush and, ultimately, the shock paddles to the chest. The problem? More than one hundred pages passed before the main character first suspected that another doctor, his old mentor, had practiced euthanasia on the coded patient. So the opening didn't mention anything about this to the readers. I suggested that the author have the doctor feel some doubts about the code immediately after it happened, so readers would realize that the code was actually the beginning of the story.

FINESSING THE OPENING

Of course, some novels are impossible to open with a pertinent attention-grabbing scene. Some murder mysteries have to introduce a number of different suspects before the first body drops. Some romances have to show the couple meeting and getting to know one another before the real tension in the relationship starts. How do you get your readers involved in your story if they need to know a lot of background before the story makes sense?

First, make sure that your readers do, in fact, need to know all the background you're giving them. In the Vietnam novel, readers didn't need to know the nurse's whole story before they saw how it affected her. In fact, discovering what drove her to give birth under her hospital bed rather than on it gave the story an air of mystery that actually increased the tension.

So maybe your readers don't need to know all the details of the con man's real-estate scam before they see his body floating facedown in the pool. They just need to know the scam cost people a lot of money, and you can fill that in during the investigation. Perhaps they don't need to see your lovers meet to understand how things are between them, and you can start the story where each begins to realize the other isn't as perfect as they thought. In short, if your story has a slow beginning, try starting in the middle.

If this won't work, you might want to consider a prologue, where you move part of the middle to the beginning. If you open with a prologue of one of your young lovers attempting suicide, for instance, then your readers will know that the happy relationship they see in chapter one will turn tragic at some point. And if your prologue doesn't make it clear whether or not the suicide succeeds, you give your readers a reason to keep reading.

I once worked on a mystery in which the victim moved into a small town and started throwing money around irresponsibly, creating a lot of anger and greed and making enemies. Since the various motives were pretty intricate (and the detective was also caught up in the victim's financial machinations), it would have been awkward to bring all the details out through flashbacks or during the investigation. The author was essentially saddled with giving the readers 150 pages of story before the detective found a body. A prologue in which the detective found the body solved the problem. To add to the tension, the author didn't identify *whose* body was found—before he dies, the victim drives one or two characters, including the detective's oldest friend, to the point of suicide. Readers were left trying to guess who the body in the woods would turn out to be, and that uncertainty kept them reading until the story caught up with the prologue.

CHARACTER AND TENSION

As with any other plot problem, the best solution to a late-starting story may lie in your characters. An opening that presents sharply drawn and engaging characters may lure readers into the story more quickly than an anonymous bit of adventure. "Call me Ishmael" became a legendary opening line because those three words tell you volumes about who the narrator is and how he feels about his life; you want to find out what kind of story this man has to tell. Sue Grafton's Kinsey Millhone mysteries simply open with Millhone talking to her readers in her charmingly irreverent voice. By the second page of *"G" Is for Gumshoe*, we learn that Millhone cuts her own hair with a nail scissors and, if asked to rate her looks on a scale of one to ten, wouldn't. A character that intriguing leads most readers to keep reading.

Dick Francis is another master of this technique. *Whip Hand*, for instance, opens with a prologue in which the only thing that happens is that an ex-jockey dreams about a race. We don't even learn the man's name, yet the dream shows his deep passion for racing; when he wakes to the realization that he'll never race again, readers share his crushing sense of loss and resignation. The main story starts quickly after that—he is involved in the investigation that is the center of the plot by the end of the first chapter—but readers are hooked from that dream alone.

Of course, most authors get to know their characters as they write them, which means characters are at their most flat and uninteresting in chapter one. But there are a few easy solutions to this problem: One is to simply scrap your first-draft opening and rewrite it once you know who your characters are. Or you could add a prologue that, like the prologue in *Whip Hand*, showcases your main character's personality. Or you could write out the events that happened during the two weeks before your first chapter, so you already know in detail who your characters are before your readers meet them. In any case, you can draw your readers into your story by giving them characters to love from the very beginning.

LAYING THE GROUND RULES

As you rewrite your first fifty pages to start your story with a strong hook and introduce your characters, remember that you're also establishing the ground rules for how you will tell your story. By the end of those fifty pages, your readers should know what genre you're writing in (if any) and what stylistic techniques you'll use, and even have some idea of the metaphysics behind the world you've created. You need to give them a comfortable set of expectations about your mechanics and worldview so they can concentrate on your characters and events. If you later shift those expectations without reason, you run the risk of driving your readers back out of the story.

So if you write from several different points of view, make sure you switch POV at least once early on to let your readers know what to expect. If your world includes occasional magic and miracles, let your readers know such things are possible from the beginning. If the resolution of your story hinges on one particular character, make sure your readers meet that character quickly.

A client once had one of her characters come back as a ghost at the end of the manuscript. Unfortunately, up until that point, her story didn't hint that ghosts were a possibility, so the ghost's appearance shifted her readers into a different sort of universe without any warning. I suggested that the author give the future ghost a mystical bent from the beginning, with occasional premonitions and glimpses of the spirit world. These hints were enough to alert readers that they were in the kind of universe where magic happened.

Of course, there are cases, most often with mysteries, where you can't alert your readers that a given character or plot element is important without giving away your plot twists. One client's manuscript opened with her main character, a corporate lawyer who had just joined the legal team of a major oil company, mourning the apparent suicide of her lover, a researcher for the same company. But because the first few chapters introduced various company managers and showed details of the company's organization, readers knew the company was going to play a role in the plot. It came as no surprise, then, when the lawyer discovered that her lover was actually murdered because he'd uncovered a conspiracy within the company.

The author had to introduce her readers to the company before she hit them with the truth—plot twists are always more satisfying when there's a sense of the familiar about them. But the company had to have some reason for being in the first fifty pages. She could, for instance, give the lawyer some close friends in the oil company hierarchy, friends who would comfort her over her lover's death. Or the lawyer could deal with her lover's death by throwing herself into her work, which would let the author show the company's organization while readers are watching the lawyer's emotional state. Or the lawyer could suspect that the lover's apparent suicide had something to do with the company—excess tension from overwork, say—and delve into it, only to discover the conspiracy. In any case, the author had to give the company a false reason for appearing so early in the story so readers wouldn't suspect the real reason.

Your readers are willing to take you on faith at the beginning, to invest some effort in learning who your characters are, what your story is about, what your world is like. Pay back their effort quickly. Let them know as early as possible that you're giving them a story, characters, and a world that are worth reading about. If you can do that, then they'll stick around for more than just fifty pages.

DAVID KING is an independent editor who has worked with such authors as Sol Stein, Susan Loesser, and Fran Dorf. He's the co-author of *Self-Editing for Fiction Writers*.

CHAPTER 21

PACE YOURSELF

BY NANCY KRESS

If you're writing a thriller, mystery, Western or adventure-driven book, you'd better keep things moving rapidly for the reader. Quick pacing is vital in certain genres. It hooks readers, creates tension, deepens the drama, and speeds things along.

If you're a writer (or an hourly worker or dancer), you've probably heard the phrase "pick up the pace" many times. But how do you do that? And why should you?

Let's start with a definition. For writers, pace is the speed at which events unfold and characters are introduced. It can be expressed as a ratio: the number of story events divided by the page count. The higher the ratio, the faster the pace.

PACE AND GENRE

Writing fast-paced fiction isn't for everyone. So the first question is: What kind of book are you writing? If it's one of the aforementioned genres, you should plan on keeping the story moving briskly.

For instance, all of the following events occur in the first seventeen pages of James Patterson's best-selling thriller *Cradle and All*: two immaculate conceptions, a polio-like plague, a murder, an attempted abortion, the hiring of a private investigator, and the dispatching of a papal envoy from Vatican City. This varied action takes place in three countries among at least two dozen characters. Now that's a high pace ratio.

The advantage of this is that it raises many questions in the reader's mind, so he pushes on to seek answers, interested in the connection among these events and their possible outcomes. And if one question doesn't intrigue him, another will.

If you're writing women's fiction, character-driven science fiction or a historical novel, you can take more time to develop scenes and introduce events. With literary fiction, you can go slower still.

The slower pace, however, requires that your style be more polished and your characters more complex. Pace, like everything else in writing, involves a trade-off. If you're not offering the reader a lot of action to keep her interested, you must offer something else in its stead.

Slow pace is ideal for complex character development, detailed description, and nuances of style. In contrast to *Cradle and All*, consider the first seventeen pages of Carol Shields's *The Stone Diaries*, which won a Pulitzer Prize in 1995. The only "event" is that Mercy Goodwill, while preparing a pudding for supper, experiences an attack of what she thinks is indigestion. Shields uses this time to set up her story—and she's in no hurry about it. The advantage here is that the reader can form a deep interest and concern for each developed event and character.

TENSION

Picking up the pace increases tension in two ways. First, when events happen more quickly, you can more quickly get your characters into trouble. Conflict drives fiction; no one wants to read a four-hundred-page novel in which everything rolls along smoothly. Conflict also creates and sustains tension. Characters under stress are usually searching for ways out.

For instance, the first fifteen pages of Tess Gerritsen's mystery novel *The Apprentice* include four deaths, three of which are murders, at three separate locations. Even for a mystery, that's a lot of homicide crammed into a low word count. Here, the quick pace allows for a rapid increase in tension through the rapid increase in problems faced by the main character. Gerritsen's protagonist, Jane Rizzoli of the Boston Police Department, is forced to experience several kinds of tension at once:

- At the first death, which is especially grisly, she's afraid of looking weak in front of her fellow detectives—all male.

- The second two murders appear to have the same *modus operandi* as a serial killer that Jane put away once before, awakening terrible memories.

- Then there's a death threat that Jane isn't aware of—but we are. And she's the target.

The second way that a quick pace increases tension is that it sets opposing scenes close enough so that readers can draw unstated connections between them, even when characters don't.

Suppose, for instance, that your protagonist is a girl whose mother has just died. An uncle she's never met before attends the funeral and they converse briefly. He's sympathetic but reserved. After a few scenes concerning the girl's school life, the uncle reappears—not sympathetic to her at all, but instead brusque and even abusive.

If one hundred pages had passed between the uncle's first and second appearances, we might have remembered his name (maybe) but probably not much else, because both brevity and reserve marked his initial arrival. But a quick pace means that this encounter was not one hundred pages ago, but only twenty. It's still fresh in our minds, enabling us to ask, "What made him change so much toward her?" Now the uncle isn't just another minor character—he's a problem for the reader (if not yet for the girl), and problems increase tension.

BREVITY AND SPEED

So how do you quicken the pace of your story? Here are some suggestions:

- Start your story in the middle of a dramatic action, not before the drama commences.

- Keep description brief. This doesn't mean using no description, but rather choosing one or two telling, brief details and letting the reader's imagination fill in the rest.

- Combine scenes. If one scene deepens character by showing a couple at dinner and a few scenes later they have a fight, let them have the fight at dinner. Better yet, have them fighting at dinner and then have a cop burst in to arrest the wife.

- Rely on dialogue. A lot of story can be carried by spoken conversation. Readers seldom skip dialogue, especially brief exchanges, and it reads rapidly.

- Keep backstory to a minimum. The more we learn about your characters through what they do now, in story time, the less you'll need flashbacks, memories and exposition about their histories. All of these slow pace.

- Keep chapters short.

- Squeeze out every unnecessary word. This is the best way of all to increase pace because, as I noted before, pace is events divided by word count. If you consistently write "The sun set" rather than "The sun sank slowly in the bright western sky," your story will move three times as fast. Of course, there are times you want the longer version for atmosphere—but not many. Wordiness not only kills pace; it bores readers.

Not all of these suggestions will work for every story. Again, it depends on your genre and individual preference. Faster isn't always better, but frequently it's more salable.

 NANCY KRESS is the author of twenty-six books, including *Write Great Fiction: Characters, Emotion & Viewpoint.*

CHAPTER 22
THE PERFECT TITLE

BY STEVE ALMOND

It happens every semester I teach fiction, usually on the day we distribute stories for the first workshop. A student will raise her hand and offer the following caveat: "So I just wanted to, like, apologize for my story not having a title. I totally hate titles."

To which her classmates will inevitably respond with a chorus of amens about how much they, like, hate titles, too! To which I'll respond with a roar of anguished disbelief: "Are you *kidding* me? Guys, titles are the coolest part of the whole process! They're like the cherry on top of the sundae! They're the sign over the gate! A story without a title is like a doll without a head!" This statement hangs in the air for a disturbed moment. Then I launch into my lecture on titles, which I have titled: "Who Wants to Play With a Headless Doll? No One, That's Who."

I'm going to summarize that lecture here, and I'll restrain myself from threatening to flunk you. Instead, I'll entreat you (as I do my students) to think of titles not as a burden, but among the greatest opportunities you as a writer are afforded.

A title should serve three purposes: an introduction to the story's crucial images and ideas, an initiation into the rhetorical pitch of the prose, and an inducement to keep reading. It's important to note that a title need not serve all of these purposes at once but the best ones manage to nail this trifecta. A few gimmes:

- *The Catcher in the Rye*: Salinger not only highlights the book's most striking image, but underscores the preoccupation of his wry teenage hero—to save children from the corrupting artifice of adulthood. It's impossible not to be intrigued.

- *Pride and Prejudice*: An oddly formal name for this exquisite comedy of manners. But Jane Austen was determined to stress the serious themes bubbling beneath the drawing-room banter.

- *Lord of the Flies*: William Golding forces us to reckon with the most disturbing symbol in his novel of boys run amok—the pig's head that serves as a prophet of evil. The title makes fruitful allusion both to the Old Testament and *King Lear*. And bonus points for spawning an Iron Maiden song.

"So fine," you're saying. "Those dudes make it look easy. That's why they're *famous*." Don't be fooled. Sometimes the right title comes to you in a flash. Other times, you have to struggle.

F. Scott Fitzgerald spent months fretting over the title of his great American novel. He considered a bunch of howlers: *Among Ashheaps and Millionaires* (precious), *The High-Bouncing Lover* (all wrong tonally) and, most famously, *Trimalchio in West Egg*, the reference being to a character from an obscure Roman novel. The book would still have been great, even saddled with such a pretentious name. But it would have lacked the tragic irony of Gatsby's self-mythification and the spirit of keen observation that Nick Carraway's narration brings to the book.

At the eleventh hour Fitzgerald reportedly tried to change the title to *Under the Red, White and Blue*. He wanted to pound home the book's connection to the American dream. But he went for something far too broad, a name that could have applied to any one of a hundred books. Thankfully, he failed.

Like any aspect of your fiction, a title should feel organic, not imposed. It should arise from the vernacular of the piece itself. Raymond Carver's short story "What We Talk About When We Talk About Love" doesn't just tell us what the story is about, but *how* it's going to be told—in colloquial, prolix outbursts. The same can be said of Karl Iagnemma's wonderful short story "On the Nature of Human Romantic Interaction," the chronicle of a lovesick engineer. Or Lorrie Moore's short story "Which Is More Than I Can Say About Some People," which captures the oppressive chattiness of our heroine's mother.

I've chosen these exuberant titles for a reason: to emphasize that there's no word limit on titles. I'm not suggesting that longer titles are better, only that there's no prevailing orthodoxy.

But titular mistakes are easy to make. Don't name your story after a character. This is a failure of imagination. It tells us nothing we don't already know. Don't recycle the last line of the story. It's like hitting the same nail twice. A title should do original work on behalf of the piece. Don't use obvious or clever puns. If you write a story about a couple who can't conceive a child, please don't call it *Fruitless* or *Womb Without a View* or, worst of all, *Grin and Barren It*. Finally, don't quote William Shakespeare or the Bible. How many tepid short stories entitled *Brief Candle* or *Let There Be Light* have I read? Too many.

Of course, rules were made to be broken.

How did William Faulkner get away with *The Sound and the Fury*? Well, for one thing, he was Faulkner. (It helps to be Faulkner.) But the quote he lifts from Macbeth's famous soliloquy travels to the heart of his novel, which is a "tale told by an idiot," about the loss of dignity, and the futility of life.

Or consider Vladimir Nabokov's *Lolita*. Why does it work? Because the book is about how Humbert Humbert transforms his stepdaughter into a fetish object. The chief indicator of his obsessive love is the lurid-sounding name he gives her, the one he rolls around his mouth like a morsel.

So where do great titles come from? For the most part, they're right under your nose. I tell students to consider details, or even snatches of dialogue that jump out at them and that resonate.

A few years ago, for instance, I had a brilliant student named Ellen Litman. She turned in a story about a family of Russian immigrants newly arrived in America. Her original title was something like "How to Survive in America." But as we went over the piece in class, we kept returning to a scene in which the narrator's father, set adrift in a huge American grocery store, clutches a chicken "like it was the last chicken in America." This image seemed to encapsulate the story: its blend of black humor and pathos, of bewilderment and neediness and courage. Not only did the story get a new name, but (at

Ellen's instigation) it became the title of her wonderful debut novel, *The Last Chicken in America*.

Another student looked to dialogue as a source of inspiration. She came up with the title *Look Who Decided to Show Her Face*, which captured the tough feel of the working-class milieu she was writing about, but also the tentative self-examination of her heroine.

Part of what keeps writers from finding strong titles is embarrassment. They may be ready to write a story, but they're not ready to name the thing, or openly woo readers. They view titles as a form of advertising for a product they don't quite believe in yet.

Well, folks, titles are a form of advertising. (Think about it: What makes you turn to a particular story when you read a magazine's table of contents?)

That's not an invitation to histrionics; it's an exhortation. The search for a title should be a means of interrogating your story, trying to discern the heart of the thing you've created. It's a promise you're making to the reader.

If you can't come up with a title, or find yourself relying on the gambits cited above, it might be that you simply need a loudmouth like me to enable you. But it may also be that your story or novel isn't ready for the world yet. I'm convinced that the right title is like the right romantic pairing: You'll know when you've found it, even (and especially) when it forces you deeper into life's mysteries.

EXERCISES

1   Take a look at your most recent work. Underline the phrases that feel most resonant to you. Test them out as titles. Do any of these change the way you envision the story?

2.   Make a list of your favorite novels and/or stories. Consider how the titles operate in each case. What work are they doing? What promises do they make?

3. Consider what expectations—in terms of plot, theme and tone—the following titles provoke: *The Day I Became a Virgin*; *Blue Falls*; *First Month, Last Month and Security*; *Sacrifice Fly*; *Sylvia Plath Is My Love Goddess*.

STEVE ALMOND (stevenalmond.com) is the author the story collections *My Life in Heavy Metal* and *The Evil B.B. Chow*, and the nonfiction books *Candyfreak*, *(Not That You Asked)*, and *Rock and Roll Will Save Your Life*.

CHAPTER 23
WHAT YOUR STORY SAYS

BY NANCY KRESS

Theme. The most fraught word in literature. You can call it central concern or reader resonance or some such thing, but it still conjures memories of ninth-grade English: What is the book's theme? Concisely state the theme, and be sure to support your statement with specific examples in a well-written essay .... No wonder so many writers go out of their way to announce their fiction has no theme. They don't want students forced to reduce their works to twenty-five words or less of platitudes.

Nonetheless, every work of fiction does have a theme. And, as a writer, it's helpful to know what yours is.

Three paragraphs into this article, and I know I'm already in trouble with hordes of would-be dissenters. Yes, writers frequently aren't particularly articulate about the larger implications of their own work. Yes, the text itself is what matters. Yes, a story can "mean" different things to different people. But I'm going to discuss theme anyway, because the lack of it is what I see crippling so many new writers' work.

But let's not call it theme, after all. Let's call it *worldview* for reasons I hope become clear as we go. And let's see why you need to think about it—if not during the first draft, then later—in order to make your work successful.

YES, MRS. MARBLEHALL, THERE IS A PATTERN

First, it's impossible to write a story, or even a few significant paragraphs, without implying a worldview. This is because the writer has always chosen to include some details and to leave out others. Furthermore, the writer has—wittingly or not—chosen a tone in which to present those details. That tone, too, implies a worldview.

Here, for example, are two descriptions of the same person. The first is from a police report. The second is from a short story, Eudora Welty's "Old Mr. Marblehall":

> Caucasian female, thirty-eight, 5'1", 175 pounds. Mole on left cheek, near eye. Described by neighbors as possessing thick shoulders, small round head. Last seen by neighbor, on own front porch, wearing sleeveless loose brown cotton dress, green bedroom slippers, size four.
>
> There's his other wife, standing on the night-stained porch by a potted fern, screaming things to a neighbor. This wife is really worse than the other one. She is more solid, fatter, shorter, and while not so ugly, funnier looking. She looks like funny furniture—an unornamented stair post in one of these funny houses, with her small monotonous round stupid head— or something like a woodcut of a Bavarian witch, forefinger pointing, with scratches in the air all around her. But she's so static she scarcely moves, from her thick shoulders down past her cylindered brown dress to her stubby house slippers. She stands still and screams to the neighbors.

The police report, through its tone and choice of details, says this about the world: Reality can be objectively observed and numerically described. The physical world is our common ground in interacting with each other. Missing persons are sometimes able to be located and therefore it is rational to devise paperwork and procedures to do so. On the other hand, the Welty description—like the story from which it's taken—implies a different view of the world: The best way to understand something is through subjective contrast and metaphor ("like funny furniture," "like a woodcut of a Bavarian witch," "so static" even though she's screaming). Ways of interacting are grounded in some unseen judgment ("This wife is really worse than the other one") that carries with it a tone of both contempt and mystery. A factual account of what the wife is shouting at the neighbors is never explained; it's the overall subjective impression that counts.

It's not hard to imagine a third way of describing the second Mrs. Marblehall that would be different from both these. Her view of herself as a wronged woman, perhaps. Or the view of her through the eyes of her six-year-old son as Mama, warm and loving and dependable. Each of these would imply yet another view of the world by emphasizing different aspects of reality.

What does all this have to do with theme in your writing? Hang on. We're getting there.

It's not only description that implies a view of the world. So does the choice of story events and the way they play themselves out in your work. Detective stories, for example, almost always end with the murderers being identified. If they did not, most readers would get quite upset. The choice of events—investigation, deduction, resolution—carries the metaview that the world is rational, and the further theme that crime doesn't pay. Romances, on the other hand, all offer the reassuring theme that although the road to winning love may be rocky, love is possible and worth it. This is true even when the lovers end up losing each other, as in Robert James Waller's best-selling *The Bridges of Madison County*.

It's possible, however, to visualize a different choice of ending for Waller's novel. Suppose his two lovers had still ended up parting, but after Robert leaves, Francesca's husband discovers their affair. Shocked and betrayed, he divorces her. Francesca then hunts down Robert who, nomad that he is, has meanwhile taken himself to Argentina and fallen in love with a Spanish girl named Rosaria. There is a confrontation, and Rosaria shoots Francesca. In that book, the view of love—the theme—would be much different than in the one that Waller actually wrote.

So, on a macro level, the events you choose to include in your story form an overall pattern that implies a worldview. If you know what worldview you're actually creating, it can help you choose events that support it, descriptions with telling details and evocative tone, and characters who bear out your beliefs. All this gives your fiction a wholeness, a consistency born as much of patterned emotion as of rationality, which can vastly improve it.

But there's more. Pattern operates on a micro level as well as a macro level, and there, too, you have more control than you may think.

GUNS AND CASSEROLES

A famous writing maxim attributed to Anton Chekhov says that if you have a gun going off in the third act of a play, it had better sit on the mantelpiece during the first two acts. Conversely, if a gun is clearly visible on the mantelpiece for two acts, it had better go off during the third. In other words, critical plot developments and people must be clearly foreshadowed, not dragged in from left field at the end of your story. And if you spend time and verbiage on something early on, we can reasonably expect that thing to figure in the climax or denouement.

Suppose, for instance, you give four early pages of a thirty-page story to Aunt Mary's shoplifting. She stole a candy dish and a bath towel. The incident is amusing, well-written, and characterizing. Is that enough? No. You're letting us know that this incident will be part of the overall pattern of your story, and so it had better turn out to be just that. You'd better use that candy dish, that towel, or some other aspect of the escapade at Macy's as an important element of your climax. A story, like an Oriental carpet, is a pattern, and everything in it is supposed to contribute to the design.

However—and here's the critical point—not all patterns are equally tightly woven. Your theme gains or loses credibility partly on the basis of the weave you create.

In commercial fiction especially, *everything* in the story usually contributes directly to the plot. The shorter the story, the truer this is. Objects that receive more than one mention, secondary characters, symbols, events, lines of dialogue, all relate directly to the main point in a tightly woven pattern. Such fiction pleases us at least partly because it says to us that life contains patterns, order, design.

But each of us knows, in our heart of hearts, that life doesn't really add up so neatly. A real person's day (or week, or year) includes hundreds of small things unrelated in any pleasing, orderly way. Real life is messily patterned, if it's patterned at all. Aunt Mary's shoplifting occurs right in the middle of a daughter's illness, a cousin's wedding, a business triumph, a lawn-care crisis, and it's unrelated to any of them. It's not a pattern; it's a distraction. Real life is disorderly.

As a result, fiction that is too neatly patterned will not feel real. When everything in a story works out exactly, and each detail we see has a neat place in the overall scheme, we may enjoy the story but we don't really believe it. It has a sterile, manufactured feel.

Some writers, especially literary writers, compensate for this by including elements that are connected indirectly, often thematically, but not directly woven into the main plot. Anne Tyler is especially good at this. Her novel *The Accidental Tourist* abounds with subplots and digressions connected only loosely to the main plot of Macon's romances. One recurring element is Macon's sister Rose's cooking. Rose cooks casseroles, desserts, a turkey. All of this could have been left out, but it serves several purposes. It deepens our understanding of Macon's background. It creates thematic design; much of the book concerns how people nurture each other (or don't). And it gives the book the feel of the multidistraction that is real life.

However, fiction in which there is no order whatsoever—in which things just seem to happen without connection or thematic implication—isn't satisfying either. Why should it be? It may look like life, but we want something more from fiction. We already have life.

The result is that every writer walks a tightrope between arranging the elements of his story in too tight a pattern or too loose a pattern. Too tight, and the story feels contrived. Too loose, and it feels pointless. And, to complicate matters more, different kinds of fiction define "too tight" and "too loose" in different ways. Romance novels usually require tight patterning; literary short stories allow very loose design.

Theme is how much order, how stringently you've imposed on your fictional universe. It's also what kind of order: happy, malevolent, despairing, random, hidden-but-there, and so on.

Some writers find that they don't know their themes until they've finished the first draft (I am one). They then rewrite with an eye toward balancing on that tightrope: not too contrived, not too rambling; does what I'm saying about the world below me actually add up to anything? Other writers pay attention to these things as they write the first draft. Either way, an awareness of the macro and micro levels of theme can provide one more tool for thinking about what you should write, and how.

 NANCY KRESS is the author of many short stories and books, including *Dynamic Characters* and *Beginnings, Middles & Ends*.

Part Two

THE WRITING PROCESS

BEST-SELLING ADVICE: Getting Started

"Two questions form the foundation of all novels: 'What if?' and 'What next?' (A third question, 'What now?', is one the author asks himself every ten minutes or so; but it's more a cry than a question.) Every novel begins with the speculative question, What if 'X' happened? That's how you start."
—Tom Clancy

"I think my stuff succeeds, in part, because of what it's about—a diagnosis by attempting the adventures oneself of universal American daydreams. Now, I'm not saying that any writer who decided to select that device or notion could have written a bestseller; you have to add ingredients that are very special, I agree, but I think I started out with a good pot to make the stew in." —George Plimpton

"When I start on a book, I have been thinking about it and making occasional notes for some time—twenty years in the case of Imperial Earth, and ten years in the case of the novel I'm presently working on. So I have lots of theme, locale, subjects, and technical ideas. It's amazing how the subconscious self works on these things. I don't worry about long periods of not doing anything. I know my subconscious is busy." —Arthur C. Clarke

"Beginning a novel is always hard. It feels like going nowhere. I always have to write at least 100 pages that go into the trashcan before it finally begins to work. It's discouraging, but necessary to write those pages. I try to consider them pages -100 to zero of the novel." —Barbara Kingsolver

"An outline is crucial. It saves so much time. When you write suspense, you have to know where you're going because you have to drop little hints along the way. With the outline, I always know where the story is going. So before I ever write, I prepare an outline of forty or fifty pages." —John Grisham

"I do a great deal of research. I don't want anyone to say, 'That could not have happened.' It may be fiction, but it has to be true." —Jacquelyn Mitchard

"Being goal-oriented instead of self-oriented is crucial. I know so many people who want to be writers. But let me tell you, they really don't want to be writers. They want to have been writers. They wish they had a book in print.

They don't want to go through the work of getting the damn book out. There is a huge difference." —James Michener

"I have a self-starter—published twenty million words—and have never received, needed or wanted a kick in the pants." —Isaac Asimov

"Don't quit. It's very easy to quit during the first ten years. Nobody cares whether you write or not, and it's very hard to write when nobody cares one way or the other. You can't get fired if you don't write, and most of the time you don't get rewarded if you do. But don't quit." —Andre Dubus

CHAPTER 24

BABY STEPS

BY BILL O'HANLON

Many therapists related to the movie *What About Bob?* and laughed at the pop psychiatrist's prescriptive program called Baby Steps. Take small steps out of problems and into mental health. As silly as it sounded, many writers have successfully used the same strategy to get their writing done. A Chinese proverb makes the point: Enough shovels of earth—a mountain. Enough pails of water—a river.

You *can* break up the task of writing a novel into smaller pieces and smaller increments of time, take small actions, and break the mental barrier. Here's how.

SMALL ASSIGNMENTS

First, focus not on the whole task but on the smallest piece of the task. "I've been struggling with 'bookus interruptus' for years," says Sandy Beadle, a co-author of one of my books. "My next book got waylaid when the energy went away. It had taken far too long and I lost focus. I knew that there was nothing like a deadline to get me focused, so I asked someone in my seminar if I could send her a page or a chapter every week. She didn't have to comment, or even read it—just catch it. That was eighty-three weeks ago, and I just mailed her my seventy-ninth file. Sometimes it's just a paragraph; sometimes it's a whole chapter. I recently told her I was going to arbitrarily call it finished when I got to one hundred items, so that's not far off."

To divide your project up into bite-sized chunks, first make a simple outline. Next, make a more detailed outline with ideas for anecdotes, quotations, exercises, scenes, plot points, which characters are in the scene, and where it takes place. Then transfer each of those detailed points onto index cards that you can carry with you everywhere and write on. Keep them bundled with a rubber band in chapter or section order. "It's like driving at night in the fog," E.L. Doctorow once said. "You can only see as far as your headlights, but you can make the whole trip that way."

SMALL INCREMENTS

Big things can get done in small amounts of time. Max Barry wrote two novels—*Company* and *Jennifer Government*—during his lunch hours while working at Hewlett-Packard. It took him several years but he finally made enough money writing that he could quit his job and begin writing full time.

The most common strategy to get yourself to write when you're not writing is to commit to small amounts of time. Choose five or fifteen minutes. You can write more if you want. But you must write at least that amount of time per writing session. Writing begets writing, and not writing begets not writing. If you can trick yourself into writing a little, that trickle often creates a bigger flow.

Decide on a minimal amount of time and a realistic number of words or pages you're willing to commit to writing each week. Because the human mind often works better with a limited and achievable finish line, make limited time commitments as well. Decide you'll write every day for one month, or that you'll write three times per week for two weeks. If it works for you and is producing the writing you want, you can recommit or commit to a longer time period.

An experiment: For the next week, sit down with a kitchen timer and write for five minutes without lifting your fingers from the keyboard. Write on a particular pre-selected part of your book. No matter how busy you are, devote five minutes. Most people can write about 250 words in five minutes. That's about one page of a double-spaced manuscript.

Do that every day for a year and you'll have a book.

BREAK THE MENTAL BARRIER

One of the reasons the small-steps method can be so useful is that it makes big projects seem less mentally and emotionally daunting. When my friend, psychologist Stephen Gilligan, was an adolescent, his father was an alcoholic. They would occasionally exchange harsh words, and his father's favorite put-down was, "Who the hell do you think you are?"

Many years later, his father sobered up and their relationship improved, and Stephen discovered that he had internalized his father's criticism. As he sat down to write his first book, he was stopped by a voice that asked, "Who the hell do you think you are, that you could write a book?" The voice stopped Stephen for some time until one day it occurred to him that if the question wasn't used as a put-down, it was actually pretty useful for self-exploration. "Who the hell do I think I am?" Stephen wondered. This take on the question broke the mental barrier and Stephen finally completed the first of several books he's written.

One way to change your counterproductive view of writing is to discover where you're focusing your attention and shift that attention to something else. For example, if you're focusing on the idea that you'll never get published or get an agent, and that stops you from writing, shift your focus to writing for the pleasure of it or getting the words down on paper. If you're focused on how you're not as good a writer as John Irving and that stymies you, compare yourself to a writer you think is bad but who still got published. If you're focused on getting all the words and ideas perfect and that paralyzes you, focus instead on the number of words you write each day.

In psychotherapy we use a technique called externalizing. First, identify unhelpful inner voices or ideas that mess up your motivation to write. Then, begin to consider them as external. That is, instead of thinking, *I really sabotage myself by telling myself I'm not a good enough writer to get published*, think of that voice or idea as an external influence. Try thinking, *self-doubt is trying to convince me that I'm not good enough*. Or, *self-criticism is whispering unhelpful things into my ear today*. This change can help you shift your relationship to those undermining voices and ideas and, at times, make it easier to challenge them.

For a more physical way of dealing with your internal criticisms, write your unhelpful thoughts or ideas on a piece of paper or draw some representation of them, and then burn, tear up, or bury them. For example, if you're having writer's block, write the words "Writer's Block" on a piece of paper, burn it, and flush the ashes down the toilet.

Here's another variation on this idea: Carry a heavy rock around with you (in your purse, backpack, or briefcase) to represent your barriers, fears, or problems in your writing. Carry it for several days until you become really annoyed with the burden. Then—without getting caught—place the rock in the garden of someone who annoys you. Or, on a more positive note, throw the rock in a lake and enjoy watching your fears symbolically sink out of sight.

There's something in the human psyche that can actually use this method to purge unhelpful influences. (If you want to find out more about this method, search the term "narrative therapy" on the Internet.)

DEVELOP YOUR IDENTITY AS A WRITER

Before I wrote my first book, I'd never known anyone who had written a book and published it. I was clueless about how to proceed. But these days, I think of myself as a writer.

That identity shift took time. At first I thought of myself as "someone who had written books," not "a writer." I kept thinking I wouldn't be a writer until I developed writerly habits: writing every day from 8 A.M. to noon; wearing corduroy blazers with patches on the elbows; smoking a pipe and sipping bourbon while pounding at the typewriter keys. None of these things ever happened and yet I kept cranking out books. Eventually I began to list "writer" on my immigration and customs cards when returning from overseas—that was the first element in stepping into an identity as a writer. Next I began to say, "I write books," when someone asked me what kind of work I did. That gradually shifted to "I'm a writer."

You may have known early on that you were a writer. Or maybe you weren't so lucky or clear. You have to move toward thinking of yourself as a writer.

It really supports the process of writing—opens the possibilities of writing and completing books—if you begin to think of yourself as a writer. One friend says she thinks of herself as "a thinker, not a writer." She has, at times, shared her thoughts and ideas with someone, only to later see them in print with the person taking credit. She gets annoyed when she sees them writing what she didn't, but still can't imagine herself as a writer. She's afraid no one will read what she writes. Contrast her self-image with that of Isaac Asimov, who once said: "If my doctor told me I had only six minutes to live, I wouldn't brood. I'd type a little faster."

Do whatever it takes to convince yourself you're a writer. Get a mock-up of a book cover with your title and name. Get published in the local rag. Whatever it is, start doing those things and someday, in the near future, you'll live your dream of being a writer. To do that takes action. Don't just dream it, do it.

BLOG YOUR BOOK

Julie Powell began a blog while working as a secretary in New York. Each day for a year, she wrote about her experience of cooking every recipe from Julia Child's *Mastering the Art of French Cooking*. She began the blog because she was dissatisfied with her life and wasn't confident she would follow through on the project until she began to hear from readers who urged her on and gave her confidence. And she did hear—in the hundreds, then thousands. The resulting book, done in small pieces daily on her blog, was called *Julie and Julia: 365 Days, 524 Recipes, 1 Tiny Apartment Kitchen.* It was published by Little, Brown and Company and has sold more than 100,000 copies.

The blog *Baghdad Burning*, written pseudonymously by an Iraqi woman in order to keep the author safe, was turned into a book and went on to win the Samuel Johnson Prize in Britain, with an award of $53,000.

A blog by Jessica Cutler called *The Washingtonienne*, a juicy D.C. insider's online gossip column, was turned into a novel and published by Hyperion in 2005.

Blogs can be a nice way to get yourself to write every day or once a week. Even if your entire blog doesn't fit perfectly into a book, you can take pieces of the entries and use them to begin or create a book project. You also get writing practice and, because blogs are so informal, you probably lose that performance pressure felt by most when first writing. In addition, if you make a mistake, your readers are sure to let you know. They might even suggest new topics or a new slant on your topic.

Blogs can also be self-indulgent time-wasters, so be wary. Sometimes you can't tell at first whether it's a bane or boon for your writing. But if, after some months, you find you're doing nothing with your book and the blog itself isn't going to turn into a book, drop it or spend less time on it for a while and get cracking on more productive writing.

BILL O'HANLON (billohanlon.com) has authored or co-authored twenty-eight books, regularly speaks about writing and offers seminars for people who want to write and publish books.

CHAPTER 25
WRITE LIKE POE

BY MORT CASTLE

While teachers urge beginning writers to find their own voices and critics praise established authors for their unique styles and sensibilities, I've experienced considerable success in "borrowing" other writers' voices and, ahem, "emulating" their literary techniques.

I've been faux Hemingway and fake O. Henry, donned the dark cloaks of twentiety-century horror masters H.P. Lovecraft and Robert Bloch, borrowed Samuel Pepys' parlance and Dr. Samuel Johnson's dictionary, and, it sometimes shames me to admit, made more money writing as (pseudo) Edgar Allan Poe than the tragic genius himself.

I've taken the concepts of these and other literati and added to them, extrapolated from them, or reshaped, revised, and reimagined them.

I've written pastiches.

So can you.

THE COPYCAT

The pastiche prose form openly mimes the content and mannerisms of another written work. It's a respectful, if often jocular, homage to the work that inspired it. (Its literary cousin is the parody, but that imitation subtly or savagely satirizes its source material.) The pastiche implicitly says, "I appreciate this author, the characters, and the fictive world ... and my imitation is sincere flattery."

The affection for Sir Arthur Conan Doyle and his immortal Sherlock Holmes is evident in August Derleth's stories about brilliant, deerstalker-wearing Solar Pons of 7B Praed St.

Bloch, Ramsey Campbell, Lin Carter, and many other fantasy and horror writers have provided us with their take on the "cosmic monstrosities" of Lovecraft's Cthulhu Mythos universe, often liberally borrowing from Lovecraft's pseudo-Gothic literary techniques. Philip José Farmer, a Tarzan devotee, has given us Lord Grandrith, a loin-clothed jungle Übermensch, as well as Doc Caliban, a pastiche clone of the pulp era's crime-busting Doc Savage, a character who also motivated mystery novelist Michael A. Black to create his own Doc Atlas.

Right off the bat, your pastiche should proclaim what it is and invite the reader "in" on your literary joke. The title of my novella "A Secret of the Heart," originally published in the anthology *Lovecraft's Legacy*, is plainly an allusion to "The Tell-Tale Heart."

Early in the story, I let the reader know that we're journeying into a Poe mindscape of madness by selecting the opening of "The Tell-Tale Heart" as my model:

> True! Nervous, very, very dreadfully nervous I had been and am; but why will you say that I am mad? ... I heard all things in the heaven and in the earth. I heard many things in hell. ... Hearken! and observe how healthily—how calmly I can tell you the whole story.

This "Who you callin' crazy/'I'm no wacko,' said the wacko/doth protest waaaaay too much" opening is associated with Poe by anyone who earned at least a C- in junior high English. Here's the "A Secret of the Heart" rendering of it:

> Regard me! Madmen sweat and shake; they mutter to themselves and shout at delusional wraiths only they can apprehend ... Madmen rage, they fume, one moment seeking to slyly cajole the listener to belief, then threatening him the next.

Look into my eye to find therein not a glimmer of inner turmoil ...

THE ELEMENTS OF STYLE

Authors' styles grow from all the basic elements of prose: vocabulary, sentence length, structure, rhythm, narrative point of view, imagery, figures of speech, and lots more. Style reflects a writer's line-by-line, moment-to-moment decisions about what to leave in or what to leave out, what tone to adopt and what mood to induce in the reader. Style is the summation of "how" a story is presented.

Naturally, you'll find it easier to craft a pastiche if the writer you are honoring or aping is a strong stylist. Many popular writers aren't considered stylists, and they seek what's termed a "transparent style" that focuses exclusively on plot. But the styles of such diverse writers as Nathaniel Hawthorne, Herman Melville, Franz Kafka, Gertrude Stein, J.D. Salinger, Norman Mailer, and William Styron are unquestionably distinct; a paragraph from any one of these writers will let you know who you're reading, just as the opening notes of a pop song will quickly tell you if you're listening to Frank Sinatra, Tony Bennett, Barry Manilow, or Tom Waits.

And there are authors who have their own marked idiosyncrasies of style, which can easily be incorporated into your pastiche. Be ready to observe and use these little tricks.

For instance, in his National Book Award-winning novel *Cold Mountain*, Charles Frazier eschews the use of quotation marks, instead employing the "En dash" to let us know we're getting a direct quote:

>   –That would be easy to toss into my story, Peter Pastiche said.
>   –Oh? said Carmela Clone.

Yes. It's a device that promptly suggests the origin of my pastiche *Tepid Hill.*

When I wrote my Charles Bukowski pastiche (less-than-cleverly titled "Hank Crankowski"), published in 1976 in *Samisdat*, I tried for the author's borderline psychotic-deadpan fatalistic tone—and made good use of Bukowski's habit, in early works, of using only lowercase letters. Here, the protagonist of that story tells a would-be author the secret of crafting literature:

>   expose yourself to feel what wretches feel. get beat on the head by cops and get thrown in jail. get drunk and become a pacifist. ... crash an old chevrolet into a taco bell stand ... kick in a television set, howl at the moon, roar against the wind of being ... never use capital letters.

SAY WHAT?

No matter how renowned authors may be for stylistic skills and original mannerisms, it is *what* they say, the subject matter and theme, that we come to associate as the personal territory of writers. We pick up an Agatha Christie novel expecting a murder mystery with the accent on mystery, the clues there for us to discover (if we have "little gray cells" equal to those of her detectives, Hercule Poirot and Jane Marple). No rapacious extraterrestrial ever abducted Miss Crumbcake from the cozy village of Slothful-upon-Avon in a Christie novel, and we don't expect to read the story of the "Monocoled Prussian Assistant" in a collection of Flannery O'Connor's southern Gothic tales. The forest primeval and its Native American, French and English settlers—and Hawkeye!—belong to James Fenimore Cooper, just as the faraway galaxies and distant futures belong to the man who created them in the Foundation novels, Isaac Asimov. Elsewhere, dreamy and deceitful 1930s Los Angeles, its grifters and shysters and the lone PI following his own moral compass, is owned by Raymond Chandler.

Ernest Hemingway is credited with transforming the American prose style, but he's sometimes criticized for a "narrow" range of subject matter and theme: sports and war, machismo and violence. (In our politically correct times, I don't want to push that bright red button marked "bullfighting!")

I'm a card-carrying fan of Papa; I've read his collected short stories at least once a year for many years. When I was asked for a contribution to the anthology *Still Dead*, stories set in the world of flesh-eating zombies inspired by George A. Romero's *Night of the Living Dead*, I saw an opportunity to do *my* Hemingway story.

I called the novella "The Old Man and the Dead." With that obvious allusion to *The Old Man and the Sea*, I told the reader what I was doing, and then I underscored it with these opening lines:

> In our time there was a man who wrote as well and truly as anyone ever did. He wrote about courage and endurance and sadness and war and bullfighting and boxing and men in love and men without women. He wrote about scars and wounds that never heal.

Later in the tale, I introduce the characters Adam Nichols (a young man not unlike Hemingway's Nick Adams), Jordan Roberts, who, like the American Robert Jordan in *For Whom the Bell Tolls*, is fighting for the Republic in the Spanish Civil War, and a tough female guerilla leader named ... Pilar.

Here's the final scene of the pastiche, my moment of memorial for a writer who has profoundly influenced me:

> It was early and he was the only one up ...
>
> He went to the front foyer. He liked the way the light struck the oak-paneled walls and the floor. It was like being in a museum or in a church. It was a well-lighted place and it felt clean and airy.
>
> Carefully, he lowered the butt of the Boss shotgun to the floor. He leaned forward. The twin barrels were cold circles in the scarred tissue just above his eyebrows.
>
> He tripped both triggers.

I know there are writers who've come to live in your mind. Your pastiche will be your way to acknowledge, learn, and pay tribute to them. The passage above summarizes why I write in the style: It's my grateful tip of the hat to someone whose words mean so much to me.

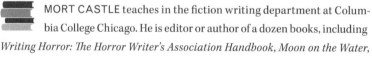 MORT CASTLE teaches in the fiction writing department at Columbia College Chicago. He is editor or author of a dozen books, including *Writing Horror: The Horror Writer's Association Handbook*, *Moon on the Water*, *Cursed Be the Child*, and *The Strangers*.

CHAPTER 26
BREAKING THROUGH WRITER'S BLOCK

BY OCTAVIA E. BUTLER

Writer's block is a deadness. Any writer who's had it knows what I mean. Writer's block is that feeling of dead emptiness and fear, that "can't write!" feeling that isn't quite on a par with "can't breathe!" but is almost as unnerving.

But the feeling is a lie. Can't write? Of course you can. Short of real physical or mental disability, you can research and write whatever you like. If you know your craft, you may even be able to write well in spite of writer's block. What's missing is not your ability to write, but your ability to feel any joy, any passion, any satisfaction in your writing.

But as writers, we should use everything that touches us. It's all ore to be refined into story. I'm more aware of that now than ever before because I've just spent almost ten years alternately fighting and using writer's block while working on books called *Parable of the Sower* and *Parable of the Talents*. I've never before written so slowly. The two books stalled and stalled and stalled. Each time I thought I had found a way to tell the story that I wanted to tell, I would hit another wall—or the same wall. And usually that was because I was unknowingly trying to do something that was wrong for the story.

The books are the near-future story of one woman's obsessive struggle to spread a belief system—a religion—that she feels will focus humanity on a specific, constructive goal and turn it away from the chaos into which it has descended.

Knowing that much, at least, I knew that I had a story. I had a character—sometimes homeless, sometimes a community leader, sometimes on the run—who, against all likelihood and common sense, was trying to do something she believed in while her world took casual, lethal swipes at her.

So if I had a story to tell and a passion to tell it, where were the blocks? They were near the beginnings of each book. As I began *Parable of the Sower*, I found it difficult to develop any empathy with my main character. I didn't like her. I didn't like the fact that to do what she wanted to do, she had to be a kind of power-seeker.

CHANGING POV AND OTHER TRICKS

I've written much about power in my earlier novels. It fascinates me— what it does to people, what they do with it. I've had characters inherit power or get handed power in the shape of heavy responsibility, but before the Parable books, I had never written about a powerless person who sought great power. I discovered that I found such a person morally questionable at best. Without realizing it, I had bought into the idea that anyone who wanted power probably shouldn't have it.

On an intellectual level, I realized that power was just one of humankind's many tools, like education, like technology, like money, like a lawn mower for goodness' sake. Power is a tool. It's what we do with it that's good or bad. But knowing this didn't change my feelings—thus the block.

I tried distancing myself from the character by writing about her from the point of view of first one, then another of her relatives. But each of these efforts dragged, then died. So I tried telling her story from an omniscient point of view, another way of not getting too close. When this failed, I froze.

Desperately, I tried some of my favorite block-breaking tricks— writing at different locations, for instance (at the library, on long bus rides, at the beach). I tried taking a break from my writing and reading other people's work. I read several best-selling novels and some fiction and nonfiction from that ever-growing stack of books that I had always meant to read. That was good. And I tried writing as my main character, writing for practice, not for publication in my character's voice. I tried to force myself into her skin. This works most of the time. It feels mechanical and artificial at first, but after a while it gets easier, more natural.

Not this time.

Finally, I began to write bits from my character's religious book so that I could quote them in the novels. I didn't know at that point that I would begin each chapter with such quotes. And I was surprised to find myself writing in verse. I realized that the research I had done was beginning to kick in.

A POETIC LIFT

There comes a time for me within each of my novels when what I know from research becomes such a natural part of the story that I forget that I haven't always known it. In this case, I had been glancing through books of a number of actual religions. I needed a form for my character's religious book and I worried about making her religion too much like one of the existing religions. I found that I liked the form of the *Tao Te Ching*—a slender little book of brief, seemingly simple verses. I began to write my own, quite different, quiet little verses. I'd written no poetry of any kind since I was in school, and even then, I only wrote it under duress. But time seems to have eased my resistance. The stuff I came up with at first was terrible, but it was fun to write, then to rework into something less terrible.

The change of genre helped me to break my block. Suddenly I was working on the novel in a whole different way, and it was intriguing.

One of my early inspirations helped move me along too: the news. The ugly things in the novels happened because today's dangers—drug use, the popularity of building prisons coupled with the unpopularity of building and maintaining schools and libraries, and the yawning rich-poor gap—grow up to be tomorrow's disasters.

At last, I began to write more successfully as my character—to write in her voice. But it was her voice as a young girl. When we meet her in *Parable of the Sower*, she has already come up with some of her religious ideas, but she's just a kid at home with her family. She isn't a power-seeker yet. She hasn't done anything questionable and nothing terrible has happened to her. Yet.

Terrible things do happen to her, though, and she must respond to them.

Eventually she is stripped of home, of family, of everything except her beliefs. She rebuilds her life and begins a community several hundred miles north of where she grew up. She turns a horrible situation into a hopeful one. She begins to attract people to her beliefs. And that's where *Parable of the Sower* ends. I thought I was rolling. I really did know the story I wanted to tell, and I didn't expect to have any trouble finishing it in *Parable of the Talents*. I did a publicity tour with *Sower*, and wrote an introduction and several afterwords for *Bloodchild*, my short story collection. Then I began to work seriously on *Parable of the Talents*. I had already written a few chapters. Now, working steadily, I wrote about 150 pages. Then I realized I was going wrong. Normally, I don't rewrite whole novels. I don't do a rough draft, second draft, third draft, and so on. I do one complete draft. Then I do line corrections. This works for me because I can't go on writing when I know something's wrong. I've got to fix the problem as soon as I realize it's there. If that means I have to dump sixty or eighty pages, so be it. I've learned the hard way that I lose interest in a novel if I write the whole thing and then go back to try to fix things.

So after I'd written the first 150 pages and realized that there was a problem, I had to go back and try to fix it. Eventually, I had to go all the way back to the beginning. The problem was this: My plot and my character were going nowhere near where they should go. In fact, they went nowhere at all. No doubt this had something to do with the fact that I felt, at this point, exactly the opposite of the way I'd felt when I began *Sower*. I had gone from not liking my character at all and trying to distance myself from her, to liking her far too much. I identified with her. And I didn't want to hurt her anymore. Character in conflict is the essence of story, but liking a character too much to give her trouble is one of the most ordinary hazards of writing. It was the cause of a serious block. I knew what I needed to do, but every time I tried to do it, I failed somehow. The story slipped away from me and went wrong. And when it did, I couldn't go on. I wrote the first 150 pages over and over and over again, getting nowhere. I had never done that before. The worst thing was that with each repetition, I proved to myself that I couldn't get it right. It was impossible. I couldn't do it. It was as though I had forgotten how to write. Very scary. And yet, I couldn't let the novel go.

If there's any single talent a writer needs, it's persistence. If you can keep at your writing and you can learn as you write, you can tell any story you want to tell. I used to say this before I began the Parable books, and I say it now that they're written, but there were times while I was writing them when I wasn't sure it was true.

DIVERSIONARY BREAKTHROUGH

Years passed. My life changed. I bought a house. I finally broke down and bought a computer. I'd written eleven books on manual typewriters and they were high-tech enough for me. But my editor didn't much like them, and I was beginning to feel left behind by the world in general. As soon as I began to use the computer, it became a nastier enemy than the novel had ever been. In fact, the computer made me forget how impossible the novel was. And, nastily, I found that giving my character trouble got easier since I was getting so much trouble myself. Again, learning to do something new helped me break the block. My unconscious mind needed the vacation from the novel—or needed the new and different opponent. Once it had both, the block was broken.

Writer's block, then, has been a guide and a goad to me. It's stopped me from writing badly. Like power, it's been a tool. It isn't a tool that I would want to use, but writers can't always be choosers. And if we're serious, we do use everything.

OCTAVIA E. BUTLER has won Hugo and Nebula awards for her science fiction writing. She was named one of the one hundred best writers of the twentieth century by Writer's Digest readers, editors, and advisory board members. She is the author of *Kindred*. Her final novel, *Fledgling*, came out in 2005. She passed away in 2006.

BEST-SELLING ADVICE: Rituals & Methods

"I try to write a certain amount each day, five days a week. A rule sometimes broken is better than no rule." —Herman Wouk

"I think that the joy of writing a novel is the self-exploration that emerges and also that wonderful feeling of playing God with the characters. When I sit down at my writing desk, time seems to vanish. ... I think the most important thing for a writer is to be locked in a study." —Erica Jong

"I threw the thesaurus out years ago. I found that every time you look up a word, if you want some word and you can think of an approximately close synonym for it and look it up, you only get cliché usages. It's much better to use a big dictionary and look up derivations and definitions of various usages of a different word." —James Jones

"I think writing verse is a great training for a writer. It teaches you to make your points and get your stuff clear, which is the great thing." —P.G. Wodehouse

"When I really do not know what I am saying, or how to say it, I'll open these Pentels, these colored Japanese pens, on yellow lined paper, and I'll start off with very tentative colors, very light colors: orange, yellow, or tan. ... When my thoughts are more formulated, and I have a sharper sense of trying to say it, I'll go into heavier colors: blues, greens, and eventually into black. When I am writing in black, which is the final version, I have written that sentence maybe twelve or fifteen or eighteen times." —Gay Talese

"I like to say there are three things that are required for success as a writer: talent, luck, discipline. ... [Discipline] is the one that you have to focus on controlling, and you just have to hope and trust in the other two." —Michael Chabon

"If I'm at a dull party I'll invent some kind of game for myself and then pick someone to play it with so that I am, in effect, writing a scene. I'm supplying my half of the dialogue and hoping the other half comes up to standards. If it doesn't, I try to direct it that way." —Evan Hunter

"I'll tell you a thing that will shock you. It will certainly shock the readers of *Writer's Digest*. What I often do nowadays when I have to, say, describe a room, is to take a page of a dictionary, any page at all, and see if with the words suggested by that one page in the dictionary I can build up a room, build up a scene. This is the kind of puzzle that interests me, keeps me going, and it will even suggest how to describe a girl's hair, at least some of it will come, but I must keep to that page. I even did it in a novel I wrote called *MF*. There's a description of a hotel vestibule whose properties are derived from page 167 in W.J. Wilkinson's *Malay English Dictionary*. Nobody has noticed this. The thing you see, it suggests what pictures are on the wall, what color somebody's wearing, and as most things in life are arbitrary anyway, you're not doing anything naughty, you're really normally doing what nature does, you're just making an entity out of the elements. I do recommend it to young writers." —Anthony Burgess

"The conclusion to be drawn is that I am happiest writing in small rooms. They make me feel comfortable and secure. And it took me years to figure out that I need to write in a corner. Like a small animal burrowing into its hole, I shift furniture around, and back myself into a cozy corner, with my back to the wall ... and then I can write." —Danielle Steel

"I try to keep my space very, very contained, because I feel that inspiration and the spirits and the story and the characters live there for as long as I'm writing." —Isabel Allende

"Write. Rewrite. When not writing or rewriting, read. I know of no shortcuts." —Larry L. King

CHAPTER 27

THE USE OF THE JOURNAL IN WRITING A NOVEL

BY SUE GRAFTON

The most valuable tool I employ while writing a novel is the working journal. The process is one I began in rudimentary form when I first started work on *"A" Is for Alibi*, though all I retain of that journal now are a few fragmentary notes. With *"B" Is for Burglar*, I began to refine the method and from *"C" Is for Corpse* on I've kept a daily log of work in progress. This notebook (usually four times longer than the novel itself) is like a letter to myself, detailing every idea that occurs to me as I proceed. Some ideas I incorporate, some I modify, many I discard. The journal is a record of my imagination at work, from the first spark of inspiration to the final manuscript. Here I record my worries and concerns, my dead ends, my occasional triumphs, all the difficulties I face as the narrative unfolds. The journal contains solutions to all the problems that arise in the course of the writing. Sometimes the breakthroughs are sudden; more often the answers are painstakingly arrived at through trial and error.

One of my theories about writing is that the process involves an ongoing interchange between Left Brain and Right. The journal provides a testing ground where the two can engage. Left Brain is analytical, linear, the timekeeper, the bean counter, the critic and editor, a valuable ally in the shaping of the mystery novel or any piece of writing for that matter. Right Brain is creative, spatial, playful, disorganized, dazzling, nonlinear, the source of the Aha! or imaginative leap. Without Right Brain, there would be no material for Left Brain to refine. Without Left Brain, the jumbled brillance of Right Brain would never coalesce into a satisfactory whole.

In addition to the yin/yang of the bicameral brain, the process of writing is a constant struggle between the Ego and the Shadow, to borrow Jungian terms. Ego, as implied, is the public aspect of our personality, the carefully constructed personna, or mask, we present to the world as the "truth" about us. The Shadow is our Unconscious, the Dark Side—the dangerous, largely unacknowledged cauldron of "unacceptable" feelings and reactions that we'd prefer not to look at in ourselves and certainly hope to keep hidden from others. We spend the bulk of our lives perfecting our public image, trying to deny or eradicate the perceived evil in our nature.

For the writer, however, especially the mystery writer, the Shadow is crucial. The Shadow gives us access to our repressed rage, the murderous impulses that propel antisocial behavior whether we're inclined to act out or not. Without ingress to our own Shadow, we would have no way to delineate the nature of a fictional killer, no way to penetrate and depict the inner life of the villain in the novels we write. As mystery writers, we probe this emotional black swamp again and again, dredging in the muck for plot and character. As repelled as we may be by the Dark Side of our nature, we're drawn to its power, recognizing that the Shadow contains enormous energy if we can tap into it. The journal is the writer's invitation to the Shadow, a means of beckoning to the Unconscious, enticing it to yield its potent magic to the creative process.

WHAT GOES INTO THE JOURNAL AND HOW DOES IT WORK?

At the outset of each new novel, the first thing I do is open a document on my computer that I call "Notes" or "Notes-1." By the end of a book, I have four or five such documents, averaging fifty single-spaced pages apiece.

In my first act of the writing day, I log into my journal with the date. Usually I begin with a line about what's happening in my life. I make a note if I'm coming down with a cold, if my cat's run away, if I've got company coming in from out of town. Anything that specifically characterizes the day becomes part of the journal on the theory that exterior events have the potential to affect the day's work. If I have a bad day at work, I can sometimes track the problem to its source and try correcting it there. For instance, if I'm consistently distracted every time I'm scheduled for a speaking engagement, I can limit outside events until the book is done.

The second entry in the journal is a note about any idea that's occurred to me in the dead of night, when Shadow and Right Brain are most active. Often, I'm wakened by a nudge from Right Brain with some suggestion about where to go next in the narrative or offering a reminder of a beat I've missed. Sometimes, I'm awakened by emotion-filled dreams or the horror of a nightmare, either one of which can hold clues about the story I'm working on. It's my contention that our writing is a window to all of our internal attitudes and emotional states. If I sit down to write and I'm secretly worried about the progress I'm making, then that worry will infuse the very work itself. If I'm anxious about an upcoming scene, if I'm troubled by the pacing, if I suspect a plot is too convoluted or the identity of the killer is too transparent, then the same anxiety will inhibit the flow of words. Until I own my worries, I run the risk of self-sabotage or writer's block. The journal serves as a place to off-load anxiety, a verbal repair shop when my internal writing machine breaks down.

Generally, the next step in the journal is to lay out for myself where I am in the book. I talk to myself about the scene I'm working on, or the trouble spots as I see them. It's important to realize that the journal in progress is absolutely private—*for my eyes only*. This is not a literary *oeuvre* in which I preen and posture for some future biographer. This is a nuts-and-bolts format in which I think aloud, fret, whine, and wring my hands. There's nothing grand about it and it's certainly not meant to be great writing. Once a novel is finished and out on the shelves, the journal can be opened to public inspection if I so choose.

In the safety of the journal, I can play "Suppose ..." and "What if ..." creating an atmosphere of open debate where Ego and Shadow, Left Brain and Right, can all be heard. I write down all the story possibilities, all the pros and cons, and then check back a day or so later to see which prospects strike a chord. The journal is experimental. The journal functions as a playground for the mind, a haven where the imagination can cavort at will. While I'm working in the journal, I don't have to look good. I can be as dumb or goofy as I want. The journal provides a place where I can let my proverbial hair down and "dare to be stupid," as we used to say in Hollywood.

USING YOUR JOURNAL AS A JUMP START

The beauty of the journal entry is that before I know it, I'm sliding right into my writing for the day. Instead of feeling resistant or hesitant, the journal provides a jump start, a way to get the words moving.

To demonstrate the technique, I'll include a few sample pages from the journal I kept during the writing of *"G" Is for Gumshoe*. I do this without embarrassment (she said), though I warn you in advance that what you see is a fumbling process, my tortured mind at work.

"G" Is for Gumshoe is essentially a "road picture." In this seventh novel in the series, Kinsey Millhone discovers she's on Tyrone Patty's hit list, targeted for assassination in retaliation for her part in his arrest and conviction. The following passages of the journal begin some three chapters into the novel. Earlier notes, unfortunately, were lost to me in the transfer of the work from an old computer system to newly acquired equipment. My intention here is not to try to dazzle you with my song-and-dance work, but to demonstrate the mundane level at which the journal actually functions.

> 1-2-89
>
> Just checking in to have a little chat. I'm in Chapter 3 and feeling pretty good, but I'm wondering if I don't need some tension or suspense. We know there may be a hit man after her. She's currently on her way to the desert and everything seems really normal ... nay, even dull. Do I need to pep it up a bit? She's almost at the Slabs. I've been doing a lot of description but maybe I need to weave it into the narrative better. Flipping back and forth from the external to the internal.
>
> What other possibilities are there? I've noticed that with Dick Francis, sometimes when nothing's happening, you sit there expecting something anyway. I could use the external as a metaphor for the internal. I know I'll be doing that when Dietz enters the scene. What could Kinsey be thinking about while she drives down to the Slabs? She's talked briefly ...

1-4-89

Can't remember what I meant to say in the paragraph above. I did some work last night that I'm really happy with. I'm using a little boy with a toy car at the rest stop. Added a father asleep on the bench. Later, he turns out to be one of the guys hired to kill her.

Want to remember to use a couple of things.

When the mother dies, Kinsey goes back down to the desert with Dietz. They search, finding nothing ... maybe a few personal papers. What they come across, in an old cardboard box under the trailer, is some objects ... maybe just old cups & saucers (which may trigger memories in Irene Gersh ...). But the newspapers in which these objects are packed dated back to 1937 ... Santa Teresa. Obviously, the mother was there at some point.

When Kinsey checks into the mother's background, she realizes Irene's birth certificate is a total fake. The mother has whited out the real information, typed over it, and has done a photocopy. All the information has been falsified. She's not who she says she was during her lifetime ... father's name is wrong ... I was thinking it might be Santa Teresa, but then Irene would know at the outset she had some connection with the town. Better she should think she was born in Brawley or someplace like that.

Kinsey tries to track down the original in San Diego ... or wherever I decide to place the original ... no record of such a birth. Once Kinsey finds the old newspapers, she decides to try Santa Teresa records, using the certificate # which is the only thing that hasn't been tampered with. Up comes the true certificate.

Must remember that a social security card ... first three digits indicate where the card was issued. That might be a clue.

Irene Gersh is floored. If mom isn't who she claims she was, then who am I?

Must also remember that mom is frightened to death. That would be a nice murder method.

USING YOUR JOURNAL TO RECORD RESEARCH

In addition to storyboarding ideas, I use my journal to record notes for all the research I've done. I also make a note of any question that occurs to me while I'm writing a scene. Instead of stopping the flow of words, I simply jot down a memo to myself for later action.

Journals often contain the ideas for scenes, characters, plot twists, or clever lines of dialogue that don't actually make it into the book I'm working on. Such literary detritus might provide the spark for the next book in the series.

Often, too, in the pages of a journal, I'll find Right Brain leaping ahead to a later scene in the book. Since I don't actually outline a novel in any formal or detailed way, the journal is a road map to the story I'm working on. If dialogue or a descriptive passage suddenly occurs to me, I'll tuck it in the journal and come back to it when I reach the chapter where the excerpt belongs. This way, I find I can do some of my writing in advance of myself. Right Brain, my creative part, really isn't interested in working line-by-line. Right Brain sees the whole picture, like the illustration on the box that contains a jigsaw puzzle. Left Brain might insist that we start at the beginning and proceed in an orderly fashion right through to the end, but Right Brain has its own way of going about its business. The journal is a place to honor Right Brain's ingenuity and nonconformity.

Sometimes I use the journal to write a note directly to Shadow or Right Brain, usually when I'm feeling blocked or stuck. These notes are like writer's prayers, and I'm always astonished at how quickly they're answered.

In the *"G" Is for Gumshoe* journal, you can see that by March, some three months later, the book has advanced almost magically. I'll do a hop, skip, and jump, picking up entries here and there.

> 3-12-89
>
> Finally got Dietz & Kinsey on the road. They've stopped for lunch. She's asking him about his background & he's being good about that stuff. Want to keep them moving ... let information surface while they're heading for Santa Teresa. Don't

want the story to come to a screeching halt while they chit chat. Must keep defining his character through action ... not just dialogue. Once I get the book on body-guarding techniques, I can fill in some technical information that will make him seem very knowledgeable. For now, I can do the small touches. At some point, he should give her some rules & regulations.

What else do I want to accomplish on the way up to Santa Teresa? Don't need any action at this point ... don't need jeopardy per se. Must keep in mind that Dick Francis plays relationships very nicely without jamming incessant screams and chases into the narrative.

3-13-89

I wonder if chapter nine will last all the way to Santa Teresa. What does Kinsey do when she gets home? She'll call Irene to make sure Agnes has arrived, which she will very soon. She'll introduce Dietz to Henry Pitts who'll be briefed about the situation re: the hit man. Security measures (if I knew what they were ...).

Want to dovetail "A" & "B" plots so both won't come to a ragged stop simultaneously.

Within a day, Agnes Grey will have disappeared from the nursing home.

Soon after, her body will be found.

Haven't quite solved the problem of how Kinsey gets hired to track down the killer.

Can't quite decide what the next beat is in the attempt on Kinsey's life. Dietz will get her a bulletproof vest. Does he jog with her? She won't really feel like it, and he'll advise against. He'll have her take a different route to the office & home every day ... always in his company.

Maybe Dietz has to make a quick trip to Carson City ... or someplace. Papa sick? Mama sick? An unavoidable personal emergency. If I played my cards right, his absence might coincide with Kinsey's second trip to the desert. I guess I'll map all this out as I get to it but it does feel like a tricky business to make the story move smoothly through here.

Why do I worry so much about boring the reader? I don't want it to look like I've sacrificed the mystery and the pace for mere romance.

And skipping ahead to August ...

8-12-89

Trying not to panic here. In the dead of night, Right Brain suggested that maybe Kinsey gets locked in the very storage bin Agnes was locked in. Nice claustrophobic atmosphere.

As a reader, I don't object to being privy to the reasoning process a detective goes through as long as it makes sense to me and seems logical. When the leap comes too fast, then I object. I like for the detective to consider every possible alternative.

My problem here is one of transitions ... forging the links between the scenes I know are coming up.

8-15-89

Book was due today but so be it. Just closed out Chapter 23 and opened 24. I'm going to write notes to myself for a while and then print pages 30-35 so I can have them handy.

Need to set up "It used to be Summer ... ."

Maybe Kinsey & Dietz go back to Irene's & confront her with the true information on the birth certificate. If these aren't my parents, then who am I?

8-16-89

God, I'm tired today. I'd really love to sleep. Let's see what I can accomplish in a stupor. Can't wait for this book to be over and done.

Dear Right Brain,

Please be with me here and help me solve and resolve the remaining questions in the narrative. Help me to be resourceful, imaginative, energetic, inventive. And patient.

Look forward to hearing from you.

Sincerely,

Sue

I could pull up countless other samples, but you get the point I'm sure.

LOOKING BACK

One comfort I take from my journals is that regardless of where I am in the current private eye novel, I can always peek back into the journals I've kept for previous books and discover I was just as confused and befuddled back *then* as I am today. Prior journals are reminders that regardless of past struggles, I did somehow manage to prevail. Having survived through two novels, or five, or even twelve, in my case, there's some reason to suppose I'll survive to write the next.

If you haven't already incorporated a journal or its equivalent into your current bag of writing tricks, you might try your hand at one and see how it works for you. Remember, it's your journal and you can do it any way you choose. If you don't use a computer, you can write yours in crayon on sheets of newsprint. You can type it, write in longhand, use a code if you need to feel protected. You can log in every day or only once a week. You can use it as a launching pad and then abandon the practice, or use it as I do, as an emotional tether connecting me to each day's work.

To help you get started, I'll give you the first entry just to speed you on your way:

Enter today's date.

Just sitting down here to try my hand at this weird stuff Sue Grafton has been talking about. A lot of it sounds like California psychobabble, but if it helps with the writing, who really cares?

In the book I'm working on, what worries me is .... .

SUE GRAFTON is the author of the best-selling Kinsey Millhone series, the most recent of which is *"U" Is for Undertow*. She is a past president of the Private Eye Writers of America and is the editor of *Writing Mysteries*..

CHAPTER 28

RESEARCH IN FICTION

BY KAREN DIONNE

Novelists are naturally drawn to write about the subjects that interest them. Doctors pen medical thrillers. Lawyers turn their hands to courtroom dramas. Suburban soccer moms write about—well, suburban soccer moms. Some add to their experiences by arranging to ride along in patrol cars, or taking flying lessons, or traveling to the locations where their novels are set, all in the name of research. Others spend hours combing through resources in libraries and on the Internet.

But just because an author is deeply interested in a topic doesn't mean her readers will be. You've probably read novels in which you skipped over dense paragraphs of exposition or lengthy descriptions to get to the "good stuff."

What went wrong? And more important, how can you incorporate your own research into your novel without distracting or overwhelming readers?

BE OBJECTIVE ABOUT WHAT YOU ALREADY KNOW

When your novel deals with obscure or difficult topics, assume your readers are on the fringes of knowledge. Don't talk down to your readers, but don't show off what you know, either, thinking that copious details and technical jargon demonstrate authority. You're writing a novel, not compiling a research paper.

To someone who has only a mild interest in science, reading a detailed explanation of some obscure scientific phenomena in the middle of a novel is like biting into a lump of salt in a cookie. Facts add seasoning to any narrative, but no matter the genre, good fiction transports the reader into another world because the reader cares about the *characters*, not the subject matter, or the novel's time period, or its location. It's better to err on the side of simplicity than to delve too deeply.

It's not easy to step outside of yourself and "become" your reader, but that's exactly what a novelist has to do. Step back and consider: If you knew nothing about this subject, would there be enough information in your novel for you to understand it clearly? And, conversely: Have you included unnecessary details simply because *you* think they're interesting?

Readers love learning something new, but above all, a novel is a *story*. Your job is to entertain. Don't let your enthusiasm for your material turn your novel into the literary equivalent of three hours of vacation pictures.

USE SECONDARY SOURCES WISELY

Sometimes the subjects that fascinate authors fall outside their areas of expertise. "I was a lawyer, but I didn't want to write about the law," says *New York Times* best-selling thriller author Steve Berry. "I like conspiracies, secrets, history, international settings, action, and adventure, so that's what I wrote."

Authors like Berry spend many happy hours digging through books, newspaper archives, scientific papers, websites, and blogs. They post questions to community research sites like Ask MetaFilter (ask. metafilter.com) and to specialized e-mail lists and usegroups.

All of that is necessary, and has its place. (See the sidebar on Page 204 for tips on effective research strategies.) But how can your legwork yield more colorful material, the kind you can't seem to find elsewhere—the kind of insider details that will enhance your story and captivate readers?

"For a sense of plausibility, we always turn to experts," says Joe Moore, an international best-selling writer whose thrillers, co-authored with Lynn Sholes, have been translated into twenty-three languages. In researching their novels, Moore and Sholes have consulted with such experts as Secret Service agents, Navy commanding officers, and professors. "The most remarkable thing we've discovered is that expert advice is easy to get," he says. "Almost everyone we've approached has been eager to provide fictionalized theories and futuristic details that help make our often outlandish premises ring within the realm of possibility."

To approach experts, send a brief e-mail explaining your project in a sentence or two, with a short list of three to five key questions. Express appreciation for any help you receive, and it's likely your expert will offer even more. (Be sure to note the names of all such expert sources so you can thank them later in your acknowledgments.)

Regardless of how you glean information from secondary sources, because they're one step removed from your own experience, it's important that the details you choose to include in your novel don't sound stilted—especially if you're regurgitating material you don't fully understand. Readers balk when a character conveniently cites a book she just happens to have read as the source of her random wisdom, or when a character without a college education starts spouting detailed scientific explanations. Anything that smacks of the obvious or the contrived spoils the mood and takes the reader out of the world you've created.

BE TRUE TO YOUR STORY

"The common wisdom is that only about 1 percent of a novelist's research ends up in his or her book," says Gayle Lynds, *The New York Times* best-selling author of eight international espionage novels. "In my experience it's even less—closer to a tenth of a percent."

Facts are fun, but if a detail doesn't move the story forward by establishing the setting, advancing the plot, or shedding light on the characters, it doesn't belong. If you're not sure whether you should include a particular section, take it out. If the story doesn't suffer, paste the discarded section into an "extras" file for the day you might find a use for it, and move on.

"My books are both research intensive and dependent," Berry says. "That usually means two to three hundred sources per novel. The hard part comes in deciding what to use and what to discard. Unfortunately, there's no formula. It's a matter of practice, practice, practice, and it's something I struggle with every day. Always remember, the story never takes a vacation."

Research is for the author, not the reader. The main function of research is to ground you in your subject, so you can write your fiction with authority. The rest is up to you.

ALWAYS BE BELIEVABLE

"The reason we use truth in fiction is so we can tell a bigger, better lie," says David Hewson, best-selling author of the Nic Costa thriller series. "It's the lie—how big, convincing and 'real' it is—that matters."

Readers expect novelists to be as accurate as possible. Yet in their authors' note for *Cemetery Dance*, *The New York Times* best-selling co-authors Douglas Preston and Lincoln Child admit, "Readers familiar with upper Manhattan may notice that we have taken certain liberties with Inwood Hill Park." Admissions like this raise the question: Is changing reality or embellishing the truth dishonest?

"In a novel," Preston answers, "something doesn't have to be true; it only has to be believable. The word 'fiction' is a marvelous cover for all kinds of shenanigans, distortions, manipulations, and outright fabrications."

There will always be literal-minded readers who object to authors changing historical dates or moving mountains. But a novel is by definition fiction, an artfully contrived blend of plot, setting, and characters.

"Ninety-five percent of the geography, science, and history in our novels is accurate and true. But we have no intention of imprisoning ourselves inside reality," Preston says. "The novel I'm currently writing, *Impact,* takes place on the real coast of Maine in a real place called Muscongus Bay—but I've added a few islands that don't exist, some currents that aren't present; I moved a reef about forty miles northwest and shifted an old radar installation from Cutler, Maine, down to Muscongus Bay.

"It's that other 5 percent that makes it a novel. And that 5 percent is the magical ingredient which transforms all the rest."

Whether your research springs from your own experience or from hours of painstaking effort, remember: Your story doesn't have to *be* real, it just has to feel that way. Incorporate your facts smoothly into your fiction, and you'll create a compelling, believable world.

THREE STRATEGIES FOR SOLID RESEARCH

Before you can incorporate your research into your writing, you first need to be as smart as possible about the research itself.

Develop a system for tracking your legwork. "Take a digital camera with you, photograph everything, dictate notes ... never lose anything. *Never* lose anything," says David Hewson, international best-selling author of the Nic Costa thrillers. "I keep a journal on every book I'm writing that notes down ideas, locations, characters, themes—and I keep a running diary on the book as I'm writing it. This is separate from the draft, so it acts as a left-brain perspective on the whole exercise."

Get in the habit of vetting your research as you go—particularly research conducted online. Verify facts from multiple reputable sources before you record them. This way, you'll already know that all your notes are accurate when it comes time to incorporate them into your work.

Be wary of cutting and pasting research nuggets directly into your manuscript. You don't want to become guilty of plagiarism by letting someone else's words get inadvertently mixed in with your own. If you do feel the need to paste in a block of research while you're writing, be sure to highlight the copied text in a different color so you can go back and remove or rewrite it entirely later.

KAREN DIONNE (karendionne.net) is the author of *Freezing Point*, an environmental thriller *RT Book Reviews* calls "A fascinating blend of science fiction and fact."

CHAPTER 29
YOUR NOVEL BLUEPRINT

BY KAREN S. WIESNER

Writing a novel and building a house are pretty similar when you think about it. For instance, most builders or homeowners spend a lot of time dreaming about their ideal houses, but there comes a time when they have to wake up to the reality of building by analyzing what they expect from a house, and whether the plans they've selected will meet their needs. Architects argue that it's better to build from the inside out.

This is where a home plan checklist comes in handy. This list assembles the key considerations to keep in mind when deciding on a plan, including what are called external monologues, relating primarily to the outside of a house and its environment, and internal (interior) monologues. (The word *monologue*, in building, refers to a single facet of overall composition on the inside or outside of a house, such as flooring material or landscaping aspects.) Writers spend a lot of time dreaming about their ideal story. Eventually they have to face reality and analyze whether or not the story will work.

Authors, too, usually build from the inside out—in other words, they know what they want at the heart of their stories and they build around that.

This is where a Story Plan Checklist becomes essential, because it targets the key considerations necessary when building a cohesive story that readers will find unforgettable. The checklist has basic external and internal monologues. Monologue, in writing, refers to a single facet of overall composition concerning the internal or external elements, such as conflict and motivation. Generally, these are composed individually in free-form summaries, but they need to develop and grow cohesively.

The Story Plan Checklist can ensure cohesion between character, setting, and plot. This checklist connects all the dots between internal and external conflicts, and goals and motivations, thereby guaranteeing the cohesion all stories require. In its most simplified form, a Story Plan Checklist—which you can find an example of at writersdigest. com/article/first-draft-finish-novel—includes free-form summaries (or monologues) covering each of the topics in this chapter.

I call this list a Story Plan Checklist not only because of its correlation with a home plan checklist, but because if you haven't considered each of these areas, written something solid about them, and checked them off, your story may not be fully fleshed out and cohesive enough. Sooner or later, the basic structure will begin to fall apart.

PART 1: THE BASICS OF A STORY PLAN

While you're in the beginning stages of forming a story plan, sit down and figure out some of the working details (which may change throughout the process).

Title and Genre Specification

First, come up with a preliminary title. All you need here is something to reference the project. While you don't want to lock in your genre too early (stories evolve in unpredictable ways), get started with genre specification. For now, list all the genres this story could fit into.

POV Specification

Now, start thinking about what point of view you want to use for your book. It's very important to start your Story Plan Checklist with this because the identities of your main characters will play a huge part in your characterization and, subsequently, each of the areas you'll be summarizing on your checklist. Most stories spark with a character who may end up becoming your main character. Your best bet for deciding which character's viewpoint to use: In any scene, stick to the view of the character with the most at stake—the one with the most to lose or gain.

High-Concept Blurb

The high-concept blurb is a tantalizing sentence—or a short paragraph with up to four sentences (one or two is ideal)—that sums up your entire story, as well as the conflicts, goals and motivations of the main character(s). It's no easy task. Here's a simplified explanation of what your sentence needs to contain:

> A character (the who) wants a goal (the what) because he's motivated (the why), but he faces conflict (the why not).

Or you can simply fill in the blanks—whichever works best for you:

> (name of character) wants (goal to be achieved) because (motivation for acting), but she faces (conflict standing in the way).

Story Sparks

At this point in the checklist, we've established the basics of the story and we're ready for the beginning spark—so crucial to drawing a reader's interest—followed by the initial external and internal monologues on the Story Plan Checklist. Here, you'll begin the cohesive development of your story. Most authors start strong because the idea that initially fascinates them guides them through this first portion of the sequence naturally.

A story spark is something intriguing that ignites a story scenario and carries it along toward fruition. It's that "aha!" moment when a writer thinks up something that completely captures his imagination, and he must see how it unfurls and concludes. I dare say there's not a writer alive who hasn't come up with one idea that blows the mind. However, most don't realize that a story has to have more than one of these sparks to sustain it. A story spark must infuse and re-infuse the story, and a new one must be injected at certain points in order to support the length and complexity of the story.

Most novels up to 75,000 words have three story sparks: one for the beginning, one for the middle, and one for the end. The beginning spark sets up the conflict. The middle spark (or possibly more than one middle spark) complicates the situation. Finally, the end spark resolves the conflict and situation. Short stories, flash fiction, and novellas usually have only one or two sparks (beginning and ending). All of these sparks absolutely must be cohesive to ensure a solid story.

Estimated Length of Book/Number of Sparks

The more sparks you include, the longer and more complex your book will be. It's hard to get around that, so plan accordingly. But don't consider it the end of the world if your "little" idea evolves into something big and beautiful. With that in mind, a story of more than 75,000 words may have an excess of three basic sparks, especially in the middle, because a longer story needs complexity to sustain it. A middle story spark can appear anywhere after the beginning one—before the end—though it usually appears somewhere toward the halfway mark of the book.

To give you a basic idea of how many sparks you'll need for a novel, you can figure that if you have an estimated 250 words per page:

- up to 75,000 words = 300 pages (3 sparks)
- 90,000 words = 360 pages (4 sparks)
- 100,000 words = 400 pages (4+ sparks)

You might also make a note about where you want to place the extra spark(s). In general, extra sparks should come in the beginning or middle of the book.

There's a tendency for authors to include too much backstory and action in the beginning, but you don't want your story to be overdone from the get-go. Starting with focused action and backstory is the best way to do it. Then, dribble more in when the story is capable of accepting it in the middle. The end won't need more than one spark because you're winding down at that point, rather than introducing new ideas.

PART II: EXTERNAL MONOLOGUES

In your quest to form a cohesive story plan, sit down and figure out the working details (which may—and should—evolve throughout the progression of the story).

Identifying the Main Character(s)

If you have no idea who your main characters are, chances are this particular story needs a lot more brainstorming. Even if your story is more plot than character oriented, brainstorming on your characters until you can fully envision them—i.e., filling out character sketches and writing a Story Plan Checklist—will help immensely.

In this section of the checklist, simply list the names of the main characters. While a complex book will have more primary and secondary characters (in fact, that seems to be a trend I'm not sure I can get on board with, considering how difficult it is to keep up with ten-plus POV characters in a single book), most 75,000 to 90,000-word stories have, at least in terms of main characters, a hero, a heroine, and/or a villain.

Character Introductions

The introduction of a character in the Story Plan Checklist is a springboard into finding out more about him. It's like meeting someone for the first time—you say your name and a few pertinent details about yourself. In the checklist, you list a name and the character's role in the story. Each of your main characters will have particular skills that are shaped specifically for the plot, and that's really what you're introducing in this section of the checklist. Some of these could and should be carefully selected occupational skills, but most will go far deeper than that.

Character Descriptions From Outside Viewpoints

If you're using a third-person omniscient POV, chances are your main characters will be described by other characters. Although this kind of description can include physical appearances, it should always incorporate impressions made by your characters upon the ones around them. You can (but don't have to, as the checklist is only for your own use) describe the main characters from each individual viewpoint in the book. Or your summary can simply encompass the most basic impressions without ascribing them to the person offering them.

Character Descriptions From Self Viewpoint

Very few people describe themselves the same way others do. That makes it even more important for main characters to describe themselves, because the reader gets a strong sense of who your players are with both outside and inside descriptions. In essence, these are like mini first-person profiles. The characters talk about themselves, and sometimes give their impressions of others.

Character Occupational Skills

Especially in a work of fiction, what the characters do is pivotal to their personalities and motivations. Just about everything hinges on these interests, hobbies, or jobs. What the character does for a living (or doesn't do, if he doesn't have a job), gives him the necessary skills to deal with the conflicts he's facing in the story. To build the form of cohesion we've been talking about, the character's skills should be directly related to either his internal or external conflicts. In the best-case scenario, his skills will connect to both in some way.

Enhancement/Contrast

If you want to create a truly unique character—and what writer doesn't?—the best way to do so is by providing his personality with enhancements and contrasts. Enhancements are the subtle, balanced, or extreme elements that complement what the writer has already established as traits for that character. Enhancements are personality traits that make a character uniquely larger than life. A writer can't create a truly average Joe because he would be boring to read. In the fictional world, an author may present a hero who seems ordinary at first glance, but something makes him stand apart. This something may not be revealed until later, when his quality is tested.

A contrast, which can also be subtle and quite nuanced, balanced, or extreme, is an element that's in opposition to what the writer has already established as traits for that character. A personality contrast is one of the best and most frequently used ways of making a character rise memorably to the spotlight. Few readers want to know a hero who advertises "Hero for Hire—Inquire Within" on a sign outside his office.

The hero who's optimistic to a fault, whiter than snow, and perfect in every way is dull.

Flawed (but likeable!) characters are the ones readers root for, because a character without flaws or fears is a character without conflicts. Readers know that true courage is facing what you fear most, pursuing your goals, and not giving up even when there's little chance of success. Readers go crazy for a rough and raw, imperfect hero with more baggage (of the emotional kind) than a pampered socialite. An eternal pessimist, he wants nothing to do with the title, let alone the job; he's only forced into it by an oft-buried sense of nobility, or because something or someone he cares about deeply is in danger.

One way to develop a main character is by introducing another main, secondary, or minor character (love interest, family member, friend, or villain) who either enhances or contrasts his personality. You'll see the saving-herself-for-marriage woman paired with a slutty best friend. The street-smart guy with the 4.0 GPA buddy. The happily married accountant with 2.5 kids, living vicariously through his footloose, unfettered college buddy who's been to every corner of the globe on one hair-raising adventure after another.

As a general rule, a character who's an extremist in any regard (whether hard, obsessive, ruthless, etc.) will need someone or something to soften him. In a character who's more balanced, an enhancement or contrast may be more subtle, but should be just as effective. Whatever you do, choose characteristics that'll be necessary at some point in the book, that don't hit the reader over the head and that advance each story element.

Symbolic Element (Character and/or Plot-Defining)

Another effective means of developing character is to give him a symbol that defines him, defines the situation he's in, or both. These symbols are sometimes called by the music term *leitmotif.* In the writing world, we use them to associate characters, objects, events, and emotions. Each appearance makes them more intense and meaningful.

Whether you make symbols subtle or well defined, they take on layers of meaning each time they're mentioned, and they become an integral part of the story. As a general rule, every character should have only one associated symbol, but if you have a total of two in the book, one of them should be subtle, while the other should be well defined. The point is to enhance or contrast, not take over the story so the symbol becomes the focal point when you have no desire for it to be.

The symbol can be tangible, in the form of something that defines the character, setting, and plot in some way—a piano, pet, flower, key, map, or necklace—but it doesn't have to be. It can be a trait or mannerism the character uses frequently that says something about him and/or develops the character, setting, and plot. It can also be a hobby or vice, or a disability or disfigurement, such as a scar. This tangible or intangible symbol also must be cohesive and not thrown in for the fun of it. In one way or another, it has to enhance or contrast—and thereby develop—your story in deeper ways.

Build in symbols to make your plot, setting, and characters a seamless trinity. The nice thing about incorporating cohesive symbols is that while it's ideal to do this before you begin writing the book, it's never too late to come up with this kind of enhancement.

Setting Descriptions

Your setting is a basis for building your story—it enhances the characters, conflict, and suspense, and provides a place for all three to flourish. If your setting doesn't match the other elements, you'll work harder at creating fitting characters and plots. Additionally, it will be hard to create the appropriate mood. In any case, you'll have to find a skillful way to play against the contrast of setting.

The importance of creating a setting cohesive with character and plot can be illustrated by imagining different settings for classic novels. What if *Moby-Dick*, instead of being set at sea, had been set in, say, a lighthouse? *Moby-Dick* wouldn't have been the novel that's become so well known if the setting had been anywhere else but where the author put it.

Describe your setting in such a way that it not only becomes evident how the characters and plot fit there, but super-charges your whole story. What does the setting reveal about the character's personality? What in the setting means the most to him? How will this setting create the stage for conflict and suspense? How can you make it so real that your reader will believe the place actually exists?

The purpose in writing setting descriptions is to allow the reader to "see" what the main character sees, as well as to give a sense of the characters. Very few characters will notice every detail of their surroundings. A character notices the things in his setting that are important to him at the moment. In other words, focus the description. Describe only what means the most to the character, what enhances the mood you're attempting to create. If the description doesn't advance some part of the character, setting, or plot development, it's probably unnecessary.

PART III: INTERNAL MONOLOGUES

The crucial need for cohesive character, setting, and plot becomes boldly evident in these next steps—which are truly the heart of your story. Life is conflict, and fiction even more so. Without conflict, you don't have a story. For every spark your story has, you'll check off one of each of the following items for all the major characters. This is optional for secondary and minor characters.

Character Conflicts (Internal)

Internal character conflicts are emotional problems brought about by external conflicts that make a character reluctant to achieve a goal because of his own roadblocks. They keep him from learning a life lesson and making the choice to act.

In fiction, character conflicts are why plot conflicts can't be resolved. Simply put, the character can't reach his goal until he faces the conflict. (Sounds a bit like not getting dessert until the vegetables are eaten, and that's pretty accurate.) The audience must be able to identify with the internal and external conflicts the character faces in order to be involved and to care about the outcome. Character growth throughout the story is key to a satisfactory resolution.

Keep in mind that clearly defined conflicts are ones that won't hit your reader over the head or frustrate her. If you as the writer don't quite understand the conflicts in your story, your instinct will be to compensate by bombarding the story with unfocused ideas. The reader won't find it any easier to sort through them and identify the true conflict. Vaguely defined conflicts usually lead to the reader putting down a book for good.

Your first story spark will usually suggest what the character's conflicts are, and they're almost always based on someone or something threatening what the character cares about passionately. In some instances, a loved one is in jeopardy, or something the character wants, needs, or desires above all is at risk of being lost. It's your job to give the character incentives not to give up until everyone is safe and he has what he's fighting for.

Internal conflicts are different than external ones, but they're related causally—the best definition of conflict I've heard is "can't have one without the other." Internal and external conflicts depend on each other, and therefore they need to be cohesive. Internal conflicts are all about characters, and external conflicts are all about plot. But keep this in mind, lest confusion creep in: Both internal and external plots belong to the main character(s). After all, if both didn't affect him in some profound way, they wouldn't be conflicts, and therefore wouldn't even be part of his story.

Evolving Goals and Motivation

Goals are what the character wants, needs, or desires above all else. Motivation is what gives him drive and purpose to achieve those goals. Goals must be urgent enough for the character to go through hardship and self-sacrifice.

Multiple goals collide and impact the characters, forcing tough choices. Focused on the goal, the character is pushed toward it by believable, emotional, and compelling motivations that won't let him quit. Because he cares deeply about the outcome, his anxiety is doubled. The intensity of his anxiety pressures him to make choices and changes, thereby creating worry and awe in the reader.

Goals and motivations are constantly evolving (not changing, necessarily, but growing in depth, intensity, and scope) to fit character and plot conflicts. Your character's goals and motivations will evolve every time you introduce a new story spark because he's modifying his actions based on the course his conflicts are dictating.

Beginning goals and motivations don't generally change as much as they become refined to the increasing intensity of the conflicts—though this must be clarified when looking at complex novels, especially mysteries that must include red herrings and foils to keep the reader guessing.

Plot Conflicts (External)

External plot conflict is the tangible central or outer problem standing squarely in the character's way. It must be faced and solved. The character wants to restore the stability that was taken from him by the external conflict, and this produces his desire to act. However, a character's internal conflicts will create an agonizing tug of war with the plot conflicts. He has to make tough choices that come down to whether or not he should face, act on, and solve the problem.

Plot conflicts must be so urgent as to require immediate attention. The audience must be able to identify with both the internal and external conflicts the character faces in order to be involved enough to care about the outcome. Plot conflicts work hand-in-glove with character conflicts. You can't have one without the other, and they become more intense and focused the longer the characters struggle. The stakes are raised, choices are limited, and failure and loss are inevitable.

The first layer of a story is created when you plan for and lay the foundation. By using a checklist and analyzing the monologues, you'll be prepared to craft an extremely strong initial layer—one capable of supporting everything you build on it afterward.

 KAREN S. WIESNER is author of more than fifty books.

CHAPTER 30
MAP YOUR NOVEL

BY N.M. KELBY

We can all benefit from a sense of organization. I like to think of a novel outline as the bones of a story. As a child, your bones grow to the place where they'll support who you are meant to be on this planet. If your genes determine that you're tall, your bones will form that foundation, and your flesh will grow accordingly. As you grow older, you need calcium, and bones provide it to the point where they become brittle and can easily break.

This is the same with outlines. You need to create the basic framework for your story to grow on, but not so much that it takes away the energy from the work.

So where do you begin? Arthur Miller once said, "If I see an ending, I can work backward." So start with the end.

KNOW YOUR ENDING BEFORE YOU START

If you start with the end of the story, the ending won't be set in concrete; it can change. But starting with what you think is the end allows you to have a firm idea of where you are going when you begin a journey with 60,000 to 80,000 words in tow. And you'll need that. Once you decide on your ending, everything in the book will be shaped to arrive there. None of your characters should be superfluous, nor should your scenes. It's all about bones.

Of course, the most difficult part of writing any story, long or short, is ending it.

In order to write your ending, you have to ask yourself what action you want to set forth in the start. But be careful not to create a "purse-string" ending—with all the elements brought together in a tidy bundle.

At the end of your story, you don't want to give readers the sense that all there is to know is already known. You really just want to give them a whisper and a dream, and send them on their way.

Once your ending is in place, you can weave your tale. Novelist Tony Earley always says, "A story is about a thing and another thing." So it's your job to plan your story so that you give your reader the satisfaction of getting closure from one "thing," the most obvious thing, but keep the mystery of the other "thing" intact.

A good example of this can be found in Sherman Alexie's "What You Pawn I Will Redeem," the short story about a homeless Spokane Indian's circular attempts to raise $1,000 to redeem his grandmother's powwow regalia from a pawnshop. The shop owner would like to give it back, but he paid $1,000 for it himself. So he gives the homeless man $5 as seed money and twenty-four hours to raise the rest of the cash.

In the first paragraph, Alexie gives the reader notice and sets up the ending of his story:

> One day you have a home and the next you don't, but I'm not going to tell you my particular reasons for being homeless, because it's my secret story, and Indians have to work hard to keep secrets from hungry white folks.

The idea of a "secret story" is the key to the ending. While the protagonist does manage to earn money, he drinks, gambles, or gives it away. After twenty-four hours, the money has not been raised, but the pawnbroker gives him the regalia anyway. The last paragraph of the story is this:

> Outside, I wrapped myself in my grandmother's regalia and breathed her in. I stepped off the sidewalk and into the intersection. Pedestrians stopped. Cars stopped. The city stopped. They all watched me dance with my grandmother. I was my grandmother, dancing.

Because the regalia is given back, the story does seem to tie itself up (that would be the first "thing"), but this really isn't about getting a stolen dress back. It's about the struggle to regain one's spirit—and that could be seen as the "secret" story (or the other thing) wrapped in this tall tale.

The ending that satisfies the reader, or ties things up, is never the real ending of the story. We discover that the grandmother's regalia is returned, and yet the story continued on for a moment to put the act into context. Alexie left the readers with a whisper and a dream and sent them on their way.

OUTLINE YOUR STORY SIMPLY AND BRIEFLY

There is no set amount of pages in an outline because it all depends on how large a story you're going to tell. The story of *Harry Potter and the Order of the Phoenix* had thirty-eight chapters that spanned 870 pages. Its table of contents provides an interesting look at the bones of an outline. It begins: *One: Dudley Demented; Two: A Peck of Owls; Three: The Advance Guard.*

If you were J.K. Rowling, and this was your outline, all you'd have to do is write a short summary paragraph after the title of each chapter. In the first chapter, you would tell us why Dudley is demented and make sure that there are bits in your description that set the action of the book in play. Then move on to the next chapter.

To build the bones of your own outline, begin by writing a short description of what happens in the last chapter, and then move to the first chapter. After that's done, divide the rest of Act 1 into as many chapters as it takes to properly introduce your protagonist and the conflict—the "who," "what," "when," and "where" of the tale.

Move on to Act 2 and, again, create as many chapters as it takes to explain the crisis, complications, and obstacles that present themselves on the protagonist's way to the climax. Make note of the emotional challenges that he faces.

Once you've written the climax, it's time to create as many chapters as you'll need to lead to the final chapter.

Try not to get too fancy with the writing. If your agent is going to pitch your outline, he's going to take fifty pages of the draft with him, so you don't need to show any style in the outline. This is all about bones.

GIVE YOUR STORY IDEA A LITMUS TEST

Find out if you can turn your initial story idea into a real novel.

Step One: Answer these questions to the best of your ability. There are no wrong answers, but there are answers that inspire you to write on ... and that's what you're looking for.

1. What about the idea draws you in? What's the most important element of it to you?

2. Who could the players be? Not just the people who inspired you to follow your idea, but the supporting characters. Who are the friends? Who are the enemies? Create a quick biography of each. Explore their relationships to one another and to the protagonist. Add physical descriptions, what they sound like, their aspirations, and any other details you "know."

3. Where and when does the story take place? Keep in mind that the details that sparked you may not be where you choose to set your novel. Whatever you do, make the setting as concrete as possible.

4. What are the possibilities for conflict? Now that you have a chance to imagine this idea in a more fleshed-out manner, ask yourself what could happen given who the characters you've created are, in addition to where they are in this world that you've made.

Step Two: Write. This is the difficult part. Begin with what you think is the first chapter. Or, just write a couple of chapters out of sequence. When you reach fifty pages, try to write your outline. If you can't, keep writing until you can't any more, and then try again.

You're not looking for publishable pages, you're just looking to unlock the possibility of story and give yourself an understanding of the depth of the project.

N.M. KELBY (nmkelby.com) is a novelist and the author of *The Constant Art of Being a Writer* and the story collection *A Travel Guide for Reckless Hearts*.

CHAPTER 31

ROUGH UP YOUR FIRST DRAFT

BY ELIZABETH SIMS

As Ernest Hemingway famously said, "The first draft of anything is shit." For years, I didn't understand. When I started writing fiction seriously, I kept trying to get it right the first time.

Every night after clocking out from my job in a bookstore, I'd sit at my favorite coffee shop with a yellow pad and the pens I collected from publishers' reps, and carefully work on my first novel. I'd write my minimum 300-word requirement, staying inside the lines and squeezing out every word with great thought and deliberation. Grant me, at least, that I was disciplined: I counted my words, and if I got to 299, I wouldn't go back and add "very" to a sentence—I had to at least begin the next one.

By that method, I managed to produce quite a lot of pages. But guess what? My prose didn't consistently swing, sizzle, or startle. It took me a long time to figure out Hemingway's hidden meaning, and longer still to apply it. Over time, as I got rougher with my first drafts, my finished work got better and better.

BE HONEST

Why does a coherent first draft give birth to a stilted finished product? Because it means you haven't let it flow. You haven't given yourself permission to make mistakes because you haven't forgiven yourself for past ones. Admit it: Unless your throttle's wide open, you're not giving it everything you've got.

One day I realized that creativity in writing isn't a linear process, even though we read in a linear fashion and the words must go on the page one after the other; even though we must put our thoughts and words in order so the reader can make sense of them.

Writing, in fact, is the only art that is literally one-dimensional. If you can be gut-level honest with yourself, you've really got a shot at your readers. And the only way to find that honesty is to not overthink it.

For your writing to come alive—to be multi-dimensional—you must barter away some control. The rewards are worth it.

LEARN TO LOVE ANARCHY

Ignore sequence while writing your first draft. Beginning writers will often say, "I've got the basic story figured out, but I don't know how to present it so it hangs together. I'm never sure what should come next."

Nothing is as freeing as writing *what comes to mind next*, not necessarily *what must come next*. Transitions are unimportant. Hey, don't take my word for it—trust John Dos Passos, Patricia Highsmith, Mark Twain, and William Shakespeare. Exposition is always less important than you think it is. Just focus on what happens next.

Hemingway didn't mean, though, that if you begin with crap, dung or merde, you'll end up with something far better without much effort. He also didn't mean that it's okay to start with a weak premise.

He meant that the first execution of your ideas must be as unfettered as possible. Which will result in—yes!—some crap: false starts, pretentiousness, clunky images, and clichés. Fine. Get them out now. They'll contaminate the good stuff only until you get around to your second draft.

GET LOOSE

Relax, physically and mentally. If, as I do, you write your first drafts longhand, consider your pen a paintbrush. Hold it relaxed in your hand and move it from your shoulder, instead of with your fingers. Your whole arm will move freely, and you'll pour out the words, as well as banish carpal tunnel syndrome all to hell.

Legibility is overrated. Remember that.

The common wisdom in writing workshops is that you shouldn't stop to revise. But let's be honest: That's unrealistic because sometimes you really do see another possibility right away, and you should be free to pursue it. I recommend over-writing as you go.

If, in a single moment, you think of two different ways of saying something, just write both, one after the other. Later you'll be able to decide which is better.

Write a box around a phrase; stack two competing adjectives atop each other; make notes in the margin. I use the margins for research notes such as, "what's position of Sirius over L.A./August?"

Fresh sheets aren't just for motels. Use paper! I'm a big believer in using exactly the amount of natural resources you need, and no less. If you want to go off on a new tangent that's longer than a sentence, rip off your current page and start a fresh one. Never crowd a new thought into a crevice of the page you're on.

And for the love of God, don't wait for the new thought to fully form before you put it down. More often than not, as soon as you write the first shard of that new thought, it'll work itself to fullness as you write. And that's the magic we all live for, isn't it?

If you want to add a word or a block of text, don't stop at using carets to show an insert. Circle stuff, draw arrows, loop one piece of text into the middle of another. And keep going. If it's instantly obvious that one version of a word, sentence, or graph is better, strike out the bad one and go on without looking back.

If you compose on a keyboard, make the "return" button your best friend: Set off a new idea by hitting two carriage returns. Let your fingers splash on the keyboard. Let typos stand. Don't use the cut-and-paste functions while creating a first draft.

Note that I'm not telling you to write as fast as you possibly can, as in speed for speed's sake. No. Take time to pause and reflect. Then take whatever comes without judging it too much.

Why's it so important to suspend judgment when writing? Because that freedom opens you to the surprising stuff you never saw coming; stuff that makes you smile as you sit there in the coffee shop, your mug of joe cooling because you've forgotten to take a sip in 15 solid minutes.

When beginning a writing session, new authors often feel that they must jump off to an excellent start, when all they really need is to start. In this, there's no difference between me and you.

Often I have to slog through crap to produce decent writing, especially if I've laid off from it while doing revisions. But I never despair, having learned that if I just keep going, I'll get to someplace worthwhile.

FACE YOUR SECOND DRAFT

If you've practiced slovenliness with a liberal hand, you'll be delighted at how much fun your second draft will be. After I've got a chapter or two roughed out, I go from my handwritten pages to my PC, where I edit and rewrite as I go, adding new text and omitting what—I can now clearly see—doesn't work.

Thus I establish the rough rhythm that works for me: a couple of days writing longhand, then a day at the old PC. Some authors work through their entire manuscript in longhand before sitting down to type, and that's dandy, too. Most beginning writers cling to every word they've written. But if you practice looseness and receptivity when writing your first draft, the day will come during revisions when you realize you have a surplus of good writing to sort through. You'll know joy.

I just took a spin through a couple of my old *Writers at Work* volumes (*The Paris Review* Interviews). Along with George Plimpton's interview of each famous author, the *Review* reproduces pages from their drafts.

I studied some of these:

Cynthia Ozick: Her handwritten draft page is a beautiful mess, containing almost more strike-outs than unscathed text.

Ralph Ellison: He used a typewriter, then marked up his pages with a ruthless hand.

Ernest Hemingway: His handwritten page from "The Battler" shows only one cross-out. However, between that and the published story, the passage shows subtle but significant differences.

During the course of writing six novels, I realized that the days when the truth shone brightest were the days my pen flowed the freest and messiest across the pages. And I was rewarded with longer and longer satisfactory passages.

It's paradoxical that giving up control rewards you with what you seek most: concise, insightful work.

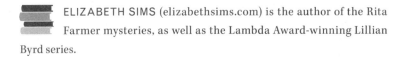 ELIZABETH SIMS (elizabethsims.com) is the author of the Rita Farmer mysteries, as well as the Lambda Award-winning Lillian Byrd series.

BEST-SELLING ADVICE: Revision & Editing

"I do not rewrite unless I am absolutely sure that I can express the material better if I do rewrite it." —William Faulkner

"I almost always write everything the way it comes out, except I tend much more to take things out rather than put things in. It's out of a desire to really show what's going on at all times, how things smell and look, as well as from the knowledge that I don't want to push things too quickly through to climax; if I do, it won't mean anything. Everything has to be earned, and it takes a lot of work to earn." —Peter Straub

"If you're writing for a magazine or a newspaper, then you're a guest. It's as if you're a guest violinist in some great conductor's orchestra. You play to his rhythm, to his audience. You're invited in and he edits you and tells you what he wants. On the other hand, when you're writing a book, the only reason you're writing it is to say it your own way, in your own words, and tell the story the way you see it." —Teddy White

"... Falsely straining yourself to put something into a book where it doesn't really belong, it's not doing anybody any favors. And the reader can tell." —Margaret Atwood

"I'm a tremendous rewriter; I never think anything is good enough. I'm always rephrasing jokes, changing lines, and then I hate everything. *The Girl Most Likely To* was rewritten seven times, and the first time I saw it I literally went out and threw up! How's that for liking yourself?" —Joan Rivers

"I've always felt that my 'style'—the careful projection onto paper of who I think I am—was my only marketable asset, the only possession that might set me apart from other writers. Therefore I've never wanted anyone to fiddle with it, and after I submit an article I protect it fiercely. Several magazine editors have told me that I'm the only writer they know who cares what happens to his piece after he gets paid for it. Most writers won't argue with an editor because they don't want to annoy him; they're so grateful to be published that they agree to having their style—in other words, their personality—violated in public. But to defend what you've written is a sign that you are alive." —William Zinsser

CHAPTER 32

A FOUR-STEP PLAN
FOR REVISION

BY RAYMOND OBSTFELD

Revising can be daunting. There's so much to look for—pacing, characterization, plot, theme, style. When I sit down to write the first few versions of a chapter, the jumble of clumsy words appearing on the screen is a far cry from the perfect passages I'm imagining in my mind.

Early drafts lay down the basic story and characters while the final drafts fine-tune what's already there. In the early stages of writing and revising, you're more daring because the area is still uncharted. But once you've charted it—that is, once you have the characters you want, doing and saying the things you want, in the order you want—now you're ready for the final draft.

GROUND RULES

First, compartmentalize your approach. The strength of the following four-step method of revision is that by doing only one step at a time, you're fully focused on that one area. Don't give in to the temptation to fix something that's not part of the step you're pursuing. Keep in mind that each step has an ultimate goal, and achieving that goal is the whole point of a particular revision.

Second, apply this process only in short, self-contained sections. If you're revising a long story or novel, use this method on scenes or chapters. I strongly discourage writing the full draft and then going back to revise. That's because the act of revising sometimes involves rethinking what you're writing about, what you want to say, whom these characters are, where you're going with the story. Sometimes you only discover the answers to these questions during a rewrite. There's usually a reason you get stuck in a particular place: You realize something is wrong with what you've written or intend to write. You just don't yet know what that something is. You need to take the time to figure out the exact element that's bothering you to know what comes next.

STEP ONE: STRUCTURE

- Goal: Develop a clear and compelling plot.
- Look for: Too passive, talking-head characters; no plot buildup/anticlimactic action.
- How to fix: Basically, you're looking to see that events are in the right order and that, if they are, the scene builds toward a satisfying climactic payoff.

The passive/talking-heads scene occurs when characters are sitting around yammering back and forth without any tension to the scene. They're called talking heads because what they're saying seems removed from any sense of characterization. It's as if they are puppets speaking the author's words rather than real people speaking their own minds.

One simple way to fix this is to change the setting so the scene is more active. Instead of a husband and wife sitting in the airport waiting for his mother to arrive and discussing how horrible she is, put them in a car stuck in horrendous airport traffic that may make them late. This additional element shifts the readers' focus to the urgency of the couple being late, which makes the readers anxious and therefore more apt to pay attention to the dialogue. Also, it gives the couple more to talk about (the awful traffic, his or her awful driving) so the conversation seems less contrived and more natural. And it gives a concrete focus to the mother's character by introducing the fact that she hates it when people are late; this shows us who she is and replaces long descriptions of how controlling she is.

Each scene is like a ministory: It has a beginning, middle, and end. The beginning introduces the conflict of the scene, the middle complicates it, and the end resolves it. That means every scene has to have a "hot spot," a point in which the action and/or emotions reach an apex. When revising for structure, make sure you locate the hot spot and make sure it generates enough heat to justify the scene. One of the main reasons scenes weaken here is that writers end the scene too early, as if it were a TV show and they were breaking for a commercial. An argument doesn't end when someone makes a witty or stinging comment; it keeps on going to the point where people are uncomfortable, frustrated, at a loss for words. So must the scene.

So far, I've discussed revising structure within a scene or chapter. However, once the whole story is completed, you must also revise the structure of the larger work. This means making sure all the scenes are in the best order. Before moving scenes around, I suggest you create note cards for each scene or chapter. Record who is in the scene, what happens in it, and how many pages it is. Tack them up in order on a bulletin board. Do you have too many passive scenes together? Are the settings too similar? By studying the cards, you can sometimes discover structure problems. Move the cards around; see if changing the order helps. Or perhaps you'll find you need an additional scene between a couple characters.

STEP TWO: TEXTURE

- Goal: Sharpen descriptive passages to make characters, setting, and action more vivid.
- Look for: Too much or too little description, research "info dump," too many adjectives, information in wrong place.
- How to fix: This step has a lot to do with defining your own style.

Some writers use a lot of description, others use very little. There's no right way. But when there's so much description that the story's momentum bogs down, that's too much. Or if there's so little that the characters or settings are bland and nonmemorable, that's too little. Most writers, myself included, have many descriptive passages that they love but that must go because they call too much attention to themselves and detract from the story. Anytime you see a passage of description that is so poetic and involving that the reader stops to admire the author, cut it. Save all those wonderful passages you cut in a folder; you may be able to use them in another story.

Telling the reader too little can be equally annoying. Even though the writer may tell us the scene takes place in an alley, if the reader emerges from the scene and still doesn't have a feel for the setting, the reader never experiences the alley and therefore is never fully involved.

Directly related to this is the dreaded "info dump." This is where the writer decides to stop the story cold to give a lot of details about the history of the house that the characters live in or how to pilot a plane. Yes, sometimes those details are important to your story and add a level of credibility. But novice writers either include too much information or too many such passages. One of my students is writing a novel that involves sailing a yacht. This author has sailing expertise, so he includes page after page of description about the technical aspects of sailing. Workshop reaction to these scenes is always the same: There's so much technical information that the readers get lost and no longer care about what's happening to the characters. However, there's another student in the same class who is also an expert sailor and writing a novel about sailing, but reaction to his work is always enthusiastic because we get just enough information to accept the realism of the scene, but not so much as to numb us.

Aside from adjusting length, writers can vastly improve the impact of the texture by concentrating on word choices. Read through the manuscript once and circle words that could be stronger. Then go back and take your time replacing them. Don't rely on a thesaurus; many times you'll just trade one dull word for a more complex and even duller word. The word you're looking for often isn't a synonym; it's just something richer, more evocative.

A common reason that passages can bog down or lose their snap is that the writer has burdened them with too many adjectives. Most of the time when there are several adjectives together, at least two of them have the same meaning. For example: "She was a quiet, introspective, shy girl." Think of every adjective as a one hundred dollar bill and spend wisely.

STEP THREE: DIALOGUE

- Goal: Elicit character personality through conversation.
- Look for: Too many tag lines, too few tag lines, tag lines in the wrong place, bland or melodramatic lines.
- How to fix: Tag lines are the "he said" and "she said" parts of dialogue. If there are only two speakers, several lines can go on without telling us who the speaker is; the reader already knows.

To add tag lines in such a situation is really nothing more than a crutch to avoid making the characters' voices so individual that the reader can recognize their cadence and tone without being told.

Yet there are times when the reader does have to be told who is speaking. This can be because there are several speakers, or the dialogue is interspersed with action or interior monologues, or it's needed for the sake of the rhythm. The following are several examples of the same line of dialogue:

> "Hi," she said, moving toward me.
>
> "Hi," she said. She moved toward me.
>
> She moved toward me. "Hi."
>
> "Hi." She moved toward me.

The first two examples are friendlier because the "she said" slows the pace, taking away some of the energy from her act of moving. The second two examples are more dramatic because they present just the dialogue and the action, which now seems more deliberate and aggressive.

Where the tag line goes affects the emphasis on the dialogue. Look at the following variations. Which has more impact?

> "This is yours. That is not," he said.
>
> "This is yours," he said. "That is not."

The second version is stronger because the emphasis is now on "That is not." Placing the emphasis there adds an ominous tone. The first version has the lines together, which doesn't emphasize either and makes the dialogue seem breezier.

Sometimes you need to identify the speaker, but you don't want to use the word said for the millionth time. You can substitute an action instead:

> "You always do this to me," I said.
>
> I said, "You always do this to me."
>
> I shook my head. "You always do this to me."

Don't overdo this technique, otherwise every line of dialogue will have a gesture attached and the characters will all seem like they're on a caffeine buzz.

Finally, keep your tags simple. The more complex the tag line, the more it detracts from the actual dialogue. Avoid adverbs (e.g., she said angrily).

One of the things I do before editing my own dialogue is to read a passage by someone whose dialogue I admire (Elmore Leonard, Ross Thomas, Lorrie Moore, Jane Smiley, Peter De Vries). Which writer I choose to read depends on the tone I want to achieve. If the scene calls for fast-paced, edgy dialogue, I may read Leonard. If I want playful and desperate, I may read playwright David Mamet. Read the dialogue passages until you have a feel for the language, then go right back to your work and start editing.

STEP FOUR: EDITING

- Goal: Tighten pace and continuity.
- Look for: Repetition through implication, slow passages.
- How to fix: Cut. Cut. Cut.

This is often the hardest part for writers because they've worked so hard on every word. But this final step is the one that gives the work its final shape. Much of what you will cut is repetition, words that repeat what the reader already knows because it's been directly said or implied elsewhere.

Once you've finished editing your manuscript, go through again to make sure that there are clear transitions bridging your cuts.

A FINAL WORD ON FINAL DRAFTS

Although the phrase "final draft" suggests the last time you'll revise, that really isn't the case. Final draft really refers to the final process of revising. It's when you're satisfied with the basics, but want to erase any persistent flaws.

However, there is a point at which every manuscript must be abandoned, sent out to publishers, and the next work begun. This four-step revision method will allow you to reach that "final" draft more comfortably because you will know you have examined every aspect of the work possible. But if you've completed these four steps and you still feel the work needs something, begin again with step one.

 RAYMOND OBSTFELD received an Edgar nomination for his novel *Dead Heat*. He has written forty books and a dozen screenplays.

CHAPTER 33
DEALING WITH CRITICISM

BY LAURA HENDRIE

I'm sitting at a bar with a young man who's recently taken to calling himself a writer. After throwing back a shot of whiskey, he turns to me and says, "I think the greatest thing about writing is the honesty of the response you get back. Nobody hedges. Nobody tries to be polite. It's exhilarating. Know what I mean?"

I look at him with curiosity. We've just spent an hour together in a class where he was told by several writers, including me, that his novel—despite interesting characters, sharp-paced dialogue, and a real eye-opener of a plot—doesn't work. As far as I could tell from his reaction at the time, he wasn't all *that* thrilled by honesty, and now, though he smiles warmly at me before he turns to motion for another drink, I notice a tic in the muscle at the side of his neck.

A negative response from your readers—especially when they've taken the time to be conscientious about it—is always a shock. It's like getting kicked in the behind while bending over to pick up the penny. It's not the kick that hurts, it's the humiliation of having bent over for the penny. True, your voice may not quiver when you're thanking them for their honesty. Your hands may be steady when you're opening that letter of advice from the editor you've always admired. You may even be able to agree with your favorite author when he tells you that he thinks your new book isn't half as interesting as the last one you wrote. But your whole face is on fire, there's a roaring in your ears, and behind that pleasant, puppet-strung "uh-huh" of yours stands an infuriated, tic-faced little dictator demanding to know this instant one of three things: (1) how you could allow these half-wits near your best work, (2) why you ever thought you could get away with calling yourself a writer, or (3) how you're ever going to write again. And this may be where you stop. But it shouldn't be. In fact, the difference between the writer who's going to add up to something in a few years and the writer who's not may have less to do with the quality of the work than with the way each one handles criticism.

USING CRITICISM TO YOUR ADVANTAGE

Some writers *use* criticism. Experienced writers do it all the time. They selectively choose whom to listen to, selectively listen for what they need to hear, and selectively use the information they're given. They do this with the same skill and concentration they use in their writing. Some writers will panic and toss out everything readers didn't like while embalming for worship everything they praised. Either that or balk at the very idea of changing a word or comma. A successful writer will panic, too, but then he will flounder onward, pondering this criticism and sweating out that compliment, trying all the wrong advice and being thoroughly disgusted with himself when he can't seem to make it work, until somewhere along the line, if he's open enough, he turns almost by accident to the advice he needed to hear in the first place—the advice he was too biased or nervous or green to understand before—and wham! He's invented something new. Not only that, but he's learned things *not* to invent along the way as well.

Writers who realize that feedback can be a valuable tool use it often and with growing dexterity and gratitude. And why not? Writing is a lonely enough experience without summarily refusing all help and input from outsiders. To do so simply because the reader may be wrong, the advice might upset you, or you don't like to be told what you didn't think up yourself is not only stubborn, but ultimately foolhardy.

If you're thinking, "Yes, but writers who can jump at a chance to receive feedback don't get the kind of feedback I get; they don't have to put up with the grunting manuscript-eaters I've got to deal with," you're wrong. Everybody gets their share of negative feedback and everybody gets their share of nonobjective, incompetent criticism. So don't think you're being unfairly picked on when even the most unskilled reader you know calls to tell you how to fix your story or poem, when even the silliest little free pamphlet-magazine sends you a rejection. It comes with the territory.

Writers who use critical feedback are not less egocentric or thicker-skinned or more flexible than writers who can't. Writers are by definition egocentric, thin-skinned, and highly sensitive to criticism. They write to be understood and when they are not, no matter how they may try to hide it, it hurts.

But while one writer may walk off from a negative response to his work looking like a suicide headed for the bridge, another writer can leave the same situation with a sense of excitement, even eagerness. Why? Not because he enjoys humiliation. And not because he is, in John Wayne's words, a damn fool. He just hasn't lost sight of his priority in the process. His priority is and always should be, even at the cost of pride and temporary pleasures, *to improve the writing.*

Okay, so you want to improve your writing, too. So you want to be able to learn from readers even when they start sucking the air out of the room. How do you manage it?

STEP ONE: ASK YOURSELF WHY

The way to handle criticism is to know *why* you're asking for it. You should know the answer to this *before* you ever send out a piece of work to be read.

This is not as easy as you might first suppose. Writers may be notoriously honest, but when it comes to the question of why they're sending out their work to be read, they tend to hold their hands over their mouths when they speak. Or as Logan Pearsall Smith explained it: "Every author, however modest, keeps a most outrageous vanity chained like a madman in the padded cell of his breast."

So the first question you should answer has two parts, one for the writer in you and one for the madman: (1) What do you think you want?, and (2) What do you *really* want? "I know!" you chirp like the good child. *"To improve the writing!"* But to do that you must be as honest about your weaknesses as you are about your strengths. This can be extremely difficult when your weaknesses are being pointed out to you by someone else. Honest readers know this. That's why there are so few of them. They know how likely it is that when you say you want honesty, your preference is praise. Yet the irony is, you know you have to have that dose of honesty once in a while. You can't live without it, not if you're to become any sort of "real" writer.

The best way to get honesty from your readers is by asking for honesty from yourself. This is why *before* I send off a story or poem, I clear a place on my desk and sit down with a clean sheet of paper and a thick, black felt-tip pen to work out the reasons *why* I'm about to send out my work to whatever reader(s) I've chosen. I start at the top with the word:

Priorities

Some days, this in itself is enough to make me feel virtuous. Below that, I write:

Why do I need to send out this piece?

Priorities are more like eternal laws than personal decisions. They do not change much and they are as easy to remember as the memory of your mother's voice telling you to sit up straight or that brussels sprouts are good for you. I have two priorities: "to improve the writing" and "to get honest feedback." My only other priority is when I'm sending my manuscript out to be published, and then I'll naturally include, "to have the story published."

Notice how I avoid using personal pronouns in priorities. I like to keep them sounding as noble and unselfish and thoroughly martyred for the sake of the writing as the mother who offers to crawl to Bethlehem for the sake of her children.

When I'm done with that, I move down to the middle of the page. There I draw a heavy black line similar to the River Styx and below that I take a breath and write: *Preferences.* Then, I write: *What else do I want?*

This is where it gets tricky. You'll do anything but admit what you *really* want, right? To get around this, write your answers in the form of questions.

What else do I want?
To show my readers that:
I'm a living treasure?

I've led a fascinating life? (had fascinating parents? children? dogs?)

I'm not afraid of a little criticism?

I should be published soon in some magazine their mother works for?

I'm nothing like them?

I'm just as good as them?

I'm ten times better than them?

I try to put the preferences that sound most vulgar right at the top of the list. That way I offer myself the chance to be honest from the start. I also think it's helpful to go over each item and ask yourself, "If I could ever be so grossly self-centered as to want that and then the opposite actually happened, I wonder how I'd feel?" Then close your eyes and imagine it. If you feel anything like nausea or dizziness, you're probably close to the truth. Keep going. When it comes to preferences, i.e., vanity-driven motives that have absolutely nothing to do with good writing, still waters run deep. And what do you do with all this truth? Examine your options:

Forget about sending out the story.

Forget about getting honest feedback and send the story to your aunt who "always loves anything" you write.

Send it out to honest readers but ask them to read only for grammar and spelling errors. Or better yet, tell them to read it "only for enjoyment." (Don't worry; they'll get the point.)

Send it out and prepare yourself for the possibility of seeing every one of your preferences shot for the sake of improving the work.

If you choose the last option, remember two things. One is that the reason you're asking for feedback is that you are still learning to write. (If you're smart, you'll spend your entire life learning and still never be able to admit you know how.) The other is Marcus Aurelius's quote: "It is not death that a man should fear, but he should fear never beginning to live." Which in my neck of the woods translates to mean that if I'm fully prepared to get bucked off my horse in a negative critique and then I actually *get* bucked off, I'm a lot less stunned about it than if I assumed my horse wasn't the bucking type. Plus I'll be able to get back on faster and decide which direction to go in next with a great deal more clarity and eagerness.

The surprising thing is this little pregame self-exam can make a big difference. Let's say, for example, that I've given my fiction to my most honest reader, who then informs me that she thinks the main character is insipid. If I'm not aware of my preferences, if I've deluded myself into thinking that honest feedback was my *only* expectation, I may get the desire to, let's say, snap off her head at the neck. Why? Because the story was so *obviously* all about me and my incredible childhood! Granted, I *called* it fiction instead of autobiography, granted I *asked* for her honest opinion—but *really*!

But if, on the other hand, after admitting to myself that my desire to send out my poem about Miami was influenced not only by my desire to improve the work but also because the reader I chose just happens to edit a magazine called *Miami Monthly*, I can't be all that upset with her if she spends her time talking about the heavy-handedness of the setting. After all, she's kept her priorities straight—to give honest feedback. I'm the one who bent the rules, who tried to submit to her magazine without her realizing it. But I can forgive myself—wanting love is only human, right? I'll look at the poem some more, try to see what she saw, maybe even change the setting to something I know more about. And in the meantime, I've discovered a gem: The reader who insists on being honest.

STEP TWO: ASK YOUR READERS QUESTIONS

Contrary to what many people believe, giving a manuscript to readers for a critical discussion does not mean the writer gives up control of it. Far from it. In most cases, readers look to the writer for direction. If they sense the writer's priority is to improve the work, they'll try to deliver; but if they sense the writer is fishing for compliments or expecting a browbeating, they're likely to do that, too. It's hard not to. So if you don't want to leave your next critique feeling duped, take charge. Teach your readers how to teach you.

One way to do this is to come to the discussion with a carefully planned set of what I call writing-oriented questions about your work. Asking writing-oriented questions accomplishes several things. It makes you an active participant in the feedback process, provides a framework for you and your readers to address particular concerns about the work, and helps organize your readers' discussion into themes that are easier for you to grasp, understand, and use later.

But most important, writing-oriented questions clarify for everyone concerned why the critique is taking place. Not because the writer is hoping to be coddled and not because the readers want to toot their horns about how much they know. No, this discussion is taking place for one reason and one reason only: *To improve the writing.* Most readers appreciate being reminded of this.

Which is why, if you want your questions to be writing-oriented instead of self-oriented, they should be written down *before* you enter the critique, before that little madman imprisoned in your breast—your ego—starts shrieking and rattling his chains too loudly for you to think.

A writing-oriented question sounds exactly like what it is. It's the same kind of open-ended question English teachers pose for their students on a piece of literature, and it demands the same sort of response from readers, i.e.:

Clearly stated ideas backed by concrete examples;

Objectivity in arguments;

A strong sense of respect for and deference to the work (i.e., a writing-oriented question asks the reader for a clear description of what is on the page, not a prescription of what to put there next);

Examination based on two bigger issues: What works? What doesn't work?

Now let's put this to the test. Suppose that as the author, you're curious to know if the complexity of your main character translates onto the page. If you ask something like, "Did you like the main character?" or "Didn't you think that ending was confusing?" the reader feels trapped. The questions are close-ended and ego-oriented. They plead not for an honest response from the reader, but an ego-mollifying, uninformed, and uninformative, knee-jerk response like "yeah" or "sure."

A writing-oriented question, however, might be, "Can you describe the kind of person the main character is?" Now you are asking an open-ended question that demands objective information based not on opinion but on what is on the page. *You* as author know the answer. You know it because it's your work, but see if your readers know it, too. If they don't, and you know they're careful readers, then the character is obviously not as fully realized on paper as he is in your head.

Here are some other examples of writing-oriented questions:

> Can you tell me why the man does what he does?
>
> Can you tell me why or why not the point of view (the pace/voice/ setting/dialogue/whatever you're concerned about) works for this particular piece?
>
> Can you tell me what the strongest images were in the piece and why? The weakest? Why?
>
> Can you explain why I changed from third person to first?

Adapt questions to your specific needs, your specific style, and your specific readers. Then make sure to open your ears. Good listening begins with respect. Write down everything, even if you don't agree with it. (If your critique occurs through the mail, copy down the comments from your readers in your own hand.) Listen not only to what is said, but also to what is not said. Be courteous. Be sure you understand. Encourage them if you think they are holding back. And *never* argue. You are there to improve the writing, and no matter how far off the mark they are in this regard, they are trying to help. Remember this: The more you're able to hear what they're saying and why they're saying it, the more you'll understand the worth of it later.

STEP THREE: WHAT TO DO WITH FEEDBACK

After you come out of a critique of your work, you've got, as you know, several choices. If you don't believe what you hear, you can throw a fit and send the story to someone else. If you believe it, you can throw a fit and destroy the piece. Or you can throw a fit and then hide the piece in the back of your closet for a while.

But most writers—even the ones who don't throw fits—end up wanting to rewrite. The question is how to do it when every voice is yammering at you except the original one that told you to write the piece in the first place. Here are some methods that have helped me:

- Pace problems: I learned this method from Andre Dubus and I still use it, especially when I think my work may need to be heavily edited. I clear out the furniture in my living room and then lay out my manuscript, page by page, on the floor, like tiles. I then get down on my hands and knees and, starting at page one, skim the content and then paraphrase it in one short sentence. I do this with every page, using ditto marks and arrows where the idea doesn't change from one page to the next. It is much like dismantling and cataloging a skeleton, studying the shape and weight of each bone so as to better understand the body and how it works. When I'm done, my list can tell me how much space each idea/character/scene takes up and how they fit and move (or don't fit and move) together. This has, at times, clearly mirrored for me what my manuscript as a whole needs in terms of trimming here and fattening there.

- Story development problems: I prefer free-form writing. The purpose is to suspend critical judgment by writing down whatever comes into your head, whether it's related to the subject or not. Be silly. Be crazy. Write fast and judge nothing. This can lead you to stumble over your subconscious memory and onto the missing key, which will once again unlock the sound of the story you want.

- Character development problems: Any long-married person will tell you that after you've grown accustomed to someone, no matter how much you love them, you can sometimes lose sight of who they are until you take a break from your regular surroundings, when that person becomes suddenly strange and wonderful all over again. Therefore, if you're having trouble getting interested in or understanding one of your characters after a critique, remove the character from the situation you had him in and try him out in something else. Describe him in front of the mirror brushing his teeth. Put him to bed, or if he's already there, put him in the kitchen in his pajamas staring into the refrigerator for something to eat. Use any small, mundane act (new action is not what you're looking for, it's new insight into personality) and see how he does it. Study movements, look for revealing details, listen to what he thinks. Whole new personality quirks for characters have come to me in this way, sometimes even whole new characters. And even when they don't, it's a good exercise anyway.

- Morale problems in general: When I get so bogged down by negative feedback that I don't know where to begin, I sometimes give myself an absolute three-week deadline to finish the story and an absolute order to stop writing anything but random notes to myself for a week.

This may sound crazy and it certainly can make you feel crazy, but it's like turning on the heat under a pot of water and then putting a tight lid on it so the pressure builds, making the water boil faster. In my case, it makes me both acutely aware of and eager to foster the idea that everything I do and see and feel is related to what I'm going to write, whether or not I'm writing it at the time. What I see happening around me, what I read, the way I talk, what I eat, what people say to me, sometimes even what I dream—if I believe all of it holds messages for my writing in all sorts of mysterious and coincidental ways, when I am truly focused on that, it works. I'll pick up a magazine in the local laundry with a quote in it that is exactly what I was trying to get at; I'll hear a conversation at the store that is stunningly like what my fictional character wants to say; I'll sit down to write a letter to the editor of a newspaper and suddenly know how the story, which is in my bottom drawer, will end.

The more aware I can make myself of the possibility of the answer coming to me unannounced, the more it does. This is not magic. It has nothing to do with New Age affirmations. It is simply allowing the mind to imagine what it wants while keeping tabs on the priority of improving the writing.

You'll have more success with a holistic, work-oriented approach to rewriting than the simplistic types of problem-shooting the how-to books suggest. A story is a living, breathing organism with all kinds of angles and textures and private, changeable moods to it, and it should be viewed as such, from a cubist's vision, seeing all different sides at once. This doesn't apply just to writing it. You can dictate it to a tape recorder. Read it in a voice other than your own. Shout it at the wall. Whisper it to your cat. Make it into a poem. Draw a picture of it if you can. Anything, anything that will *let the story speak*.

Because in the end, that is exactly what will happen. The story will speak. It will make your decisions for you, either by becoming too awful to work on another moment or by becoming too interesting not to. You can count on it. No matter how badly it's written in its first draft, no matter how much negative and/or uninformed criticism it gets buried under, no matter how cruel and barbaric your ego behaves when left alone to rewrite it, if the story has something worthwhile in it, it is indestructible. Throw a good idea away and it will emerge in the next story you write. Hide a good character in your closet and sooner or later you will hear him telling you to take him out again, whether you want to or not. You can't stop it.

Writers in the critiquing process too often forget this. They think they're in charge of the story or the readers are in charge of the story, but the truth is, *the writing is in charge*. It is the top priority. Treat it as such, listen to it as such, honor it as such, and from the day you get back the results of your first critique to the day you sit down to rework the final draft, you will be better able to make wise decisions.

 LAURA HENDRIE is the author of the short story collection *Stygo* and the novel, *Remember Me*.

Part Three

EXPLORING NOVEL GENRES

BEST-SELLING ADVICE: Style & Craft

"You have to follow your own voice. You have to be yourself when you write. In effect, you have to announce, 'This is me, this is what I stand for, this is what you get when you read me. I'm doing the best I can—buy me or not—but this is who I am as a writer.' " —David Morrell

"I think I succeeded as a writer because I did not come out of an English department. I used to write in the chemistry department. And I wrote some good stuff. If I had been in the English department, the prof would have looked at my short stories, congratulated me on my talent, and then showed me how Joyce or Hemingway handled the same elements of the short story. The prof would have placed me in competition with the greatest writers of all time, and that would have ended my writing career." —Kurt Vonnegut

"What a writer has to do is write what hasn't been written before or beat dead men at what they have done." —Ernest Hemingway

"Oftentimes an originator of new language forms is called 'pretentious' by jealous talents. But it ain't watcha write, it's the way atcha write it." —Jack Kerouac

"I'm very concerned with the rhythm of language. 'The sun came up' is an inadequate sentence. Even though it conveys all the necessary information, rhythmically it's lacking.

The sun came up.

But, if you say, as Laurie Anderson said, 'The sun came up like a big bald head,' not only have you, perhaps, entertained the fancy of the reader, but you have made a more complete sentence. The sound of a sentence." —Tom Robbins

"I guess I believe that writing consists of very small parts put together into a whole, and if the parts are defective, the whole won't work." —Garrison Keillor

"You should really stay true to your own style. When I first started writing, everybody said to me, 'your style just isn't right because you don't use the really flowery language that romances have.' My romances—compared to what's out there—are very strange, very odd, very different. And I think that's one of the reasons they're selling." —Jude Deveraux

"Writing is like being in love. You never get better at it or learn more about it. The day you think you do is the day you lose it. Robert Frost called his work a lover's quarrel with the world. It's ongoing. It has neither a beginning nor an end. You don't have to worry about learning things. The fire of one's art burns all the impurities from the vessel that contains it." —James Lee Burke

"We, and I think I'm speaking for many writers, don't know what it is that sometimes comes to make our books alive. All we can do is to write dutifully and day after day, every day, giving our work the very best of what we are capable. I don't think that we can consciously put the magic in; it doesn't work that way. When the magic comes, it's a gift." —Madeleine L'Engle

CHAPTER 34
LITERARY LUST VS. COMMERCIAL CASH

BY JODI PICOULT

I remember the moment I crossed over to the Dark Side.

It was after I'd published my second book at a big New York publisher with a reputation for publishing classics or works that would one day *become* classics. As with most literary contracts, they had the right of first refusal on my next novel.

"Well," they said after they read it, "we'll publish it if no one else wants to."

Not exactly a ringing endorsement.

My agent took the manuscript to a publishing house that, philosophically, was diametrically opposed to my current one. It was known for its domination of *The New York Times* best-seller list, with so many brand-name authors under its roof that I was convinced my agent's exercise was futile.

The editors offered me a two-book deal. They wanted to pay me two times what I'd made before. There was only one catch: Could I cut out some of that Native American stuff in the novel and beef up the Hollywood scenes?

I was too excited that a publishing company wanted the kind of stories I wrote to realize that, well, they actually *didn't*. They wanted to groom me to join their highly profitable stable of writers, turning out bestsellers and beach reads. All I had to do was agree that, from that moment on, I was going to be a commercial writer.

The difference between a commercial writer and a literary writer is, at first sight, painfully clear. Literary writers get clout. They get reviews in *The New York Times*. They win National Book Awards. Their stories haunt you, change the way you think about the world, are destined to be part of college curricula. These authors teach at prestigious universities. When they do readings, it's at a place like Carnegie Hall. Their print runs are in the tens of thousands, and they don't make gobs of money, but that doesn't matter, because a literary writer is "above" mundane things like that.

By contrast, a commercial writer's books *sell*. They're given marketing and advertising budgets. They don't get reviewed in *The New York Times* but have big, splashy full-page ads inside, and they grace the peaks of its best-seller list. Commercial books are the ones you trip over when you walk into a bookstore, stacked in enormous displays. They're the stories you can't put down at night and can't remember in detail after you've read them. Their print runs are in the hundreds of thousands; their advances are dissected in "PublishersLunch" reports.

As a beginning writer, I'd labored under the misconception that I could surely be both literary and commercial at the same time. Why couldn't I write books that changed the world … and still make enough money to pay my mortgage? Did those two criteria have to be mutually exclusive?

Yes, but not for the reasons you'd think. At some point in your career, you'll be forced to choose either the commercial path or the literary one. You can start by straddling the two, but eventually, as they veer apart, you're going to tumble onto one side or another. And—here's the big stunner—what makes a writer literary or commercial has far less to do with her writing than it does with marketing. We live in a publishing world that's made up of bottom lines, which means every book must have a target audience. Whereas literary fiction is made up of masters with oeuvres, commercial fiction is made up of genres. It makes sense for a publisher to pitch a writer as the new James Patterson—it tells bookstore owners that mystery lovers will buy the book. The same goes for romance novels, family dramas, and horror. When you label a commercial writer by her genre, you've already sold her.

Interestingly, the distinctions are arbitrary. For years, half of my books were shelved in the mystery section at Borders; the other half were shelved in literature. There was no salient plot difference between the books in either category; they'd just been pitched to two different corporate buyers by my publisher. Although many people compare my writing to Anita Shreve's, she's considered literary by the chain stores, whereas I'm commercial, because, again, we're pitched to two different buyers. My mentor from the creative writing program at Princeton University, Mary Morris, writes books that I can't put down and is (along with Sue Miller, Anne Tyler, and Alice Hoffman) one of the finest detailers of human relationships, but because she's a literary writer, she isn't as well known as they are.

Or, in other words, it's not that you won't find literary writers enjoyable. It's just that you won't *find* them, period. Part of the marketing strategy for commercial fiction involves co-op advertising at chains and box stores—namely, a contract between the store and the publisher to pay for the spot where a book is placed (much like at a supermarket when Cheerios pays for the end-of-aisle display for a week). Commercial fiction is far more likely to be in the front of a store than literary fiction, which will be tucked into the side shelves—and therefore is less likely to be an impulse purchase.

All writers wish for commercial success. But at what price? If you sell your soul to the devil of profitability, you have to be able to look in the mirror every day and be able to say, without flinching, that you're a commercial fiction writer. You have to be aware that your books may not have the lasting power of a literary novelist's. Naturally, no one plans to be a hack when they set out to write the Great American Novel, yet digestible reads are the ones that sell best. If you ask me, the trick is to be a commercial writer—but don't sell out. Write for a wide audience, but don't compromise what you write.

I'm living proof that you can have your literary cake and eat it commercially, too. Although I get letters all the time from fans who say things like, "I read only mystery/romance/courtroom drama, and you're my favorite mystery/romance/courtroom drama writer!" I really am none of those things—and all of them. My books are a combination of commercial genres, and I have no inclination or intention to narrow it down.

Frankly, I don't care what genre a reader thinks my book is, as long as it gets him to pick it up. Does this make my books a harder sell for my poor beleaguered publisher? You bet. It may be the reason it took me twelve years to be an overnight commercial success. But it also has allowed me to defy the logic of the literary/commercial split: My genre has become the very lack of one.

Because readers have become accustomed to me not writing the same book twice, my publisher expects me to do something new every time, which gives me the freedom to try new things and to use fiction to explore moral and social conundrums—a trait more commonly associated with the literary writer. And, in one of the greatest ironies of my career, I've heard of new commercial novelists being pitched as the next Jodi Picoult.

I admit that when I dove headfirst into the sea of commercial fiction, I made mistakes. When that publisher asked me to "pump up the Hollywood," I did. In retrospect, I wish I hadn't. I was too naïve to stick up for my writing; to understand that a commercial novel could still be resonant and relevant; that I didn't have to dumb it down to the masses. See, here's what the publishers *won't* tell you: You don't have to write to the lowest common denominator if you're a commercial author. You can up the ante; your readers will rise to the occasion.

When you reach that junction—and you have to pick the literary high road or the crowded commercial one—remember that you're standing in front of a mirage. Let the business folks at the publishing company slap a label on you, but write what you want and need to write. The label can't dictate what's between the covers; that's up to you.

And for those compatriots who choose to join me on the commercial side of fiction, take heart in our forebearers: William Shakespeare was a commercial hack who cranked out his plays on deadline. Charles Dickens was paid by the word and was wildly popular with the masses. By the same token, Ian McEwan and Joan Didion and Philip Roth have all enjoyed recent crossover success as huge literary bestsellers. Maybe that means what's commercial today might be literary tomorrow or vice versa. Or maybe—just maybe—it means that when you're talking about good writing, there simply are no divisions.

 JODI PICOULT is the bestselling author of seventeen novels, including *My Sister's Keeper, Vanishing Acts,* and *House Rules.*

CHAPTER 35
WRITING THE WORLD OF FANTASY

BY TERRY BROOKS

I remember vividly, twenty years later, what Lester del Rey repeatedly used to tell me about writing fantasy. Lester was a longtime writer, critic, and editor in the fantasy/science fiction field, and I was fortunate enough to be able to work with him during the first fifteen years of my professional career. Most of what I learned about being a commercial fiction writer, for better or worse, I learned from Lester. Lester used to say that it was harder to write good fantasy than any other form of fiction. Why? Because a writer of fantasy is free to invent anything, unfettered by the laws and dictates of this world and limited only by the depth of imagination and willingness to dream. The temptation to free-fall through a story chock full of incredible images and wondrous beings can be irresistible—but, when not resisted, almost invariably disastrous.

What he was telling me was that in creating a world populated by monsters and other strange life forms, reliant on uses of magic and shimmering with images of childhood tales, legends, and myths, a writer runs the risk of losing touch with reality entirely. Given the parameters of the world and characters that the writer has created, something of that world and those characters must speak to what we, as readers, know to be true about the human condition. If nothing corresponds to what we know about our own lives, then everything becomes unbelievable. Even the most ridiculous farce must resonate in some identifiable way with truths we have discovered about ourselves. Even the darkest sword and sorcery epic must speak to us of our own harsh experience.

Achieving this end as a fantasy writer demands mastery of a certain skill, one not uncommon with that required of a ship's captain charting a course at sea. When putting together a fantasy tale, a writer must navigate a treacherous passage that bears neither too hard to starboard nor too far to port in order to avoid arriving at an unforseen destination or, worse, ending up on the rocks. Fantasy writing must be grounded in both truth and live experience if it is to work. It can be as inventive and creative as the writer can make it, a whirlwind of images and plot twists, but it cannot be built on a foundation of air. The world must be identifiable with our own, must offer us a frame of reference we can recognize. The characters must behave in ways that we believe reasonable and expected. The magic must work in a consistent and balanced manner. The book must leave us with a feeling of comprehension and satisfaction at having spent time turning its pages to discover its end.

How does a writer accomplish this? Fantasy stories work because the writer has interwoven bits and pieces of reality with imagination to form a personal vision. Understanding the possibilities is a requirement to making choices. Those choices might include various forms of magic, types of weapons and armor, fantasy races and creatures, and ancient societies on which speculative fictional worlds and characters can be based. Each writer must choose the ones that work and make them the building blocks of a story's foundation.

Description lends weight and substance to ideas, and nowhere is that more important than in a world that doesn't exist—at least outside the pages of the writer's story. So giving the reader an understanding of how a world looks, tastes, smells, sounds, and feels is crucial. In fantasy, more than in any other form of fiction, the reader must feel transported to the world being created, while at the same time readily comprehending what it is he is experiencing. When an otherwordly character is introduced, the reader must be made to see the differences, but must recognize the similarities as well. Details ground the story's larger images and keep the reader engaged.

I happen to favor rather strongly the practice of outlining a book before trying to write it, and I would recommend it to beginning writers, in particular, for two reasons. First, it requires thinking the story through, which eliminates a lot of wasted time chasing bad ideas. Second, it provides a blueprint to which the writer can refer while working on a story over the course of months or even years. Use of an outline is not a popular practice because it is hard work. It isn't easy thinking a story through from start to finish. But writing a hundred pages that have to be discarded because they don't lead anywhere is a whole lot more unpleasant. Moreover, outlining gives a writer a chance to add to the details of the book, to pen notes in the margins, to decide how all those bits and pieces of reality I mentioned earlier will fit with those grand landscapes of imagination.

This seems a good place to stress the importance of "dream time" in the creative process. All good fantasy requires a certain amount of gestation, a period before pen is set to paper or fingers to keyboard, in which a writer simply gives free rein to imagination and waits to see where it will go. After a path reveals itself, a writer should start to map that path, carefully noting which side roads are offered, what travelers await, where dangers might lurk, and how lessons could be learned. If the writer is patient enough, eventually a story will present itself. If it is the right story, it will demand to be written. It simply won't stand to be cooped up. But this is a process that is difficult to rush and one in which the writer must trust. It sounds a bit mystical, but it really isn't. It's puzzle building without a box cover. It's outlining in your mind.

There is one final lesson Lester taught me that I want to pass on before I end this. Some years back, I was fussing to him about finding an idea for a story that hadn't been used before. I wanted something new and original. He gave me one of his patented smiles—the ones that always made him look like a cross between your kindly uncle and Jack Nicholson in *The Shining*—and told me in no uncertain terms that new ideas did not come along that often and that when they did, they came in disguise. It was better to take old, established ideas and just turn them over and over in your mind until you found a new way to look at them. Then write about what you saw.

It was good advice then. It's good advice now. Go forth, and write something magical.

TERRY BROOKS has more than fifteen million books in print worldwide. He published his first novel, *The Sword of Shannara*, in 1977. His most recent novel is *Bearers of the Black Staff*.

CHAPTER 36

STORY STRUCTURES FOR SCIENCE FICTION & FANTASY

BY ORSON SCOTT CARD

All stories contain four elements that can determine structure: milieu, idea, character, and event. While each is present in every story, there is generally one that dominates the others. Which one dominates? The one that the author cares about most. This is why the process of discovering the structure of a story is usually a process of self-discovery. Which aspect of the story matters most to you? That is the aspect that determines your story's structure. Let's take each element in turn and look at the structure that would be required if that were to be the dominant element in your story.

STRUCTURE 1: THE MILIEU STORY

The milieu is the world—the planet, the society, the weather, the family, all the elements that come up during your world-creation phase. Every story has a milieu, but when a story is structured around one, the milieu is the thing the storyteller cares about most. For instance, in *Gulliver's Travels*, it mattered little to Jonathan Swift whether we came to care about Gulliver as a character. The whole point of the story was for the audience to see all the strange lands where Gulliver traveled and then compare the societies he found there with the society of England in Swift's own day—and the societies of all the tale's readers, in all times and places. So it would've been absurd to begin by writing much about Gulliver's childhood and upbringing. The real story began the moment Gulliver got to the first of the book's strange lands, and it ended when he came home.

Milieu stories always follow that structure. An observer who sees things the way we'd see them gets to the strange place, observes things that interest him, is transformed by what he sees, and then comes back a new person.

This structure is most common in science fiction and fantasy, but it also occurs in other types of novels. James Clavell's *Shogun*, for instance, is a milieu story: It begins when the European hero is stranded in medieval Japan, and it ends when he leaves. He was transformed by his experiences in Japan, but he does not stay—he returns to his world. Other stories are told along the way—the story of the shogun, for instance—but regardless of how much we're drawn into those events, the real closure we expect at the end of the story is the main character's departure from Japan.

Likewise, *The Wonderful Wizard of Oz* doesn't end when Dorothy kills the Wicked Witch of the West. It ends when Dorothy leaves Oz and goes home to Kansas. As you conceive and write your own story, if you realize that what you care about most is having a character explore and discover the world you've created, chances are this structure is your best choice.

When writing a milieu story, your beginning point is obvious—when the character arrives—and the ending is just as plain: when she leaves (or, in a variant, when she decides not to leave, ending the question of going home).

Such stories are typically most effective when seen through the viewpoint of the arriving character, as she'll be surprised by and interested in the same strange and marvelous (and terrible) things that engage the readers.

STRUCTURE 2: THE IDEA STORY

Idea stories are about the process of seeking and discovering new information through the eyes of characters who are driven to make the discoveries. The structure is very simple: The idea story begins by raising a question; it ends when the question is answered.

Most mysteries follow this structure. The story begins when a crime takes place. The question we ask is, "who did it and why?" The story ends when the identity and motive of the criminal are revealed.

In speculative fiction, a similar structure is quite common. The story begins with a question: Why did this beautiful ancient civilization on a faraway planet come to an end? Why are all these people gone, when they were once so wise and their achievements so great? The answer, in Arthur C. Clarke's "The Star," is that their sun went nova, making life impossible in their star system. And, ironically, it was the explosion of their star that the wise men saw as the sign of the birth of Christ. The story is told from the point of view of a Christian who believes that this must have been a deliberate act of God, to destroy a beautiful civilization for the sake of giving a sign to the magi.

When writing an idea story, begin as close as possible to the point where the question is first raised, and end as soon as possible after the question is answered.

STRUCTURE 3: THE CHARACTER STORY

Character stories focus on the transformation of a character's role in the communities that matter most to him. Sure, in one sense, stories are almost always "about" one or more characters. In most stories, though, the tale is not about the character's character; that is, the story is not about who the character is.

Take, for example, the Indiana Jones movies. These are not character stories. The story is always about what Indiana Jones does, but never who he is. Jones faces many problems and adventures, but in the end, his role in society is exactly what it was before: part-time archaeology professor and full-time knight-errant.

By contrast, Carson McCullers's *The Member of the Wedding* is about a young girl's longing to change her role in the only community she knows—her household, her family. She determines that she wants to belong to her brother and his new wife; "they are the we of me," she decides. In the effort to become part of their marriage, she is thwarted—but in the process, her role in the family and in the world at large is transformed, and at the end of the story she is not who she was when she first began. *The Member of the Wedding* is a classic example of a character story.

The structure of a character story is as simple as any of the others. The story begins at the moment when the main character becomes so unhappy, impatient, or angry in her present role that she begins the process of change; it ends when the character either settles into a new role (happily or not) or gives up the struggle and remains in the old role (happily or not).

STRUCTURE 4: THE EVENT STORY

In the event story, something is wrong in the fabric of the universe; the world is out of order. In classic literature, this can include the appearance of a monster (*Beowulf*), the "unnatural" murder of a king by his brother (*Hamlet*) or of a guest by his host (*Macbeth*), the breaking of an oath (*Havelock the Dane*), the conquest of a Christian land by the infidel (*King Horn*), the birth of a child portent who some believe ought not to have been born (*Dune*), or the reappearance of a powerful ancient adversary who was thought to be dead (*The Lord of the Rings*). In all cases, a previous order—a "golden age"—has been disrupted and the world is in flux, a dangerous place.

The event story ends at the point when a new order is established or, more rarely, when the old order is restored or, rarest of all, when the world descends into chaos as the forces of order are destroyed. The story begins not at the point when the world becomes disordered, but rather at the point when the character whose actions are most crucial to establishing the new order becomes involved in the struggle. Hamlet doesn't begin with the murder of Hamlet's father; it begins much later, when the ghost appears to Hamlet and involves him in the struggle to remove the usurper and reestablish the proper order of the kingdom.

Almost all fantasy and much—perhaps most—science fiction uses the event story structure. Nowhere is it better handled than in J.R.R. Tolkien's great trilogy. The *Lord of the Rings* begins when Frodo discovers that the ring Bilbo gave him is the key to the overthrow of Sauron, the great adversary of the world's order; it ends not with the destruction of Sauron, but with the complete reestablishment of the new order—which includes the departure of Frodo and all other magical people from Middle-earth.

Notice that Tolkien does not begin with a prologue recounting all the history of Middle-earth up to the point where Gandalf tells Frodo what the ring is. He begins, instead, by establishing Frodo's domestic situation and then thrusting world events on him, explaining no more of the world than Frodo needs to know right at the beginning. We learn of the rest of the foregoing events bit by bit, only as the information is revealed to Frodo.

In other words, the viewpoint character, not the narrator, is our guide into the world situation. We start with the small part of the world that he knows and understands and see only as much of the disorder of the universe as he can. It takes many days—and many pages—before Frodo stands before the council of Elrond, the whole situation having been explained to him, and says, "I will take the ring, though I do not know the way." By the time a lengthy explanation is given, we have already seen much of the disorder of the universe for ourselves—the Black Riders, the hoodlums in Bree, the barrow wights—and have met the true king, Aragorn, in his disguise as Strider. In other words, by the time we are given the full explanation of the world, we already care about the people involved in saving it.

Too many writers of event stories, especially epic fantasies, don't learn this lesson from Tolkien. Instead, they imagine that their poor reader won't be able to understand what's going on if they don't begin with a prologue showing the "world situation." Alas, these prologues always fail. Because we aren't emotionally involved with any characters, because we don't yet care, the prologues are meaningless. They are also usually confusing, as a half-dozen names are thrown at us all at once. I have learned as a book reviewer that it's usually best to skip the prologue and begin with the story—as the author also should have done. I have never—not once—found that by skipping the prologue I missed some information I needed to have in order to read the story; and when I have read the prologue first, I have never—not once—found it interesting, helpful, or even understandable.

In other words, writers of event stories, don't write prologues. Homer didn't need to summarize the whole Trojan War for us; he began the *Iliad* with the particular, the private wrath of Achilles. Learn from Homer—and Tolkien, and all the other writers who have handled the event story well. Begin small, and only gradually expand our vision to include the whole world. If you don't let us know and care about the hero first, we won't be around for the saving of the world. There's plenty of time for us to learn the big picture.

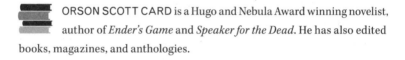 ORSON SCOTT CARD is a Hugo and Nebula Award winning novelist, author of *Ender's Game* and *Speaker for the Dead*. He has also edited books, magazines, and anthologies.

CHAPTER 37
INNOVATION IN HORROR

JEANNE CAVELOS

When I teach creative writing and ask my students what they believe their strengths and weaknesses are, almost all of them include creativity as a strength; almost none include it as a weakness.

As a result, few developing writers spend a lot of time and energy on *making* their work creative. They feel, by the very act of typing in words, they already are being "creative." After all, they are creating something new.

But there's the rub: How *new* is it?

Horror is a genre, a type of literature that has certain identifiable characteristics. When people who enjoy horror read your story, they are not reading it in a vacuum. They are reading it as part of a genre, constantly comparing your story to other horror stories they have read. If I have never read Edgar Allan Poe's "The Tell-Tale Heart" and I write a story very much like "The Tell-Tale Heart," readers who know Poe's story may not be as thrilled with my Big! Surprise! Ending! as I had hoped. To them, it's no surprise. They've read it before and they've read it better (you can't beat Poe).

To be a creative, innovative horror writer, you must read a lot of *everything*, and a lot of that everything must be horror. You may be thinking, How can I be creative and original with all those other authors' ideas floating around in my head? But this is critical: The sheer amount of material floating around in your head will prevent you from copying any one author.

Instead you will find a tiny piece of character from this book, a tiny piece of plot from that book, a certain stylistic technique from that other, which you will combine into something totally new. It is the writer who reads only Stephen King who will turn out stories that sound like Stephen King—on a very, very bad day.

If you can accept the need to know the horror writing that has gone before, you might still have difficulty with the idea of extensive reading *outside* the field. Simply by the law of averages, more great writing has been done outside the field of horror than within it. Another law of averages: The more great writing you read, the more will rub off on you. Read works from different periods of history, from different cultures. Read fiction and nonfiction. Many innovations arise from taking ideas outside the genre and bringing them in. Some of our favorite stories even mix genres.

When a story is innovative, it brings fresh ideas and techniques to the genre. It helps enlarge the genre and renew it. It helps keep the genre exciting and alive for future generations of readers. And it creates one hell of a great story.

INNOVATE OR IMITATE?

Why do so many people think John Carpenter's *Halloween* is a great movie? (I'm using a movie rather than a novel as an example because I think more of you will be familiar with a particular movie than a particular novel. But my point holds equally true for novels and stories.) If you watch it now, it may seem a rather tame and predictable slasher movie. But when it came out, nothing quite like it had ever been done before. It was intense, tightly plotted (the whole story takes place in one night), concerned itself very little with explanation (we have no idea why the killer goes after Jamie Lee Curtis with such determination), and had an incredible amount of suspense (every scene either had the killer in it or had in it evidence of something the killer had done, like a dead body). It didn't spend half of its length building up to killings, as so many movies of the day did. A murder occurs in the first five minutes. Each of these elements was not new, but this combination of them was, and it was very powerful, touching off a whole series of sequels and imitators. *Halloween* expanded and renewed the genre.

Stephen King has had a similar effect. He combined elements in a totally new way. Never before had classic horror archetypes, like the vampire (*Salem's Lot*) or the haunted house (*The Shining*), seemed so possible in our mundane, middle-class world. He brought these horrors down to earth, making them not the province of unstable minds and rarefied atmospheres, but of Anytown, U.S.A., in the plumber's house, the son's room, right under the bed. In the early 1980s, King had a huge impact on the genre, expanding and renewing it and spawning hordes of imitators. Even today his influence is strong on many developing horror writers; there are more than a few who believe that to write horror is to write "Stephen King horror"—since they've never read anything else they've liked.

The question is, do you want to be an innovator or an imitator? It's normal for young writers to be inspired by books or movies and to begin writing by emulating those sources. But horror that simply reflects the source that inspired it is not going to be rich and powerful; it's going to be a pale reflection of its source. A writer must take various sources of inspiration and filter them through his own unique sensibilities.

There are, of course, an infinite number of ways you can make your story innovative. Writing is a layered and complex process, and each story combines multiple elements. In creating new combinations and new patterns, you are innovating.

INNOVATIVE PLOTTING

What will the plot of your story be? What fear will it focus on? Many writers choose a plot by choosing a horror archetype to write about. Maybe you decide to write a vampire story, or a ghost story, or a serial killer story, or a zombie story. That's okay. These archetypes have developed and persisted over the years because they tap into our fears and have a strong, resonant effect on us. But they also present a serious challenge to today's writer: What is *your* vampire story going to do that no other vampire story has done before? (This is quite a question, considering how much material has been written about vampires.) What unique sensibility do you bring to a vampire story? If you don't have a powerful, significant difference to offer in your story, you probably shouldn't write it.

Maybe you decide to center your plot around a specific fear—one of *your* specific fears. This can be a wonderful technique, because if you are afraid of "it," chances are you can also make the reader afraid of it. But when I ask writers what they are afraid of, they usually come back with answers like "cockroaches." That's a perfectly valid answer, and if you are truly afraid of cockroaches, perhaps that can play a part in a story sometime.

But that's not a very deep-rooted fear. What I want to know is what frightens you at all levels, not only at the surface but at the deepest levels. That way, perhaps cockroaches cannot only be scary and gross, but can symbolize a deep fear, the fear, perhaps, of chaos, of forces beyond your control. Most of us fear this a lot more than we fear cockroaches. Don't just throw a ton of cockroaches in a story and assume your reader will be horrified (how many cockroaches are in a ton, anyway?). The cockroaches need to tie into a deeper fear: *Why* do they scare you so much? Becoming aware of the unique way that you see things and writing a story that reflects your unique sensibility is the key to writing innovative horror.

Once you have a basic concept for your story, you need to develop it into a plot. Now, the great thing about the horror genre is that, unlike other genres, it allows infinite possibilities. The horror genre has only one requirement for membership: The story must make the reader feel ... *horrified*. Many writers don't realize how revolutionary this is. In other genres, a fairly strict plot is imposed. In a mystery, a crime must occur, usually a murder, which must then be solved by the end of the story. In a romance, two people must meet and fall in love. But the plot of a horror story can be anything, as long as it makes the reader feel horror. So why is it that the plot of so many horror novels can be summarized like this?

> *Prologue:* Evil creature is awakened and kills one or more victims in spectacularly gruesome fashion.

Chapter 1: Introduction of thirty-something family man (often a writer) who's carrying around a problem from his past.

Chapters 2–15: Evil creature creeps into life of family man, killing numerous other victims on its way (in spectacularly gruesome fashion) and threatening members of the family man's family. The family's pet usually gets it at this point. Family man continues to suffer over problem from his past.

Chapters 16–19: Family man recognizes the threat of the evil creature, fights the evil creature, figures out the secret to killing it and triumphs, killing the creature in spectacularly gruesome fashion and simultaneously resolving his problem from the past.

Chapter 20: Family man and his family (minus pet) live happily ever after. Creature is dead (or is it . . ?).

If horror, as I said, puts no constraints on plot, why does this darned thing sound so familiar? As an editor, I have read this plot more times than I can count and many more than I want to remember. These days, any horror manuscript with a prologue makes an editor sigh in despair. Reading a lot in the field will help these old, tired patterns become more apparent to you. Then as a writer, you can decide to avoid them, or you can play off them, beginning your novel in a way that makes us think we know exactly what is going to happen and then surprising us by taking the plot in a totally different direction.

INNOVATIVE STYLE

So one important method of innovating comes from choosing and developing your plot, in deciding *what you are going to say.* The other method arises from deciding *how you are going to say it.* Your writing style, or your voice, reflects your personality, your beliefs, your concerns. In writing, you are commenting on life, the human condition. What do you believe? What do you want to say?

Just as each person has a distinctive speaking voice, a distinctive tone and timbre, a distinctive way of putting words together and certain preferred words, so do we each have a distinctive writing voice. This is often more difficult to develop. Beginning writers tend to write like the authors they have read. One of my students told me she would write like Stephen King when she was reading King, like Harlan Ellison when she was reading Ellison, and on and on. She had no style or voice of her own. And truth to tell, she wasn't really writing in King's style one week and Ellison's style the next (a writer could have worse problems). She was writing in a style that was a pale, inferior reflection of King's style, or Ellison's style, or ... . She could never write King's style as well as King, because King's style reflects who he is, how he thinks, and how he expresses himself. Your style, if it is to be *your* style, must do the same for you.

How you say something is just as important as *what* you say. Critics today bemoan the elevation of style over substance, but style is critically important in powerful and innovative writing. In fact, much of the innovation in horror in recent years has come in the area of style. While Stephen King introduced a style that was immediate, concrete, accessible, and down-to-earth, post-King authors are introducing literary, postmodern, experimental styles.

Perhaps you don't understand what I mean when I say style. In the following two passages, the plot is the same, but the style is very different. In other words, *what* is said remains the same, but *how* it is said changes drastically. Here's an example of a very familiar, overused style of horror writing:

> Colin stared at the razor, shiny and sharp, that Robert held above him. *OH MY GOD*, Colin thought. *HE'S GOING TO KILL ME!* The hairs on the back of his neck prickled.
>
> Robert prodded the knife into his neck. "I will kill you. I will leave no one alive to talk about me after I'm gone."
>
> Colin's brain sent an urgent message—*Push Robert out of the way! Scream! Do something!* But shock had frozen him still.
>
> Robert laughed, his breath an execrable stench hanging in the air like a cloud of corruption. He fixed Colin in his hypnotic gaze, the twin black orbs holding him immobile.

Colin realized sickeningly that he was helpless. *I'm going to die (oh God please help me God). I'm going to die! And when they're finished with me, they'll kill my beloved Mary!*

With a snarl of rage, his lips drawn back from his teeth, Robert brought the razor down across Colin's throat. He let out a demonic yell.

Colin's world went black.

I'm afraid I don't have the space here to tell you all that's weak and derivative and clichéd in the previous example, which I wrote myself, but if you've read a fair amount of horror, this probably sounds about as familiar to you as the plot outline I gave earlier. If something sounds quite familiar, then you know it's not innovative. Many developing writers, having grown up on the horror of the 1980s, think that this is the *only* way horror can be written.

Let me give you another example, this one by the fine author Ian McEwan from *The Comfort of Strangers*:

Mary was watching the object Robert clasped in his hand. Suddenly it was twice its length, and she saw it clearly, and though every muscle in her body tightened, only the fingers of her right hand clenched softly. She shouted, and shouted again, and all that left her was a whispering exhalation.

"I'll do whatever you want," Colin said, the level tone all lost now at the sound, his voice rising in panic. "But please get a doctor for Mary."

"Very well," Robert said and reached for Colin's arm, and turned his palm upward. "See how easy it is," he said, perhaps to himself, as he drew the razor lightly, almost playfully, across Colin's wrist, opening wide the artery. His arm jerked forward, and the rope he cast, orange in this light, fell short of Mary's lap by several inches.

Mary's eyes closed. When she opened them Colin was sitting on the floor, against the wall, his legs splayed before him. Curiously, his canvas beach shoes were soaked, stained scarlet. His head swayed upon his shoulders, but his eyes were steady and pure, and blazed at her across the room in disbelief. "Mary?" he said anxiously, like someone calling in a dark room.

"Mary? Mary?"

"I'm coming," Mary said. "I'm over here."

The main difference here, for the purposes of our discussion, is that the first author is trying to emulate the voices of other authors she has read; the second author is trying to reproduce his vision of life—and has developed his own voice to do so.

To get a better idea of the possibilities for innovation in horror, read these genre-stretching works: Patrick McCabe's *The Butcher's Boy*, Jennifer Lynch's *The Secret Diary of Laura Palmer*, Ian McEwan's *The Comfort of Strangers*, or Tim Lucas's *Throat Sprockets*.

Innovation is a critical component in any strong work of horror, and it does not come easily or automatically to us "creative" souls who write. Strive for innovation in your writing and never give up. If you can express what concerns you in a way that reflects your own unique sensibility, you are being truly innovative, and the horror you create will be truly special.

JEANNE CAVELOS is the former senior editor at Bantam Doubleday's Abyss horror imprint. She is the author of the best-selling Passing of the Techno-Mages trilogy, as well as the highly praised *The Science of Star Wars* and *The Science of the X-Files*.

CHAPTER 38
WRITE THIS, NOT THAT

BY ELIZABETH SIMS

Just as eating a balanced diet represents an endless series of good choices, so does writing a successful mystery. And just like anyone else, we authors are constantly tempted by junk. It's true: When crafting a story or chapter, you can opt for the cheap, first-thing-to-hand alternative, or you can push yourself toward something that may be less convenient, but that will ultimately be more fulfilling for both you and your readers.

Think of it this way: As an author, you're feeding your readers. Those readers come to a mystery hungry for certain elements, and they expect to feel satisfied at the end. They don't want formulaic, predictable stories that are the equivalent of fast food; they want substance, flavor, verve, and originality. If you want to keep them coming back for seconds, you need to nourish them with quality prose, cooked up with skill and caring.

Here's how to make smart choices in your writing (with apologies to the *Eat This, Not That* diet book) when it comes to the five key ingredients readers expect from a good mystery.

1. COINCIDENCES

Write This: A coincidence that arises organically from a solid plot.

In Richard Condon's *The Manchurian Candidate*, a crucial plot point is protagonist Ben Marco finding out that he isn't the only member of his platoon having strange recurrent nightmares about New Jersey garden club ladies who morph into Communist Chinese officers. This is key because it's the first evidence of the soldiers' brainwashing. Condon crafted the story so that Marco learns of another soldier's dreams when his platoon leader, Raymond Shaw, mentions a letter he received from the soldier. Better still, when Shaw reveals the key information in the letter, he does so without realizing its significance. The reader puts two and two together, right along with Marco—and is completely hooked. If Marco had just happened to meet another nightmare sufferer somehow, readers may have had a hard time suspending their disbelief.

Not That: A contrived coincidence that has nothing to do with what came before.

A prime example is the off-duty detective who just happens to be walking past the abandoned warehouse at the precise moment the torture gets going on the abducted coed.

How to Do It

Mystery writers are constantly tempted to solve a plot problem by putting in a coincidence. After all, mysteries tend to have complex plots, and complex plots are challenging to write.

Fortunately, readers love coincidences—provided they work. Life is full of real ones, so to turn your back on them in your writing would be to reject a reasonable plotting technique. The key is to generate realistic coincidences rather than contrived ones. So how do you do it?

You'll find that organic coincidences will suggest themselves if you populate your story with enough strong, varied characters. Let's say you have a damsel in distress, that coed in the warehouse, bound and gagged by the bad guy. You need this exciting scene; your plot hinges on her survival. Some of your most interesting possibilities hinge on the characters themselves. Take the bad guy, for instance. What if there's more than one?

What if one of them is holding a secret grudge against the leader? Can you immediately see where this could go?

Or, rather than drawing on your villains, say you want a hero to stop by and bust up the party. Make this more than a ploy to get your damsel out of trouble: Make it a real subplot that twines throughout the story.

For example, perhaps the building has been scheduled for an inspection. The inspector knows the building is a blight and has been fighting with the mayor to get it torn down; the bad guy knows the building is a perfect hideout. The plots about the inspector and the bad guy (who, let's say, were best friends in high school but haven't met in years) can be parallel and separate, with the building being the piece in common. This way, you can make both characters converge on the scene at the same time, resulting in a natural coincidence. Written just so, the arrival of the building inspector with the bolt cutters will make readers slap their foreheads and go, "Oh, *yeah,* the building inspection! Oh boy, what's gonna happen next?"

2. DYNAMIC DESCRIPTIONS

Write This: A description based in unconventional comparison.

"More cop cars pulled up, more cops came in, until it looked like they'd been spread on with a knife." (This from my first novel, *Holy Hell.*)

Not That: A description you've read a dozen times: "The place was crawling with cops." I almost think I became a crime fiction author so I could write whole books without using the sentence, "The place was crawling with cops," thus proving it can be done.

How to Do It

I believe many aspiring mystery writers fall into clichéd descriptions because of the genre's deep roots in pulp, work-for-hire, and cheap magazines. These outlets served, it must be admitted, less-than-discriminating audiences. (The Twinkie-eaters of mystery readers, metaphorically.) Today's mystery readers demand better.

Constantly be on the lookout for clichés in your writing. Welcome the occurrence of a cliché in your rough draft, because now you've got an opportunity to show off!

I learned from best-selling author Betty MacDonald (*The Egg and I,* among other golden oldies) to compare people with nonhuman entities, and nonhuman entities with people. She wrote things like, "As evening fell, the mountain settled her skirts over the forest." That's a great technique, a terrific cliché-buster.

Let's say you're describing a man who storms into a room, and you just wrote, "He was like a bull in a china shop." You stop in horror, hand to your mouth with the realization: *I have just written a cliché.*

Brainstorm other comparisons as well as other contexts for your description. What if he was like a garbage truck with no brakes? What if he was like a ballplayer driven insane by the worst call he'd ever seen? What if (simply describing what he does) he tears off his shirt, and the sound of the popping buttons is like a burst from an Uzi?

3. FALSE CLUES

Write This: A red herring that's built into the plot from the get-go.

Agatha Christie did it beautifully in her famous short story, "The Witness for the Prosecution," which later became a classic Billy Wilder film. The protagonist, Leonard Vole, is on trial for murder. He's a sympathetic character, and you find yourself rooting for him from the beginning. The evidence against him is circumstantial but heavy; even his wife testifies against him.

The wife is the red herring. She appears to be trying to send him to jail; she says she hates him and presents marvelous evidence for the prosecution. You begin to focus on her, wondering, *gosh, what's her angle?* Dame Agatha stokes your high suspicion. All of a sudden, however, Mrs. Vole's testimony is discredited, and Vole goes free. *Aha*, you think, *I was right: She had it in for him!*

But then (spoiler alert!), in a wonderful twisted ending, the wife reveals that she'd been working for that result all along; she herself provided the discrediting evidence, knowing the jury would be more easily manipulated that way. We learn that Vole had indeed committed the murder. Because our attention had been drawn to the wife, the heart-stopping moment we learn of Vole's guilt is the stuff mystery readers long for.

Not That: A false clue that's isolated.

In too many amateur mysteries, we get red herrings like a creepy next-door neighbor who turns out to be a good guy. You know you're being cheaply manipulated when you realize the neighbor has nothing to do with the plot; he simply appears to frighten us from time to time.

How to Do It

Mystery writers are always in need of red herrings to shake readers off the scent. A terrific test for these false clues is to ask yourself: "If I removed this clue from the story, would I have to change anything else to accommodate the cut?" If the answer is no, you've got some work to do.

Let's say you've got multiple suspects in your murder mystery. One is the proverbial creepy next-door neighbor who someone reports having heard arguing with the victim the night of the crime. (Of course, he'll later be revealed to be innocent.) This is a typical false clue to plant; readers have seen it before. So, why not expand the clue to give it some deeper roots—say, by making the argument part of a long-running feud, one that's now taken up by the victim's family members who've shown up for the funeral? Suddenly this isn't an isolated clue, but a part of the story.

You might also further consider the neighbor character himself. What if he is revealed to have been the victim's first husband? Did he kill her out of jealousy? Or did he rent the house next door so that he could protect her because he loved her so truly? This can turn an ordinary red herring into a satisfying subplot.

4. ACTION-PACKED DIALOGUE

Write This: Dialogue that arises from action, emotion, or necessity.

One of my favorite Arthur Conan Doyle stories is the Sherlock Holmes novel *The Valley of Fear*, which is packed with textbook dialogue. Here's the character Jack McMurdo responding with calculated disbelief to a workingman's offhanded comment that a gang called the Scowrers is a murderous bunch. Thus he goads the man into giving him specifics:

> The young man [McMurdo] stared. "Why, I am a member of that order myself."
>
> "You! I vould never had had you in my house if I had known it ..."
>
> "What's wrong with the order? It's for charity and good fellowship. The rules say so."
>
> "Maybe in some places. Not here!"

> "What is it here?"
>
> "It's a murder society, that's vat it is."
>
> McMurdo laughed incredulously. "How can you prove that?" he asked.
>
> "Prove it! Are there not 50 murders to prove it? Vat about Milman and Van Shorst, and the Nicholson family. ... Prove it! Is there a man or a voman in this valley vat does not know it?" ....
>
> ... "That's just gossip—I want proof!" said McMurdo.
>
> "If you live here long enough, you vill get your proof."

Not only does this passage give McMurdo the information he's looking for, it also advances the story in a natural way.

Not That: Dialogue in which one character tells another something they both already know, just so the reader can know it as well. We've all read stuff like this:

> Hero: "Hurry! We've got to move fast!"
>
> Sidekick: "How come?"
>
> Hero: "Because we've got to sabotage that convoy!"
>
> Sidekick: "You mean the one that's carrying 40,000 gallons of deadly radioactive bacteria straight toward the vulnerable entry point in the New York City water system?"
>
> Hero: "Exactly! Yes!"

Ludicrous, no?

How to Do It

Weak dialogue in mystery can often be pinned on the easy habit of telling too much too soon. Did you notice that in the above example, McMurdo learns a lot (and tells a lot about himself) simply from the way he *reacts* to something the other man said? Having a character make friends with another for a specific purpose can work well; the reader can pick up on the manipulation and enjoy it.

Masterful writers have long known that emotion is a great dialogue engine. When a character is outraged, or dying to get laid, or seeking pity or admiration, that's when she might let something slip, or unleash a whole tirade, which can trigger explosive action, be it a counter-tirade from another character, violence, flight, you name it.

You can engineer a juicy hunk of dialogue by writing down the result you want, then setting up a convincing sequence of events for the characters to reach that point. Expect dialogue to be a springboard for your characters.

And finally, here's a rule of thumb I've found transformative: *When in doubt, cut the talk.*

5. CHARACTER MOTIVATIONS

Write This: Characters motivated by almost unbearable forces.

In "The Monkey's Paw" by W.W. Jacobs, one of the most perfect short stories ever written—and one of the scariest—maternal grief is the reason Mrs. White interferes with fate and meddles with the terrible three-wish charm.

After receiving this supposedly magic paw and wishing upon it for two hundred pounds sterling, she and her husband come into the money, but they are horrified to get it as compensation for the death of their son Herbert, who is mangled to death at work. Mrs. White, deep in grief, finds the paw and wishes for her son to be alive again. Mr. White, however, saw what was left of Herbert, and now Herbert's been in his grave for a week, and now something is pounding at the front door, and there's one more wish left in the paw.

Not That: Character motivation that boils down to … not enough.

"So, exactly why is this character risking his marriage, his children, and his career as a doctor by serially murdering mafia chieftains?" I once asked a student in a mentoring session.

"Um, see, he wants to keep the streets safe."

Wanting to help strangers may be a plausible motivation for lying, but not enough for murder.

How to Do It

Making your characters take drastic risks is good, but this works only if their motivations are rock-solid. In fact, the biggest favor a good agent or editor or writing group will do for you is challenge your character motivations. Internal motivation can work, but external motivation is better.

For example, it's conceivable a cop or a P.I. could risk his life to find the truth because he loves the truth—but if the truth involves finding out why his partner was murdered in cold blood, as Sam Spade felt driven to do in Dashiell Hammett's *The Maltese Falcon*, now you've got something.

Do like Hammett did: Combine motivating factors. Not simply love, not simply money, but love *and* money. Hate and glory. Envy and shame. Sex and loss.

The possibilities are limitless. And, as with so many of the healthy choices listed above, you'll find substantial combinations to be much more satisfying than quick and easy fixes. Feed your readers with them well, and they'll keep coming back for more.

 ELIZABETH SIMS (elizabethsims.com) is the author of the Rita Farmer mysteries and Lillian Byrd mysteries.

CHAPTER 39
THE WHO IN WHODUNITS

BY J.A. JANCE

Even though I was never allowed in a college-level creative writing class, I did pick up that age-old golden rule of writing: Write what you know. So how does someone who has never been a cop or a lawyer know enough to write murder mysteries?

Part of the answer, of course, lies in doing research—in talking to law-enforcement officers, reading law-enforcement manuals, and keeping up with current events. (For example, I discovered that Freon smuggling is big business on the U.S./Mexico border by reading about it in *The Wall Street Journal*.)

Doing that kind of research, however, is only part of the answer—the easy part. The rest of it comes from living life. True, my characters Sheriff Joanna Brady and Detective J. P. Beaumont are both law-enforcement officers, but they're people first. In order to make my characters seem like living, breathing people, it's my job—the author's job—to know everything about them.

I'll be the first to admit that my characters are an outgrowth of everything I am and everything I've done. I learned to be a detective by having a houseful of adolescent children. My working career may not have included any stints in law enforcement, but I have been a teacher, a librarian, an insurance agent, and a mother. All of those occupations require people skills, and knowing how people think and work is essential to creating believable characters. After all, characters are people, too. At least they should be.

PEOPLE INTO PLOT

When it's time for me to start a book, the first thing I have to come to terms with are the people involved in the story. Once I know who they are and what made them that way, then I'm able to place them in fictional situations, all the while understanding how and why the characters behave as they do. For me, plot evolves from character, not the other way around.

With Joanna Brady, for example, in writing *Desert Heat*, I found myself launching a new series having already written nine Detective Beaumont books. I met Joanna at the same place my readers did, having a conversation with her daughter. Joanna and Jenny are sitting in the breakfast nook of their cozy ranch house, waiting for Joanna's husband to come home and take Joanna out for their tenth-anniversary dinner. Jenny, a precocious nine and a half, asks her mother whether or not she was a preemie since the required nine months between her parents' wedding and Jenny's birthday had been shortened to six. Faced with this disturbing question, Joanna has no choice but to answer truthfully, and she does.

That conversation told me several things about Joanna Brady, the most important of which was that she wasn't perfect. Headstrong and opinionated, she and Andy are still living with their small-town lives tainted by the shame of having had a shotgun wedding. The fact that Joanna doesn't dodge the issue let me know that she was a good mother, one who cared enough and had the moral fortitude to tell the truth even when the truth made her uncomfortable.

All those traits taken together—Joanna's everyday honesty, her straightforward way of looking at life, her willingness to acknowledge her own infallibility, her resilience—serve her in good stead in the hours and days ahead when Andy's shooting and eventual death plunge her into an entirely different life. Even so, several chapters into the book, I was still struggling to understand her when I came upon a pivotal scene.

Joanna and her best friend, Marianne Maculyea, are in a hospital waiting room where they have just been told that Joanna's wounded husband has pulled through surgery but is still in critical condition. The doctor suggests the two women go somewhere to sleep. Refusing to leave the hospital, Joanna and Marianne prepare to bed down for the night in the hospital waiting room. Struggling with her own fear, Joanna asks Marianne to pray for her. Marianne does so, reciting the words of comfort found in a simple childhood prayer.

Those words appeared through a veil of tears. In that moment, I realized that I really knew who those two women were. I understood what made the two of them tick as well as the depth of their friendship. Six books later, I'm confident that I still do.

When I sit down to write a Joanna Brady book, I have to think about what's happened to her in the previous books and how those events may have changed and influenced her. I also have to know about her life prior to the books. I think part of what makes Joanna believable and likable is the fact that she doesn't remain static. She changes from book to book. She learns from her mistakes even as she makes new ones. After all, learning from mistakes is part of what makes people human.

STRAW INTO FICTIONAL GOLD

For me, in order to create believable characters, I need to feel strongly about them one way or the other. While attending the University of Arizona in 1964, the creative writing professor wouldn't allow me in any of his classes because I was a girl. I've never forgotten what he told me: "Girls become teachers or nurses. Boys become writers."

Those words had a profound effect on my life. When that professor walked into one of my books nearly twenty years later, it's hardly surprising that it was in the guise of Andrew Philip Carlisle, the crazed killer in my psychological thriller, *Hour of the Hunter*. Carlisle, a former creative writing professor from the University of Arizona, returns to Tucson looking for the two women who sent him to prison six years earlier. As a writer, it was easy for me to turn my old nemesis into a terrifying character—easy and gratifying both.

The same thing could be said for the dead dentist in Beaumont number five, *Improbable Cause*. He's dead on the first page for no other reason than the fact that one of the few dentists in my hometown didn't believe in using Novocain.

In the early seventies, my life was touched and changed by a chance encounter with a real-life serial killer. Over a period of several months, I watched a Pima County homicide detective grab hold of that case with a such a fierce tenacity and concentration that even his twenty-year marriage couldn't compete and survive. When it came time to write my first mystery, I used that detective as a model for J.P. Beaumont.

Beau first walked into my books in *Until Proven Guilty* to investigate the death of a child. Angel Barstogi had been strangled and her remains tossed into an overgrown blackberry bramble in Seattle's Discovery Park. By the time readers first meet Beau, his marriage has already fallen victim to both his job and to his ongoing love affair with booze. As he follows the case to its conclusion, Beau is drawn into the orbit of the haunting and mysterious Anne Corley, whose profound impact on his life changes everything that happens to him after that—in thirteen books and counting.

Like Joanna Brady, J.P. Beaumont isn't static. He, too, changes over time and from book to book. His battle with the bottle, his difficulties with keeping and losing partners, his disdain for the "brass" upstairs, along with his gradual reconciliation with his family all serve to make him seem "real" both to me and to readers.

In writing about Joanna Brady, it helps that I know what it's like to be a struggling single mother. With J.P. Beaumont, I write with the dubious benefit of having spent eighteen years of my life living with a man who subsequently died of chronic alcoholism at age forty-two. For Diana Ladd in *Hour of the Hunter*, I drew on my frustration at being cornered into teaching school when what I really wanted to do with my life was write.

Seeing how those realities turn up in my books makes me feel a bit like Rumplestiltskin: I take the straw from my life and spin it into gold—gold with a very strong basis in reality. And the truth is, that reality is important to me. If it doesn't seem "real" to me, I can't write it.

CARING ABOUT YOUR CHARACTERS

I once read a series of unpublished manuscripts for a writers conference. In one of the manuscripts—purportedly an intergalactic murder mystery—none of the ethnic-sounding names given to the characters seemed to jibe with who they were or how they behaved. When I questioned the author about this, he told me, quite seriously, that he'd written the story using words like *Protagonist* and *Villain* and *Officers One, Two, and Three*, then went back and used his computer's search-and-replace command to name the characters.

I tried to explain to him that it hadn't worked. I wanted him to understand that, as the author, it was his responsibility to know everything about his characters before he started to write. He needed to know about their favorite foods, their relationships with their parents and siblings, where they went to school, and whether or not they attended Boy Scouts or CYO when they were kids. I hope the young writer heard what I was telling him, but I doubt it. His next question was, "But is it still publishable?" The truth is, his story wasn't publishable—far from it.

The author's responsibility goes far beyond simply naming. Caring is also essential, and that goes for minor characters every bit as much as it does for major ones. Several years ago, a good friend of mine was killed by a drunk driver. After years of effort, her husband finally saw to it that her killer was sentenced to prison—for a total of sixteen months, with time off for good behavior. At the time, I was getting ready to write Joanna Brady number four, *Dead to Rights*.

The real-life situation so offended me that I had to put a drunk driver who gets a judicial slap on the wrist into my book. What happens in the story isn't exactly what happened to my friends, but it's close enough that I'm moved to tears by it, and so are my readers. It's hardly surprising that when we next see the drunk driver, he's back at home and getting on with his life. It's also not surprising that he doesn't make it through the second chapter of the book.

The lesson I learned from that situation is that, as a writer, I may have an obligation to "care" about my victims, but I sure as hell don't have to like them. Once the drunk driver was dead, then it was simply a matter of choosing the right killer from among the several people who, justifiably or not, wanted the man dead.

FROM WRITER TO DETECTIVE

Some writers begin their books by doing detailed outlines of all the action. If that works for them, fine, but it doesn't work for me. I've never mastered the art of outlining, perhaps because I have an abiding distrust of Roman numerals. I usually start with someone dead and then try to get a grip on the various people involved in the story. That goes for the killers and victims as much as it does for the detectives investigating the case. I can't write believably about a murderer until I understand that person's motivation for taking the life of another human being.

Sometimes while I'm writing, the story will grind to a halt partway through. I sometimes refer to this phenomenon as my "Chapter Eleven Wall." Over the years, I've come to understand that if a story stops and won't move beyond a certain point, it probably means I have a problem with one or more of my characters' motivations. Once I go back and tweak the motivations, or look around and find the character who "really" did it, then the story gets back on track.

How does one go about "tweaking" a character? You think about him, day and night. Sometimes for hours on end. That kind of concentrated and specific thinking counts as some of the hardest work I do in the job because often it requires me to do the unthinkable—to change my mind. Revising text is child's play compared with the hard work of rethinking, but that's how I sometimes arrive at the conclusion that the person I originally thought was the killer didn't do it.

When that happens, I have my own opportunity to play detective. I look through my cast of characters. Finding the real culprit gives me an essential "eureka!" experience. Maybe people who do detailed outlines have those same exhilarating moments of discovery, but it seems to me they would be harder to come by if the writer knew in advance everything that was going to happen.

With no formal training in writing but with an extensive background in reading and a good foundation in grammar and spelling, I started my writing career in March 1982. My first book never saw the light of day. My second book was accepted and published by the second editor who saw it. *Rattlesnake Crossing*, published in July 1998, was my twentieth book. Three more are written and not yet published with six more under contract beyond that. This far into my career, I have some confidence that once I start a book, I will be able to finish it. Part of that confidence comes from what I now regard as the Amended Golden Rule of Writing: Write what you know, and know your characters best of all.

 J.A. JANCE's newest books are *Trial by Fire* and *Fire and Ice*.

CHAPTER 40
WRITING KILLER SUSPENSE

BY CAROL DAVIS LUCE

You're about to begin a scene in your story that you hope will set your readers' hearts racing. This scene takes special care to execute. This is a ... *suspense scene.*

By the time readers get to this scene, you've already laid the groundwork for conflict (you'd better have, anyway). Through dialogue, narrative, and actions, readers have been primed to expect a confrontation of some kind, somewhere. And now it's time to deliver. You want to do it right. You want to pull it off. Want to know how? I won't keep you in suspense.

TENSION COMPREHENSION

Tension is the act of building or prolonging a crisis. It's the bump in the night, the ticking bomb; it's making readers aware of peril. (A baby strays from its mother and toddles onto the railroad tracks. Tension begins when, in the distance, a train whistle is heard. *High tension* occurs when the baby plops down in the center of the tracks and begins to play.)

To write effective suspense, you need not see menace in every corner. But you must be aware of the potential threat of menace. You—and, through you, your readers—must feel the tension. As you set the scene, sense the danger, and anticipate the perilous outcome.

Use the following techniques to set your scenes aquiver.

THE "BIG BANG" TECHNIQUE

One way to write a dramatic, tension-filled scene is with the element of surprise. The big bang is just that. The scene appears innocuous:

Our protagonist is enjoying a pleasant walk in the woods when BANG! Disaster strikes. Both protagonist and reader are jolted by the sudden attack. With the big bang, the big moment begins and ends with the bang. This type of scene lacks genuine suspense, which is best built slowly. It is, however, extremely effective when used sparingly. Use it too much and readers won't be shocked for long—they'll feel cheated. And they'll come to expect these explosions, which is certain death when trying to lay the ground work for suspense. In fact, I'm mentioning it first here so we can get it out of the way and move to much more effective techniques.

THE "JACK-IN-THE-BOX" TECHNIQUE

I prefer to take readers slowly and steadily along the dark and sinister path of suspense, allowing them to experience firsthand the sights, sounds, smells, and pending peril. The jack-in-the-box technique beats the bang because it builds suspense. To maximize the suspense you must emphasize the tension (bring it to a higher level); you must stretch readers' stress and emotions.

It's those critical moments before Jack the clown springs from the box that generate high tension. We turn the crank, the music plays, we know he's coming ... we just don't know when. Think of building suspense this way: Blow up a balloon in front of some friends. Inflating it is a simple, nonthreatening action—anyone can do it. But when the balloon appears to be fully inflated, keep on going. Now, in a deliberate manner, you've taken it beyond a nonthreatening act, and those watching will begin to feel a sense of uneasiness. Apprehension. Tension. With each breath, their tension increases. Bracing for the inevitable does no good, for when the bang finally comes, everyone jumps. And once it's over, the relief is obvious. The tension has burst along with the balloon.

Although the balloon was filled with nothing more than hot air, it's the premeditation, along with the obvious intent to inflict a certain amount of suffering, that makes for high tension. Fill your balloon with trepidation and you will turn something that bobs merrily in the wind into something that grabs you by the throat and won't let go.

In a suspense novel, stretch these jack-in-the-box scenes to different degrees. Do this by varying the pace. The suspense can be quick or it can be drawn out, depending on how fast or slow you want the crank to turn. Too quick and the tension is gone before it even begins. Too drawn out and the tension dissipates through sheer tedium. If too much time passes from the point when you first introduce the threat to the actual execution of that threat, readers may simply forget about the initial threat, thus destroying the dramatic tension.

And sometimes attempts at generating suspense fall apart completely. In my novel *Skin Deep*, I wrote a scene where a killer with a straight razor, wearing a ski mask and gloves, breaks into the heroine's apartment and hides in her bedroom closet. The heroine, true to the story line, comes home and soon enters the bedroom (the tension builds; readers know he's behind that door, waiting to pounce). She begins to unbutton her blouse as she moves toward the closet. She reaches out, places her hand on the knob and ... .

In an early draft of this scene, I had my heroine abruptly turn and leave the room, leave the apartment even, to visit a friend downstairs. Still in the closet, our killer sweats it out in his wool ski mask and thick leather gloves until she finally returns some time later to begin the chain of events all over again. The only death here was the death of any suspense I'd started to build.

The scene was changed in the final draft to let the action flow uninterrupted. Also, to further enhance the suspense, I had the heroine's "peril detector" kick in just as she reaches for the doorknob. Something (a gut feeling, perhaps) tells her she is in danger. Readers experience first her trepidation, then her terror, as she turns to run.

And that "peril detector" is important. In another novel (not mine, this time) a killer stakes out the heroine's nightly route and waits in the shadows for his chance. On three occasions (three times!) the heroine strolls within several yards of her attacker-to-be yet manages to avoid any confrontation. Each time she comes a little closer, but one thing or another keeps her out of harm's way.

The serious suspense flaw here lies not only with repetition without repercussion, but that the heroine never sensed she was in any danger.

It made her appear too lucky for words and made the killer appear foolish and inept. Too-lucky heroines and too-inept killers will have readers reaching for the light switch.

Remember, you might get away with something like this once, possibly twice, but never three times.

THE "SHIFTY EYES" TECHNIQUES

Shifting from scene to scene and from viewpoint to viewpoint often increases tension. Switching from the antagonist (the bad guy) to the protagonist (the good guy) can effectively set up the forthcoming conflict. It works best if the scenes are kept short. This technique should be used only in setting up the conflict, such as bringing the two 'tagonists together in a direct confrontation. Here's how it works:

> Scene A: The protagonist is in her car, driving home.

> Scene B: The antagonist breaks into the protagonist's house. (You can show his sinister intent through an action, such as his killing a pet or breaking a cherished antique.)

> Scene C: The protagonist arrives home and enters her house.

At this point, the remaining action is carried out in one scene, one viewpoint, preferably the protagonist's.

Early in my novel *Night Stalker*, heroine Alex Carlson is aware that she's being stalked (anonymous calls, a break-in, threats, and so on) by a psychopath. She lives alone in a secluded hillside house, and to make matters worse, she's afraid of the dark. The scene played out like this:

> Antagonist's point of view:
> He worked the glove off his right hand with his teeth, then pulled the butane lighter from his pants pocket ... . The phone rang ... . Between the first and second ring he heard her key in the lock. He stepped back into the dim recesses of Alex Carlson's painting alcove.

> Protagonist's point of view:

Alex shifted the grocery bag to her left hip and opened the door. The telephone rang again as she hurried downstairs to the study ... . [Following a brief telephone conversation, Alex hears a soft click on the line after her friend hangs up.] Goose bumps rose along her arms. Standing at the desk, the grocery bag clasped tightly to her chest, she shivered. The click on the line, she tried to assure herself, had been Greg's secretary—nothing more.

THE "THROUGH YOUR EYES ONLY" TECHNIQUE

If you're using a strict first-person viewpoint, you can build suspense by planting "clues" through your protagonist. It can be as simple as hearing a click on the line, as Alex did, and going from there. Suppose that after hanging up the phone, Alex feels a chilling breeze at her back. She notices an open window that she was certain she'd closed before going out. On the table by the window, a small potted plant lies on its side. The wind? The cat? Alex's "peril detector" begins to kick in. She remembers that Greg's secretary is out of town; if someone picked up the line, it had to be someone in her own house. On the floor above she hears footsteps, followed by the soft thunk of the dead bolt on the front door being engaged. And then the lights go out ... .

Alex's own trepidation fuels the tension for the scene. Her ensuing terror after the lights go out (she knows now the killer is in the house with her) will propel the tension to its climactic end.

Study scenes in suspense movies, too. In *Sleeping With the Enemy*, protagonist Sara Burney, an abused wife, has staged her own death to escape from her deranged husband. She changes her identity and moves to a small town to start over. But she can't stop looking over her shoulder. We watch as the husband gets closer and closer, wreaking havoc as he goes. And just when Sara begins to feel safe, he finds her. Remember the chilling scene where Sara is reclining in the bathtub, all bad thoughts cleared from her mind by thoughts of her new love? That's when suddenly she notices that all the towels and washcloths (her husband was phobic about neatness and order) are in perfect alignment. Her worst fears are confirmed when she sees all the canned goods in the kitchen are similarly arranged. He knows she is alive. He knows where she lives. He's been in her house. Where is he now?

Even animals can be utilized to convey a sense of doom. Here's the protagonist's cat in *Night Stalker.*

> Alone in the house now, Blackie paced fitfully, his tail twitching in spasmodic bursts. He jumped onto the counter, jumped down. He scratched at the glass of the slider, meowing. Suddenly he stopped, his body stiff. With ears pointed and alert, he looked upward, listening. His tail bristled. Then, even more agitated, he resumed his scratching at the glass door.

Cats, killers in closets, and balloons stretching to bursting. Suspense is a state of mind. How you build that suspense can make the difference between your readers chucking your book for a good night's sleep or nudging their spouse to say, "the suspense is killing me."

 CAROL DAVIS LUCE has published a number of suspense novels with Zebra Books. Her latest is *Night Passage.*

CHAPTER 41
CLUES, RED HERRINGS, & MISDIRECTION

BY HALLIE EPHRON

Investigation is the meat and potatoes of mystery fiction. The sleuth talks to people, does research, snoops around, and makes observations. Facts emerge. Maybe an eyewitness gives an account of what he saw. A wife has unexplained bruises on her face. The brother of a victim avoids eye contact with his questioner. A will leaves a millionaire's estate to an obscure charity. A bloody knife is found in a laundry bin. A love letter is discovered tucked into last week's newspaper.

Some facts will turn out to be clues that lead to the killer's true identity. Some will turn out to be red herrings—evidence that leads in a false direction. On top of that, a lot of the information your sleuth notes will turn out to be nothing more than the irrelevant minutiae of everyday life inserted into scenes to give a sense of realism and camouflage the clues.

THE INVESTIGATION: OBSERVING AND INTERROGATING

Asking questions and observing are any sleuth's main investigational activities. If your sleuth is a professional detective or police officer, investigating might include examining the crime scene, questioning witnesses, staking out suspects, pulling rap sheets, checking DMV records, and going undercover. If your sleuth is a medical examiner, we're talking autopsies and X-rays, MRIs, and DNA analysis. If your character is an amateur sleuth, it's going to be about sneaking around, asking a lot of questions, and cozying up to the police.

How your sleuth investigates should reflect his skills and personality quirks. Take the extreme example of TV sleuth Adrian Monk. A former star detective, Monk was traumatized after the murder of his wife. Now he has an extreme case of obsessive-compulsive disorder and is plagued by an abnormal fear of everything from germs to heights. His obsessions lend a comic touch to the stories, but his compulsive attention to detail is the hallmark of his investigative technique, enabling him to notice what police investigators miss.

Our character, Peter Zak, is a psychologist. He doesn't know beans about fingerprints or blood spatter. He knows behavior, so he's a keen observer of people, and psychological tests are part of his interrogation arsenal. Here's an example from *Amnesia* where Peter uses a "mental status test" to question Marie Whitson, a patient who is suffering delirium from a self-administered drug overdose. As you read the excerpt, think about how dialogue and observation fuel investigation, and try to spot the possible clues in the passage.

Think about:

- Dialogue—how are questions used to drive the scene?
- Observation—how do physical details, gestures, and body language add information?
- Clues—what sticks out as potential clues?

Excerpt from *Amnesia*

"Ms. Whitson? Could you put your right hand on top of your head?"

A hand floated upward and rested on top of her head. White lines scarred her wrist. Her head tilted sideways. She met my eyes. Then her gaze shifted to the faces of my colleagues and on to the flat, gray expanse of a window shade. The hand remained planted on top of her head.

"Ms. Whitson, could you wave your left hand and stick out your tongue?"

Now a definite smile appeared. Her lips parted and the tip of her tongue emerged. But the right hand on her head and the left one in her lap remained still.

I went through the other silly-sounding questions designed to take an instant picture of that mish-mash we refer
to as mental status. Near the end, although I already knew the
answer, I asked, "Have you ever thought about taking your own
life?" This got her attention. She jerked slightly and then narrowed her eyes. I waited, wondering if she trusted me enough
to answer.

Hesitantly, she nodded.

...

Finally, I asked her, "Do you feel safe here?"

Slowly and deliberately, she nodded. A smile tugged at
the corners of her lips. It was an odd moment. I had the distinct
impression that she was enjoying a little private joke.

This excerpt demonstrates some pointers to keep in mind as you
write investigation:

- Make interrogation physical as well as verbal. Did you notice
  that Maria Whitson doesn't say much? Peter asks questions and
  notes her responses; more importantly, he observes her gestures,
  facial expressions, and demeanor. When your sleuth investigates,
  be sure to dramatize the body language he observes.

- Don't spoon-feed the reader. You don't have to explain the significance of every fact uncovered. For instance, Peter notices,
  White lines scarred her wrist. He doesn't give the reader the
  obvious news bulletin: This character has survived a suicide
  attempt. It's not necessary. Remember, your reader wants to
  solve the puzzle, too. So let the reader do some of the work.

- Establish the to-be-connected dots. There should be details that
  make your sleuth sit up and take notice but leave questions unanswered. For example, Maria nods when Peter asks if she feels
  safe. Then Peter thinks: *I had the distinct impression that she
  was enjoying a little private joke.* It's a tantalizing observation,
  and the reader and the sleuth tuck it away. Later, that observation pays off. So as your character investigates, establish the
  dots that you'll later connect.

- Nip and tuck—summarize to avoid monotony. Real psychological tests can take hours to administer. Notice how we summarized to shorten the testing scene: *I went through the other silly-sounding questions designed to take an instant picture of that mish-mash we refer to as mental status.* Many aspects of real investigations—crime scene examination, interrogations, stakeouts, fingerprint analysis, and so on—are painstaking and time-consuming. Abbreviate. Dramatize the interesting parts, and write only enough detail to make the investigation feel real.

- Stay out of the future. Notice that the point-of-view character stays in the moment. There's no sudden flash of 20/20 foresight: "If I'd known what was going to happen, I never would have left her alone in that room." Writers sometimes do this, thinking that it heightens suspense, but in fact it can rob a story of its surprise.

CREATING CHARACTER DYNAMICS IN THE Q&A

Whether your sleuth schmoozes over tea with the victim's neighbor, makes telephone calls to witnesses, formally interrogates a suspect, or huddles with colleagues to discuss blood spatter, your sleuth asks questions and gets answers. Talk, talk, talk. It can get pretty boring if all you're doing is conveying information. By creating a dynamic between the characters during the Q&A, your story continues to hold the reader's interest.

Take this example of investigation from Laura Lippman's *By a Spider's Thread.* PI Tess Monaghan questions her client.

> "How much do you know about him if he didn't participate in the group?"
>
> "Baltimore's Jews live in a small village, especially those of us in the clothing business. There's lots of gossip we keep to ourselves, so people in the city at large won't cluck their tongues. It was shocking, seeing Nat go to prison."
>
> "Did you know him before he went in?"

"After a fashion." Rubin gave her a lopsided smile.

"The pun was intended."

"Only it wasn't really a pun," Tess said.

"Excuse me?"

"It was a play on words, but it wasn't a pun, which involves changing a word in some way so it takes on a double meaning." It was fun, correcting Rubin for once.

"You know, Mexican weather report—chili today—"

"Hot tamale. Groucho Marx." He moved his eyebrows up and down, wiggling an imaginary stogie.

Interrogation becomes interesting when the relationship between the characters has some kind of electrical charge, some inner dynamic, as it does here. Tess asks questions (*How much did you know about him..?*) Her client gives evasive and misleading answers (*after a fashion*) because he's unwilling to face certain truths himself. But what makes this scene work is the dynamic between the characters. There's mental sparring (*... it wasn't really a pun ...*) and humor (he imitates Groucho Marx) as their relationship shifts at this point in the novel from adversarial to cautious, mutual appreciation.

It's all in the subtext. The relationship between characters makes this investigation dialogue interesting—the clues that get conveyed are a bonus.

MIXING UP THE CLUES AND RED HERRINGS

A clue can be just about anything: An object the sleuth discovers (a bloody glove). The way a character behaves (keeps his hands in his pockets). A revealing gesture (a woman straightens a man's collar). What someone says ("Julia Dalrymple deserved to die"). What someone wears (a locket stolen from the victim). An item that doesn't fit with the way the person presents himself or his history (a suspect's fingerprint lifted from a room that the suspect says she was never in).

Here are some techniques that enable you to play fair and, at the same time, keep the reader guessing:

- Emphasize the unimportant; de-emphasize the clue. The reader sees the clue but not what's important about it. For example, the sleuth investigates the value and provenance of a stolen painting and pays little attention to the identity of the woman who sat for the portrait.

- Establish a clue before the reader can know its significance. Introduce the key information before the reader has a context to fit it into. For example, the sleuth strolls by a character spraying her rose bushes before a neighbor is poisoned by a common herbicide.

- Have your sleuth misinterpret the meaning of a clue. Your sleuth can make a mistake that takes the investigation to a logical dead end. For example, the victim is found in a room with the window open. The sleuth thinks that's how the killer escaped and goes looking for a witness who saw someone climbing down the side of the house. In fact, the window was opened to let out tell-tale fumes.

- Have the clue turn out to be what isn't there. The sleuth painstakingly elucidates what happened, failing to notice what should have happened but didn't. The most famous example is from the Sherlock Holmes story "Silver Blaze." Holmes deduces there could not have been an intruder because the dog didn't bark.

- Scatter pieces of the clue in different places and mix up the logical order. Challenge your reader by revealing only part of a clue at a time. For instance, a canary cage with a broken door might be found in the basement along with other detritus; later the sleuth has a "wait a minute!" realization when he discovers the dead canary with its neck wrung.

- Hide the clue in plain sight. Tuck the clue among so many other possible clues that it doesn't stand out. For example, the nylon stocking that was the murder weapon might be neatly laundered and folded in the victim's lingerie drawer. Or the sleuth focuses on the water bottle, unopened mail, pine needles, and gas station receipt on the floor of the victim's car and fails to recognize the significance of a telephone number written in the margin of the map.

- Draw attention elsewhere. Have multiple plausible alternatives vying for the reader's attention. For example, the sleuth knows patients are being poisoned. He focuses on a doctor who gives injections and fails to notice the medic who administers oxygen (toxic germs can be administered in a nebulizer attached to an oxygen tank).

- Create a time problem. Manipulate time to your own advantage. For example, suppose the prime suspect has an alibi for the time of the murder. Later the sleuth discovers that the time of the alibi or the time of death is wrong.

- Put the real clue right before a false one. People tend to remember what was presented to them last. For example, your sleuth notices that the stove doesn't go on properly, and immediately after that discovers an empty bottle marked "poison" wrapped in newspaper stuffed in with the trash. Readers (and your sleuth) are more likely to remember the hidden poison bottle than the malfunctioning stove that preceded it.

- Camouflage a clue with action. If you show the reader a clue, have some extraneous action happen at the same time to distract attention. For example, your sleuth gets mugged while reading a flyer posted on a lamppost; the mugging turns out to be irrelevant, but the flyer turns out to contain an important clue.

DON'T CHEAT

You can't withhold from the reader information that a point-of-view character knows. The reader and the sleuth should realize the identity of the culprit at the same time. So how do you keep the mystery from unraveling before the end of your story?

Along the way, your sleuth can be bamboozled, blindsided, only partially informed, or flat-out wrong. What I find infuriating is when an author withholds, even temporarily, some important piece of information that the point-of-view character knows.

Why do authors do it? To create suspense. But it's cheating. Not only that, it breaks character as the author intrudes by withholding information. I know, I know, mystery authors get away with this kind of shtick all the time and laugh all the way to the bank. But it's a cheap trick, and my advice: Don't succumb.

This is why guilty narrators are problematic in a mystery. They know too much. Some mystery writers manage to pull off a guilty narrator by keeping the character's identity hidden. But it's cheating to spend chapter after chapter in a character's head, only to reveal in a final climactic scene that she's been hiding one small detail: She did it. You might get away with it if the character turns out to be an unreliable narrator who can't remember (amnesia?), doesn't realize (delusional? naïve? simple minded?), or refuses to admit even to herself that she's guilty.

CONFUSION: INTEREST KILLER

Your goal is to misdirect, but never to confuse. Lead the reader down a series of perfectly logical primrose paths—your reader must always feel grounded, even if it's on a false path. Set too many different possible scenarios spinning at once, or overwhelm your reader with a cacophony of clues, red herrings, and background noise, and your baffled reader will get frustrated and set the book aside … permanently.

As you write, keep track of the different scenarios and the clues that implicate and exonerate each suspect. Also, be sure to keep track of who knows what—particularly if you're writing from multiple viewpoints.

COINCIDENCE: CREDIBILITY KILLER

All of us are tempted, from time to time, to insert a coincidence into a story line. Wouldn't it be cool, you say to yourself, to have a character happen to run into the twin sister she never knew she had in a hall of mirrors at a county fair? Dramatic, yes. Credible, no.

Coincidence is most likely to creep in when you find yourself having to maneuver your character into position in order discover some piece of information your plot requires. Maybe your character needs to find out when and where a crime is going to occur—so you have him happen to find that information in a letter someone drops on the sidewalk. Or maybe your character needs to find a buried clue—so you have her get the urge to plant petunias and dig in just the right spot. Or maybe your character needs to know the scheme two characters are hatching—so he happens to pick up the phone extension and overhears them planning.

It may be more difficult, but it's much more satisfying if you come up with logical ways to maneuver your character into position to find the clues and red herrings your plot requires. Repeat after me: Thou shalt not resort to coincidence, intuition, clairvoyance, or divine intervention. In a mystery, logic rules. If you do put coincidence in your story, at least have your point-of-view character comment on the absurdity of the coincidence. I don't think that gets you off the hook, but at least it will keep the reader from dismissing you as a hack.

 HALLIE EPHRON is a writer, book reviewer, and writing teacher.

CHAPTER 42
INSIDE CHRISTIAN FICTION

BY PENELOPE J. STOKES

"Jesus," Madeleine L'Engle says in *Walking on Water*, "was not a theologian. He was God who told stories."

And good stories they were, too—stories that shook the religious status quo to its foundations, stories that made people think, that made them wonder and question and reevaluate their own relationships with God. Sometimes they were stories that made his listeners angry. Stories about death and rebirth, about sin and redemption, about a God who cares enough to go after one wandering sheep or to search the entire house for a single lost coin. Stories about an outcast who becomes a model of godliness by helping a wounded enemy. Stories about a father who forgives even before his wayward son has repented. Intriguing stories. Disturbing stories. Stories that comforted the afflicted—and afflicted the comfortable.

If you don't believe stories have power, watch what happens in your church on some sleepy Sunday morning. The pastor drones on about justification and sanctification and nearly every other religious term you can think of, and then suddenly says, "Let me tell you a story." Heads pop up, spines straighten, and eyes open. Ah, here it is. Not doctrine or law or history, but a story. We can relate to a story. We can hear it, glean its meaning, and make our own applications. We can find our own truth in its words—truth that may have more influence for change than all the shoulds in Christendom.

MAKING IT IN CHRISTIAN FICTION

Writers who hope to succeed as novelists in the Christian market need to understand how the CBA (formerly known as the Christian

Booksellers Association) works, and to take into account a number of primary considerations before attempting to sell a proposal.

Like any other marketplace, the Christian publishing market has its benefits as well as its limitations. For the Christian who wants to write high-quality moral fiction, CBA publishers offer the opportunity to publish in an environment open to spiritual truth, and to reach an audience hungry for that truth. In most cases, a writer does not need to have an agent to get a reading from a CBA editor, although many Christian writers these days are opting to ally themselves with literary agents who specialize in marketing to CBA publishers. Many Christian publishers are smaller than the New York megahouses; thus, a writer may find that the atmosphere in a Christian publishing company is warmer and more intimate, and that Christian companies tend to give more attention to their writers. In general, Christian publishers are a bit more open to untested writers and more willing to take a chance on a new writer if the author's work shows promise.

The limitations of publishing with a CBA house relate primarily to theological and financial issues. Theologically, the more conservative publishers expect fiction to have a strong evangelical content and an overt moral lesson or spiritual "take-away value." Other less conservative companies emphasize quality of writing and development of plot and character, but still demand a certain level of theological rectitude: characters who are identifiably Christian (or who come to Christian faith during the course of the story), a biblically based representation of God, and a worldview that reflects the justice and mercy of God, where the good get rewarded and the evil get punished.

In financial terms, many of the smaller evangelical publishers do not have sufficient working capital to invest enormous amounts of money in marketing and advertising. Advances, particularly for new writers, are generally minimal, and first print runs tend to be small. But the larger, more profitable big-name companies in the CBA are beginning to match some of the New York houses, offering substantial advances, good royalty schedules, and excellent marketing.

DISTINCTIVE FEATURES

A writer who wants to publish novels in the religious marketplace needs to have a clear idea of the distinctive features that separate Christian or evangelical fiction from general-market fiction. In general, the Christian market is geared toward the conservative end of the evangelical spectrum. Readers, booksellers, editors, and publishers expect a certain level of conservative Christian theology. This perspective does not always have to appear in the form of decisions for Christ, sermons, or prayers, but it must be visible in some form.

Some Christian publishers provide a detailed doctrinal perspective for potential writers in their writers guidelines; others require the use of specific Bible translations for any Scripture passages that may be used. And almost all publishers are looking for particular kinds of books that fit into their publishing grid. In addition to genres that fit the specific niche of each evangelical publisher, most CBA publishing houses will be looking for the following issues in the novels they acquire.

- A clearly articulated Christian worldview. A Christian worldview is based on the assumption that God is in control of the universe, and that true meaning and fulfillment in life are based on a relationship with the Almighty. This does not mean that bad things never happen, but that evil will be punished in the end and good will prevail—either in this world or in the world to come. A Christian worldview offers a perspective of a universe that includes spiritual vision, order, and moral resolution. Christian writers do not have to blind themselves to reality, but their writing must hold out the possibility of hope.

- A familiar but intriguing setting and/or time frame. According to a survey conducted by a major CBA publisher, readers are most often drawn to settings they feel comfortable with or that are familiar: American rural/small-town environments (as in Janette Oke's nostalgia novels), and well-known historical time frames such as World War II, the Civil War, or

Victorian England. These settings and time frames attract audiences because readers feel they already know something about the era and the environment.

- Universal themes and subject matter. Novels usually work best in the CBA market when they connect with some issue of current interest or universal appeal: love, suffering, injustice, moral challenges, or family relationships. Contemporary novels often approach controversial issues directly (abortion, for example), but these issues must also be approached carefully lest they become extended sermons.

- Action orientation. Action-oriented books that include intrigue, movement, suspense, danger, and ultimate resolution usually work best in the CBA market. This general principle does not eliminate the value of character-oriented books, but it's a good idea to steer clear of psychological novels comprised mostly of self-awareness, internal insights, or relationships. Something has to happen for a book to be successful in the Christian market.

- Viable Christian characters. Conservative Christian readers look for characters they can relate to—"good Christian people." Characters do not have to be perfect (who is, after all?), but main characters—heroes and heroines—are generally most acceptable when they have a clearly identifiable evangelical faith, along with some kind of memorable "conversion" in their history. Most Christian readers are looking for a conflict of good vs. evil, one of the universal themes described previously. At the very least, the central character must have redeeming faith values, an intrinsic goodness or nobility—perhaps a "lapsed Christian" with a background of faith that ultimately leads to recommitment. Some of the more conservative Christian publishers tend to be wary of characters who are too Catholic in their expressions of faith.

- Series plans or potential. Although some companies are now successfully publishing stand-alone novels, many publishers have found that a series is more marketable than a single novel, particularly with historical fiction.

Compelling characters or intriguing plots lead the reader to anticipate the next book, and the series creates its own natural marketing momentum. Plans for a trilogy, a four- or five-book series, or even a single sequel can be a major selling point for a proposal.

- Strong evangelical perspectives. Certain Christian publishers insist on a strong conservative perspective that goes beyond a basic Christian worldview. These publishers will respond positively to characters who pray and see obvious answers to their prayers, who make decisions based on Scripture, and who have significant changes wrought in their lives and attitudes by the power of God working in difficult circumstances. Most CBA publishers expect their authors to refrain from writing scenes that include gratuitous sex or overt sensuality, obscenity and profanity, humanistic philosophy, or excessive violence (particularly toward women).

ACCEPTABLE COMPROMISES

Some of these limitations present significant problems for novelists in the Christian market. Since real life contains violence, sex, and profanity, how do you write "real" fiction and create "real" characters under such constraints? Perhaps the key to that dilemma lies in the Christian novelist's perceptions—that Christian worldview. The fact is, spiritual growth and the search for truth are also integral issues in human life, issues that are sometimes ignored altogether in general-market fiction.

When personal religious compromises are necessary, they should be evaluated on the basis of the author's own belief system. Some issues can simply be soft-pedaled, as Jan Karon has done so well in the Mitford books; others can be addressed head-on through characters who exhibit growth and change as the novel progresses. I would never advise authors to try to write something that is in direct contradiction to their personal values, but I often encourage authors to find the common ground between their own beliefs and the perspectives of their readers.

The challenge to the Christian writer, then, is to create fascinating, memorable characters and gripping plots, and still represent the validity of Christian faith in human life. Writers who employ sound principles of good fiction can find ways to communicate a clear Christian worldview without compromising the artistic and literary demands of high-quality fiction.

Jesus was "God who told stories." And we, as writers who bear Christ's name, have the same calling: to tell our stories with skill and craft and passion, and to allow God to use our words in the lives of others.

It is a gift and a calling. But it is also a job.

Work hard. Listen. Learn. Grow.

God is in charge of the outcome.

PENELOPE J. STOKES holds a Ph.D. in Renaissance Literature and has taught literature and writing at the college level. She is the author of numerous novels and nonfiction books, including *The Complete Guide to Writing & Selling the Christian Novel*, from which this article was adapted.

CHAPTER 43

WHAT IS CHRISTIAN ROMANCE?

BY GAIL GAYMER MARTIN

With romance permeating all areas of the music, film, and TV industries, it's not surprising that the Christian romance novel is a major fiction genre. At its simplest, romance is the story of boy meets girl, boy loses girl, boy finds girl, boy and girl have a happy ending. The element of the happy ending is what truly defines romance.

My personal expanded definition of Christian romance is the story of two people with individual goals and needs, the physical and emotional attraction that holds them together, the conflict that separates them, and their coming together, through a deeper purpose and God's guidance, to embrace in love and commitment.

The main elements of Christian romance are: believable characters, realistic conflicts, a solid faith message, and, as with all romance, a happy ending. Most are written through the eyes of the hero and heroine (two points of view), have few subplots, and run from 45,000 to 80,000 words.

DIFFERENCES BETWEEN SECULAR AND CHRISTIAN ROMANCE

Though Christian romance follows the basic pattern of a secular romance, it differs significantly in a variety of ways. While secular romance develops two story threads (personal growth, which is the characters' struggles to obtain their goals; and romantic growth as they fall in love), the Christian romance applies three threads: personal, romantic, and spiritual growth. Spiritual growth is the characters' deepening relationships with God and greater understanding of their spiritual needs as they work through their problems.

Four other major differences between secular and Christian romance deal with the use of: violence, profanity, physical sensuality and explicit sexual content, and spiritual elements and a take-away faith message.

Violence

Christian publishers are opening the door to forms of violence in some genres; for example, Ted Dekker's thrillers. However, readers have expectations of what is appropriate in Christian romance and will avoid purchasing books that present offensive scenes. Further, they often will be wary of the publishing house's books in the future.

Some violence can be found in most thrillers, suspense, police procedurals, and war stories. Violence is necessary, to a degree, in Christian romantic suspense, and most publishers allow violence if it is needed for the story line and handled in a nongraphic manner. The difference between secular and Christian novels is the level of detail. Gratuitous violence, explicit descriptions, details of blood and gore, and any scene depicting violence to women and children must be handled with extreme sensitivity.

If violence is part of a story, it is important to include the elements of righteous justice for the criminal, meaning punishment for the crime, and justice and redemption for the hero and heroine who may have had violent tendencies in their pasts.

There are ways to handle violence in Christian romantic suspense while avoiding details; for example, begin a scene with the aftermath of the violent action, or focus on the internal struggle of the character as he battles against the impending evil. Let the emotion, rather than the physical description, provide readers with the drama of the scene.

Even in romance, topics such as rape, unfaithfulness, domestic violence, and other acts of immorality are found; but again, details can be communicated without a real-time, play-by-play account. Dialogue, introspection, or nightmares can provide enough information to understand the event's impact on the character. In *Upon a Midnight Clear*,

I chose to have a rape in the heroine's past become known through dream scenes. With each dream, the image moves closer to the rape. The final dream provides the rape scene, but without detail: "... she couldn't breathe; she was sinking into some deep swirling ocean of icy black water. She heard her blouse tearing and felt her skirt rising on her thighs, and she died beneath the blackness."

Readers know what has happened without the physical details. They experience the pain, fear, and humiliation of the rape and how it has affected the heroine's life. Dwelling on the emotion and providing only a suggestion of detail allows readers to use their imaginations as much or as little as they want to fill in the blanks.

Profanity

Many people, even some Christians, use swear words out of habit or when angry. In secular fiction, profanity is common in the dialogue of both the average cop and the "bad guy." In Christian fiction, however, the use of profanity is unacceptable. Find a way to work around those words and instead show the anger through action, internal monologue, or acrid dialogue that jumps from the page with bitter sarcasm or caustic comments.

Christian fiction authors should not fall back on common euphemisms—indirect or vague terms used to replace cursing—to suggest profanity. Gosh, gee, gee whiz, geez, and golly are all words created to replace God and Jesus' name; dang, drat, heck, shucks, shoot, and numerous other four-letter words are euphemisms for words like damn, hell, and other offensive phrases, and they are as inappropriate as their original counterparts. Some publishing houses prohibit euphemisms, so avoid their use. Instead, let readers imagine the language by using such lines as his filthy words filled the air, he bombarded the room with vile language, or he cursed under his breath.

Physical Sensuality and Explicit Sexual Content

Sexual desire is a natural part of human emotion, but the ideal approach is to provide the emotion without exploitation. Christian romance stresses chastity for the unmarried, and married couples close the bedroom door when it comes to sexual intimacy. Allow the writing to be evocative rather than explicit. Handholding, embraces, gentle caresses, and tender kisses can create a touching love story without details of body parts and descriptive scenes of lovemaking. The romance can be tasteful while still recreating the delightful emotion of falling in love.

Award-winning author Gayle Roper says this about sensuality: I have a catch phrase I use for Christian romance: chaste but promising. Christian romance need lack nothing in emotional impact. In fact, the restraint on the part of the characters can heighten the tension. In spite of the strong physical and emotional pull of genuine affection, the characters choose to remain chaste because they believe this is right, this is what God asks of them.

Spiritual Elements and a Take-Away Faith Message

Christian fiction is built on the spirituality of the hero and heroine and shows their struggle to remain true to their beliefs while dealing with the life issues and problems that challenge them. The story shows the spiritual growth of characters, whether believers or nonbelievers. Christian characters should present a realistic look at Christians in everyday life so readers can relate and apply the message to their own lives. Basing stories on a scripture lesson will present the theme or focus of the novel; the Bible verse and message become a take-away for the reader.

WRITING REAL

Christian romance provides a modern-day parable to assure readers of God's promises and give them hope and comfort. When Christian fiction was new, publishers were guarded. They wanted to be trusted, and offending a reader was the last thing they wanted to do. When books are returned for refund, the publisher loses money and, Christian or not, publishers are in a business to make a profit. So the early stories, while pleasant, were often less than exciting—enjoyable tales of families and stories of love with happy endings, but with predictable plots and conflicts too easily fixed. Die-hard fiction readers couldn't sink their teeth into the stories and stayed with secular fiction, where the subject matter often captured real-life issues. Today, however, Christian fiction has grown into a dynamic force of realistic stories that tackle deep and devastating human problems.

Relevant Plot Topics

A recent survey taken by a group of Christian authors illustrated the topics they considered relevant. The long list included unfaithfulness, divorce, infertility, abuse, domestic violence, physical disabilities, cancer, Alzheimer's, drug addiction, pornography, aging, abortion, isolation, alcoholism, lying, pride, depression, mental illness, racism, promiscuity, prostitution, homosexuality, and many other real-life issues.

Talented Christian romance writers are challenged to dig deep into the world and create stories that touch readers' hearts and souls. They create characters with serious problems and real flaws, present complex emotions based on human experience, delve into major struggles of life and faith, and deal with the heartache that affects thousands and thousands of Christians—all while remembering Christian fiction has a happy ending.

To break into the Christian romance market, it is necessary to understand your audience and the parameters set by the various publishing houses. Read books from several Christian publishers to see the depth of conflicts and characterization that go into Christian romance novels today and learn what works and what doesn't. The problems in the stories cannot be solved with easy answers or by a miracle from God. Instead, they must challenge the characters to use the gifts God has given them to resolve their own problems and, in so doing, find happiness. Writing books about real-life issues and faith struggles common to all Christians is writing "real."

SINGLE-TITLE VS. CATEGORY CHRISTIAN ROMANCE

More Christian romance novels are published in the category genre (sometimes called series or formula romances) than in Christian single titles (also called stand-alone or mainstream romance). A novel written as a category romance might have a greater chance of selling than a single title. Because of this, it is important to understand the differences in these two Christian romance formats. In order for you to decide whether to write a single-title or category romance, you will need to weigh the pros and cons of both.

Single-title romance refers to novels that stand alone and are placed on the bookstore shelves independently, usually by the author's last name. In the CBA, these books are usually printed in trade-book size, about 8½" × 5½", and are substantially longer than category romance. A single-title romance remains in the bookstores as long as it is selling. If it sells well, the book may go back for subsequent printings.

While single-title books have a longer shelf life, their success depends on the author's name and established readership. Therefore, single titles are much more difficult to sell because fewer are published each year. Single-title romances are not formula-driven, but instead depend solely on the author's ability to consistently create a compelling story that hooks readers.

Category-style romances are mass-market size, 6½" x 4", and are published with a series number and released a month at a time. At the end of the month, any books remaining in the bookstores will normally be removed and returned to the publisher to make room for the next month's category books. These books are found in the bookstores on the category shelves under the publisher's Christian romance line rather than the author's name. They can also be sold directly to readers who order each month's releases in advance from the publisher's direct mailing programs. Direct mailings differ from publisher to publisher, but they can be anywhere from 30,000 to 100,000 copies above and beyond the retail sales.

Category books are not reprinted the way a single title might be. Once the books have sold, they are out of print. If a category book is taken off the shelves but has not yet gone out of print, it may be ordered from the publisher or through online bookstores. Some publishers, such as Steeple Hill, will sometimes reissue the out-of-print books a few years later in either an anthology, a duet (two novels in one volume), or as a special stand-alone.

Category also differs from single-title romance in that it has a basic formula expected by editors and readers. Novels that do not fall into this formula will likely be rejected by publishers. The formula is as follows:

- The hero and heroine meet within the first couple of pages of the story. Awareness should be immediate, but the romantic journey should be slow and based on Christian attributes as opposed to physical attraction.

- A meaningful need brings the hero and heroine together, something more than being neighbors. Something important connects them so they must work or spend time together.

- Every scene should involve the hero and heroine. If they are not together, the scene includes their thinking or talking about the other.

- Subplots are limited because of the book length. If a subplot is included, it must make a direct impact on the faith or romantic journey of the hero and heroine.

- Lengthy details and flashback scenes are avoided.

The fact that more category romances are published each year than single titles may make it slightly easier to break into the industry. Though the royalty rate to the author is a smaller percentage than for single titles, retail sales and direct orders can result in receiving more money overall.

The success of category romance is based on a book line that is enjoyed by readers, allowing books to sell without the author being well known. But whether writing single-title or category romances, your goal is to write a compelling story that readers will remember.

FINDING A STORY

I am frequently asked where I find my ideas. My imagination is triggered in all kinds of ways. Sometimes song lyrics create word pictures, or newspaper and magazine articles offer a nugget for a plot idea. Life experiences, special occasions, or events can present scenes or a skeleton plot.

Listening to scripture in church or reading the Bible can present a theme or central truth that I want to explore in a novel. Sometimes the new settings of vacations have captured my imagination, or my own talents and abilities have evoked a storyline.

Imagination is amazing. You are not limited by boundaries, only by possibility. You've heard that sometimes truth is stranger than fiction; allow your creativity to turn everyday life situations into meaningful fiction stories. Don't limit your vision to the tried-and-true plotlines, but search those tried-and-true ideas to create the unexpected, then weave them into creative narratives.

Having a unique ability, talent, or hobby can provide fodder for the creative mind and supply details that bring a story to life. My husband's military experiences and background in music, stained glass, catering, and cooking allow me to go beyond my own expertise and extract information and ideas from his background.

The lives and faith struggles of family and friends can also produce new ideas, but their privacy must be respected. This can be done by putting a twist on the true incident or premise and making it new.

When I interviewed Louise Gouge, author of the historical Christian romance trilogy *Hannah Rose*, *Ahab's Bride*, and *Son of Perdition*, she said her idea came from doing a study of Captain Ahab in *Moby-Dick* during graduate school. She formulated her thoughts around what kind of woman Ahab would have married: "What I've done in all of these stories is play off of something already written, first Melville's character and then my own."

Marta Perry, whose novel *Hero in Her Heart*, a finalist for the Romance Writers of America RITA Award, says she found her winning plot reading a short newspaper article on service animals, which included brief mention of seizure alert dogs:

> The article didn't have nearly enough information, but once I started researching I found so much that I wondered why I'd never heard of it before.
>
> I even found online diaries kept by people who trained with seizure alert dogs, which provided exactly the sort of

> information I needed and sparked so many ideas for my char-
> acters that I couldn't keep up with them. An initial tidbit plus
> a lot of research can add up to a winning plot!

Lyn Cote, author of The Women of Ivy Manor series, says, "I always begin with setting, which gives me the type of people (characters) who would live there, which gives me what they would be doing in that area and what challenges they'd be facing, and that leads me to their conflicts and then I have a story."

Christian author Lenora Worth says, "I've gotten several ideas singing in church. My In the Garden series came to me while we were singing that song."

Kathi Mills-Macias, author of *The Ransom,* says, "Plots usually come first in the form of a 'niggling' thought, chewing on my poor, overworked brain. When I can no longer ignore it and start actively exploring it, excitement starts to set in." Kathi continues on to say that her niggling thought is often a theme:

> An idea came to me one day as I was walking against a very
> stiff wind. It was a difficult time in my life, and the wind
> seemed to symbolize my struggle. The thought expanded to
> the Christian walk, but instead of symbolizing the struggle,
> it spoke of the never-changing One who has walked the hard
> road ahead of us and triumphed. The novel was my very first
> sale, *Yesterday, Today, and Forever*, published in 1989. I believe
> all creativity originates from Him.

Stories come in a variety of ways, and research can add to the plot, so let your mind and notebooks collect ideas. One day, these ideas can connect to form wonderful Christian romances that touch readers' lives and spirits.

GAIL GAYMER MARTIN is the award-winning author of more than forty Christian romance novels and *Writing the Christian Romance*, from which this chapter is adapted. She is a cofounder of American Christian Fiction Writers.

CHAPTER 44
THE BASICS OF ROMANCE

BY RITA CLAY ESTRADA AND RITA GALLAGHER

WHAT IS ROMANCE?

Let's start from the beginning. What is a romance? With all the books out there, why is one called a *romance* while another is labeled *women's fiction* or *Western* or science fiction or mystery or techno-thriller or ... well, you get the point.

It's so simple, and so very complicated. A romance is present in every book that has a man and woman falling in love, but all of those books are not part of the romance genre. A story is only a romance when the main theme of that book is romance!

In other words, it doesn't matter whether it's a Western, mystery, or science fiction as long as the main theme is romance. Then, and only then, can it be called a romance.

> *The expanding marketplace for romances has allowed the genre to evolve into formula fiction without the formula.*
>
> —Debbie Macomber

What Is Not a Romance?

If the main theme of a story is a man and woman fighting for their lives against the Mafia as they fall in love with each other, it's probably a thriller. If the man and woman fight *each other* as they try to flee the Mafia, it's probably a romance. See the difference?

Whatever the emphasis is, that's what the book is. Think of movies: *Star Wars* was a science fiction story with a romance growing between the action. *Pretty Woman* was a romance set in the powerful elite of the corporate world. The basic rule is that for a book to be a romance, the romance must be the most important element in the story.

Now, to throw in a monkey wrench.

Danielle Steel-types of books aren't romances. They're known as *soaps*. Why? Because they're problematic—one heart-kicking dilemma after another. One life-threatening quandary after another. One tear-jerking, emotional death and divorce after another. The romance is secondary to the problems, growth, and tears of the heroine. That's a soap. Danielle Steel created the written form and made it her genre. Many have followed, but few have had the success she has.

Maeve Binchy and others have created another genre ... and you guessed it, these books are not romances either. This genre deals with women—the problems and quiet realities of their lives. These women experience growth, new beginnings, raising children alone and doing it to the best of their ability, leaving husbands and winning the economic war, going back to school, opening businesses and going to work for the first time. Through all of this, they make a success of their lives. This genre is called *women's fiction*.

In an equal, more knowledgeable world, this would all be called just good plain fiction. It used to be, but not now.

The publishing industry has an odd view of fiction sales. If you took away genre and subgenre fictions, you'd have what the market supports today: general fiction and women's fiction. General fiction is anything written by a male that both men and women read. Women's fiction can be written by men or women, but is aimed at women, since most American men don't (yes, you may read "won't" here) read women fiction writers unless it's in a genre they can publicly relate to—a genre like mystery.

We hope we can explain all about the romance genre by starting at the heart of romance. And that place is called *category romance*.

Category—The Heart of Romance

Category books are produced in *lines*. Lines come out with new titles monthly, and a set amount of books are usually published each month. All books in a line carry the same theme. They also have a set word count and topic, and each line has a very personal tone. Each line is different, although sometimes the differences are subtle. Any books published in the Harlequin lines (Temptation, American, Presents, Romance, etc.) or Silhouette lines (Desire, Romance, Intimate Moments, etc.) are category books. Also, almost all category lines are contemporary romances, and most have word counts of 75,000 words or less. Therefore, category romance is often referred to as "short contemporary" romance.

Categories are very important for the romance genre. They not only have very loyal fans, but they introduce new trends in fiction that are exploding or sneaking in the back door. What you see now in the microcosm of category romance, you can bet you'll see in stand-alone books in the near future.

Any story where the main theme is love between a man and a woman is a romance.

Basic Plot of Romance

In a romance, there is One True Love for the heroine, and once he comes on the scene early in the book, there are no other men for her—just as, from that point on, there are no other women for him (especially in category romances). The hero doesn't cheat on the heroine, and although there are times he may want to throttle her, he never, ever lays a hand on her. That's the basic backdrop for the plot.

For every rule we've just stated, you can find an exception in the nearest bookstore. However, those writers have already sold their work. The very word *exception* tells you how hard it would be to sell an out-of-the-mainstream story until you sell your first. Then, when you have a book or two under your belt and your editor wants another, you can try something out of the ordinary. It's easier to slip a foot in the publishing door when it doesn't have a ten-ton ball and chain attached.

Now, when we say middle-of-the-road story, we certainly don't mean middle-of-the-road characters. They need to be original and spicy, with distinct personalities. Characterization is where you can get creative and really show your style.

Let's face it. You need two main things to write a good story: a tight plot and realistic characters who live on after the book is put down. It can be 60–40 or 40–60, but it's best when it's 100–100.

By the way, a lot of good published stories have had better characters than plots, but no one cared because the characters *were* so good that the reader suspended disbelief.

A romance novel is ...

- about a woman trying to achieve her heart's desire, facing and fighting obstacles to reach it—and succeeding in the end.

- about a woman learning who she is, finding her place in the world, then fighting to gain (or keep) it.

- about the uncertain and confusing feelings that go with that most important part of women's emotions—love!

- about the irresistible physical and emotional attraction between male and female. Some lines (such as Harlequin Romance or Steeple Hill) deal subtly with this aspect of romance. Others, such as Harlequin Temptation and Silhouette Desire, are more descriptive about sexual attraction—and about sex. However, whether subtle or descriptive, romance with all its joys and many-faceted complications is what makes the world go around.

> *My first editor, Vivian Stephens, once told me, "When you get the world's attention, you'd better have something good to say." That has stuck with me to this day, twenty years later. A writer's priority must be the book. Invariably, other publishing idiosyncrasies—poor distribution, lousy covers, sloppy editing, promotion or the lack thereof, scathing reviews—become distracting factors. But the writer's primary focus must forever and always be the manuscript. If it's not good, nothing else matters.*

> —Sandra Brown

A romance novel, like any other kind of book, should have a wow start, something that instantly pulls the reader into the story. The first sentence should make the reader care about what's going to happen and curious enough to race through the pages to satisfy that curiosity.

FROM ROOT IDEAS TO CHARACTER GROWTH

So far we've given you a general idea of what a romance novel is all about. Now let's go a little deeper. What follows is an overview of what it takes to actually write a romance novel.

Writing a Story With Purpose

The first thing to think about it is, what is my story about? *Theme. Root idea. Premise.* What do those words mean? They mean there must be a reason or purpose for your story. If you know what you're trying to prove when you write your romance novel, the words will flow easier, your characters will respond better, and the entire design of the book will fall into place. Are you trying to prove that a woman who once loved and lost can love again? Or that a woman who loves her own child enough to kidnap her isn't really a criminal?

No matter what your purpose, jump into the middle of the problem. Then, after briefly sketching the backstory, show step-by-step why (as in the first example) a woman *can* love again. Or why the kidnapping mom *isn't* a criminal.

As you proceed, don't forget that this is a *romance* novel. The hero must be introduced almost immediately, and he should complicate things for the heroine, not make them easier. Ultimately, the heroine has to solve her problems for herself and reconcile her attraction to this man who is making her goal more difficult. And since love, though sometimes difficult, is balanced with joy, your character's perspective will change during your story; she will be able to resolve her problem on her own, strengthened by the hero's love.

How she responds to this change in her life—how, because of love, her focus changes, converges, then tries to readjust—is the heart of your story.

Premise Is the First Step to Plotting

The plot is the map or the blueprint of your book. Knowing your premise and sticking to it will keep your story from losing energy and direction. Premise will keep your story on what editors call "the main thrust" and help each step, incident, and reaction evolve logically. Although the reader doesn't know where you're heading, you need to know at all times. Sometimes that's easier said than done, like when you're in the middle of a great scene and the dialogue gets away from you, but it's worth the effort in a well-plotted story.

The Rules of Sexual Awareness/Tension

A romance novel has two more important ingredients:

- sexual awareness
- sexual tension

Rule One: From the first time they meet, the hero and heroine are deeply aware of each other. They don't have to like each other instantly, but they do have to be aware. This awareness escalates, changes, and rearranges throughout the story and culminates in the resolution.

Rule Two: The hero and heroine should be together as much as possible. In scenes where they are necessarily apart, the absent one should be kept in the reader's mind through memories, yearnings, and so on.

Rule Three: Each time they are together, their feelings should take on another aspect. Their emotions will strengthen, shake, threaten, and, as the book progresses, solidify the relationship.

Rule Four: The senses of hero and heroine are sharpened when they are together. Whether they are fighting or on the verge of making love, sexual tension escalates with each scene.

Conflict

A woman betrayed by love decides to give up all men for the rest of her life. Then, having charted her course, she is suddenly confronted with the hero, who shatters all her previous conceptions about the opposite sex. Both inner and outer conflict will appear here. And again, senses, feelings, and emotions are the three parts of the engine propelling the story to a satisfactory conclusion.

Conflict is the engine that moves the story forward. There is no story without it. Conflict forces the characters to modify their different traits and perspectives. It forces the hero and heroine to rise above the situation, to become strong, to find themselves and their self-esteem. In a romance, just like in any other well-written novel, conflict is the crux of the story.

A romance novel is about two very different people who meet and, despite differing perspectives, fall in love. Throughout the book, they overcome their differences, learn from each other, and draw closer together.

A romance novel is about two halves becoming a whole—then joining forces to become two joined wholes. (This is our personal philosophy, but history has proven that every well-received book holds the same premise.)

Why? Because one of the things we've learned over the years is that the best romance novels are not about codependence; they are about finding love in equality. The female has problems to work out and a process to learn from. She will make him fall in love with her and help teach him his own lesson. Now that's a *woman*—not a dainty flower or a codependent wimp who can't live without a man to guide her!

> *Hey, I've been rejected by some of the best.*
>
> —Jo Beverley

That is one of the most important points we can make to you. These female characters are stronger than they know, are more inventive than they give themselves credit for, and are number-one survivors. The man is the extra. He is not the only way to go.

And we don't believe that one character flaw should be used to illustrate the fullness of true love. It's not the right image to demonstrate in this form of print. We said image because we think romances help strengthen minds and resolves, defining what is right and good about men *and* women.

Characters Make the Conflict

Before writing about your characters, get to know them. Give them opposite backgrounds, personalities, and traits. For example: A fragile, gentle woman owns a china shop. She falls in love with a muscle-bound, former football player who doesn't know Limoges from Wedgewood. Each time he enters the shop, he creates disaster. But when he takes her in his arms for a passionate kiss, she is treated like rare porcelain.

He is a hamburger and beer man; she is a caviar and champagne lady.

Result—conflict!

She loves the symphony and ballet; he finds them terribly boring. She loves attending theater parties on opening night; he hates to wear a tux. In every aspect of her life (except for her choice in a man), she is rigidly formal.

Result—conflict!

What does he have to learn from her?

What does she have to learn from him?

If you know the personality of the heroine and hero, you will know which traits will draw them together and which traits will create conflict between them.

With some skill and thought, you can even turn these character tags around and still have a strong story.

Expressing Character Through Point of View

Point of view (POV) is the person who's telling the story. If it's the female, you're writing as if you're in her head, thinking her thoughts, and feeling her desires, needs, and wants. You do the same thing if it's the male point of view.

A long time ago, writers (especially new writers) were told to stay in one viewpoint forever: the female point of view. Now editors and readers alike want to see both sides of the main characters.

Note: This does not mean that you skip from one head to another to another and then back again. For reader identification and ease, stay in one mind for each scene.

Because women relate best to basic female emotions, the heroine's viewpoint is usually presented. Every woman understands the pain of lost love or betrayal, whether or not she has experienced it. Women also understand the determination to seek a goal and the joy of achieving it, regardless of whether the goal is fame, fortune, or a man.

In a romance novel, another key word is *man*. If a woman thinks that all she wants is fame, fortune, and a career, a man will usually pop up to complicate her life and give her more than she bargained for. That's what a romance novel is all about: Goal (whatever she wants or strives for) = achievement and love.

Now let's talk about the male point of view.

> *Writing is an action verb. Do it, don't just talk about it.*
> —Marie Ferrarella

What is important about the hero? The hero is the catalyst for the heroine. Like a powerful magnet, he enters her life and creates physical and emotional chaos. (So what's the difference in real life? Not much!) The heroine is drawn to him, and all her prior ideas about life and love are turned topsy-turvy. How she deals with this hero and her own private, conflicting emotions are what the story is all about.

There is another reason for explaining the thought processes of the hero in a romance novel. Within those pages, a reader finds the hero of her dreams: the man that she married or wants to marry. Not that he's perfect—he can't be perfect, and neither can the heroine. But the interaction and growth they experience, no matter how abrasive at the beginning, brings out the best in each of them by the story's end.

The greatest joy women find in the hero's role is seeing what makes him tick. For years, men were seen as gods, strong and virile. They ruled the woman's world and many women were intimidated by their power. In romance novels, the reader is given a peek inside those Lords of the Realm. Many female souls rejoice when they see that men are also vulnerable. Men can be hurt, they can yearn, suffer, and even cry. And miracle of miracles, when true love takes over a man's heart, he can change. He can grow and become as strong as the women we admire. The heroine he loves can smooth his rough edges.

She can teach tenderness where there was insensitivity, compassion where there was heartlessness, and selflessness where there was selfishness. She can show him the strength in being vulnerable. And the reader identifies.

> *Romance heroines aren't "women who love too much," nor are they perfect. They tackle their problems head-on and stand by their convictions. These are women of courage, risk-takers. Women as real as you and me.*
>
> —Debbie Macomber

Prevailing Over Conflict!

By their very natures, your characters create story energy through conflict. What she wants isn't what he wants. What he thinks isn't what she thinks. He disagrees with what she does and vice versa.

With all that conflict, what, you ask, could possibly hold these two people together? These five points:

1. A strong physical (chemical) attraction.
2. The fact that opposites attract.
3. The hero's surprise to find a woman who isn't so blinded by his charm that she keeps her opinions to herself.
4. Or, though intrigued by the hero, the heroine fights being told what to do, when to do it, how to think, and so on.
5. Committed love! All the push/pull of likes, dislikes, fights, and make-ups forces both hero and heroine to look, not only at each other, but at themselves.

Because the heroine is a strong and worthy adversary, the hero grows strong and worthy, too. You can also reverse the theory, but we like it this way best.

What Is Character Growth?

With every painful hit life hands us, we adjust and grow, change our perspective, and try to avoid making that same hurtful mistake again. If you realize this, you already know about character growth.

While we create, experience, and live with our characters, we may forget that with each impact, each mood swing, each reaction to the hits along the road to the character's goal, that character is changing. We also change as we react to life's lessons through our own personal disasters. With each problem, we change our perspective, our methods of coping, and we find new means to reach our goals. There isn't a time when we aren't constantly shifting to meet whatever specific goal we have set.

The same thing applies to your characters. A book is a slice of life, and real live characters react in the same way as real live people.

Keep in mind that your characters will never again be the same as they were at the beginning of the story. Their story lives will force them to change and grow.

Giving Your Characters Goals and Motivations

Just like you, if a character has a strong goal, she is strongly motivated to reach it.

Ask yourself these questions:

1. Are your main characters goal-oriented?
2. Do they have the inner strength, motivation, and persistence to fight for their goals?

Note: Perhaps at the beginning of the story, the two main characters have very different goals. But as they interact through conflict and disasters, they are drawn together and, in the end, achieve happiness with just a slight modification of their original goals

3. Remembering that a reader doesn't want to read about weak, insipid characters, have you shown enough *present* strength and potential in your hero/heroine for them to grow and, through constant striving, achieve their goals?

4. As your characters progress and persist, are they taking honorable chances that will make them grow and try new things despite whatever obstacles they encounter?

5. Have you stayed away from the old and tired "victim of fate"? Remember, readers want ever-strengthening characters getting a handle on life while focusing on cherished goals.

Now, what are you supposed to do to keep your writing alive and well?

READ, READ, READ

Read everything and anything that piques your interest. Read fiction from the best-seller list. Read anything and everything from your general genre. Category romance? Read a couple from each category, then go back and read a couple more from each category. Get a good, overall flavor of the various lines and how they speak to different topics.

> *Write what you like to read most; it is what you will write best.*
> —Susan Kyle, aka Diana Palmer

Read nonfiction, any type you like: bios, poetry, narrative prose, do-it-yourself books, Westerns, spy stories, classics that weren't introduced to you in school ... the entire gamut. Read anything that will educate you on living. On becoming better at anything. On writing.

> *The most important research you can do is read. Read everything, especially the category in which you want to write. Every writer I know is an avid reader. Reading is the first love; then writing comes naturally.*
> —Mary Tate, aka Tate McKenna

 RITA CLAY ESTRADA is a founding member of the Romance Writers of America and has published more than thirty romance novels.

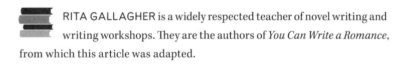 RITA GALLAGHER is a widely respected teacher of novel writing and writing workshops. They are the authors of *You Can Write a Romance*, from which this article was adapted.

CHAPTER 45

SEXUAL TENSION & LOVE SCENES

BY LEIGH MICHAELS

The love scenes in a romance novel are different from those in other kinds of fiction. Love scenes in romance novels are integral to the plot and to character development, thus they're more important than love scenes in most other fiction. Since the love developing between the main characters is such an enormous part of a romance novel, the physical expression of that love is a crucial element of the story.

Like many components of romance novels, however, love scenes and all their particulars are difficult to sum up in a few words. People who haven't read a lot of romance novels are apt to ask, "Is there always a love scene?" or "How many love scenes are there in the average romance?" or "Where are the love scenes placed? Should there be one in the first chapter?"

The answer to all these questions is "It depends on the kind of romance novel." There are many varieties of romance novel, and physical affection is handled a bit differently in each one. A wide range of love scenes from many different kinds of romances appears later in this chapter.

LOVE SCENES

It's important to understand that a love scene isn't the same as a sex scene; a love scene in the romance novel can be any physical expression of affection between the main characters. A kiss, a hug, a touch between hero and heroine are all love scenes on a smaller scale. Even a look can sizzle with sensuality, and a foot massage—if well written—can be as arousing for the readers as a sex act.

Relatively speaking, sex is a very small part of love, and romance novels—even those toward the erotic end of the spectrum—are love stories, not sex stories.

While it's hard to picture two people falling in love without displaying any physical affection at all, a romance novel might include nothing more than a touch of the hand here and there, and a single chaste kiss on the last page. Or it may include mind-bending and intimately described oral, vaginal, and even anal sex in every chapter.

Physical attraction between the characters is important, of course, but when their attraction is deeply emotional as well, the love scene will be far more involving for the readers.

To be effective, love scenes have to fit into the course of the story and heighten the tension and conflict. Even if the actual love scene is a calm interlude in the conflict between the two main characters, the act of loving should lead to increased difficulties later. Every love scene should have a purpose in the development of the overall story, not just be there to titillate the readers.

If the love scene can be removed without destroying the story, it shouldn't be there in the first place.

Two people who have slept together are going to behave differently afterward. They will not hop out of bed the next morning acting as if nothing happened the night before. Their actions have changed them and the situation—and, inevitably, the rest of the story. Once your lovers have kissed, touched, or made love, they may try to pretend it never happened—but they, and the readers, can't forget. In many beginning writers' stories, love scenes are like frosting on a cake. Frosting is applied to the surface, and it adds nicely to the taste. But essentially it changes nothing—the cake is still the same underneath. A good love scene is more like applying heat to the cake batter—once it has started to bake, the cake gets a lot tastier, and there's no way to reverse the process.

SEXUAL TENSION

The most sensual romances aren't necessarily those in which there's a lot of sex, but those in which there is a high level of sexual tension.

Beginning writers often mistakenly consider foreplay synonymous with sexual tension. The characters do not need to be touching in order to create sexual tension; they certainly do not need to be kissing or in other intimate contact.

Sexual tension is the unsatisfied attraction of the hero and heroine for each other. The key word here is *unsatisfied*. Why can't they act on their attraction to each other? What's keeping them from getting together? The stronger the reason, the more emotionally involving the story will be.

Sexual tension begins at the moment the main characters meet, with their first awareness of each other. They might be angry, interested, wary, or tense, but their heightened sense of awareness of the other person provides the first stirrings of sexual tension.

In her sweet traditional *The Billionaire Takes a Bride*, Liz Fielding uses the conflict between the characters—and a slow cleaning of a pair of glasses—to increase the sexual tension:

> Rich forgot all about the fact that Ginny Lautour was ransacking his wardrobe looking for a spare key to his desk and instead found himself wondering what she'd do with her hands if she didn't have her spectacles as a prop. If she didn't have them to hide behind. And what were they hiding? ...
>
> He removed them—ignoring her gasp of outrage—and held them up out of her reach, checking them against the light, reassuring himself that they weren't just that—a prop, a disguise.
>
> They were real enough, he discovered ... he opened a drawer, took out a clean handkerchief and began to polish them.
>
> Her fingers twitched as if it was all she could do to stop herself from grabbing them back.
>
> He finished one lens, moved on to the next, taking his time about it so that he could get a good look at her eyes.
>
> He hadn't been mistaken about them. Grey and green intermingled in a bewitching combination beneath a curtain of dark lashes that were all hers. No magic mascara to lengthen

or curl them, they'd be soft to the touch, silk to his lips, he thought. And he wanted to touch. ...

He restrained himself. ... More exciting than the most blatant of invitations, this veiled promise of hidden fire tugged at something deep inside him. Or was it simply a mask to hide her true purpose?

If Rich weren't hesitating to get closer because he found Ginny trying to break into his desk, Fielding's scene would be flat—because they're pretty obviously attracted to each other.

In this passage from Nicola Cornick's historical novella *The Season for Suitors*, her hero is ostensibly teaching the heroine how to avoid being taken advantage of by an unscrupulous man:

The path was narrow here and wended its way through thick shrubbery. Even in winter the trees and bushes grew dark and close overhead, enclosing them in a private world. It was a little disconcerting to discover just how alone they were in this frosty, frozen wilderness.

[The Duke of] Fleet was smiling gently. "Take this as a free piece of advice, Miss Davencourt," he said. "Always pay attention to your surroundings. The aim of the rake will always be to separate you from company so that he may compromise you."

He put up a hand and touched one gloved finger lightly to her cheek. Her gaze flew to his as the featherlight touch burned like a brand.

"And once he has you to himself," the duke continued softly, "a rake will waste no time in kissing you, Miss Davencourt."

For what seemed an age they stared into each other's eyes. Clara's heart twisted with longing and regret. ... Her body ached for him with a sudden, fierce fire. His presence engulfed her. She felt shaky, hot with longing. She raised her hand and brushed his away. Her fingers were not quite steady.

"Your point is well made, your grace." Her voice was husky and she cleared her throat. "I shall guard against that possibility."

Notice that the only touch is his gloved finger to her cheek; there's not even skin-to-skin contact. Cornick has used the rules of society—which at the time forbade an unmarried woman to be alone with a man—to build sexual tension. If the Duke had gone ahead and kissed Clara, much of the tension in the scene would evaporate, because we'd no longer have to wonder what that kiss would be like and wait for it to happen.

In her erotic contemporary novella *Out of Control*, Rachelle Chase uses a great deal more touching, but the sexual tension is increased because of what the couple doesn't do:

> He chuckled. There was no humor in the sound. "If I let you leave, Ms. Thomas, you'll talk yourself out of it before you reach the lobby."
>
> If he let her leave? Tingles skipped up her arms at the forcefulness of that statement. His warm breath bounced off her lips, enticing her, drawing her closer. A slight tilt of her head and she would be able to taste him, just as she'd fantasized about doing. One tiny movement.
>
> Unwillingly, her eyelids lowered, her head tilted, and her lips brushed ... his cheek. Her eyes flew open.
>
> His tongue flickered against her earlobe.
>
> "Did you want me to kiss you, Ms. Thomas," he whispered huskily into her ear. "Like this?" he asked, letting his lips nibble and his tongue swirl their way down her neck. Astrid shivered, a moan escaping her.
>
> "Was that a yes?" he rasped, his mouth moving across her collarbone and up her throat.
>
> What was happening to her? "Oh ..."
>
> He suckled her chin. "Say it."
>
> Kiss me.
>
> She wouldn't say it.
>
> His tongue moved up, tracing her lower lip. "Say it," he said hoarsely.
>
> She struggled to free her hands.

> His grip tightened.
>
> Kiss me.
>
> If she didn't get away from him, she was going to say it. She was going to arch toward him, strain to meet his lips ...
>
> His hold on her hands loosened, lightly caressing, no longer restraining. He pulled back and stared unsmilingly at her. The hunger radiating from his gaze stunned her.
>
> Abruptly, her hands were free. "You've got ten minutes," he said. His voice sounded rusty.
>
> "Ten minutes?" she asked drunkenly.
>
> "To think about it." He left the room.

If Astrid had given in and asked the unnamed hero to kiss her, Chase's couple would have been well on their way to admitting their attraction, and we'd have been cheated out of the fun of figuring out why she can't or won't surrender.

Three very different styles—traditional, historical, erotic—and in all three cases, withholding a kiss creates much more interest and tension in the scene. But it's not just that the hero and heroine don't kiss; the sexual tension is increased because there's a real reason they don't.

DISSIPATING SEXUAL TENSION

One of the easiest ways to dissipate sexual tension is to let the lovers admit their feelings too early in the story. Once the readers know that he's wild about her (and he knows it) and she's wild about him (and she knows it)—even if the hero and heroine haven't told each other—the sexual tension evaporates. The resulting warm, cuddly feeling is highly desirable at the end of the book, but it's murder if it happens halfway through.

Another way to lose the sexual tension is to let the lovers consummate their relationship too early in the story. The unwritten rules of the romance novel don't allow casual sex, and the readers know those rules, even if they can't enunciate them.

Even in chick-lit, which technically allows the heroine to make love with more than one man, it's a rare heroine who actually does. In chick-lit, if there is more than one man, sex with the wrong one is perfunctory, ho-hum, even clinical rather than enthusiastic. With the hero, the heroine has meaningful, emotional, special sex that indicates that a serious and lasting relationship has begun. Erotica, too, is a special case. In erotica, the characters are making love—or at least having sex—frequently throughout the story. The most effective erotica presents characters who, though they are liberated sexually, have good reasons to avoid permanent commitments, so the readers are kept uncertain about how the couple will end up together.

Because of the no-casual-sex tradition, once the hero and heroine have made love, the readers know that at some level they're committed to each other, even if they're still shown as having doubts about their relationship. So the sexual tension is reduced, and only a very strong conflict will keep the readers' doubts going at that point. If, however, the problem between the hero and heroine is still so deep and so threatening after they have made love that they may not reach a happy ending no matter how good their lovemaking is, the sexual tension still exists. In fact, it may even be stronger, because they're no longer just fantasizing about what it would be like to be together. They know exactly what's at risk, and that raises the stakes even higher.

DELAYING THE LOVE SCENE

A delayed love scene is nearly always a more effective love scene, one that keeps the readers eagerly reading as they wish for more.

But don't break off a love scene just to frustrate the readers, or just to keep the story from progressing too fast. There has to be a darned good reason why two people who are ready to make love—or even kiss, for that matter—suddenly change their minds.

Delaying a love scene doesn't mean avoiding the subject. Don't send the hero off to fight in the wars, leaving the heroine knitting at home. Instead, dangle the idea in front of the readers: Show the lovers' feelings developing; show them sharing their questions and their doubts; play on their uncertainties about each other, using every moment they're together to heighten their desire for each other. If the hero and heroine don't know whether they can trust the other person, the readers don't know either—and they have to keep reading to find out.

Keep in mind that a couple's second sexual encounter is seldom as exciting as the first for the readers. You may be tempted to set the scene in an unusual location or add a slightly kinky twist to keep the excitement level high, but many times the result of that approach isn't exciting at all to the readers—just disquieting. It may be better to delay the important first lovemaking scene than to try to pep up a second one in order to maintain anticipation.

An alternative is to delay the second lovemaking scene. Sometimes after the hero and heroine make love once, they have good reason not to repeat the experience, and this too can increase the sexual tension. Because they know what making love together is like, their desire is piqued and the readers' interest level is even higher.

In her single title *You've Got Male*, Elizabeth Bevarly's heroine attempts to entrap the villain through online sex, but she and her partner in the investigation lose control and make love. Then they have to deal with what's happened:

> "We should talk about that," she said. "... about what happened between you and me last night."
>
> "We had sex," he said flatly. ...
>
> "And that's all it was," she said emphatically. ... "It won't happen again."...
>
> That remark seemed not to surprise him at all. It also seemed to piss him off. Not that she cared.
>
> Nevertheless he sounded agreeable enough. ... "Sounds like we're both on the same page then. Let's get to work."
>
> Gee, Avery thought, it was just so great when two people could talk like grownups and get right to the heart of a matter. ...

Because their lovemaking was unforeseen and unprofessional, and a repetition would interfere with their investigation, this couple has an excellent reason for calling a halt to further intimacies. Does she really think it's wonderful? Is he really agreeable? Of course not—and every time they look at each other for the rest of the book, they (and the readers) will remember that night.

THE SATISFYING LOVE SCENE

Love scenes are most effective when they build in intensity from the start of the book to the end. If your romance novel will contain several consummated love scenes (as erotica and short contemporary category romances often do), the first one should not be the most exotic, the most titillating, the most intense. When you plan the first love scene, think about where you're going to go from that point in order to build the emotional intensity between the couple—and for the readers. Save some of the good stuff for later.

No matter how sweet or spicy the level of sexuality in the story, the most important factor in a love scene is the emotions experienced by the lovers. It isn't who puts which hand where, it's how their feelings—and those of the readers—are touched. The goal of the love scene is to make the readers feel good, warm, and cherished. That can best be done by using sensual language—words and images that evoke the readers' five senses. Sight, scent, sound, taste, and touch are all important and can be used to great effect.

Avoid euphemisms (his throbbing shaft or her womanly fullness) and clinical descriptions (it's hard to make words like cervix and scrotum sound romantic).

The very best love scenes aren't expressed in generic images of fire or lightning but in terms and images appropriate to each character's outlook, mindset, and past experience—even his hobbies or job. A gymnast will think in physical images, while a chef may compare lovemaking to food.

In her chick-lit novella *Return to Sender*, Lisa Cach uses all five senses to create an effective seduction scene:

> Ten minutes later a fire was crackling happily, sending heat and an amber glow into the room. He found the sound system, tuned the radio to a station playing Christmas carols, and turned the volume down low. The first flutter of a nervous tremor went through me as he then started turning off all the lights in the room. He left a single dim table lamp lit in the corner, then ignored the vacant rocking chair and sat down beside

me, his weight making the cheap futon creak, his body beside me large and warm. He stretched his arm over the back of the futon, his fingertips draping down to brush my shoulder.

Half-lit room. Wine. Fire. Quiet music. Couch. The classic setup for a smooth slide from conversation to kissing to petting and to that moment when he drew back with a question in his eyes, wanting to know if tonight meant sex. ...

But oh, he did smell so very good.

Sight, sound, taste, touch, smell—all are used, some of them multiple times, to create a picture the readers can relate to on many levels.

The level of sensuality and physical description in love scenes varies from category to category, and even more from category books to single titles. But no matter what the type of story, the emphasis in romance is on feelings rather than on technical description. A catalog of body parts is pornography, not a romance novel.

How much detail is too much? Sometimes even well-established authors aren't sure where the limits are. Jacqui Bianchi, editorial director of Harlequin's Mills & Boon division in the 1980s, told of sitting down to lunch with an experienced author at the Ritz Hotel in London, in the early days of spicy romances. Just as the waiter was setting her appetizer in front of her, the author leaned across the table to her young editor and boomed, "So tell me, dear, just how much sex can I have?"

The answer, of course, depends on the publisher and the type of romance. But it depends even more on the kind of story, the age and experience of the characters, the setting (for example, a couple stranded alone in the wilderness vs. a couple staying in a family member's house, where respect for the host and the lack of privacy have an impact), and the readers' comfort level (for instance, many readers are uncomfortable with unmarried lovers when there is a child nearby).

Today's heroine—no matter where her story falls in the spectrum of romance novels—is far more likely to go to bed with her hero before the wedding than was a heroine of twenty years ago. (Inspirationals are the exception here; in that case, "bedding before wedding" is forbidden.) But common sense is the key. An older and more experienced heroine is more likely to have premarital sex than a younger, virginal one. The heroine's actions must be consistent with her character and her circumstances.

No matter what variety of romance, how explicit the scene, or how experienced or inexperienced the lovers, sex in romance novels is always better than average and usually of medal-winning caliber. Heroes always make sure their heroines are satisfied, even virgins are always ready for the next round, and everybody climaxes every time they make love.

But the most important thing of all about love scenes in romance novels is that heroes and heroines don't just have sex. In fact, they cannot simply have sex—they make love.

LEIGH MICHAELS is the author of nearly one hundred books, including eighty contemporary novels and more than a dozen nonfiction books. Six of her books have been finalists for Best Traditional Romance novel in the RITA contest sponsored by Romance Writers of America. She is the author of *On Writing Romance.*

CHAPTER 46
CRAFTING HISTORY INTO FICTION

BY JAMES ALEXANDER THOM

The world's oldest profession isn't what you might think. Storytelling is older. In fact, the words *history* and *story* come from the same Latin root and mean almost the same thing. But we've come to think of "history" as stories of times past. And not only is it old but it's said to be the "truth," so we're obliged to know it. But if you know how histories get written, you suspect that the truth of history is often dubious, at best. In fact, the title subject of the genre makes me smile and shake my head: *Historical Fiction*. The phrase is redundant. Most history is more fiction than we like to admit.

Most historical accounts were written by fallible scholars, using incomplete or biased resource materials; written through the scholars' own conscious or unconscious predilections; published by textbook or printing companies that have a stake in maintaining a certain set of beliefs; subtly influenced by entities of government and society—national administrations, state education departments, local school boards, etc.—that also wish to maintain certain sets of beliefs. To be blunt about it, much of the history of many countries and states is based on delusion, propaganda, misinformation, and omission.

It's a problem at least as old as the Athenian historian Thucydides, who qualified his history of the Peloponnesian War by admitting "the want of coincidence between accounts of the same occurrences by different eyewitnesses, arising sometimes from imperfect memory, sometimes from undue partiality for one side or the other."

One of the first lessons I learned as a newspaper reporter long ago was that there will be at least as many descriptions of any simple incident as there are witnesses. Add more versions as time passes and as the eyewitnesses rethink their memories. Apply that lesson to deliberate or motivated events like crimes, battles, love affairs, and public hearings, and you come to understand that history might be, as Thomas Carlyle put it, "a distillation of rumor," or, as Napoleon said, "a set of lies generally agreed upon."

A novel, or so-called "fiction," if deeply researched and conscientiously written, might well contain as much truth as a high school history textbook approved by a state board of education. But having been designated "historical fiction" by its publisher, it is presumed to be less reliably true than that textbook. If fiction were defined as "the opposite of truth," much of the content of many approved historical textbooks could be called "historical fiction."

But fiction is not the opposite of truth. Fiction means "created by imagination." And there is plenty of evidence in literature and art that imagination can get as close to truth as studious fact-finding can.

This claim is not intended to belittle historians. Most of them do their best to find and state the truth. I like and admire historians, and even associate with some of them. I've had the pleasure of dining, drinking, and conversing with a few of the very best of them, and I've learned a lot from them. Some are even my pen pals, and I cherish their friendship. Why, if I had a daughter who wanted to marry a historian, I wouldn't object on the basis of any innate prejudice against historians. But I might advise her, "Tell him you're the daughter of a historical novelist and see if he still wants to marry you." The fact is, more historians look down on historical novelists than vice versa. And with good reason: There are even more bad historical novelists than bad historians. My hope is that you will be respected by good historians.

It can happen. If we study and work conscientiously to raise our image from the old, licentious, stereotypical "bodice-rippers" of our raffish past, we may eventually become comrades-in-arms with the historians who have traditionally scorned us.

Then we can fight proudly alongside them against the common enemy: ignorance of history.

A ROSY PAST

Nostalgia ain't what it used to be. That statement might sound like a gag, but, actually, it's a smart way to look at the past. I would describe *nostalgia* as "looking at the good old days through rose-colored glasses." But to tell the truth, the good old days *weren't*.

A longing for the good old days is a main motive for writing and reading historical fiction. It's similar to a child's love of fairy tales. Finding it ever harder to anticipate a rosy future, we take refuge in a rosy past: a past when men were chivalrous and brave and honorable, when women were virtuous and neither obese nor anorexic, when our founding fathers were idealistic and selfless, when the happy slaves on the old plantation adored their Massa, when hardy frontiersmen strode into the wilderness to create civilization and enlighten the ignorant savages, when men shouldered their muskets for the one noble purpose of throwing off tyranny and bringing Freedom to all.

The trouble with a rosy past, though, is that it doesn't stand up very well under research. Specifically in the case of American history, greed was at least as powerful as idealism: The founding fathers (many of them slaveholders) set up a form of government designed to protect their own advantages; women were chattel; a large percentage of frontiersmen explored new terrains to get beyond the influence of the law, or simply as real estate speculators, like George Washington and Daniel Boone; and many frontiersmen shouldered their muskets because they either yearned to kill "savages" or were afraid of being labeled cowards; they even went to war to defend their right to own slaves.

Clear-eyed research, alas, turns up warts and all. True, our nation was the first ever to be created out of whole cloth, right out of the aspirations of enlightened men, and it became the richest and most powerful nation in world history. Americans' inventive genius developed material wealth and creature comforts that the Old World had never imagined. But progress was ruthless, cruel, hypocritical, venal, and relentlessly violent—in other words, no more noble then than now. As one of my favorite essayists, Hal Crowther, puts it, "No one can trump Americans for self-righteous amnesia."

Others agree. "Turning a blind eye to ugly aspects of the past can be a bad habit that carries over into the present," writes columnist Norman Solomon. "Back in 1776, all the flowery oration about freedom did nothing for black slaves, women, indentured servants, or Native Americans. If we forget that fact, we are remembering only fairy tales instead of history."

A good historical novelist has the same obligation as a good historian: to convey a truthful history, not perpetuate pretty myths.

The greatness of America isn't diminished by the recognition that it was made like sausage: the grinding up of human meat—Native American flesh, slave muscle, women's bodies, soldiers' limbs (Redcoat, Yankee, and Rebel), laborer sinew, souvenir Filipino fingers .... Telling the truth, even when it's ugly, isn't unpatriotic. Showing the "other side" isn't revisionism; it's a widening of vision.

Therefore, the yearning to tell a great historical narrative isn't an excuse to cherry-pick the glorious parts or ignore the brutality that forms empires.

Much as you the historical novelist might hate to do it, you might have to portray your dashing Virginian protagonist as a male white supremacist, because many such men of the past were. They were brought up that way. Many believed blacks and Indians were inferior, less intelligent races that didn't have souls, an easy excuse to mistreat or kill them with impunity. Between Thanksgiving dinners, those quaint Pilgrims with their white collars and buckled shoes occasionally massacred villages full of Indian women and children, decapitated their chiefs, and displayed their heads on tall poles. Racism was even less subtle then than it is now. Most early American white men thought women should be seen but not heard. As a historical novelist, you might wish to make your hero "politically correct" by today's standards, but if you do that, you'll be lying to your readers.

My wife, Dark Rain, who is also a historical author, spent much of her early life idolizing a brave, beautiful, statuesque female Shawnee Indian chief named Nonhelema. Being of that same tribe, Dark Rain had esteemed her as a heroine. White girls had Clara Barton, Helen Keller, Eleanor Roosevelt, and Amelia Earhart as inspiration;

Nonhelema was about the only well-known role model for an Indian girl in Ohio. In the 1990s, my wife got a publisher interested in a novel about Nonhelema and began researching her long, spectacular life story in great detail.

Now and then I would hear my wife mutter in her office, "Oh, no!" Or growl, "You damned fool! How could you?"

"Who's the damned fool?" I asked.

"Nonhelema!" she replied. "This woman did some of the dumbest things! Got involved with no-good palefaces. Believed their promises. Kept doing things for them that were bad for her own people! Drank like a fish! I didn't know this. She's got feet of clay! What kind of a 'heroine' is this, anyway? I'm so disgusted, I'm not sure I even want to write a book about her!"

I sat for a minute with my fingers steepled, amused and musing, then said, "You realize, of course, that your novel keeps getting better."

She saw my point and didn't like it. "Well, if you like this kind of a life story so well, you write it!"

"She's your heroine," I reminded her. "It's your book contract."

Eventually she came to terms with it. She asked herself, "So, Self, you've never made a bad decision? You've never followed your heart and got into a mess?" She decided to continue writing about the real Nonhelema, warts and all, not the idealized one she'd admired in childhood naïveté.

As it turned out, we got a better contract for the book from another publisher, and co-authored the novel, adding my knowledge of the battles and treaties in Nonhelema's life to my wife's understanding of her culture, spirituality, femininity, and conversion to Christianity. The book, *Warrior Woman*, was anything but a fairy tale about an ideal heroine. My wife ended up understanding her better than she ever had—and admiring her more because she persevered through all the problems she caused herself. As we know, real life is like that.

Even a story about a beautiful woman is better if it includes warts and all.

FACTUAL AND FICTIONAL FUDGING

One way to compare historians and historical novelists might be like comparing brunettes and blondes: Novelists have more fun.

Even historians seem to think so. Some admit that they envy us. It's not just the fun of being free to make up stories. It's also that we don't have to take ourselves quite as seriously as historians do. Not *quite*.

To be really good historical novelists, we have to take our obligation to historical truth just as seriously as the historians do theirs. But we don't have to bear the burden of being the authority on every factual detail. Our disclaimer is right there on the cover: *a novel*.

My friend and colleague Lucia St. Clair Robson isn't a blonde, but she's one of the good historical novelists, one who makes the work seem like fun. She expresses her attitude about the genre in an almost frolicsome tone: "After all, we really are making stuff up!"

She loves to find factual incidents that add humor and picturesque images to her historical novels, such as an incident in the Second Seminole War when a chieftain named Wild Cat and his warriors attacked a troupe of Shakespearean actors and carried away eighteen trunks full of Elizabethan costumes. The Indians showed up later at treaty talks dressed as Hamlet and his entourage.

It was delightful imagery, but there was a chronological problem: The costume caper occurred after her novel, *Light a Distant Fire*, ended. Says Lucia: "I took a poll among my friends. They all agreed I would be crazy not to use it." So she used it. It was one of only two times she ever "deliberately fudged dates." She explains to me, "I can only plead youth and inexperience as cause for the malfeasance and throw myself on the mercy of the court."

That wasn't even making stuff up. It was simply juggling time to make use of a colorful and amusing scene. In other words, a novelist can have more fun and wiggle room than a historian—although a historian could have put it in parenthetically or as a footnote.

Fun, yes, but notice what Robson said: Only two times did she ever deliberately fudge dates.

The other was when she placed Sam Houston and Davy Crockett simultaneously at the Battle of Horseshoe Bend, when actually they had missed each other by only a short while. That's only two conscious "time cheats" in a long career of novel writing. Many historical novelists take much greater license. Some twist historical chronology in knots to enable historical figures to encounter each other for dramatic effect. The great novelist E.L. Doctorow has felt free to alter just about any historical fact to improve a story, and his works become eminently readable bestsellers. But you certainly wouldn't want to use them as reference books.

Lucia Robson's facts can be trusted if, say, you're a teacher assigning her novels as supplemental reading in a history class. "Researching as meticulously as a historian is not an obligation but a necessity," she tells me. "But I research differently from most historians. I'm looking for details of daily life of the period that might not be important to someone tightly focused on certain events and individuals. Novelists do take conscious liberties by depicting not only what people did but trying to explain *why* they did it."

She adds, "I depend on the academic research of others when gathering material for my books, but I don't think that my novels should be considered on par with the work of accredited historians. I wouldn't recommend that historians cite historical novels as sources." But, she adds: "I think historical fiction and nonfiction work well together. ... I'd bet that historical novels lead more readers to check out nonfiction on the subject rather than the other way around," she says, and then notes:

> One of the wonderful ironies of writing about history is that making stuff up doesn't mean it's not true. And obversely, declaring something to be true doesn't guarantee that it is. In writing about events that happened a century or more ago, no one knows what historical 'truth' is, because no one living today was there.

That's right. *Weren't* there. But *will be*, once a good historical novelist puts us there.

JAMES ALEXANDER THOM has written nine deeply researched American frontier books. He is the author of *The Art and Craft of Historical Fiction*.

Part Four

FINDING & CULTIVATING A MARKET FOR YOUR WORK

BEST-SELLING ADVICE: Publishing

"The most important thing is you can't write what you wouldn't read for pleasure. It's a mistake to analyze the market thinking you can write whatever is hot. You can't say you're going to write romance when you don't even like it. You need to write what you would read if you expect anybody else to read it.

And you have to be driven. You have to have the three D's: drive, discipline and desire. If you're missing any one of those three, you can have all the talent in the world, but it's going to be really hard to get anything done." —Nora Roberts

"Inevitably, you react to your own work—you like it, you don't like it, you think it's interesting or boring—and it is difficult to accept that those reactions may be unreliable. In my experience, they are. I mistrust either wild enthusiasm or deep depression. I have had the best success with material that I was sort of neutral about; I didn't think it was the greatest thing in the world, nor did I think it was bad; I liked it, but not too much." —Michael Crichton

"One of my agents used to say to me, 'Mack, you shouldn't submit anything anywhere unless you [would] read it aloud to them.'" —MacKinlay Kantor

"I would advise anyone who aspires to a writing career that before developing his talent he would be wise to develop a thick hide." —Harper Lee

"If you have the story, editors will use it. I agree it's hard. You're battling a system. But it's fun to do battle with systems." —Bob Woodward

"Publishers want to take chances on books that will draw a clamor and some legitimate publicity. They want to publish controversial books. That their reasons are mercenary and yours may be lofty should not deter you." —Harlan Ellison

"It's wise to plan early on where you'd like to go, do serious self-analysis to determine what you want from a writing career. ... When I began, I thought I'd be comfortable as a straight genre writer. I just kept switching genres as my interests grew. I've since been fortunate that—with a great deal of effort—I've been able to break the chains of genre labeling, and do larger and more complex books. But it's difficult, and few people who develop straight genre reputations ever escape them." —Dean Koontz

"There's really a shortage of good freelance writers. ... There are a lot of talented people who are very erratic, so either they don't turn it in or they turn it in and it's rotten; it's amazing. Somebody who's even maybe not all that terrific but who is dependable, who will turn in a publishable piece more or less on time, can really do very well." —Gloria Steinem

"There's no mystique about the writing business, although many people consider me blasphemous when I say that. Whatever else my books are, they're also products, and I regard and treat them as such. To create something you want to sell, you first study and research the market, then you develop the product to the best of your ability. What happens next? You market it." —Clive Cussler

CHAPTER 47

A STEP-BY-STEP GUIDE TO THE PUBLISHING PROCESS

BY JERRY D. SIMMONS

It might sound like an unfair stereotype, but it's true: Those of us who have worked in publishing can attest to the obvious fact that few first-time writers have the slightest idea of what goes on behind the scenes at their publishers. And it's not because it's top-secret information that agents and editors don't want you to know. In fact, the opposite is true: Developing a basic understanding of the process with a realization of how you can impact the sale of your book is crucial to your success. If you dream of a career as a writer, the more knowledge you have about the marketplace and the publishing process, the better your chance of making your dreams come true.

There are two crucial parts to every writing career: The first is the writing and completion of your manuscript and preparing it for acquisition and publication, and the second is everything that goes along with the production, marketing, sale, and distribution of your book. Knowing how all this comes together doesn't just increase your odds of crafting a submission that will get you a deal—it also gives you a better chance of impacting the decisions that can make or break your book's success.

Here's how it works, why you need to know, and how you can enter into a publishing agreement as an author with influence.

FIRST THINGS FIRST

Before getting into the specifics of how publishing works, you need to start with the basics. And that means that even while you're in the stages of completing or revising your manuscript, you need to make a habit of visiting your local bookstore regularly. Your goal: marketplace research. Browse the aisles, make observations, and read similar books in the same broad genre as your own.

Pay special attention to the books in your section written by authors you don't recognize. Notice how they're packaged and priced. Take note of the cover design, jacket copy, and sources of the endorsement blurbs—anything that went into the process of publishing what you see in front of you.

Bookstores are laboratories for marketing and selling books. Writing is a craft, but publishing is a business. To become a successful author you must develop a knowledge of that laboratory. Being able to intelligently discuss books and authors with professionals who make their living in publishing builds your credibility as a market-savvy author—especially if you can demonstrate an understanding of where your own book will fit in. Once you know exactly where your work belongs on the shelf, be sure that knowledge is reflected in the query or cover letter accompanying your submissions to agents or editors. It will increase your chances of getting one.

ACQUISITIONS

Publishing is an extremely competitive business. Houses compete to sign the best manuscripts possible. The major houses, as a rule, do not accept unsolicited submissions. They rely on agents to supply them with a steady stream of publishable possibilities. Once an editor agrees to read a manuscript, it has passed a critical test. If the editor likes what she reads and thinks it's a good fit for her list, she will then move forward with a proposal to acquire the book. But this doesn't mean it's a done deal.

Every publisher has an acquisition committee of editors, publishers, and sales and marketing representatives dedicated to finding manuscripts that can, to put it bluntly, make the company money. There are three broad criteria publishers use to make these selections. The first is whether or not they feel the manuscript is well written and informative or entertaining. The second is whether or not they think it can secure a wide enough distribution to booksellers—and then attract enough consumers to generate sufficient revenue. The third is whether or not the author has a platform and is promotable. Each manuscript must meet all three criteria, almost without exception, to be seriously considered. Timing (and, let's be honest, luck) also plays an important role: If your book is salable but the company recently acquired two similar titles, yours may get the bump. Publishers go to great lengths to produce a well-rounded list of titles. Each imprint has a certain editorial expertise by genre, and the company is focused on producing a group of quality books that fill every category.

If your submission meets the committee's approval after all of this has been considered, you'll be offered a contract.

THE MEETING

Consider for a moment that even once you've made it past the gate-keepers, your book is just one of hundreds—or even thousands—your publisher releases each year. The more you can separate yourself from all the other authors up front, the better chance you have of making an impact on the publication of your book. So once you sign the contract (after negotiations and the expert consult of your agent or another legal professional, of course), plan a trip to your publisher, set up a meeting with your editor, and ask him to invite the appropriate parties of all the departments involved with the book. Whether or not this request is honored—and if so, who exactly attends—will speak volumes about where you are in the pecking order of other authors. For example, if it turns out to be just your editor, or a group of bright young "assistants," you're probably near the bottom of the list (along with almost all the other first-time authors). If that happens, don't take it as a bad sign. Just understand where you rank in the grand scheme of things so you can set realistic expectations.

The moment that contract was signed, you lost rights and control over how your manuscript will be published. But if you develop solid relationships up front with the key people involved in making your manuscript a marketable book, you have a better chance of at least having your ideas heard. This meeting is your first and, arguably, most important chance to do that. (It may even be the only one you get.) So *don't skip this step.* The secret to being effective: Base your comments on the realities of the marketplace, and acknowledge the time constraints these players have in balancing their work on your book among all the others. This is where all those visits to the bookstore begin to pay off.

EDITORIAL

Today's book industry is so competitive that most acquired manuscripts don't require significant editorial overhauls. Those needing lots of attention—whether they're riddled with technical errors or in need of heavy restructuring—rarely make it past the agent.

Today's editors more often request minor rewrites or reworks and otherwise polish the manuscripts they acquire. The secret to starting off right: Recognize that when an editor asks for editorial changes, you are under contract to rewrite and deliver on time. You are the author and always maintain your copyright, but ownership of your writing has transferred to your publisher, which is paying you for those rights and control. Similarly, when it comes to your book's title, know that it could very well be changed, and it's your publisher's prerogative to do so.

Beyond the obvious editor/author relationship, every smart writer knows his editor is also his main contact (and advocate) for *all* things relating to the publication of his manuscript. Conduct yourself accordingly. Don't come off as "needy," but don't neglect this relationship, either.

SCHEDULING

Once a title is scheduled for publication and a release month has been set, the work begins in earnest. The time from a book's acquisition to the day it hits shelves is typically anywhere from one to two years. It depends on how timely your topic is, how many titles are under contract in your category, and when your publisher thinks your book will have the greatest chance of success in the market.

Publishers meet often to discuss the seasonal schedule and position their titles to maximize sales potential. The biggest consideration is competition, both in-house and from other companies. Publishing competitive titles concurrently dilutes the sales potential of the entire list. This is another reason it's essential to meet all your deadlines for rewrites, revisions, and reviews: Failing to do so can endanger the carefully choreographed timing designed to maximize your book's sales prospects.

NUMBERS

Publishers work from a set of numbers that is developed during that initial acquisition meeting. Upon agreeing to publish your manuscript, your publisher already knows the number of copies your book needs to sell to be profitable—for the house and for you. Profitability is the cornerstone of everything the company does with regard to publication, and it's often referred to as the "budget number" for each book. This number is the basis of how much attention to detail your title receives. With limited time and resources to produce thousands of titles, the budget number is one way for publishers to prioritize.

Authors are rarely aware of their budget numbers, and questions directly relating to those numbers seldom receive a response. Again, that initial meeting with your editor or publishing team is the best indicator of where your book stands.

THE 90/10 RULE

Because publishing is a business with limited time and resources, authors should be aware of the 90/10 rule. This states that approximately 90 percent of a publisher's revenue is generated from 10 percent of the titles it publishes.

Authors whose books fall within that lucky 10 percent range are generally established bestsellers. If you are one of the 90 percent of authors whose books generate the remaining 10 percent of the publisher's revenue, this only means you have to be proactive in understanding what goes on behind the scenes and how you can positively impact your book's performance in the marketplace.

PRODUCTION

Possibly the most overlooked and underappreciated part of the publication process is the work of the production department, which develops and designs the cover and interior of each book, along with coordinating the printing and binding of the finished products. Readers do in fact judge a book by its cover, and getting it right is something the largest publishers do extremely well.

Awareness of the production schedule for your book is important; knowing when each part of the design and layout process is coming helps you determine when it's appropriate to ask any questions you might have—and to gently offer your own ideas while there's still time for them to be taken into consideration. As long as you acknowledge your publisher's control, you're likely to find the house will be receptive to your input if it's based on your keen sense of the market. Always make suggestions a few weeks in advance of the date the production schedule indicates each decision is being made. Don't be overbearing and don't be a pest. Make intelligent suggestions based on your knowledge of the need your book is filling in the marketplace, and you will be seen as an asset, not just another author looking to promote her own interests. Speak up too late, and there's no turning back. Your publisher's team is making all the decisions, remember; they bought the rights to your writing and can do what they want.

MARKETING

There are three major components to book marketing: advertising, promotion, and publicity. Advertising includes paid placements of a book in print or other media. Promotion is the creation of anything that draws attention to a book, from corrugated floor and shelf displays in bookstores to bookmark and T-shirt giveaways. Publicity is the art of generating print and media pieces about an author and her book. The key to selling copies at a high sell-through (meaning people actually buy the books off the shelves) in today's marketplace is to generate lots of publicity. The key to effective publicity is to focus on the area that will generate the most sales for your book.

One quick caveat: The stronger your author platform already is, the better equipped you will be to assist in these efforts. Marketing is not something that starts or stops at any given time. Ideally, it's an integral part of your writing career that begins long before you land a book deal and continues for as long as you call yourself a writer.

Successful marketing is all about creating the proper mixture of advertising, promotion, and publicity within the assigned marketing budget to generate interest that results in sales. Don't ask for things that are clearly outside the limits of your publisher's budget. If something is missing from the plan and you offer to help, make sure you get your publisher's approval, and be willing to work with each department to make it happen. Be prepared to invest your own money in these efforts eventually, but don't offer to do it up front until you know exactly what your publisher plans to do. Then, partner with your publisher to promote your book, keeping them informed of your own efforts and listening carefully to their expertise so that together you can present a unified marketing plan. Publishers dislike authors going off on their own without consulting them or soliciting input. They also dislike authors who are singularly focused on the writing and want nothing to do with promotion. These are the two quickest ways to lose support, and you never, ever want your publisher to turn its back on your efforts.

CONFERENCE

Most major publishers separate their list of titles into seasons. The seasonal designation is significant to the bookseller and marketing staff because each season's list is presented at one conference to the sales group. Members of this sales group then go and make seasonal presentations to book buyers at major chain and independent bookstore groups around the country.

Any changes that need to be made to your book should be completed prior to this conference. Afterward, you won't have another opportunity to speak up about your cover, interior design, jacket copy, marketing plans, or anything else. As soon as it's over, your book is already on its way to being presented, sold, and distributed to booksellers around the country.

The conference is a well-guarded place and publishers seldom allow authors to attend. If you're invited, it's a very big deal; make the most of it. If not, it can't hurt to ask about attending a portion of the conference. On the off-chance your publisher says yes, it's a great opportunity to meet people who have a tremendous impact on the success of your book. Observe, network, and learn.

SALES

Once the sales representatives leave the conference, they immediately begin making appointments and presenting titles to the buyers for the big chain bookstores (like Barnes & Noble and Borders), and for suppliers of independent ones (like Ingram and Baker & Taylor). Seasonal lists of titles are typically sold months in advance of publication, so most titles being presented are months from the actual publication and release date. This gives the publisher plenty of time to assess all orders, make adjustments as necessary, and print the right number of copies for distribution to the marketplace.

Obviously, the books at the top of the list get the most orders. If your book is positioned low on the list, there's a good chance the big chains will pass or give you a small order, which means you won't find copies on all store shelves. Don't get upset! A targeted distribution with a high sell-through trumps having your book placed inside every single store in the country. What makes distribution such a delicate dance is that books are always returnable to the publisher's warehouse if bookstores can't sell them. So while you want your book to be readily available to your audience, there's also a danger in printing and distributing too many copies. Selling large quantities to booksellers without proper marketing support is tantamount to a low sell-through and a high rate of return, which can spell doom to a promising career. (Translation: If your first book isn't profitable, your chances of publishing a second one are slim.) Be happy with what you get and work with your publisher to promote your book so you can sell those copies. Then the stores will have to order more!

DISTRIBUTION

The most misunderstood and misconstrued term in the wide scope of publishing is *distribution*. For the largest trade publishers, selling and distribution go hand-in-hand. Proper distribution is not a simple listing of a title in the database of a large book outlet or mailing postcards to bookstores around the country.

Actual distribution begins with the process of sales presentations we've already discussed, coupled with skillfully matching booksellers with books that sell copies at a very low rate of return. Different genres—as well as the publishing formats of hardcover, trade, and mass-market paperbacks—resonate with consumers who shop in specific locations. Distribution in the truest sense is matching the category, format, and price to the right outlet in quantities that make sense for both the publisher and bookseller.

ON SALE

The cycle is now complete: Books have been produced and distributed, copies are for sale online and on store shelves, and marketing plans are, with hope, bringing enough attention to particular titles that consumers are buying books. It may seem daunting, but it's actually both repetitive and consistent. As an author, understanding how your book works its way through the process gives you a head start.

Never forget the fact that publishing is a business, your manuscript is a product and you, as the author, are a commodity. When you sign that contract, your manuscript is packaged, priced, and sold to make money. Your publisher has acquired your work to profit from the sale of your writing. It's not so much about great writing as it is about a good book that can generate revenue, and how much value you as an author and your writing bring to the company. As long as your writing is profitable and you continue to produce entertaining, informative manuscripts on schedule, you have a very good chance of maintaining a career as a writer.

Best of luck.

SELL-THROUGH

Many authors think having a large print run for their book is important, when it fact it is not as important as *sell-through*. All books ordered by bookstore buyers are distributed on a returnable basis—for a full refund—if they don't sell once they land on the shelves. Because of this, sell-through, or the percentage of those copies that actually sell and are not returned to the publisher, is the key to profitability.

For example, if a bookseller receives an order for one thousand copies from the publisher and is able to sell only six hundred copies to consumers, the remaining four hundred are "returns." In this case the author's sell-through would be 60 percent. If three hundred copies were returned, the sell-through would be 70 percent. So regardless of how many copies your publisher prints and distributes, the goal is to make sure that people buy the books, plain and simple. Publishers set their print runs based on historical data and careful profit and loss calculations, so don't read too much into yours (or bother questioning it). Just know that sell-through, also referred to as "percent of sale," is the key to a successful career as a writer. The higher the sell-through, the more likely any writer will have a bright future as an author, regardless of the size of the initial print run.

JERRY D. SIMMONS is the author of *What Writers Need to Know About Publishing* and publisher of the industry newsletter "TIPS for WRITERS from the PUBLISHING INSIDER." You may contact him via his websites, WritersReaders.com and nothingbinding.com.

CHAPTER 48
"STUDY THE MARKET!"

BY MICHAEL SEIDMAN

You've heard the advice again and again, read it in every how-to book you've picked up: Read the publication you want to submit to, read recent books by the publisher you've chosen to send your proposal to, and make sure that what you've written is what they publish.

The problem with that old chestnut is that too many freelancers "read blind." They'll look at the *type* of material (mystery, science fiction, general nonfiction) being published, but won't pay attention to *how* the text is presented. I'm not talking about simple matters of format; I'm referring to language, taste, and myriad other things, including a book or magazine publisher's self-image.

OPEN YOUR EYES

In the 1980s, I was editor of *The Armchair Detective*, a quarterly devoted to criticism, review, and commentary about crime fiction. Under my predecessors, the magazine had an academic tone; wherever possible, it seemed, contributors used footnotes. Not to put too fine a point on it, I hate footnotes. I find them intrusive. I dislike seeing that superscripted number next to a comment and then having to turn to the end of the piece to see what it's all about. So when I took over the reins, I started editing pieces in inventory so as to incorporate the footnotes into the text. I made specific mention of this change of "style" in an editorial column and in the writers guidelines sheet.

I made other changes as well, and a casual browsing should have made them clear to anyone. More columns were added, written by professional mystery writers. And rather than being in-depth studies of the development of a character in a particular series (such as the growth of Poirot), these were freewheeling commentaries about anything that in any way related to the fiction under consideration. Review columns were sometimes presented as dialogues between the reviewer and a friend. Living American writers and the things having impact on their lives, from the Mystery Writers of America to newspaper reviews to fan reactions at a convention, were all fair game. Rather than a specialized version of the *Journal of Popular Culture* then, *The Armchair Detective* became a magazine that anyone who enjoyed a mystery novel would be able to enjoy. As the editor, I chose to make the magazine one I would enjoy editing and reading. And footnotes were only a small part of what I didn't like.

In all fairness, it should be pointed out that my choices were not always popular and, while we didn't lose many subscribers, we did receive more than a few complaints. *The Armchair Detective* was well-enough established by that time that certain things were expected, and my kind of rabble-rousing was not among them. At any rate, articles continued arriving festooned with footnotes. After a year, I began rejecting anything that crossed my desk in that format. I also chose fewer submissions that I considered academic or pretentious. I still attempted to maintain a balance: I couldn't ignore the people who had helped build the magazine, but I did want other folks, the people like me, to feel welcome. If the writers had paid attention to what was being published, they would have not only understood what I was looking for, but submitted what I considered publishable.

An easily recognized difference between two similar magazines can be discovered by looking at issues of *National Geographic* and *Scientific American*. Both publications might cover the same story, but the voice in the former is much more informal. Most of its articles are first-person narratives, almost casual in nature. This doesn't mean that the information isn't there; it means that the approach feels like sitting down and having a drink with the authors while they regale you with tales of their discovery. In *Scientific American*, however, the articles are more scholarly in nature. For me, reading that magazine is like sitting in a lecture hall—after having missed the first half of the lecture.

The decisions made at these magazines are a result of the editors' understanding of their markets and needs. As a writer, you have to come to the same kind of understanding. Who are you writing for, and what does that person need? The answer to this question takes priority over what you perceive as *your* needs as a writer. If a publication does not address the audience you've chosen or if you're unable to write for its audience, it is the wrong publication for you. Expecting an editor to become so enamored of your prose's brilliance that he will forgo his own vision of his publication is authorial madness.

DIFFERENCES WITHIN GENRES

I began with a discussion of nonfiction because, frankly, it's a whole heck of a lot easier to discuss—the issues are more obvious. When it comes to fiction, the nuances you must look for are no less important, but they may very well be a whole lot more diffuse.

First, you must realize that, within any category, each editor brings particular literary beliefs to the job. As a writer, though, how do you go about noticing such differences?

You do it by bringing a critical eye to your reading. What was going on in the last horror novel you read? Was it splatterpunk? Was a child at the heart of the story, either as the source of evil or the answer to it (or both)? Was the same theme driving other novels you read by the same publisher? Does that give you a hint?

Crime fiction brings the same issues to your decision-making process. Is every book from a particular publisher a hard-boiled P.I. story? A cozy? Is an editor doing mystery (in the sense that there's a puzzle built into the plot) as well as suspense? What about the levels of violence, gratuitous or otherwise? Do the criminals say *oh heck*, or do they use the kind of language criminals are like to use?

Questions about language, violence, and other aspects of the work being published by your target market have to be answered, by you, before your manuscript is put in the mail. The thing to remember, always, is that just because you're writing in a category doesn't mean that every publisher in that genre is, by definition, interested in *your* work.

WAIT, IT GETS MURKIER ...

The lines aren't always even *that* clear if one is interested in so-called "mainstream" or "literary" fiction. Especially when we consider book publishing. The first problem is defining those categories—something, fortunately for my sanity, beyond the purview of this essay. If a publisher's list indicates strong support for some currently popular fiction mode—magic realism, postmodernism, deconstruction—and you're writing something that uses Cheever or Updike as a model, you're probably spinning your wheels if you submit there. (We're also assuming that you understand terms like *magic realism*. I don't. And I don't even care to. Obviously, you wouldn't submit magic realism manuscripts to me.)

The same problems apply to magazines that publish fiction. Reading magazines regularly is an urgent part of your job. And read with an understanding of the business: When Kristine Kathryn Rusch took over from Ed Ferman as editor of *The Magazine of Fantasy and Science Fiction*, readers began talking about the differences they claimed to discover in the first issue under Rusch's guidance. The fact that was missed all too often was that the stories in that first issue (and several after that) had actually been acquired by Ferman. The lesson is simple: Never take anything for granted.

In the magazine market, the differences between literary fiction styles are a bit more clear-cut than they are in book publishing. The stories in *The New Yorker* are not the same as those in *Tri-Quarterly*. Some magazines encourage various forms of experimentation in fiction; others define literary quality as any story that doesn't have a point—vignettes taken from life. (Yes, there's a certain cynicism on my part being revealed here. But a perceptive writer will make himself aware of that kind of feeling on the part of an editor; it helps determine what he'll buy!) Again and again, read the publisher's products looking for an understanding of what is driving the selections, digging for the philosophies that guide the editorial staff.

Some specifics: Is the language rich and lush, or is it plain? Does the editor show a preference for complex constructions as opposed to simple declarative sentences?

While considerations like those may seem beside the point—after all, you've written a wonderful piece and isn't that all that counts?—the reality is that editorial taste goes far beyond simply choosing a story that fulfills a particuilar guideline. It is a function of the editor's "literary" beliefs and understanding of what makes a good piece of writing, be it fiction or nonfiction. There is no way to argue with those feelings; all you can do is try to figure them out and, most vitally, appeal to them.

Once you begin to do that, you'll have come to learn what the editor is *really* looking for: a manuscript that fulfills *all* the expectations we have when we open your envelope.

MICHAEL SEIDMAN (mseidman.com) is an editorial consultant, serving publishers and individual writers. He is the author of *The Complete Guide to Editing Your Fiction* and *Fiction: The Art and Craft of Writing and Getting Published.*

CHAPTER 49
OUTSTANDING BOOK PROPOSALS

BY DON PRUES

Many writers attempting to find an agent to represent their books perceive themselves to be a diminutive David staring down a monstrous Goliath. Even worse, they think no weapon exists to slay the giant and prove their book is worth publishing. Such folks are wrong. An effective weapon does exist: It's called a book proposal. The hitch, however, is that writers must build this weapon themselves.

And therein lies the problem: Most writers don't know which materials to use nor how to put the pieces together to stand a fighting chance. That's where this chapter comes in. We'll show you what you need to include in your proposal and how to assemble it, ultimately equipping you with the necessary weaponry to conquer even the most colossal rejection pile.

Before we get into the specifics about composing and organizing your proposal, we need to get one fact out of the way: The proposal you create depends upon what the agent wants. And the most nonintrusive way to know what she wants is to follow the submission specifications to a tee. Do nothing more, nothing less. Remember, you must play by each agent's rules if you want that agent to represent you.

THE NOVEL PROPOSAL

The golden rule in publishing fiction is your novel must be completed before you solicit an agent. Will you be permitted to send your entire novel upon initial contact? Probably not. Unsolicited manuscripts are ignored, returned, and sometimes even thrown away when sent to an agent who does not accept them. That's the catch with fiction: You need to have your novel finished before soliciting an agent, but rarely are you allowed to send the complete manuscript. Don't waste your time, energy, paper, and postage sending material to an agent who doesn't care about it.

Many agents prefer to receive a one-page query letter first, and only ask for the proposal or the manuscript after having their interest piqued by the query letter. Check the agents' guidelines to see what they accept—rarely will it be a complete manuscript, but often it will be a novel proposal.

Novel proposals are easy to put together. You can anticipate sending a cover letter, a synopsis, three consecutive sample chapters (almost always your first three chapters) or the first fifty pages, possibly an author biography, and an endorsements page. These are by far the most important—and most requested—parts of your proposal. Some agents require only a cover letter and three sample chapters because, with fiction, the writing itself (your sample chapters) matters most. Again, what you send is determined by what the agent demands.

THE COMPONENTS

Cover Letters

The type of cover letter you compose depends on whether you're sending a blind ("unsolicited") proposal or a requested ("solicited") proposal.

If the agent accepts or even prefers a blind proposal upon initial contact (instead of a query letter), you'll need to tailor a sharp cover letter to hook the agent and encourage her to dive eagerly into the rest of your proposal. A cover letter accompanying a blind proposal submission is like a tightened version of a query letter. Similar to the query letter, your cover letter lets the agent know who you are *and* what you have to offer. You don't need to spend much time arguing that your proposal is worthwhile because what you have to offer (the proposal) is actually enclosed.

If you've already sent the agent a query letter and she has requested a full proposal, keep the cover letter short—just a paragraph or two will do. Simply let the agent know what material you've enclosed, and mention whether any other agents are considering the same proposal.

Cover/Title Page

Although the title is but a small part of a large book, a telling and catchy title can be so important. The difference between an adequate title and a superb title can mean the difference between mediocre book sales and gargantuan ones. Think about some of the successful titles you know—most are under five words (excluding the subtitle) and emit something unique about the book.

For fiction proposals, the cover page, or "title page," follows your cover letter. When formatting the cover page, be sure to put the book's title in all caps about a third of the way down the page. Include your contact information (name, address, phone number, fax, e-mail) with the date in the bottom right corner. Put the word count in the top right corner.

Table of Contents

Your contents page lets the agent know precisely what's in your proposal package, and lends order and organization to all the disparate proposal elements. Be sure to list every item you're sending and the corresponding page numbers in the order they appear in your proposal. You obviously need to make your contents page neat and easy on the eyes. It should be double-spaced and organized according to its sections. The contents pages should not be numbered.

The Synopsis

A synopsis is a brief, general overview of your novel, sometimes referred to as a "short summary." The goal of your synopsis is to tell what your novel is about without making the agent read the novel in its entirety. You need to supply key information about the primary elements in your novel (plot, theme, characters, setting), then show how all these aspects work together to make your novel worthy of publication. The trick with the synopsis, however, is doing all of the above quickly.

How quickly? Well, that depends on the person you're soliciting. There are no hard-and-fast rules about the synopsis. Some agents look at it as a one-page sales pitch, while others expect it to be a comprehensive summary of the entire novel. Not surprisingly, there's conflicting advice about the typical length of a synopsis. Over the years, I've contacted numerous agents to get their take on just how long it should be, and nearly all agents prefer a short synopsis that runs from one to two single-spaced pages, or three to five double-spaced pages. Because every novel is different—with its own number of important characters, plot twists, subplots, and so on—there is obviously some disagreement among agents about the specific length of a typical synopsis. Nevertheless, every agent agrees there's one truism about a synopsis: "The shorter, the better." That's why one to five pages is generally the preferred length for a novel synopsis.

That said, some plot-heavy fiction, such as thrillers and mysteries, might need more space, and can run from ten to twenty-five double-spaced pages, depending on the length of the manuscript and the number of plot shifts. If you do opt to compose a longer synopsis, aim for a length of one synopsis page for every twenty-five manuscript pages (a 250-page manuscript should get a ten-page synopsis), but attempt to keep it as short as possible.

A few other important aspects of your synopsis:

- Write in third person (even if your novel is written in first person).
- Write in present tense (even if your novel is written in past tense).
- Only focus on the essential parts of your story, and try not to include sections of dialogue unless you think they are absolutely necessary.

Make your story seem complete. Keep events in the same order as they occur in the novel (but don't break them down into individual chapters), and be sure your synopsis has a beginning, a middle, and an ending. And yes, you *must* tell how the novel ends.

Chapter-by-Chapter Outline

An outline describes each chapter as its own entity; the descriptions range from a few paragraphs to two pages per chapter. In short, you're expanding and specifying what you've generally written in the synopsis.

Few agents want chapter-by-chapter outlines with fiction (most just request a cover letter, a short synopsis, and a few sample chapters). Therefore, you should never submit an outline for your novel proposal unless an agent specifically asks for it. Chapter-by-chapter outlines will be requested occasionally with genre fiction, which often has numerous plot shifts. When possible, limit the novel outline to one paragraph per chapter.

Author Biography

If you think aspects of your life are important and relevant to the salability of your book, then include an author biography. The goal of your author bio is to sell yourself in ways that complement the proposal. Don't include information that doesn't directly help the pitch. Do tell about your profession, particularly if it's pertinent to your book, and always highlight noteworthy publishing credits if you have any. Try to keep the author bio to one page.

Endorsements Page

An endorsements page is not essential, but having one can improve the salability of your manuscript. Your endorsements must come from noteworthy people, typically prominent industry insiders (well-known authors, agents, experts on the topic) who've read your manuscript and commented favorably on it. Unless you have contacts, though, it is difficult to obtain a quote from someone noteworthy. But don't fret if your proposal doesn't have an endorsements page—few authors include one.

A Reply Postcard

If you're a bit paranoid about whether or not your material actually makes it to the agent or publisher, you may send a reply postcard with your proposal package. Having it signed by the agent or someone on the staff and sent back to you will alleviate any worries that the package didn't make it to its destination. Two caveats: (1) Not all agents are gracious enough to send your reply postcards back, but most do, and (2) Just because you receive a postcard reply, you cannot assume your proposal has been read or will be read in the next few weeks. Your reply postcard's only function is to let you know your package has been received.

Now you have all you need to know to craft a powerful proposal. Just be smart, target the right agent, honestly acknowledge the commercial viability of your proposal, and send the agent what the agent wants to receive. Sound doable? Good. Go do it—Goliath is waiting.

 DON PRUES, former editor of *Guide to Literary Agents*, now freelance writes and edits from home.

CHAPTER 50

BUILDING A SOLID THREE-PARAGRAPH QUERY

BY ANN RITTENBERG

Like many independent literary agencies, mine is small, with only two full-time people and one part-time person and no more than fifty active clients at any given time. Yet even we receive at least fifty query letters every week. Potentially, we could replace our entire client list—which has been nearly twenty years in the making—every week of the year. And at the end of each year, we've read, processed, answered, thrown away, cried over, winced at, yawned over, or gotten excited about nearly three thousand letters about as-yet-unpublished books. That number doesn't include the e-mail queries—which we officially don't accept, but which nevertheless come in at the rate of twenty or more a week.

Out of those three thousand pleas, nearly 75 percent are about novels. And out of those, at least 90 percent are about first novels. That brings the number of queries about first novels to about two thousand every year. And in a recent year, I accepted as a client one new novelist out of those two thousand. That's not 2 percent, or 1 percent, or even one-half of a percent. That's one-tenth of one-half of a percent.

Reading statistics like those must be thoroughly discouraging. Statistics are, after all, often discouraging: The number of people who apply to certain schools vs. the number who get in is always a discouraging number. Our chances of winning a million-dollar-plus lottery are also discouraging, but many of us still buy tickets. So let's look at those numbers another way: 80 percent of those query letters about first novels never should have been sent.

That's right—a full 80 percent of the letters I read pitching first novels never should have been sent to me, or to any agent or editor. Either the writers were not ready to be published and their books were not ready to be agented, or they misdirected the query letter by writing to me about the kind of book I don't represent.

So, if we subtract 80 percent from the two thousand first-novel query letters I (and many of my colleagues) see every year, we come up with a grand total of four hundred. Four hundred letters a year is only about eight per week. I would happily read to their end eight letters a week about first novels. Yet if I still take on only one writer of those four hundred, I have taken on one-quarter of a percent of the writers who write to me about their first novels. It's still a small percentage, but 1/400th is considerably better than 1/2000th. (Try reading that sentence out loud and you'll see one reason why.)

So, with that in mind, let's make sure you have the tools you need to write a query letter that sets you apart from the pack—a letter that should definitely be sent.

QUERY LETTER BASICS

A good query letter, like the best writing, has urgency and clarity. It's not dull, but it attends to the business at hand without fuss. It is, of course, a sales pitch directed with passion, belief, and enthusiasm to someone likely to buy the product being pitched. You're trying to find a reader for your book. And because every editor and agent is first a reader, you're going to write this letter to the reader who is most likely to want to read your book.

Let's start with the basics. For instance, you've probably figured out that an effective query letter:

- doesn't state the obvious—if it does, agents will think your book is all "telling," no "showing."

- is never longer than one page—if it is, agents will think your book is overwritten.

- is not about you—if it is, agents will think your book will be too navel-gazing to invite the reader in.

- never sounds generic—if it does, agents will think your book won't have a unique or appealing voice.

- makes the book sound interesting—if it doesn't, agents will know the book isn't.

So what does a good query letter look like? Well, here's a letter that got my attention:

> Dear Ms. Rittenberg,
>
> I am seeking representation. I have won a few awards for fiction and poetry. My novel, THE CLEARING [later titled *A Certain Slant of Light*], is a supernatural love story told from the point of view of a young woman who has been dead 130 years. She's haunting a high school English teacher when one of the boys in his class sees her. No one has seen her since her death. When the two of them fall in love, the fact that he is in a body and she is not presents the first of their problems.
>
> Please let me know if you would be interested in reading part or all of THE CLEARING. I have enclosed a SASE. Thank you and I look forward to hearing from you.

Although the author, Laura Whitcomb, began the letter by saying something that might not have been strictly necessary, she said it with admirable brevity. I didn't have time to stop in the middle of the opening sentence. Before I knew it, I had read the whole letter and written the word *yes* at the bottom. (If you could see the pile of rejected query letters in my office every week, you would see how the *no* is always written at the top of the letters. That's because I didn't reach the end.) Laura's letter wasn't written with fireworks, but it didn't need to be, because the story as she described it briefly needed no embellishment. And she had enough confidence in her story to let the description be.

Let's break it down paragraph by paragraph, and see how all the pieces fit together.

THE FIRST PARAGRAPH: YOUR HOOK

The first paragraph of your query letter should skip the throat-clearing—or at least keep the opening pleasantries to a bare minimum—and get quickly to the one-line description. In that sentence you'll give the title of the novel and insert the genre if appropriate. Here's the first line of a letter I saw this year:

> [Title] is a coming-of-age novel about two young women trying to
> survive their first year of college and find their own identities.

To tell you the truth, that sentence would have been enough to describe the book, but the author went on for four more sentences in an attempt to make the novel sound dramatic. If she had taken out those four additional sentences, she would have had a serviceable description of the novel. However, she probably also would have had to face the fact that her novel was not inherently dramatic enough to interest agents and editors in a competitive marketplace. It didn't have a hook. Somewhere within herself, she knew this, and that's why she added the four sentences.

Look again at Laura's letter:

> My novel, THE CLEARING, is a supernatural love story told
> from the point of view of a young woman who has been dead
> 130 years.

The genre, the title, and the hook are in one sentence. Laura added a few more sentences to flesh out the basic idea, but she didn't go on too long and, more important, she left the reader with a cliffhanger by saying:

> When the two of them fall in love, the fact that he is in a body
> and she is not presents the first of their problems.

Your hook should be your novel's distinguishing feature. A distinguishing feature can be something imaginative in the plot—the way Laura's book was a love story featuring a heroine who'd been dead for 130 years—or it can be sheer good writing. It can be something unique about the book or about the way you describe the book. But if the one-liner doesn't make anyone sit up and take notice, all the additional plot description in the world isn't going to help.

Your letter should not describe your book at length, should not drag the reader all the way through the plot, and should not give away the ending. A real mood-killer is to use an overworked notion like redemption or a clichéd description—such as, *It's about the human condition*—when describing your book. Stick to the concrete. It's easy to see why someone might think that a one-line description is the same thing as a summary, but it's not.

THE SECOND PARAGRAPH: YOUR BIO

In your second paragraph, give some brief and pertinent biographical information. Writing courses, publications, and awards are good to mention. But more than a sentence summing up minor publications and writing study is not so good.

Remember—the immediate task of the query letter is to get an agent or editor interested in reading your novel. It's not to showcase what an interesting, fabulous, credentialed, or kooky person you are. That will come later, when your agent needs to sell you as well as your book. But for now, you need to come across as professional, serious, dedicated, and confident.

Anything you say about yourself should somehow, briefly and brilliantly, make us think we want to read your book. All Laura said of herself was, "I have won a few awards for fiction and poetry." Because she couldn't claim to have won the Pulitzer, hadn't invented nuclear fusion, wasn't married to someone famous and, more to the point, had never published a book, there was no point in giving a long résumé of her achievements.

Many query writers insert a sentence beginning, "Although I am an unpublished writer …" Doing so simultaneously states the obvious (you're writing about your first novel, after all) and dwells negatively on you—on what you haven't done. Remember that the query letter is looking to the future. The future is when someone is going to read your novel, and your job is to convince us that we will be that future someone. Say no more than one or two things:

- I received my MFA from the Columbia Writing Program, where my novel was awarded the Prize for Singular Fabulousness.

- I've worked as a taxi driver and a mail carrier while writing and publishing short fiction in literary journals.

THE THIRD (AND FINAL) PARAGRAPH: YOUR CONCLUSION

Your third paragraph should be the sign-off paragraph. Wrap up the letter with a word or two about having enclosed a SASE and looking forward to a response, and sign off. Don't drag it out. Don't give your vacation schedule with your spouse's cell phone number. If you've used a letterhead with your address, e-mail address, and telephone number, or inserted that information in a business-letter-appropriate fashion, anyone who wants to track you down will find you. Many agents nowadays don't even need you to indicate that you're making a multiple submission, because they assume you are. So stop talking, finish the letter with a complimentary closing, and hit "Save." Then prepare yourself for the next step: researching agents to find the right one for your book.

 ANN RITTENBERG is a literary agent.

CHAPTER 51

PRODUCING A KNOCKOUT NOVEL SYNOPSIS

BY EVAN MARSHALL

Your novel is finished and ready to be mailed to an agent or editor. You shoot off a query letter. The agent or editor asks to see your manuscript, *or* she asks to see a proposal: three chapters and a synopsis, or one chapter and a synopsis, or just a synopsis.

A *what*? A synopsis—a brief narrative summary of your novel. It's a vital marketing tool for a novelist, because it often has to do the entire job of enticing an agent or editor enough to want to read your novel. Think of the synopsis as a sales pitch for your book.

A synopsis has other uses, too. Later, when you sell your novel, your editor may ask you for a synopsis to be used as the basis for jacket or cover copy for your book. Other departments in the publishing house, such as art or sales or publicity, may want to read your synopsis to get a quick idea of your story.

Even later, when it's time to sell your next novel, you may be able to secure a contract solely on the basis of a synopsis and a few chapters, or just a synopsis. As you can see, the synopsis performs a number of important functions. It therefore deserves as careful attention as you've given the novel itself.

SYNOPSIS MECHANICS

The synopsis is formatted much like your manuscript. Use courier type; double-space all text; set your left, right, and bottom margins at 1¼" (3.2cm), your top margin at ½" (1.3cm). Justify the left margin only.

On every page except the first, type against the top and left margins a slugline consisting of your last name, a slash, your novel's title

in capital letters, another slash, and the word *Synopsis*, like this: Price/
UNDERSUSPICION/Synopsis. Number the pages consecutively in the
upper right-hand corner of the page, against the top and right margins.
The first line of text on each page should be about ¾" (1.9cm) below the
slugline and page number.

On the first page of your synopsis, against the top and left margins,
type single-spaced your name, address, and telephone number. Against
the top and right margins, type single-spaced your novel's genre, its word
count, and the word *Synopsis*. (The first page of the synopsis is not numbered, though it is page 1.)

Double-space twice, center your novel's title in capital letters, double-
space twice again, and begin the text of your synopsis.

SYNOPSIS BASICS

Before we get to the subtleties of writing the synopsis, be aware of a few
basic rules.

1. The synopsis is always written in the present tense (called the historical present tense).

2. The synopsis tells your novel's *entire* story. It doesn't leave out
   what's covered by the sample chapters submitted with it. Nor does
   it withhold the end of the story—for example, "who done it" in a
   murder mystery—in order to entice an agent or editor to want to
   see more. The synopsis is a miniature representation of your novel;
   to leave anything out is to defeat the purpose of the synopsis.

3. The synopsis should not run too long. An overlong synopsis also
   defeats in purpose. My rule is to aim for one page of synopsis for
   every twenty-five pages of manuscript. Thus, a four hundred-page
   manuscript calls for a sixteen-page synopsis. If you run a page or
   two over or under, don't worry.

4. To achieve this conciseness, write as clean and tight as you can.
   Cut extra adverbs and adjectives. Focus on your story's essential details. Let's say, for example, you have a section in which
   your lead meets another character for dinner at a chic French
   bistro to try to convince her to lend him some money. We don't

need to know where they had dinner or what they ate or even exactly what was said. We need something on the order of "Ray meets Lenore for dinner and tries to convince her to lend him the money. Lenore refuses." Actual dialogue is rarely, if ever, needed in the synopsis.

5. Don't divide your synopsis by chapters; write one unified account of your story. You can use paragraphing to indicate a chapter or section break.

HOW TO MAKE YOUR SYNOPSIS SIZZLE

Now, keeping all of the above in mind, translate your manuscript into synopsis. Begin with your lead and her crisis as the hook of your synopsis. Then tell how your lead intends to solve the crisis (what is her story goal?). For example:

> BARBARA DANFORTH has never been especially fond of her brother-in-law, GRAHAM, but she would never have murdered him. Yet all the clues point to her as Graham's killer. She'll have to prove her innocence if she doesn't want to end up as dead as Graham.
>
> PATRICK WARMAN, founder and director of Philadelphia's Friendship Street Shelter for runaway children, has always been careful to maintain a professional distance from the young people he helps. That's why he is especially horrified to realize he has fallen in love with PEARL, a teenage girl in his care. If he can't come to terms with these forbidden feelings, he'll lose everything he's worked for. Yet he can't bear to lose sixteen-year-old Pearl.
>
> RITA RAYMOND is delighted when an employment agency sends her to work as a companion to a man recovering from an accident. She would never have accepted the job if she had known the man was her ex-husband, AARON. And damn if she isn't falling in love with him again. Yet Aaron was the cause of everything wrong in her life.

Soon after your problem hook, give the vital details about your lead: age, occupation, marital status (if you haven't already), as well as details of time (the present? the past?) and place.

> Barbara, single at thirty-eight, has lived quietly in Rosemont, Texas, working as a stenographer and generally minding her own business. When her sister TRISH invited her to a party to celebrate the tenth anniversary of Trish's marriage to Graham, Barbara balked. She'd never liked Graham. But she accepted—her first mistake. Agreeing to let Graham take her for a moonlit walk around the couple's lavish estate was her second... .

> Patrick, twenty-eight, has been married to MARIANNE for nine years, but although she helps at the shelter, their marriage is in name only... .

> At twenty-nine, Rita has made peace with her life as a divorcée. She earns enough money as a high-school teacher to support herself and her seven-year-old daughter, ALLEGRA, though Allegra's severe asthma has been an emotional and financial strain. Even so, life these past five years without Aaron has been better than life was with him... .

Now continue telling your story, keeping to the main story points. Remember that the synopsis is not necessarily meant to convey the circumstances of *how* something happens; the happenings themselves are the concern here.

Most important, remember that *motivation and emotion are things that happen*; they are plot points, as important as any physical action a character might perform. Some of the worst synopses I've seen from would-be clients are dry and lifeless because these aspects have been left out.

Don't just tell us that Brandon tells Carla he's accepted the job in Sydney and that the next morning Carla has coffee at her friend Tanya's house and tells her the news. Tell us that when Brandon tells Carla he's accepted the job in Sydney, Carla sees her happy life collapsing around her. Devastated, the next morning over coffee she pours her heart out to Tanya.

Don't just tell us that Jake Hammond stomps into the bank and dumps a sack of money on the president's desk, announcing he's repaying his loan. Tell us that Jake, full of angry self-righteousness at how the bank has treated his sister, stomps into the bank and dumps the money on the president's desk.

The agents and editors who will read and evaluate your synopsis are looking for the same things as your eventual readers: emotion and human drama. Bear down on these life-breathing aspects of your story and you can't go wrong.

Indicate other characters' story lines in your synopsis by beginning a new paragraph and describing the character's actions. Sometimes transitions such as "Meanwhile" or "Simultaneously" or "At the hotel" can help ground the reader in time and place.

As you write the synopsis, think of it as your novel in condensed form, and present events in the same order that they occur in the novel itself. Also, reveal information at the same points you do so in your novel.

Stay "invisible" in your synopsis; by this I mean several things. First, don't use devices that emphasize the mechanics of storytelling. One of these is the use of such headings as "Background," "Setting," and "Time" at the beginning of your synopsis. All of these elements should be smoothly woven into the narrative. Another such device is the use of character sketches or descriptions at the beginning or end of the synopsis. All of these elements should be smoothly woven into the narrative. Second, they make it difficult for the agent or editor to follow your story: If he reads the synopsis first, it's meaningless because he has no information about the characters. If he reads the character sketches first, they are equally meaningless because the characters are not presented in the context of the story. Characters and story do not exist independently of each other. Give any important facts or background when you introduce a character.

In the text, type a character's name in capital letters the first time you use it—a technique borrowed from film treatments. Also, to avoid confusion, always refer to a character the same way through the synopsis (not "Dr. Martin" in one place, "the doctor" somewhere else, and "Martin" somewhere else).

Another way to stay invisible is to avoid referring to the structural underpinnings of your story. When I was a kid, we used to go to an amusement park with a scary jungle ride that went through a dark tunnel where a native jumped out and scared us silly. One day as we floated through the tunnel and the native jumped out, I noticed that the figure of the native had come loose from its metal support. I could see ugly gray metal and a tangle of electrical wires. The ride was never the same after that.

That's how I feel when I can see the scaffolding of a synopsis, for example, "In a flashback, Myron ... ." Better to simply say "Myron remembers ... ." Avoid "As the story begins ..." or "As the story ends ..."; just tell the story.

As you near the end of the synopsis and your story's resolution, quicken the pace by using shorter paragraphs and shorter sentences. A staccato effect increases the suspense.

Above all, never review your story in your synopsis, such as "In a nerve-jangling confrontation ..." or "In a heart-wrenching confession... ." This kind of self-praise is amateurish and inappropriate in a synopsis, which presents "just the (story) facts, ma'am." Let your story's attributes speak for themselves.

Once your synopsis is finished, polish, polish, polish! In many cases, your synopsis will be your foot in the door, and many agents and editors will judge your storytelling and writing style from this selling piece alone. When I receive a synopsis containing misspellings, poor grammar, and sloppy presentation, I do not ask to see the manuscript. I assume it will contain the same kinds of errors.

Writing the synopsis is an art you should become proficient in. A masterful synopsis starts telling your novel to an agent or editor before she even looks at your manuscript. In fact, a few times during my career, I have read a synopsis so well-crafted that later I felt I had read the book! That's real magic.

EVAN MARSHALL is the president of The Evan Marshall Agency. He is the author of *The Marshall Plan for Novel Writing*, from which this article was adapted. His latest book, *Dark Alley*, is part of a mystery series called Hidden Manhattan Mysteries.

CHAPTER 52
MAKE REJECTION INTO A PLAN OF ACTION

BY WENDY BURT-THOMAS

As much as you'd probably like to burn your rejection letters or mold them into little voodoo dolls of the editors who sent them, don't. There's a lot to be learned from the responses (yes, even those that arrive with nothing more than a standard checkbox of reasons the piece wasn't accepted).

Think of your rejections as reactions from first dates: Some will be very general ("Sorry, I'm just not that into you"), some will offer minimal feedback ("You talked nonstop about your ex; I don't think you're ready for a new relationship"), and some will offer detailed information to help you improve for your next attempt ("You were charming, attractive, and we had a lot in common, but I just don't date smokers").

While it might be hard to swallow, the feedback provided in these letters could be your best hope of improving your work—query, proposal, and/or manuscript—and eventually getting published. Be grateful for it. Most editors are so busy sorting through their slush piles (in addition to all their other work) that they don't have time to offer advice. So when they make time to do so, it could be either because they believe your work has potential, or because your approach is so far off the mark that they're trying to help you correct your mistakes. Either way, they wouldn't respond if they weren't trying to help.

So what are some of the specific types of responses you might get, and what can you glean from them?

First, the responses that could have been avoided if you'd done your homework before submitting:

- "No simultaneous submissions."
- "Not our genre."
- "Too long."
- "Too short."
- "No unagented submissions."
- "Not right for our audience."
- "No e-mail queries."
- "Query only" (i.e., don't send a proposal, manuscript or synopsis).
- "No anthropomorphic characters."

Lesson learned. Now, the responses that you may not have been able to predict:

"Not our style/voice/tone."

Translation: This could mean that the writing or idea was good, but the publisher doesn't print books like yours.

Your next move: Try another publishing house.

"We no longer accept this genre."

Translation: The publishing house has found that it can be more profitable in other genres. That doesn't mean your genre isn't profitable; it's just not for them.

Your next move: Try another publisher that recently printed a book in your genre.

"We aren't accepting new clients at this time."

Translation: The literary agency could be overwhelmed with clients, in the process of restructuring, or even about to fold.

Your next move: Try another agency.

"This topic has been done to death."

Translation: The editor may not be saying that her publisher in particular has covered this topic in numerous books, but rather that several publishing houses have printed books similar to yours recently and the market is saturated.

Your next move: Find a fresh angle to your story to avoid getting this response from other publishers.

"We only publish authors with platforms."

Translation: We're a small publishing house with no budget to promote new authors. It's up to you to promote yourself and your book, and because you didn't mention anything about having a platform in your query, we'll have to pass.

Your next move: Create a platform for yourself now—and mention it in your query to the next publishing house. It could be something as simple as a blog on a subject related to your book, teaching a half-day seminar on the topic, or developing an e-mail list of potential customers.

"It doesn't feel like you've zeroed in on a niche."

Translation: You were all over the map. The editor or agent couldn't understand the query/synopsis/proposal, or the topic is too broad to fit into one book.

Your next move: Get a second or third set of eyes to give you feedback on tightening the idea. Hire a book editor or join a critique club if you're serious about seeing your manuscript get published, and prepare yourself for the possibility that it could need some major rewriting.

"I really like your protagonist but just can't get on board to represent you."

Translation: You're great at developing characters, but other areas (like plot, motivation, dialogue, or conflict) are still lacking or weak.

Your next move: Ask a professional editor with expertise in your genre to give you feedback on your strongest and weakest areas. You may also want to consider taking a class (or attending workshops at a writing conference) specific to your genre.

"Numerous grammatical errors."

Translation: You either didn't proofread and spell check your piece, or your grammar skills are lacking (or both).

Your next move: Paying someone to proof your work will help with the initial step. But if you're going to finish your book, write another book, or do your own press releases, you'll need to take a few English classes and invest in a copy of Strunk & White's *The Elements of Style*.

"The book didn't quite live up to my expectations."

Translation: The first few sample chapters you sent were great; that's why I requested more. But the book lost its appeal the more I read.

Your next move: Revisit your story and see where it might be going off track. Does it change focus? Does the action slow down? Do the main characters lose their charm or do something that no longer makes them believable? Don't be afraid to cut any words that aren't working.

"I recommend you read other authors in your genre."

Translation: Your work was mediocre or did not adhere to the conventions of the genre in which you are writing, and you need to learn about basic narrative elements like plot, structure, motivation, characters, etc.

Your next move: Read several classic and contemporary books in your genre and take a writing class before heading back to revise your manuscript. Then, join a critique group or attend a writing conference where you can get feedback from an industry professional. Don't submit your book to any other publishers until someone knowledgeable about your genre has "approved" your piece. And no, your mom doesn't count.

"This isn't quite right for us, but have you tried contacting [insert name of agent or acquisitions editor]? This might be a good match for them."

Translation: This is a good, solid piece of writing. We can't publish it, but it's good enough that I'm willing to put myself out on a limb to give you a referral to another publishing house. I want them to call and thank me when they make money from your book.

Your next move: Contact the acquisitions editor at the second publishing house and tell her who referred you. Ask if you can e-mail your query/synopsis/proposal/manuscript immediately. Write the first editor a nice thank-you note and keep him updated in the process.

"You may want to consider self-publishing."

Translation: Unfortunately, this may mean that in this editor's opinion, there is nothing that can be done to salvage this book. You need to take writing classes, hire an editor, join a critique group, attend every writing conference in your area over the next three years, and then start from scratch. But it may also mean that your topic or audience is so niche that it's not commercially viable. The editor may be able to tell that this story is one that means a lot to you (like the history of your hometown or a memoir of your boarding school days), but she also knows enough about the industry to see that the book may not appeal to larger audiences.

Your next move: In case of the first scenario, ask your mom to tell you how great you are. In the second, start researching self-publishing options if you're determined to see your story in print.

 WENDY BURT-THOMAS is a freelance writer and author of *The Writer's Digest Guide to Query Letters.*

CHAPTER 53
YOUR POWER PLATFORM

BY CHRISTINA KATZ

The writing world is abuzz with one word these days—and that word is "platform." But many writers are left wondering: *What the heck is a platform? Why do I even need one?* And the biggest question of them all: *How do I start building mine?*

If this describes you, don't sweat it. Platform is a simple word to describe a complicated process—a process that's been shrouded in mystery until recently. If you're wondering what the difference is between a completely unknown writer and a well-known writer, I can tell you. The well-known writer has influence. In order for you to build influence, you need to create and launch a platform that communicates your expertise, credibility, and integrity to others quickly and concisely.

A strong platform includes things like a Web presence, classes you teach, media contacts you've established, articles you've published, public speaking services you offer, and any other means you currently have for making your name (and your future works) known to your readership. Whether you write fiction, nonfiction, poetry, screenplays, songs, copy, or even ghostwritten manuscripts, if you're not looking at your writing career as a big-picture proposition that includes platform development, you need to start now.

The benefits of having a solid platform abound. Increased media exposure, blog buzz, invitations to speak, fully enrolled classes, and a surge in readers can lead to career opportunities such as interest from agents and editors, book deals, increased book sales, and, ultimately, higher income from multiple sources. In the short run, making the decision to start becoming more visible is the first step toward long-term literary success. Once you establish a platform, it can work for you 24/7, reaching readers even as you sleep.

To start developing your platform, you'll need to make some important choices about your topic, audience, and the ways you interact best with others. No matter what kinds of writing you regularly produce, your platform development will proceed more smoothly and quickly when you take these three aspects into thoughtful consideration:

1. A clearly identified body of expertise. The first thing you need to know and communicate is what defines you and your expertise. If you don't know who you are and what you uniquely offer, how will anyone else? Think of this as cultivating your identity. Rather than the overused and impersonal term "branding," identity nods to the importance of keeping things real and staying true to yourself, even while making self-promotion a priority.

2. A distinct niche so you can stand out. With your identity in hand, how are you different from all of the other writers out there? These days, you have to communicate who you are and what you do quickly. Attention spans are getting shorter, so being able to summarize your strengths concisely is critical. Platform isn't your set of credentials or your résumé; it's current and evolving on an ongoing basis. As what you write about grows and changes over the years, you'll need to constantly revisit and rewrite the words that describe what sets you apart from the pack.

3. An ongoing relationship with a targeted audience. Clarifying who your readers are will bring your platform into perspective. If you're vague about identifying your audience, the whole writing process takes longer and typically requires more rewriting than if you zoom in from the get-go. This applies to books, blogs, and everything else you write, no matter the form or genre. Once you identify your audience and start speaking to it directly, the ongoing dialogue will spark all kinds of ideas, connections, and opportunities to catalyze your relationship over time and create community.

Peek into the weekly schedule of a writer who has influence, and you will notice that she's focused on platform growth. Very likely her planner is full of commitments, appointments, and deadlines, including scheduled time to write. You'll probably notice a steady stream of tasks to help her increase visibility, such as speaking gigs, Web editing, and curriculum, flyer, or book proposal development. Once you start working on developing your platform daily, your writing career will gain momentum. Here are ten simple steps that will take your visibility from zero to standout in a short time, while also giving you ample opportunities to flex your expertise, carve out your niche topic, and connect with your audience.

FIND YOUR TRIBES

Research five or six professional associations related to your topic, target audience, or professional goals. For example, if your topic is the magic of botanicals, your audience is gaming enthusiasts, or your ambition is to become a published author, conduct an Internet search of groups that cater to gardeners, gamers, or aspiring authors. Then narrow down your selections to the three that make the most sense for your goals. Once you're a member, get in touch with the administrators and introduce yourself. Ask how you can become fully involved. Take advantage of appropriate opportunities to share your breaking professional news. In a year, assess how well each group benefits your career. Thumb's up, rejoin and stay active. Thumb's down, try another.

DON'T NETWORK—CONNECT

Not a natural networker? If the prospect of "working the room" sounds daunting, lower the stakes. Just show up to an event or meeting. Then connect by striking up a conversation with the person sitting right next to you. "Shy writer" C. Hope Clark prides herself on overcoming her resistance and putting herself out there whether she feels like it or not. "You may hate it," she says, "but it's a necessary part of doing business." She's right. Tell yourself to just come as you are and be friendly and open. It's enough.

SERVE TO LEARN

Volunteers are smart. They know that helping out feels good, and when you feel good, everything goes better than it would if you dwelled on feeling nervous or self-conscious. There are countless literary event volunteer opportunities around the country. So volunteer—especially if you don't have the means to participate in the kinds of events and programs you'd like to. It won't hurt. In fact, it will very likely help by putting you right in the mix. Showing up is 50 percent of the secret to success. Young-adult author Susan Fletcher learned this twenty years ago at a writing conference where she was a volunteer. Her role as an airport shuttle driver led to a chance encounter with an editor who'd recently rejected her work. Rather than being resentful, she convinced him to let her view the interoffice notes about her submission. Thanks to her desire to learn what she needed to advance her career, Fletcher gained the insights necessary to adapt her submission and eventually broke in. Today, she's published several books, including the award-winning YA novel *Alphabet of Dreams*.

GIVE PUBLIC READINGS

Are you an introvert? If so, you might not believe you'll ever be able to get up in front of a crowd, much less wow an audience. But if you're in the writing biz for the long haul, you'll likely be asked to read your work. Take, for example, Sage Cohen, author of *Writing the Life Poetic*. "The first time I ever read my poetry publicly, I doubted I'd survive," she says. But she did survive, and today she uses the initial jolt of fear to "energize" her performances. Even if your instinct is to avoid such appearances, make it a rule to take deep breaths and accept any invitations that come your way. Even better, seek out smaller speaking opportunities in your area to get yourself started. Experience is the best training.

LEARN TO TEACH

Forget what you've heard. Teaching is for those who do. Teaching asks you to put yourself in someone else's shoes. What could be a better exercise for a writer? Teachers like me have built-in test markets (students) for ideas. We get to find our groove interacting with groups. We understand the importance of addressing audience needs up close and personal. Teaching and writing feed off of each other and create synergy that can increase professional momentum. Teaching has informed my career more than any other nonwriting work I do; I now work with more than one hundred writers a year, many of whom go on to achieve publication or land book deals.

SPEAK UP

Professional writers understand that speaking and selling books go hand in hand. And though not all professional writers choose to become professional speakers, many do. Certainly, if you want to spur awareness of a book, speaking on your topic to groups ranging in size from tens to hundreds is a smart choice. Author Lee Silber has written fourteen books, most recently *Rock to Riches*. "The best thing I have done—and continue to do—is speak at conventions and to corporations," he says.

START SOMETHING

I started hosting a local literary series so I wouldn't have to drive any distance to hear authors speak. In doing so, I found a way to give back to writers in my local community, added a regular event to the arts council's roster, provided a publicity opportunity for our local grocery store and Starbucks, gave an intern from the local high school something to put on her college applications, and made my local library director happy by bringing folks in on Sunday afternoons. How might you do something self-serving that might fill a need for others?

PEN ARTICLES

Allison Winn Scotch freelanced for national women's magazines for years before she landed her first book deal, a novel, *The Department of Lost and Found*. Her second novel, *Time of My Life*, quickly climbed the ranks to *The New York Times* best-seller list after its release last fall. She says her familiarity with magazine editors was a boon to sales because those editors "likely picked up my galley faster than they might have picked up someone else's, and I got a lot of great magazine exposure as a result."

Children's author Elizabeth Rusch, whose picture book *A Day With No Crayons* recently won an Oregon Book Award, published four titles in one year. She garnered interest from publishers by attaching a second sheet to her book query identifying herself as an author who had reached millions of readers over the past twelve years as a freelance writer. This demonstrated that she, like Winn Scotch, was already a more likely choice for book reviews and endorsements.

Both novelist Marc Acito, author of *How I Paid for College* and *Attack of the Theater People*, and memoirist Gail Konop Baker, author of *Cancer Is a Bitch*, became more visible by writing columns. Acito self-syndicated his humor column through gay newspapers and then mentioned his growing number of readers in his book query. Konop Baker wrote a column for the online journal *Literary Mama* and impressed an agent, who encouraged her to transform the columns into a memoir.

OFFER ASSISTANCE

As writers, we're typically good at keeping our noses to the grindstone and cranking out projects on a deadline, but we can really miss the cruise ship when it comes to what else we might be able to do with the kernels of wisdom we glean. In my book *Get Known Before the Book Deal* I explore four ways to leverage expertise that can lead to book-length projects: coaching, consulting, counseling, and training. Essentially, you need to realize when you have something to offer and then find the most appropriate way to share it.

CREATE A ONE-PAGER

Over breakfast in 2005, mental health author Julie Fast taught me how to whip up a one-pager, an easy form that summarizes your platform. I've been using it—and helping others do the same—ever since. A one-pager lists and illustrates in two columns your publication credits, media experience, speaking credentials, professional affiliations, online readership, notable education, and awards won. Carry it to conferences and literary events. Any time you're pitching a book, you'll want to include your one-pager to make a bigger impact and demonstrate your marketing savvy.

Does all of this sound like too much work? What if you're shy, reluctant, or skeptical that all of this effort isn't going to pan out? Maybe you have a full-time job in addition to your writing endeavors—and this sounds like another one. Or maybe, like me, you're a busy mom. Perhaps you don't have much money to invest, or are so focused on your writing that you shudder at the thought of growing your marketing skills simultaneously. These are common concerns. Don't let them stop you from getting started.

Platforms take time to establish, not to mention considerable energy to launch, but in the end they raise you above the pack. So make a commitment to building yours. Carve out daily time, seek out more resources on the topic or integrate platform development accountability into the format of your existing writing group. By getting off to a solid start, you'll conserve time and energy in the long run. And be sure to pace yourself—you'll be working on maximizing your visibility for the rest of your career, or at least as long as you plan to write.

 CHRISTINA KATZ (christinakatz.com) is the author of *Writer Mama: How to Raise a Writing Career Alongside Your Kids* and *Get Known Before the Book Deal: Use Your Personal Strengths to Grow an Author Platform.*

CHAPTER 54

NOVELISTS NEED PLATFORMS, TOO

BY JANE FRIEDMAN

The term author platform is a big buzz phrase in the publishing world: It typically means the way you establish yourself as a voice of authority about a subject. But don't make the mistake of thinking that having a good promotional platform is just for nonfiction writers.

It's true that nonfiction writers are different from novelists when it comes to pitching your work. Nonfiction writers almost always have to prove that they have authority/credentials, as well as a platform, that will help them market and promote the book effectively to a target audience. Nonfiction writers essentially put forth a business plan explaining the market need for the book. Novelists don't do this at the outset; the decision usually comes down to the quality of the writing and the storytelling.

However, what separates successful writers from unsuccessful writers (no matter what the genre), is platform, or visibility to a readership. If a novelist is unable or unwilling to develop a platform for her writing career, she will find that her books don't sell and the publishers lose interest fast. A novelist should never rely on the publisher to make his book sell.

Here are a few things that fiction writers need to consider in targeting their audience and developing a platform.

- **How and where you write.** How have you developed your fiction-writing chops? Through critique groups? Online workshops? Creative writing programs? Whatever writing community you participate in, that leads to a part of your platform. For example, if you are an expert critiquer in online workshop settings, and word spreads about you, then you're building a platform. Think about your interactions with other writers and how you network. These can provide the seeds.

- **Community/regional presence.** Also think about your interactions within your community or region that may or may not be connected to writing. Can you establish programs relating to reading, writing, or the themes in your work? Most writers are passionate about something connected to words; are you involved in your community, or do you work for a greater cause and have visibility that way? Usually the passions in our lives come out in our writing, and vice versa.

- **Special relationships.** Maybe you were mentored or coached by a notable writer or someone in the community. Or you have connections with people in the media (whether family or friends or colleagues), or with other influencers and tastemakers. Who do you think will be willing to help you? And how can you offer something in return?

- **Your work.** What themes or topics are explored in your work? It's likely you'll return to the same themes or topics throughout your writing career. (For example, if you write about small-town life today, it's likely you'll still be writing about small-town life in a few years.) Becoming known as someone who explores certain themes or topics can make you interesting and visible to particular audiences. And that's what platform-building is all about: knowing what audiences will be most interested in your work, always thinking about how you can be more visible to them, and reaching out to them in meaningful ways.

Keep in mind that some things that work for one author may not work for another. But it's helpful to see what's being done, to help spark new ideas and to better understand your own position and strengths.

 JANE FRIEDMAN is publisher and editorial director of the Writer's Digest community. Read her publishing blog at blog.writersdigest.com/norules.

CHAPTER 55

THE MUST-HAVE ONLINE MARKETING PLAN

BY M.J. ROSE

So you've been building your platform, and now it's time to use it. You've got a book deal. You're going to be published. Now what?

There are authors who hire expensive publicists to ensure word gets out about their books—and there are authors who never spend a dime and get the same amount of publicity. There are authors who hire top-notch design firms to build $5,000 websites to entice readers—and there are authors who use free templates, put up rudimentary sites, and get the same number of visitors. There are authors who blog and post on Twitter for hours every day (eating into their precious writing time, I might add)—and others who think Twitter is something Tweety Bird does. And in both sets you'll find bestsellers and modest sellers.

I could go on and on, but I think I've proved my point: There's no one solution to being a successful author. No one trick. No one effort guaranteed to work. The bad news is even if you do everything possible and spend $150,000 of your own money, you still can't guarantee success. (And I know an author who did just that last year, and the book didn't sell more than five thousand copies.)

Ultimately, no matter what you do, careers are made on the book, not on the marketing. But once you've written the best book you can and gotten the best agent possible and she's made the best deal she can get with the best publisher who's interested, then you need to deal with reality:

1. If no one knows your book is out there, no one will think about buying it. It's as simple as that.

2. Someone—either you or your publisher—is going to have to get the word out about the book. First, you need to find out exactly what your publisher is and isn't going to do, so you can plan accordingly. The reality: Publishers can and do spend money on advertising, PR, and co-ops (meaning paid placement on special displays in bookstores and other retailers), but they don't spend the same amount on all books. In general, publishers spend less than $2,000 on 85 percent of their titles—and that won't even make a dent in getting the word out about your book.

3. Regardless of the publisher's plan for your book, the work you put into standing out to your editor and agent doesn't end with the book deal. You need to prove you'll be a savvy companion in marketing yourself and your work to further gain their confidence and ensure your first book isn't your last.

A comprehensive marketing plan involves both online and offline efforts to use and broaden your existing platform to promote your book. But these days, a solid online marketing plan is a logical (and affordable) place to start. Here's a list of the most critical, innovative things you can do to market your book online:

Create a strong writer's website (mandatory) **and blog** (optional). *Writer's Digest* took an in-depth look at exactly how to do this in the October 2008 issue. Visit writersdigest.com/article/the-anatomy-of-a-writers-website for the complete piece.

Get involved with social networking.

Create a video trailer for your book and get it in front of your readers. Search for video book trailers on Amazon.com, bookstores' websites, authors' sites and blogs, and YouTube (youtube.com). Watch and learn. Then decide what would work best for your book and whether or not you're capable of putting it together. As with most online marketing, you can do this yourself or hire a firm (a $500–$5,000 investment), depending on your skill level and resources. Either way, there's no one solution for every book; you need to be objective about what will work best for yours. Post it on your website, upload it to YouTube, share it with your publisher, and ask others to post or link to it on their sites, blogs, or e-newsletters (offering, of course, to return the favor).

Do a blog tour. It's very expensive to go on a tour that's not online. The last one I did cost $9,000. That would buy six weeks of advertising online to more than ten million people. Of course, the great benefit to touring in person is meeting booksellers, who then put autographed copies on display, write about your book in newsletters, and, most of all, get to meet your charming self—all of which they'll remember when your next book comes out. But to an extent, this also can be accomplished online if you develop a smart strategy. And a blog tour costs nothing but time.

Find a dozen blogs that match the tone, tenor, and subject of your book. If it's a thriller about a veterinarian, search for blogs devoted to pets and offer the owners an excerpt, provide them with a free book to give away to their readers, or propose a contest idea. You can and should also target blogs devoted to books and readers as well as blogs and websites of independent bookstores—just be aware that on all of these sites you'll be competing with other books.

Get reviews of your books posted online. This is as simple as getting free copies into the hands of the right people: other writers you know, online reviewers, etc.

Podcast. Who should podcast? Anyone who wants to—it's all about you, your book, and what you want to do. Again, go to authors' websites you admire and listen to theirs. See if it's for you.

The key to podcasts—and many other successful online marketing tools—is how well you market the marketing idea. In other words, how are you going to get people to listen to the podcast that then sells the book? Make sure you have a plan to spread the word.

Become a commenter. There are great blogs read by hundreds, thousands, and millions of people, and they all have comment sections. Subscribe to a few, read these sections and take note of what authors do that works—and what turns you off. As a general rule, when you comment on a blog, make it knowledgeable or witty and, most of all, relevant to that post—then, simply sign it with your name and your book title. Resist the urge to brag or sell your book.

SEEKING PROFESSIONAL HELP

Unsure if you have the time or know-how to take on a marketing plan yourself?

Go 50/50. Offer to split advertising and co-op costs with your publisher. Write up a plan outlining what you're proposing and take it to your publisher. I find that about half of the writers who try this discover their publisher will split costs with them—especially when the author is suggesting a marketing service or effort the publisher knows and likes.

Hire a publicity pro. Hiring a publicist can be a gamble because publicists don't guarantee placements. Go this route only if you have a highly marketable book that can get publicity. This is one area where more is usually more. Hire the best publicist you can afford. Make sure you interview at least two publicists who do both on- and offline marketing and who come recommended by people you can speak to on the phone. Be certain you are dealing with someone reputable.

Get a marketing firm. If you do your homework and hire someone who comes recommended, marketing is not a gamble in the same way PR is, because marketing is guaranteed. The results, of course, aren't guaranteed, but if you pay for an ad, it shows up where it's supposed to—no ifs, ands, or buts.

 M.J. ROSE is the best-selling author of ten novels and co-author of two nonfiction books on marketing, including *Buzz Your Book*.

CHAPTER 56

FINDING THE PERFECT EDITOR

BY MARK PETERS

Anyone who has entered the online dating world and worked as a freelance writer may have noticed some spooky similarities between the two: the suspiciously vague ads, the long response waits, the frequent miscommunication, the soul-crushing self-doubt and—when you're lucky—the giddy feeling of being in a mutually respectful relationship that results in plenty of good love (or good clips).

In a frightening number of ways, an editorial relationship can feel like a romantic relationship. And many of the rules for being lucky in love will also keep you well-published and in the good graces of your editors. While I don't pretend to have any Yoda-like wisdom or awe-inspiring accomplishments as a writer or dater, I've been on about 117 dates in the last year, and my writing career is slowly moving away from the tragic and comic toward success: a book contract, a column, and articles in some major magazines. Here are some of my own discoveries and experiences that I hope will give you a knowing chuckle—or a warning of what's ahead.

SENDING E-MAILS INTO THE VOID

In about a year and a half of using the *Chicago Reader* personal ads, I've sent 258 messages and received 145. Maybe I'm pathetic (maybe?) but that actually seems like a decent percentage: If I were batting over .500 with my writing pitches, I'd be making a lot more cash than I am now.

Online dating and freelance writing both involve a lot of waiting by the computer, and the wait often results in a big fat zero. If I had a horse for every pitch that hasn't received so much as a no-thanks form letter, there wouldn't be a stable in the world big enough to hold them. Though the desire to be published and the desire for companionship aren't one and the same, in both cases, the blow-off has the same soul-diminishing, dream-crushing, woe-is-me effect.

COMPATIBILITY

Online dating sites promote pickiness, which may be a good thing, but can dating really be reduced to a bazillion-question form like eHarmony's? (Maybe reduced isn't the right word.) And how likely are you to find a suburban veteran Jewish conservative architect who likes *Arrested Development* and bubble tea? I don't know about you, but few of my former significant others would fulfill the multiple must-haves I demand online.

Much as we'd like to plug ourselves into both relationships and publications based on logic and qualifications, chemistry will always trump a list of characteristics. This can be particularly upsetting with writing. I've been rejected by publications that—in my mind, anyway—I'm perfect for. I've also been rejected by publications that are demonstrably worse (in terms of pay and credibility) than publications I've already written for. Logic would suggest they should be thrilled to have me, right?

And yet, lesser publications continue to turn me down, even as glossier publications sometimes accept my work. How could *Super-Mega-Popular Magazine* like me but not *Pissant Pretentious Quarterly?* You begin to feel like a doorman on *Seinfeld* bellyaching, "You think you're better than me?"

As with dating, "better" is a word to avoid. You'll hit it off with some publications/editors. Others, not so much. Look for too much logic and you'll go cuckoo-bananas—just keep pitching and give yourself more chances to find a match.

MIXED SIGNALS

Last year, I got a message on Match.com from a gorgeous blonde with about seventeen other attractive qualities. We had a great phone conversation, and she seemed to dig many things I liked: George Carlin, dogs, *Battlestar Galactica*, Swedish pancakes and—most importantly—me. So we planned a meeting, which she had to postpone because of work. This seemed like a sincere non-blow-off, but I never heard from her again.

Did I do the e-mail equivalent of farting in church? Did she remember she was married? Was the witness protection program involved? I'll never know.

In related news, I once sent an idea to an ultra-hip magazine that allows its writers to explore ideas in depth with great freedom. After several months, I received this e-mail from the editor: "I love this idea, and am ready to assign it instantly, but I should probably exercise a bit of restraint and first ask for some clips. Any chance you could e-mail me some?" I immediately did so, eagerly and droolingly, as I was thrilled at the chance to write for this magazine.

Much to my ulcer's chagrin, I never heard from the editor again. Were my clips that bad? Did the editor die? What happened? I'll never know.

Here's the bottom line, which is about as easy to swallow as a flaming octopus: It doesn't matter what happened. Regardless of how unpredictable, insane, or unprofessional your editor's behavior may be, analyzing the editor's actions is pointless, won't help, and that's that. The fact is, no matter how much an editor's words may have indicated otherwise, now, at the present moment, he's just not that into your ideas. That's the reality. And yep, it stinks.

DETERMINING WHO'S DUMP-WORTHY

We've all been dumpers and dumpees in our lust lives, but it can feel like dumping isn't an option in the writing biz. When you're starting a freelance career, it's common and useful to have a get-clips-at-all-costs approach. Frequently, the "no-cost" part literally describes what publications are paying for your work. Sometimes it's hard to get out of this mindset and start being selective.

Case in point: There's this glossy magazine that features music articles plus a few columns on wide-ranging subjects. This magazine seemed a likely candidate for me to pitch a language piece, and I suggested something on goofy, beauty-related terms—such as foot facelift, muffin top, bar-code hairstyle, boyzillian, umbilicoplasty, and trout pout—that happened to fit right into a fashion issue the publication was working on. As the idea evolved, the editor checked out my clips, liked the clips, and even seemed receptive to my suggestion that this could be a regular feature.

Finally, I asked that indelicate question: What do you pay?

The answer? Diddly. It sure would've been nice to know this before I exchanged a dozen e-mails with this editor, and it was tempting to write the article anyway, because it promised to be a fun one. But by this point, I already had some excellent clips, so I said no to the freebie. I regretted the whole episode, except for my decision to bail out. After you have some clips and you've been paid for your work, it's time to stop settling for some crappy website or non-paying magazine. Get paid, raise your standards, and move on.

Or, as rogue cop/dating consultant Vic Mackey once said, "Put your clothes on, get out of here and change your taste in men."

SIGNS THE RELATIONSHIP IS DEVELOPING

Along with spongeworthy, schmoopy, home-bed advantage, and conjugal-visit sex, one of the many relationship terms contributed by *Seinfeld* was the elusive quality of hand—something George Costanza seldom, if ever, could get in a relationship. Hand is control; hand is power. Those without hand wait pitifully for any scraps of affection or attention they can get.

After you've written for an editor a few times, you've got a relationship going, but it's still difficult to feel confident: Editors always have "hand." So how do you know an editor really gives a damn? Here's what I do: I submit an article to an editor I've worked for several times, and she rejects the idea, but suggests something else to write instead.

That might not sound terribly exciting, but it's significant progress, and it parallels two schmoopies discussing an evening's plans. I may want to see *Knocked Up*, while my sweetie-bag prefers *Evan Almighty*, but we're not going to break up over it. People in a real relationship make counteroffers; they don't cancel the night's plans because one doesn't like the other's first idea.

So if an editor is rejecting your pitch with a counter-pitch, that's a fantastic sign: Your editor doesn't want to send you home alone, un-loved, and with nothing to write. The editor has the hand, but the editor values having the relationship, too.

SENDING E-MAILS INTO THE VOID ...
AND THE VOID ANSWERS BACK

Recently, I received an e-mail from an awesome magazine that's been compared to *The New Yorker*—the editor accepted my article. Woo-hoo! But wait ... what article? Turns out I had sent it to this magazine two years ago, and since then I had published the piece elsewhere and even had it reprinted. Fortunately, this editor didn't mind reprinting the piece again because the other publications had different audiences.

I can't imagine what the dating equivalent of this would be; maybe if I wrote someone and said I liked her ad, followed by two years of silence that ended with a marriage proposal. Of course, that would be more of a reason to hit "block sender" than to do a touchdown dance, while my magazine surprise was an unqualified delight: I ended up in a great magazine that I had given up on, and because of the time lag, I felt like I didn't even have to work for it. Sometimes what's disturbing and wrong in the dating scene—having eleven partners, for example—is like a warm cookie in the writing world.

DATING AND WRITING: NO WIMPS ALLOWED

Let's think of two hypothetical people: The first is a Shakespearian-level writer who's kind of a wimp when it comes to rejection but is brimming with ungodly, sublime talent. The second can barely write a sentence but is tenacious and determined to succeed, come hell, hand grenades, high water, or toilet water.

Wonder who would be more successful? I don't. The determined semi-illiterate would trounce the weak genius—it wouldn't even be close. Likewise, a gorgeous, funny, intelligent, well-dressed sex god isn't going to find companionship by acting like a fragile, mopey, ostrich-like wimp.

As dating columnist Judy McGuire has lamented, "How many times do I have to tell you people that dating is not for the faint of heart?"

Neither is writing.

MARK PETERS (wordlust.blogspot.com) is a language columnist for *Good*, a euphemism-collector for *Visual Thesaurus*, and a blogger for Oxford University Press.

CHAPTER 57
THE FUTURE ROLE OF AGENTS

BY JANE FRIEDMAN

Given the magnitude of change underway in publishing, some have questioned the future role and necessity of the literary agent. Will agents continue to be the middlemen between publishers and authors? Do authors still need agents if they can get discovered or published on their own? Will publishers rely on agents when they can uncover talent through websites like HarperCollins's authonomy.com?

There are two sides to this discussion: the changing needs and roles of the author vs. the changing needs and roles of the publisher. Let's start with the publisher.

Many in the industry believe publishers need to become less horizontal and more vertical (or specialized) in their approaches. Dominique Raccah of Sourcebooks has said that targeting niche categories is the only way publishers can survive. So has publishing futurist Mike Shatzkin.

I work for a special-interest nonfiction publisher (F+W Media, parent company of *Writer's Digest*) that's been vertical in its approach all along. We serve niche audiences, know our markets better than most agents, and find authors and create great-selling books without agents.

You may agree this makes sense for nonfiction publishing, but what about fiction? Who will separate the wheat from the chaff?

First, keep in mind it's the mainstream New York houses that accept only agented submissions. If you take a look at some of the genre fiction publishers (those that *specialize*), as well as presses focusing on more literary work, many—including Harlequin, Algonquin, DAW, and Tor/Forge—accept unagented submissions.

Second, it is mandatory for publishers' survival that they develop online communities, digital content, and consumer-facing programs (rather than retailer-focused programs). Former Soft Skull Editorial Director Richard Nash suggested during a talk at this year's BookExpo America that if he were starting a publishing house from scratch today, he'd propose a community-based system that brings readers and writers together in a virtual roundtable to edit, publish, and discuss content. Such models acknowledge the disintermediation we're witnessing in the culture at large, where the middlemen are disappearing. Fiction publishing is not exempt from disintermediation, and publishers of every category need to cozy up to the particular community of readers and writers supporting them.

So I believe the future of agents will be determined more by the needs and the future of authors. What does that future look like? This is where things become less clear, but here are three critical issues.

1. KEEPING PACE WITH DIGITAL TECHNOLOGIES AND BUILDING NEW CONTRACTS AND RIGHTS STRUCTURES

Right now everyone's confused—authors, agents, publishers. Authors need agents who can make sense of what's happening, be proactive in negotiating and renegotiating contracts to take advantage of new opportunities, and navigate the increasingly complex ways content can be sold, licensed, and repackaged. Agents need to be able to do this in a way that will fairly compensate authors (so they can continue to produce great material), but also ensure publishers can sustain their business models, too.

Both Shatzkin and Nash have suggested that contracts between authors and publishers need to be revolutionized—that today's boilerplate contract is inflexible and outdated. One idea put forth by Nash is that contracts become time-based, with potential for renewal, which dodges the sticky "in print" or "out of print" question that now determines the termination of most book contracts.

Whatever happens, agents need to innovate as much as the publishers in developing a model that works, and avoid contract restrictions that make it difficult to partner and grow as the industry changes.

2. ESTABLISHING AND GROWING EMPOWERING PARTNERSHIPS AND ONLINE PRESENCES FAR BEYOND BOOK PUBLICATION

It's essential for writers to know how to use new technologies and online tools to help build and reach their readership, to create visibility and a brand around their content, and to be associated with a message or story greater than just one book or product.

For anyone in this publishing game for the long run, it can't be about the sale of one book—and this is where sometimes I see a lack of vision across the board. People get so focused on selling a title or in how that title is (or isn't) supported by a publisher, that they lose sight of the much larger goal of an author's career.

Would the architecture of an author's career be better nurtured by the agent or by the publisher, or by someone else still?

To draw on Raccah's wisdom, she has said publishers aren't in the business of producing books, but in the business of building authors' careers—and connecting writers to readers. I agree that the successful publishers of the future (whether specialized or not) will be those that offer something of tangible benefit to an author—not the ones that continue business as usual. Enterprising authors already have many viable options to publish successfully without a traditional publisher's assistance or expertise—and opportunities will only continue to proliferate.

Perhaps, in the best of all worlds for writers, vertical publishers can offer amazing networking, distribution, and business partnerships that neither authors nor agents can develop on their own (e.g., how Chronicle is master of the gift market, or how Harlequin has a mission to reach women wherever they are). But it will be the agents who can meaningfully partner and advise on authors' long-term career growth. It is, after all, the authors' responsibility to develop an online presence (isn't that much too important to be handled by a publisher?), and authors need agents savvy enough to help them shape that image apart from a publisher's business interests.

3. DEVELOPING NEW BUSINESS MODELS FOR HOW AUTHORS PAY AGENTS FOR THEIR EXPERTISE AND PARTNERSHIP

There's a final dilemma. Publishers are now paying lower advances, releasing fewer titles, and selling digital content at lower prices than print content (which in turn affects royalty payments to both agent and author). Assuming this is the new reality, there will be less money to go around for the number of agents now in business. Plus, will it be worth an agent's time and energy to sell a project that doesn't pay more than $1,500 upfront? Probably not.

One agency has quietly come out with a new model that requires authors to pay a minimum commission—i.e., the agent must earn a minimum amount on a sale no matter what advance the publisher pays, which means authors would "share" a larger part of the advance upfront (or even pay out of pocket in the case of very low advances).

Undoubtedly, there's no shortage of aspiring writers who would be ecstatic to pay more to an agent if it meant securing a publishing deal. But such a model is sure to raise ethical concerns. Agents may take projects knowing they will ultimately be paid by authors rather than by publishers. Is the industry (that includes the author!) ready to accept such a shift in how agents profit?

In the end, agents will need to do much more than make sales to publishers to remain viable. The best agents have always been career managers who know what kind of clients they should take on—and who say no to people who don't fit their strengths or values. Notable voices such as Seth Godin and Shatzkin have said that agents, like publishers, will have to survive by specializing, by being distinctive in some way.

I find that fitting—because isn't that what agents have advised authors all along? Be unique. Be distinct. Have something special to offer.

It turns out no one is exempt from that prescription.

JANE FRIEDMAN is publisher and editorial director of the Writer's Digest brand community. Read her publishing blog at blog.writersdigest. com/norules.

CHAPTER 58
HOW TO DECIPHER AGENCY CONTRACTS

BY HOWARD ZAHAROFF

Do you need an agent? Do you even want one? And what should you do if you get one?

When I was a fledgling publishing lawyer, I answered the first question by telling most of my writer clients, "probably not." That is, until I saw a good agent in action.

An editor at *Writer's Digest* had referred to me two psychologists-turned-authors who had self-published a health guide, and who were now being courted by an agent claiming she could place the book with an established publisher to round out its new line. Despite some skepticism on my part, I helped these authors negotiate their contract with the agent—who promptly netted them a six-figure advance for their already self-published tome.

No surprise: I became a quick convert to the importance of a good agent. On top of the point that many publishers won't look at unagented work, add the argument that knowledgeable agents can truly—and often dramatically—increase their clients' sales, revenues, and overall success.

Of course, that's not to say every agent does this for every client. As with any personal or professional relationship—from spouse to doctor to lawyer—the key is to find someone who is the right fit for you. The process starts with due diligence: learning more about this person to be sure she not only has the basic qualifications required for that role, but also seems to be the partner or resource you need.

So let's say you've found that agent and have been offered a contract. Now what?

There are three points to keep in mind: Agents represent *the work*; agents must *earn their keep*; and writers need an *exit strategy*.

1. AGENTS SHOULD REPRESENT THE WORK, NOT THE WORKER

As a writer, you want an agent who's committed to you and the success of your work. But you don't want to shackle yourself to an agent, certainly not until he has proven he has the drive and talent to make you a success.

This is significant because agents often offer writers, especially novices, a contract that states the agent will represent the writer and all of his literary creations, from the start of the contract until it ends (see points No. 2 and No. 3). A savvy writer should reject this approach and, if offered such a deal, require that the contract be revised to state that the agent represents the author for only the *specific identified* project(s) under discussion. Writers should avoid granting their agents an automatic right to represent them on sequels, "option works" for the same publisher, or anything else.

Obviously, if the agent (and the book) does well, both writer and agent will want to partner on other projects. But even if the writer doesn't seek additional representation from the agent, the agent typically will have been reasonably well compensated for his efforts (assuming they were successful), so he'll have little cause to complain.

Subsidiary rights are a related issue. Most agents stipulate they handle not only the sale of the book and all the literary rights associated with it, but also movie, TV, dramatic, multimedia, and other subsidiary rights. Because the sale of book rights is often the lynchpin to these others, it isn't unfair for the agent to manage these. But before you sign, just make sure your agent can demonstrate success—with experience and established contacts—in managing sub rights.

The key is to remember this: Your agent is there to promote your work, negotiate contracts, and monitor your royalties, but you don't want to give him unrestricted authority over your career. So be sure the agent agreement requires your written approval of—and preserves your right to reject—all contracts.

2. AGENTS MUST EARN THEIR KEEP

Many agents want to be compensated for any contract that arises after they've taken charge. Although an agent is generally appointed on an exclusive basis (for the particular work during a period of representation), if that period ends without success, the question arises: Should the agent still be entitled to a commission if the work is sold later, perhaps by the author's *new* agent?

If the agent had no role in the sale, no. But possibly yes, if the sale—despite occurring after (but not too long after) the contract expired—resulted from the agent's efforts during the term of the agreement. Some publishing lawyers insist the only such post-termination contracts that should earn an agent a commission are those that were under negotiation at termination. Most agents believe that's too high a bar.

A reasonable compromise is to agree the agent will collect a commission not only on contracts she negotiates and closes during the term, but also on contracts that close within one to three (but no more than six) months after the agreement terminates, provided they are with publishers with whom the agent had *material* dealings or discussions about the work during the contract period. The emphasis on "material" (or "substantive") is meant to prevent the agent from claiming a commission on any sale to a publisher to whom the agent had merely sent an e-mail or made a brief phone call mentioning the project. To earn a commission on a contract she didn't negotiate, the agent's involvement must have been more than remote or casual. (If you reach such a compromise, consider inserting language into the agreement that also requires the agent to negotiate the publishing contract even if her representation has ended. That way, she earns her keep regardless of the timing!)

The contract clause addressing this issue should also describe what happens if another agent is involved in the post-term sale. Then, to make a sharing approach work, the contract with the second agent must specifically agree to this treatment. You do *not* want to be in a situation where, by contract, both agents can claim a full commission on a particular sale (or one can claim a full commission and the other a half commission—or any situation where their combined claims exceed 100 percent of a fair commission).

3. WRITERS NEED AN EXIT STRATEGY

Even if you've done your due diligence and found an agent who seems right for you, things don't always work out as hoped. The agent may have less experience with your genre than you realized; or have too many projects at one time; or begin acting inappropriately (not returning your calls, etc.); or be dealing with personal issues; or ...

The "or" doesn't matter. What matters is that you need a way to exit the relationship if things are not working out.

On the other hand, it may be unfair to fire an agent—particularly one who contributed to the work or proposal or otherwise invested time and energy in you—before the agent has had a reasonable chance to sell the work.

The most judicious approach is generally to allow an agent a fair amount of time—say, four or six months—to market your work, as long as he's doing what he promised (at a minimum, he should be providing periodic reports about his progress and/or offering responses to your questions). But after the minimum period ends, either party should be free to cancel the arrangement by simply notifying the other that the contract is finished (perhaps subject to the agent's right to complete any negotiations in progress).

As I said before, if agents receive commissions on all contracts they negotiated and get a reasonable opportunity (e.g., thirty days) to conclude any contracts underway (or to get credit for post-termination contracts that resulted from their efforts), they have no cause to gripe.

Finally, don't forget that your agent's job is to handle the business terms and negotiations—in other words, to put deals together. Unless your agent is also a lawyer, and agrees to represent you on legal terms as well, it's often prudent to consult with folks like me.

HOWARD ZAHAROFF is a copyright and publishing lawyer. He's the author of *Stump Your Lawyer!* and his humor writing has appeared in *The Wall Street Journal, The Boston Globe, Computerworld,* and other publications.

CHAPTER 59
STRAIGHT EXPECTATIONS

BY JANE FRIEDMAN

It's time to get real. Here's our take on self-publishing as we know it.

Self-publishing is not new. It's been around at least since the days of John Milton and *Areopagitica*, and defenders of self-publishing often point to such historical works in celebration of the practice.

Businesses that offer publishing services have been advertising in *Writer's Digest* since its inception. A 1930s back-page ad suggested that a self-published chapbook of poems would make the perfect Christmas gift for friends and family, but also warned, "no fame or riches."

The advent of print-on-demand and digital printing technology in the 1990s has made self-publishing more affordable than ever before, and subsequently, the number of books published every year has skyrocketed.

Every day at the *Writer's Digest* offices, and on our travels to writing conferences, we field the same big questions about self-publishing, from new and established authors alike.

1. WHAT SHOULD I CONSIDER BEFORE DECIDING TO SELF-PUBLISH?

There are three critical factors if you're hoping to see your self-published work widely read and/or favorably received by editors and agents:

- **Editorial quality.** Never publish a book that has not been professionally edited. A self-publishing service rarely reviews your work to assess the quality of its content (or, more important, its market viability), and no service will undertake the revision and editing process unless you pay for it. Only you can ensure that your work has the best content, structure, and organization, and it's up to you to pay for copyediting, proofreading, indexing or any other polishing your work may require. Unfortunately, many self-published books have not undergone any meaningful editing, which can give the whole lot a bad rap.

- **Distribution and sales.** The thing to remember about self-publishing services is that, almost without exception, they make their money on the upfront fees that you pay before even a single copy is sold. Compare their situation to that of a traditional publishing house, which must invest a significant sum of money upfront, then recoup the investment through book sales. A traditional publisher has a sales force or a distributor who pitches books to the national chains and independent stores; the same cannot be said of self-publishing services. Plus, in a self-publishing scenario, there's rarely a supply of books to distribute and stock on store shelves because most authors use print-on-demand technology to keep costs low, printing one book at a time to fill customer orders.

  Bottom line? Self-published authors need to have a way to reach their readership directly and let everyone know a book is available for purchase. Without marketing and promotion, very few sales will occur. (Of course, the same is true of traditionally published books, but with distribution in place, it's easier for people to stumble across books on the shelf and make impulse buys.)

- **Cover, design, and packaging.** The cover (as well as the title) can be the number-one marketing tool for any book. The same can be said of the size, trim, price, and interior features. All these factors contribute to having the right packaging to make the right sale to the right audience. Traditional publishers often have considerable in-house expertise on what kind of packaging will sell to a particular consumer, and they spend numerous hours on title, design, and packaging refinement. Many self-publishing services require you take a template approach (one size fits all) for convenience and economic efficiency, which can make it difficult to compete.

Of course, if you're just looking into self-publishing for your own gratification, perhaps to have some copies for your friends and family members, these considerations don't apply—and you have more affordable options now than ever before. See question No. 3.

2. WILL I KILL MY CHANCES WITH A TRADITIONAL PUBLISHER IF I SELF-PUBLISH?

Of course not. Even if you publish what in hindsight is a terrible book, or you're embarrassed by the results, no agent or editor would turn down your subsequent work if it looked like a surefire winner in the marketplace. But, you may ask, have you ruined your chances of traditionally publishing that same work?

It depends. If your self-published book sells well and looks like it could take off with traditional distribution, agents and editors will gladly take a piece of that success. This is a huge exception to the rule, though, and no one should self-publish solely to win attention from traditional publishing houses. It's a rare occurrence, and one that usually only happens after the author has created a quality work and dedicated countless hours to self-promotion.

3. IF I SELF-PUBLISH, WHICH SERVICE SHOULD I USE?

We can't possibly recommend a service that works for everyone because every writer has a unique situation, a unique book, a unique set of resources, and unique goals. It's up to each writer to research the options carefully and make an informed decision. But what we *can* do is help you get started, so we've created an exclusive online directory of sixty self-publishers and the services they offer. Simply visit writersdigest.com, where more information about each one is just a click away.

4. I'VE ALREADY SELF-PUBLISHED. NOW WHAT?

If you're wondering if you've made the wrong decision, it's time to stop worrying and start focusing on either marketing the book you now have, or moving on to writing your next book.

5. SO WHERE DOES *WRITER'S DIGEST* STAND ON SELF-PUBLISHING?

I can't tell you how many heated discussions the *Writer's Digest* staff has had about self-publishing—its advantages or disadvantages, its past and future, its advertising presence in this very magazine. As publisher and editorial director of *Writer's Digest,* I can tell you this is where we stand: Our main goal is to inform and educate, so you make the right decision for your work. Self-publishing can be easy, affordable and satisfying—but marketing, selling and promoting can be difficult. Many authors enter into it without a full understanding of the challenges and of what self-publishing services can and can't provide. We want to help you have realistic expectations and give you the tools to succeed, no matter what road you take.

 JANE FRIEDMAN is the publisher and editorial director of the Writer's Digest community. Read her publishing blog at blog.writersdigest.com/norules.

WHAT CAN YOUR PUBLISHER DO FOR YOU?
BY THE WRITER'S DIGEST STAFF

	TRADITIONAL PUBLISHER	SELF-PUBLISHING SERVICE
Development, content and copy editing	An in-house editor offers feedback on early drafts and helps you revise. Some authors complain that today's time-pressed editors aren't as involved in this process as before.	You hire an editor independently or through your self-publishing service. (If you're serious about bringing your book to the market, do not forgo this step.)

Cover and interior design	Your publisher handles everything design-related and usually has the final say on cover and interior design, relying on in-house expertise about what sells and what doesn't.	Varies. Most basic self-publishing packages include a template-based design. Some services offer upgrades for a fee; others charge you to control the process.
Title	Your publisher's marketing and sales department, in collaboration with the editorial team, often has the final say over your title.	You have the final say.
Sales and distribution	Most publishers have an in-house team that sells your book to national chains and other retailers, or a distributor to perform the task.	Your book is usually available for purchase through the service's site, as well as Ingram or Amazon.com (sometimes at an extra charge). The rest is up to you.
Marketing and publicity	Varies greatly. It's common for publishers to rely on authors to market their work. At the least, most publishers send out review copies and include the book in their sales catalogs and promotions sent to retailers.	Completely dependent on the author, though most services offer marketing and publicity package upgrades. Some also select outstanding books for special marketing at no cost.

CHAPTER 60
AN AGENT'S PERSPECTIVE ON SELF-PUBLISHING

BY ANDREA HURST

As a literary agent, I receive hundreds of query letters every month—and reject about 99 percent of them. Many aspiring writers dream of getting a book published, but for most it's a tough road to navigate, and today's economy is making it even harder to get a deal from a traditional publisher. These factors—coupled with the increasingly affordable and accessible choices for self-publishing—are prompting many authors to get their book out there on their own.

Indeed, self-publishing can be successful. Several recent bestsellers started out self-published before landing a mainstream deal and hitting it big: *Rich Dad, Poor Dad, The Celestine Prophecy, Eragon,* and *The Shack* among them. But almost always, behind each break-out success you'll find a dedicated, highly motivated author with an extensive marketing plan that's being implemented on a full-time basis. What you hear about less often are the thousands of disappointed authors who have gone the self-publishing route only to end up with hundreds of unsold books in their garages.

When a submission to an agent states that the book was formerly self-published, that can be a red flag: If a book doesn't sell well in its first printing, regardless of who or what house produced it, it's very unlikely that another publisher will pick it up. When agents like me receive queries from a writer with a self-published book, we first ask how many copies it has sold and how long it's been in print. We're looking for one set of qualifications: a highly marketable hook and a product that has sold at least five thousand books in (preferably) just a year or less on the market.

If you've self-published and generated good profits, consider all the pros and cons before making the decision to seek an agent to take it to a larger publisher. True, a large publisher can offer you much better distribution and higher visibility. However, you'll face being put on a publisher's timeline—and having to earn back your advance before you see additional income. This may be a welcome relief from the massive job of covering all aspects of the publishing yourself, but it's also a big shift in strategy. And, of course, you'll be asked to stop selling your current self-published edition at some point before the new one comes out.

Jennifer Basye Sander, author of *The Complete Idiot's Guide to Self-Publishing,* self-published a small booklet called *The Air Courier's Handbook,* which sold five thousand copies, primarily through Internet and mail-order marketing efforts. Her total income was $40,000 with minimal expenses, so she made an excellent profit. She attributes this to finding and serving a clear niche market, planning a direct route to her audience and dedicating herself to marketing the product aggressively. Self-publishing can be the best option if you have a niche idea that's directed toward a very targeted market and may not appeal to a large publisher. On the other hand, breakouts such as *The Shack* appealed to a broad range of readers, but reaching that audience would have taken much larger campaigns than most authors have the funding, time, or expertise to undertake.

If you're up to the challenge (and equipped to meet it head-on), self-publishing may be an excellent way for you to prove your book can sell and to begin building your career. But be sure to do lots of research in advance, avoiding publishers with hidden costs and shabby, mediocre production quality. I can often spot a book that's self-published at a glance, and not for any favorable reasons. I strongly suggest investing in a superior product that can compete in the professional publishing arena.

ANDREA HURST (andreahurst.com) is president of Andrea Hurst & Associates Literary Management. She represents such best-selling authors as Bernie Siegel, Jean-Michel Cousteau, and Maureen Murdock.

CHAPTER 61
THE GROWING COMMUNITY OF SELF-PUBLISHING

BY JOE WIKERT

For someone who comes from the traditional publishing arena, I'd be the first to admit that the self-publishing world is intriguing. There's a lot to like about how the self-publishing model works, that it enables more content to reach more customers, and that it offers a great deal of flexibility along the way.

Self-publishing is all about community. New authors now see their ideas converted into books to reach audiences big or small. More important, though, the decision about whether or not a concept becomes a book isn't made by a bunch of editors and marketers around a table.

Just as with any open-market model, the weak ideas won't sell, but the great ones can become enormous hits—hits that often would have simply died on the vine without the self-publishing option.

The self-publishing world has generally been ignored by the traditional publishing industry, but that's starting to change. Success stories like *The Shack*, while still somewhat rare, have caused conventional publishers to realize the old model is far from perfect. Some are being proactive. Take HarperCollins and its Authonomy site (authonomy.com), for example. Its mission is to "flush out the brightest, freshest new writing talent around." It's a community site for authors (as well as publishers and agents) where content can be shared and critiqued. If you're willing to upload a 10,000-word sample of your work, you can join in. Best of all, it's totally free and a great way to start building a platform.

An author platform refers to the writer's reach and includes websites, blogs, speaking engagements, mailing lists, and any other ways the author communicates with potential book buyers. The bigger the platform, the greater the likelihood a traditional publisher will be interested in the author's project, because these publishers want to know how that platform can be used to sell books.

Wait a minute. Isn't it up to the *publisher* to sell the books? That used to be the case, but these days, traditional publishers are finding that author platforms move books better than old-fashioned ads and other publisher-driven promotional vehicles. If you opt for self-publishing, *all* your sales and marketing efforts probably hinge on your platform. Your book's success will depend on your ability to hand-sell as many copies as possible. Given that the vast majority of traditionally published books now benefit from very limited marketing/public relations efforts (e.g., visibility on a publisher's catalog and website), the gap between self-publishing and traditional publishing is tightening. In other words, your author platform is equally effective (and vitally important) in either model.

Distribution remains a challenge for self-publishers, though, particularly in bookstores. But this, too, may change before long, thanks to rapidly improving print-on-demand capabilities.

Because of the number of players and the interest level most have in trying new methods, I think we'll see a variety of hybrid publishing models in the future. It wouldn't surprise me if one or more traditional publishers were to partner openly with self-publishing companies, perhaps even using them as a way to extend the traditional brands in new directions.

It also makes sense for self-publishers to look for opportunities to work closer with traditional publishers, particularly since we're all going after the same audience.

Not long ago, authors were faced with extremely limited options. If you couldn't get a traditional publisher excited about your work, you were out of luck. Boy, am I glad those days are over—and I say that as both a book lover and a book publisher.

 JOE WIKERT (joewikert.com) is general manager and publisher at O'Reilly Media, Inc.

Part Five

INTERVIEWS WITH NOVELISTS

BEST-SELLING ADVICE: Readers

"Write out of the reader's imagination as well as your own. Supply the significant details and let the reader's imagination do the rest. Make the reader a co-author of the story." —Patrick F. McManus

"Always remember the reader. Always level with him and never talk down to him. You may think you're some kind of smart guy because you're the great writer. Well, if you're such a smart guy, how come the reader is paying you? Remember the reader's the boss. He's hired you to do a job. So do it." —Jay Anson

"A cop told me, a long time ago, that there's no substitute for knowing what you're doing. Most of us scribblers do not. The ones that're any good are aware of this. The rest write silly stuff. The trouble is this: The readers know it." —George V. Higgins

"You better make them care about what you think. It had better be quirky or perverse or thoughtful enough so that you hit some chord in them. Otherwise it doesn't work. I mean we've all read pieces where we thought, 'Oh, who gives a damn.' " —Nora Ephron

"I don't believe one reads to escape reality. A person reads to confirm a reality he knows is there, but which he has not experienced." —Lawrence Durrell

"We all tell a story a different way. I've always felt that footsteps on the stairs when you're alone in the house, and then the handle of the door turning, ` can be scarier than the actual confrontation. So, as a result, I'm on the reading list from age thirteen to ninety." —Mary Higgins Clark

"I don't care if a reader hates one of my stories, just as long as he finishes the book." —Roald Dahl

"The critics can make fun of Barbara Cartland. I was quite amused by the critic who once called me 'an animated meringue.' But they can't get away from the fact that I know what women want—and that's to be flung across a man's saddle, or into the long grass by a loving husband." —Barbara Cartland

"In truth, I never consider the audience for whom I'm writing. I just write what I want to write." —J.K. Rowling

"If you can teach people something, you've won half the battle. They want to keep on reading." —Dick Francis

"To gain your own voice, you have to forget about having it heard. Renounce that and you get your own voice automatically. Try to become a saint of your own province and your own consciousness, and you won't worry about being heard in *The New York Times*." —Allen Ginsberg

CHAPTER 62

A CONVERSATION WITH TOM CLANCY

BY KATIE STRUCKEL BROGAN

When asked how he was discovered, Tom Clancy says, "I was discovered on April 12, 1947, at Franklin Square Hospital in Baltimore." He says he doesn't remember the name of the doctor, "but I imagine he slapped me on the ass, and I probably let out the requisite noise."

In high school, Clancy, the best-selling author of the Jack Ryan books *The Hunt for Red October, Patriot Games*, and *The Bear and the Dragon*, knew that one day he'd see his name on a book cover. He says it took him twenty years to finally see that, "but I managed to get that dream accomplished, and then I got very lucky."

While running his own independent insurance agency, Clancy wrote *The Hunt for Red October*. A member of the U.S. Naval Institute, Clancy learned the Institute was about to enter the fiction business as Naval Institute Press. So he drove the book to Annapolis and drove home. "A few weeks later, the publisher expressed interest and so I've never had a rejection slip."

The Hunt for Red October was published in October 1984. Soon after, Gerry O'Leary, an editor with *The Washington Times*, asked Nancy Clark Reynolds, a member of the President's Commission on White House Fellowships, to take a copy of the book to the American Ambassador to Argentina in Buenos Aires. "It's a long flight to Buenos Aires," Clancy says. "And Nancy Clark Reynolds read the book on the flight."

He says Reynolds liked the book so much that she bought a case and handed them out as Christmas gifts, one of which was given to

President Reagan. "It's not widely known that President Reagan was a voracious reader. He devoured *Red October*."

On March 24, 1985, *Red October* came in at number ten on *New York Times* best-seller list. After catapulting up the list, Clancy continued to write more books about Jack Ryan, reinventing the wheel nearly every time. "Whenever Jack finds himself in a new situation, it exposes parts of his character that the reader hasn't seen yet."

The same is true in *The Bear and the Dragon*, which took him "fully six endless months" to write. Readers can expect the "latest installment in the continuing life of Jack Patrick Ryan." But that's all he'll say about the book, except, "If you want more, buy it."

What was the biggest challenge you faced while writing *The Bear and the Dragon*?

Writing a book is an endurance contest and a war fought against yourself, because writing is beastly hard work which one would just as soon not do. It's also a job, however, and if you want to get paid, you have to work. Life is cruel that way.

How do you create intricate plots while still managing to build a sharp element of suspense?

I'm probably the wrong person to ask, because I really do not think in these terms. I'm just trying to tell a story. I pace the story in the same way that the story unfolds in my mind, and so you could say that I do the important parts instinctively, or at least with a minimum of conscious thought. The virtue of my writing, therefore, is that I do not overintellectualize the production process. I try to keep it simple: Tell the damned story.

What are the most important parts in your books?

The important parts are the prime plot elements … . The peripheral elements spin off of those, sometimes affecting things directly, sometimes not, but you play them out because they are useful.

Do you think readers could understand your novels without technical details?

I think it's necessary to describe the tools my characters use to lend verisimilitude to my work, which is why I include it … . Verisimilitude provides texture that adds to the richness and plausibility of the story.

How do you maintain reader identification with Jack Ryan?

Obviously, most people perceive themselves to be "regular" people, and they're more likely to identify with a normal person than with Batman or Julius Caesar. So, you take an ordinary sort of guy and drop him into a serious situation. It's the same technique Hitchcock used, though he always seemed to use Cary Grant or Jimmy Stewart as his "regular guy." I would go so far as to say that the way I tell my stories largely results from a ninety-minute show I once saw on PBS about Hitchcock and his films. Suspense is achieved by information control. What you know. What the reader knows. What the characters know. You balance that properly, and you can really get the reader wound up.

What's your advice to aspiring writers?

Keep at it! The one talent that's indispensable to a writer is persistence. You must write the book, else there is no book. It will not finish itself. Do not try to commit art. Just tell the damned story. If it is entertaining, people will read it, and the objective of writing is to be read, in case the critics never told you that … . But fundamentally, writing a novel is telling a story.

 KATIE STRUCKEL BROGAN is the former editor of *Writer's Market*.

CHAPTER 63

CRAFTING CHARACTERS WITH ELIZABETH GEORGE

BY DAVID A. FRYXELL

If Elizabeth George were a character in one of her psychological mystery novels, figuring out her "core need" would be a snap. The core need is part of how George defines her characters, a step in a rigorous process that the self-confessed "left-brained" writer uses to unleash her creative right brain.

"My core need is that I'm dominated by the need to be really competent at what I do," says George, whose résumé includes a master's degree in counseling/psychology as well as sixteen published novels.

So, in her nightmares, she's back teaching English at El Toro High School in Orange County, California, running late or not prepared for class.

Not likely. George's success has taken her far from the blackboard. Her books sell a million copies and get translated into twenty languages. Her novel *A Traitor to Memory*, spent months on *New York Times* best-seller list. She's been nominated for an Edgar award and has won the Agatha, the Anthony, and France's Le Grand Prix de Literature Policiere. And when *Mystery* aired an adaptation of her first novel, *A Great Deliverance*, she was the first American writer ever featured on the popular PBS-TV series.

"I knew from the age of seven that I was meant to be a writer," she says. Born in Warren, Ohio, and raised in the San Francisco Bay area, George used to scan *The San Francisco Examiner* for true-crime fodder. She wrote her first novel—"Nancy Drewlike," she describes it—at the age of twelve, and collected rejection slips on five books before getting published in 1988.

Two of those rejected books starred the cerebral forensic scientist Simon Allcourt-St. James, a supporting player in her subsequent novels. It was only when George decided to see if the New Scotland Yard detectives who helped St. James—the aristocratic Thomas Lynley and his frumpy partner, Barbara Havers—could solve a case on their own that she broke through with *A Great Deliverance*.

"I wish that I had known back then that a mastery of process would lead to a product," she reflects. "Then I probably wouldn't have found it so frightening to write."

George's process for novel writing today is complex but ultimately as clear as her plots. "I have to know the killer, the victim, and the motive when I begin. Then I start to create the characters and see how the novel takes shape based on what these people are like."

Besides a core need and the rest of a psychological profile, each character gets a physical description, a family history, and what George calls a "pathology," which she defines as "a particular psychological maneuver that he engages in when he's under stress." Much of this material, written in stream-of-consciousness form, never makes it into the actual novel, but it helps George discover the truth about her characters. When she gets it, George says, she feels something right in her solar plexus.

"Creating the characters is the most creative part of the novel except for the language itself. There I am, sitting in front of my computer in right-brain mode, typing the things that come to mind, which become the seeds of plot. It's scary, though," she adds, "because I always wonder: Is it going to be there this time?"

George's plotting process is equally detailed. "I outline the plot beginning with the primary event that gets the ball rolling. Then I'll list the potentials that are causally related to what's gone before.

"I continue to open the story and not close the story, putting in dramatic questions. Any time the story stalls out on me, I know I've done something wrong—generally, I played my hand too soon, answered a dramatic question in a scene without asking a new one."

Crafting Characters With Elizabeth George

Her running plot outline might cover up to the next fifteen scenes. "The plot outline doesn't forbid the inspiration of the moment, but it does prevent a wild hare, something out of character that drags the story off in a wrong area."

For each scene, the outline notes what George calls her "THAD," short for "Talking Head Avoidance Device." The THAD that animates each scene, George says, springs from her prep work getting to know her characters.

The outline also notes the point of view for each scene. Unlike many mystery writers, George shifts her point of view among multiple characters—rather than, say, sticking with the detective's viewpoint. "In any given scene, I ask, 'Whose story is being advanced here?' " she explains. "I can usually tell the point of view by which character's part in the narrative I've gotten to."

Sometimes that's the killer. "I wanted the challenge of writing from the killer's viewpoint after the killing's taken place. The killer is thinking about the killing, but the reader never knows that's what the person is really thinking about.

"I wanted to write books that bore a second reading," George goes on. "Books that play fair with the reader but sometimes would be the kind of book where the reader wouldn't realize I'd been fair to them until a second reading. The reader is always in possession of vastly more knowledge than the investigators are."

As George has set herself more daunting writing challenges, her novels have grown longer and more time-consuming to write. She wrote *A Great Deliverance* in three and a half weeks; her latest took eighteen months. "The books are vastly more complicated now. I'm more interested in subplot, how subplots could unify the novel and reinforce the theme."

Research takes time, too, especially since all her novels are set in England, half a world away from her home in Huntington Beach, California. The most common question she gets is: Why write about England when you're an American? George can't understand why people find that so surprising. Her stock response: "It worked for Henry James."

But it does mean spending weeks at a time in England, which George first visited and fell in love with on a summer Shakespeare course in 1966. She keeps a flat in South Kensington, London, home base for research excursions armed with camera and tape recorder. For *Well-Schooled in Murder*, for example, she visited a half-dozen schools and created architectural plans and a brochure for her fictional British school setting.

"I want to ground myself in specifics, not generics. I want to force myself to deal in details. I can't make these up, that's not my talent."

Writers who want to follow in George's footsteps often complain that they don't have the time to write. George has little patience with that excuse: "Evaluate how you're using your free time every day for a week—talking on the phone, reading the newspaper, watching television, listening to the radio. All these things are bleeding away from your writing time, thinking time, preparation time. You have to structure your life to allow yourself to write.

"Writing is 10 percent inspiration and 90 percent endeavor," she adds. "It's a job and has to be approached as a job. Writers write—they don't wait for it to be fun."

Clearly writing is more than just a job to George. Yes, she allows, it helps fulfill that core need at the foundation of her character.

"Only when I write," she says, "do I feel whole and at peace."

 DAVID A. FRYXELL is the former editor-in-chief of *Writer's Digest* and Writer's Digest Books.

CHAPTER 64

FIND IDENTITY WITH JOYCE CAROL OATES

BY KATIE STRUCKEL BROGAN

As a little girl, novelist and short story writer Joyce Carol Oates used to tell stories and then illustrate them. "That's very typical of children to be extremely creative," she says. "Children are creative without any purpose other than to express their imaginations." Oates, the author of the novels *Blonde* and *Wonderland* and, most recently, of *A Fair Maiden*, has come a long way from that little girl "without any purpose."

Oates has won the National Book Award, the PEN/Malamud Award for Achievement in the Short Story, and various other awards. Known best for her short stories, many of which have been anthologized in *The Pushcart Prize* and *The Best American Short Stories of the Century*, Oates still manages to bridge the natural gap that exists between novel and short story writing. That's a feat that she acknowledges is not an easy task.

"A novel is so much more difficult than a short story. If you run, it's almost like you can think through your whole short story as you ran. Say you ran forty minutes or an hour, you can think through the whole story and have it very finite and controlled. With a novel, it's almost impossible to do that."

But that's not to say that Oates doesn't enjoy writing novels. "A novel is much more challenging, and it's also very rewarding because you stay with it for so long, you get to love your characters. I feel very close, emotionally engaged with most of my main characters."

The Complete Handbook of Novel Writing

TWO DIFFERENT SPACES TO WRITE IN

Like many writers, Oates has a specific space in which she crafts her stories and novels; however, she is unusual in that she has two spaces to write in—a generalized space and a physical space. "I write on airplanes and I write in my head a lot. I do a lot of running and walking, and I compose in my imagination. So, that's kind of generalized space."

The physical space, on the other hand, the space that she literally writes in, is in a study "with a lot of glass" and a skylight.

While in her study, Oates writes first in longhand and then on a typewriter, a somewhat ancient tool given current technology standards. "I don't have a computer. I had a computer for two years and I got very tired of looking at that little screen for so many hours.

"I didn't really want to spend the rest of my life staring at a little electronic thing. I made a conscious decision just to get rid of it."

Given that one of her writing spaces is always with her, it's no wonder that Oates has emerged as the writer she is today.

TWO NAMES TO WRITE BY

But there is one thing that some may not know about Oates—she also writes suspense, thrillers, and mystery novels as Rosamond Smith.

"I wanted to write under a pseudonym because I really wanted to have a separate identity for those novels—suspense, mystery, thrillers. They tend to be leaner and shorter than my other novels. They don't have as much sociological or political detail; they're more cinematic."

However, Oates never intended for readers to know that she was the person behind Rosamond Smith, and she still doesn't really know how the information actually got out.

"It's very hard to keep a secret today because of copyright and income tax, and certain things in our society make it difficult to have that kind of privacy that people had in the past."

Oates illustrates her point by citing that Jonathan Swift and Voltaire wrote under pseudonyms and they were never tracked down the way that she was. Still, she continues writing under the name Rosamond Smith and, in fact, has had a couple of books published that said, "Joyce Carol Oates writing as Rosamond Smith."

Oates says that writing under a pseudonym has helped her develop a separate identity, but that it has also allowed her the freedom to write "novels that were faster and leaner, more like movies." In fact, she has a unit in her writing workshop at Princeton University, where she has been a professor since 1978, in which she focuses on the process of writing under a pseudonym.

"I suggest to my students that they write under a pseudonym for one week ... . That allows young men to write as women, and women as men. It allows them a lot of freedom they don't have ordinarily."

Oates believes that writing under a pseudonym has its good and bad points, especially in relation to her role as a female writer.

"I think it's still difficult for women to be taken very seriously as writers—that there's some resistance—even though things have changed wonderfully for the better. It's very hard to be an experimental woman writer."

She says that *Blonde* was an experimental novel and almost nobody talks about that, but had she been a male writer, it would be accepted as such.

"If I had been writing under a pseudonym, just initials, I might have a different reputation, but then I couldn't be myself either.

"I think everything in life has compensation. We may do one thing and then because of that there are advantages and also disadvantages."

 KATIE STRUCKEL BROGAN is the former editor of *Writer's Market*.

CHAPTER 65

JOHN UPDIKE: STILL MORE TO SAY

BY KELLY NICKELL

Since the release of his first novel, *The Poorhouse Fair*, in 1959, John Updike has published over sixty books, written a barrage of essays, reviews, and short stories for the likes of *The New Yorker* and *The New York Times*, and received two Pulitzers—not bad for someone who says he "only meant to be a magazine writer."

With such an astounding body of work, one can't help but wonder: Does it get easier to sit down with a blank page and turn whiteness to words of power and resilience?

"No, it never gets easier. But I've written enough now that I wonder if I'm not in danger of having said my say and of repeating myself," he says. "You can't be too worried about that if you're going to be a creative writer—a creative spirit—but yeah, you do, as they say in pitching, lose a little of your fastball."

From poetry and book reviews to short stories, novels, and even a play, there's not much the author hasn't tried his hand at over the years. And each form has presented its own distinct creative satisfaction.

"I must say, when I reread myself, it's the poetry I tend to look at. It's the most exciting to write, and it's over the quickest," he says. "But they all have their pleasures. The book reviews are perhaps the most lowly of the bunch, but even they have an occasional creative thrill. I like short stories. I'm sorry that I haven't been doing so many lately, but they're very satisfying."

Whatever the form, Updike's made an art of turning life's lost and tormented souls into literary everymen by not only honing their voices, but by anchoring their societal influences and surroundings so aptly with modern thought. And as Updike wrote in *The Handbook of Short Story Writing, Volume II*:

> No soul or locale is too humble to be the site of entertaining and instructive fiction. Indeed, all other things being equal, the rich and glamorous are less fertile ground than the poor and plain, and the dusty corners of the world more interesting than its glittering, already sufficiently publicized centers.

He proves this ideology with a four-book series that includes *Rabbit, Run*; *Rabbit Redux*; *Rabbit Is Rich*; and *Rabbit at Rest* (the latter two received Pulitzers and National Book Critics' Circle awards). Using protagonist Harry "Rabbit" Angstrom, Updike offers a running commentary on middle-class America. Written between 1960 and 1990, the books explore everything from racial tension and sexual freedom to drugs and middle age. And with Rabbit, Updike illustrates that even the flawed and ordinary can become legends given the proper landscape.

"We're past the age of heroes and hero kings," he says. "If we can't make up stories about ordinary people, who can we make them up about? But on the other hand, that's just a theory, and as in America, of course, there's a democracy that's especially tied to that assumption.

"Most of our lives are basically mundane and dull, and it's up to the writer to find ways to make them interesting. It's a rare life so dull that no crisis ever intrude."

Despite saying the Rabbit series was complete with 1990's *Rabbit at Rest*, Updike couldn't resist returning to the story line one last time in *Rabbit Remembered*, a novella appearing along with several short stories in 2000's *Licks of Love*.

"It was like coming home every ten years and paying a visit," he says. "It was easy because I was at home in that world, and it was a world that I had lived through as a child, and then it was a world that I had made."

The real world Updike created for himself didn't come without a few risks. After graduating from Harvard in 1954, he went on to join the staff of *The New Yorker*. Two years later, with no other job prospects, he left the magazine and moved with his family to Ipswich, Massachusetts, to pursue freelancing full time.

"I didn't quite know what I was getting into," he says. "It's possible I might have had to find employment. But I was willing to do journalism and *The New Yorker*'s kind of journalism—I was able to carry some of it with me when I came to New England. It was a gamble, but I was young and that was the time to make it … when I was young and full of what I had to say."

What felt like a gamble more than forty years ago now seems an admirable tale of bravery—one man's pursuit of his dream. But even Updike recognizes that in these changing times, his literary start is one not likely duplicated by today's young writers.

"My generation was maybe the last in which you could set up shop as a writer and hope to make a living at it," he says. "I began when print was a lot more glamorous medium than it is now. A beginning fiction writer—Kurt Vonnegut comes to mind—could support himself and a family by selling to magazines. I'm not sure you could do that now."

With the consolidation of major publishing houses and fewer magazines embracing short fiction, up-and-coming authors may find publication even more of a challenge.

"It's harder to make a splash nowadays," he says. "When I was beginning, we weren't getting rock star-type attention, but I think now the buzz seems softer. Publishers are looking for blockbusters—all the world loves a mega-seller. And, there's less readership for fiction that isn't purely escapist."

In 1999, Updike served as editor of *The Best American Short Stories of the Century*, a compilation of stories selected from the annual volumes of *The Best American Short Stories*. While the book honors a form in which—and about which—Updike has long written, he says there seems to be less of a readership for such work.

"That kind of audience is being trained at universities, but general readers want to sink into longer works, not the stop and start of short stories."

Keeping to his frenetic pace—though he says, "I don't mean to be too overproductive"—the author is nearly always at work on another novel. But, as he writes away the mornings and early afternoons in his Massachusetts home, even Updike is tempted by the same distractions that plague so many others.

"I work at home, upstairs, so it's unfortunately handy to any number of little chores that seem to have attached themselves to the writer's trade ... answering mail or reading proofs."

Despite the fact that it may not get any easier to start each new book, Updike's long and diverse career now enables him to draw on a wealth of insight inherited from the various forms he's perfected throughout the years.

"Poetry makes you a little more sensitive to the word-by-word interest of prose, and book reviews make you a little more erudite in some regards .... Probably had I not written so many reviews, I wouldn't have tackled something like *Gertrude and Claudius*, which is a sort of bookish inspiration," he says.

"I'm generally sort of more cautious in the way I write now than I used to be, though. I write slower, try to think a little more."

And to the legions of struggling writers waiting in the wings to make a "splash" of their own, it's perseverance and dedication that Updike advises:

"It's never been easy. Books are still produced and sold, and it might as well be you. Try to develop steady work habits, maybe a more modest quota, but keep to it. Don't be thin-skinned or easily discouraged because it's an odds long proposition; all of the arts are.

"Many are called, few are chosen, but it might be you."

KELLY NICKELL is the former executive editor of Writer's Digest Books.

CHAPTER 66

KURT VONNEGUT ON FLOUTING THE RULES

BY KELLY NICKELL

Kurt Vonnegut has witnessed the evolution of fiction—and in some ways, propelled it, perhaps. From the decreasing popularity of literary magazines and the increasing price of books, to his own evolving status as a "cult figure" and "popular author," Vonnegut has been a constant observer of—and a steady contributor to—the literary world for nearly half a century. And the oft-quoted literary giant remains a vocal commentator on the changing publishing industry.

A published author of everything from novels and short stories to essays and plays, Vonnegut says fiction is an art form unto its own. "All of fiction is a practical joke—making people care, laugh, cry, or be nauseated or whatever by something which absolutely is not going on at all. It's like saying, 'Hey, your pants are on fire.'"

And with his characteristic biting wit and humor, Vonnegut often combines social satire, autobiographical experiences, and bits of historical fact to create a new form of literary fiction, as in *Slaughterhouse-Five*, which became a number one *New York Times* bestseller when it was published in 1969.

Alternating between linear and circular structures and differing points of view, Vonnegut has spent much of his life testing literary boundaries. And it's become a Vonnegut axiom that writing rules apply only to the extent that they strengthen the effect of the final piece. "You want to involve the reader," he says. "For example, *Mother Night* was a first-person confessional—the narrator ruined his life and he needn't have. But there's no way you can put together a manual about when to use first person and when to use third person.

"James Joyce broke all the rules. He's a writer like no other, and he got away with it. You have to get away with it. When I was teaching, if I gave a basic rule, it was 'whatever works, works.' I experiment, and my waste baskets are always very full of failed experiments," he says. "Can I get away with this? No. The trick is getting the reader to buy it."

It's fairly safe to assume that readers do indeed "buy it." Among his numerous honors and awards, Vonnegut has received a Guggenheim Fellowship and a National Institute of Arts and Letters grant, served as the vice president for the PEN American Center, and lectured in creative writing at Harvard University and the University of Iowa.

REMEMBER YOUR READER

"When I teach, what I'm teaching is sociability more than anything else because that's what most beginning writers, being young, aren't doing," Vonnegut says. "I try to teach how to be a good date on a blind date and to keep the reader in mind all the time. Young writers will dump everything they want to say on some poor reader, not caring whether the reader has a good time or not."

Vonnegut's early experience in journalism—he was editor of the college newspaper in 1941 while studying biochemistry at Cornell University, and later a police reporter with the Chicago City News Bureau in 1947—clearly has influenced his style. Staying true to the basic elements of journalism, Vonnegut says he tries to give readers as much information as he can, as soon as he can—a writing trait he's also tried to teach others.

"I hate a story where on page 17 you find out, 'My God, this person is blind.' Or that this happened one hundred years ago or one hundred years in the future. I tell students, 'Don't withhold information from your readers, for God's sake. Tell 'em everything that's going on, so in case you die, the reader can finish the story.'"

Another Vonnegut specialty is weaving bits of factual information into his fiction's lining, to draw in readers on an emotional level. "The facts are often useful to the reader, if they're historical events. You can expect the reader to be emotionally involved. And to make the reader believe and say, 'Oh Jesus, I guess that's right.' "

Vonnegut used both historical facts and his personal experience as a World War II prisoner of war in Dresden to create *Slaughterhouse-Five*. He says the latitude used when combining fact with fiction depends on how much the writer is willing to claim as fact: "The viewpoint character in *Slaughterhouse-Five* was Bill Pilgrim, and he was actually a real guy from Rochester," Vonnegut says. "He never should have been in the army, and he died in Dresden and was buried over there. He just simply allowed himself to starve to death. You can do that if you're a prisoner, you can just decide not to eat. He decided he didn't understand any of it, and he was right, 'cause there was nothing to understand, so he died.

"I didn't have him die in the book, but had him come home and go to optometry school. So I didn't tell the truth about his life, but I never said it was his life in the first place."

"WRITE WHAT YOU WRITE"

What's the best piece of advice Vonnegut's ever received? "Quit," he says. "It's such a relief." But he didn't. "No, I didn't quit—I'm still pooping along."

Yet there were times early in his career—when he was working as a freelancer, receiving little pay, and trying to raise a family—that the notion of quitting wasn't unthinkable. Fortunately, the author chose to follow the advice of agent Kenneth Littauer.

"I was working as a freelancer—it's a harrowing way to make a living—and I would talk to Ken about how to make more money and he said, 'Don't trim your sails to every wind, just go ahead and write and see what happens. Don't look at the market. Don't look at the best-seller list to see what's selling.' That wouldn't help anyway. You have to write what you write, or get out of the business."

Vonnegut's battle with depression following publication of *Slaughterhouse-Five* almost did get him out of the business. He even vowed never to write again. And not until 1973 did he publish another book, *Breakfast of Champions*. Subtitled *Goodbye Blue Monday*, the book certainly didn't skirt the issue of depression, but Vonnegut says he's still not sure how the whole experience influenced his work: "There used to be a theory that tuberculosis helped to make someone a genius because they ran higher temperatures. It's now believed, and I guess it's a clinical fact, that most writers are troubled by depression. And I don't know whether it helps or not, but it sure doesn't feel good."

Whether it's his seemingly natural ability to create strong characters or his remarkable modesty ("I certainly didn't expect to succeed to the extent I have. I didn't expect to amount to much"), generations of writers continue to attempt to follow in Vonnegut's legendary footsteps. And to these many aspiring writers, Vonnegut offers some simple advice: "Don't worry about getting into the profession—write anyway to make your soul grow. That's what the practice of any art is. It isn't to make a living, it's to make your soul grow."

ON THE CHANGING FICTION MARKET

"Books don't matter as much as they used to, and they cost too much," Vonnegut says of the current state of publishing. "But publishers have to sell books to stay in business. Before television, publishers would admit that what paid the freight for everything else they published, all the serious fiction, poetry, and so forth, were cookbooks, garden books, and sex books. They had to publish those or they'd go out of business."

While many of his recent books, including *Bagombo Snuff Box*, *Fates Worse Than Death: An Autobiographical Collage of the 1980s*, and *God Bless You, Dr. Kevorkian* showcase the shorter form—most have been collections of essays, interviews, and speeches—Vonnegut says short stories seem to be losing their allure as fewer and fewer prominent magazines publish high-quality pieces.

"This country used to be crazy about short stories," he says. "New short stories would appear every week in the *Saturday Evening Post* or in *The New Yorker*, and every middle-class literate person would be talking about it: 'Hey, did you read that story by Salinger?' or 'Hey, did you read that story by Ray Bradbury?'

"But that no longer happens. No short story can cause a sensation anymore because there are too many other forms of entertainment.

People can still go through old collections of short stories on their own and be absolutely wowed. But it's a private experience now."

VONNEGUT IN THE TWENTY-FIRST CENTURY

At what readers may hope is only a short break during a very prolific writing period, what is Vonnegut planning next? "Well, as I'm sitting around right now, I'm trying to think of what would be a neat idea. Most people do other things with their time. But writers, we'll sit around and think up neat stuff. Not something just anybody could do."

 KELLY NICKELL is the former executive editor of Writer's Digest Books.

CHAPTER 67

IN ANNE TYLER'S WRITING WORLD

BY JESSICA STRAWSER

Anne Tyler belongs to a disappearing generation of writers, those who came into their own in an era when it was more than enough to—well, to simply write. Intensely protective of her craft, she hasn't given an in-person interview or participated in a book tour since 1977. In an age where writers are expected to lead double lives as self-promoters to enjoy any semblance of commercial success, Tyler carries on just as she always has, remaining steadfast in her singular devotion to her writing process. And she can get away with it, too, because she's Anne Tyler—and she's just *that* indisputably good.

If Tyler's writing career sounds like a luxury, a lofty dream come to life—penning a well-received book every few years in the quiet of her home in Baltimore, eschewing the media in favor of the companionship of her characters—it's one she's earned. Tyler published her first book, *If Morning Ever Comes*, in 1964, prompting a *New York Times* reviewer to write, "This is an exceedingly good novel, so mature, so gently wise and so brightly amusing that, if it weren't printed right there on the jacket, few readers would suspect that Mrs. Tyler was only twenty-two. Some industrious novelists never learn how to write good fiction. Others seem to be born knowing how. Mrs. Tyler is one of these." Somewhat amusingly, the exceptionally modest Tyler did not agree, and has since said she'd like to disown her first four novels—in her opinion, she began hitting her stride with her fifth book, *Celestial Navigation,* in 1974.

She released her favorite of her works, *Dinner at the Homesick Restaurant*, in 1982, and cemented her status as a household name in 1985 with the publication of her tenth book, *The Accidental Tourist*, which she is still perhaps best known for today. The story—centered around a neurotic writer who makes a living penning guidebooks for travelers who, like himself, want to avoid experiencing anything unfamiliar—affirmed Tyler's reputation as a clever, charming storyteller. Her follow-up, *Breathing Lessons,* a simultaneously hilarious and heartbreaking novel that takes place in the span of a single day, won the Pulitzer Prize in 1989. But having learned that talking about her writing was prohibitive to actually doing it, Tyler would not be coaxed back into the public eye. She found she could succeed best as a wife, mother, and writer without it.

Her books are about families, and the complications therein—marital discourse, sibling rivalry, resentment, and, underneath it all, love. Tyler's eccentric and endearing characters are so intensely real, so thoroughly developed, they come to life on the page—both for her as she writes and for the reader, who suddenly can see a bit of his own mother, father, brother, or even self in their blurted-out words, their unspoken impulses, their mistakes, and, with any luck, their moments of triumph.

In anticipation of the release of her eighteenth novel, *Noah's Compass, Writer's Digest* was granted a rare interview with Tyler via e-mail—a format to which in recent years she has sporadically consented, deeming it less disruptive. She discusses her latest work, lessons learned through decades of writing, and her literary legacy.

In an interview after the 2006 release of your novel, *Digging to America*, you said, "I'd like to write about a man who feels he has nothing more to expect from his life; but it's anybody's guess what the real subject will turn out to be in the end." Is *Noah's Compass* that book? How did the story evolve?

Surprisingly, *Noah's Compass* did turn out to be exactly that book. That doesn't always happen. Even though I never base my novels on real events, I do think they often reflect my current stage of life. *Noah's Compass* began to take shape when I was in my mid-sixties. Like [protagonist] Liam, I have begun to wonder how people live after they have passed all of the major milestones except for dying.

Some of your most well-known protagonists are male, as in Noah's Compass. How do you go about writing from the perspective of the opposite sex?

I had a really good father, and two really good grandfathers, and three really good brothers—far more men in my life than women, in fact. Probably that's why I don't think of male characters as being all that foreign to me. The biggest stretch I've had to make is reminding myself that men need to shave in the morning.

Your stories often deal with matters of family and complicated relationships, and yet each one seems fresh. How do you ensure each book creates a unique world for the reader to immerse herself into?

Well, thank you, but I always worry that I'm not creating a unique world. With every novel I finish, I think, "Oh, darn, I've written the same book all over again."

How much do you consider your audience when you write? As you release a new book, do you imagine your readers to be primarily new ones, or to be "constant readers," as Stephen King calls them, who have grown with you? Or do you not imagine them at all?

I've learned that it is best not to think about readers while I'm writing. I just try to sink into the world I'm describing. But at the very end, of course, I have to think about readers. I read my final draft pretending I'm someone else, just to make sure that what I've written makes sense from outside.

At that point, I seem to picture my readers as brand-new to me. They have the neuter, faceless quality of people in dreams. It comes as a shock later when a real-life reader writes to me and turns out to be a specific human being.

Your characters seem so real, in part, because they're so flawed. You've also said your characters surprise you all the time. As you write, how do you keep even the most flawed characters endeared to the reader, rather than inadvertently portraying them as unlikable?

Sometimes I don't manage to keep them endearing, and if that happens, I ditch them. It takes me two or three years to write a novel. I certainly don't want to spend all that time living with someone unlikable.

Your books can be laugh-out-loud funny. Is it your own sense of humor we're reading, or does it come from someplace else entirely?

I'm not in the least funny personally. The funny things emerge during that stage that writers always talk about, where the characters take over the story, and more than once something a character has said has made me laugh out loud, because it's certainly nothing I'd have thought of myself.

At what point in the process do your titles come to you? How much importance do you place on them?

I think titles are hugely important, but they don't always come easily. Several times my editor, Judith Jones, has shot a title down and then I've spent ages finding a new one. Only one title—*Celestial Navigation*—came to me before I'd even written a book for it. At the time I was simply in love with the phrase; I even had a cat named Celestial Navigation.

In what ways do the longevity and experience of your career impact the writing you're doing today?

If anything, the impact is a negative one. I worry that I've done this so many times, pretty soon I'll start "phoning it in," as they say. (I love that phrase.) If that happens, I hope I will have enough sense to quit.

You seem to view writing as sacred, and to be protective of your process. Can you explain why you feel it's so essential for it to be so?

I've noticed that whenever I become conscious of the process, the process grinds to a halt. So I try not to talk about it, think about it, write about it—I just do it.

After you've won a major award for your writing—having described your reaction to winning the Pulitzer as "flabbergasted"—how does that affect the experience of writing future books? Do you ever feel pressured for each book to measure up to a certain standard or expectation?

Part and parcel of not thinking about the reader is not thinking about a book's reception in general—the critical opinions or the sales figures. So I am spared that sense of pressure you're talking about, although I admit that it's a cowardly approach.

The publishing industry has changed dramatically since you released your first book. What in your opinion is the most positive change you've observed or experienced? The most unfortunate?

I honestly have very little knowledge of the publishing industry. I have been extraordinarily fortunate in having only one publisher in my career, and only one editor, and we have jogged along together without much incident of any sort. I believe I have been in the offices of Alfred A. Knopf only twice in my life.

The expectations are increasing that young writers today do so many things in addition to writing—they are called upon to promote themselves and their work, to interact with their readers online, and the like. How do you recommend they stay true to the craft of writing while pursuing success in publishing?

I think it must be very hard. Probably they're not allowed to say "No," as writers could in the past. And I'm always sad when new young authors write letters requesting blurbs. If blurbs have to exist (and I don't believe they do), it doesn't seem to me that the writers themselves should be forced to solicit them.

You're one of only 250 members of the American Academy of Arts and Letters. What's it like to be a part of it?

It is, without a doubt, the single honor I am proudest of.

You've said that what you have to say, you've already said through your stories. When others look back on your body of work, what do you hope they hear most clearly?

It's not so much what they hear as what they remember experiencing that I have hopes for. I would love it if readers said, "Oh, yes, I was once an accidental tourist," or, "I once owned the Homesick Restaurant," and then recalled that in fact, that hadn't really happened; they had just intensely imagined its happening.

The whole purpose of my books is to sink into other lives, and I would love it if the readers sank along with me.

The first novel you submitted did not sell, and you've been quoted as saying you'd like to disown your first four published novels. Today, how do you feel you've grown as a writer?

More often now, when I finish writing a book, I feel that it comes close to what I envisioned for it at the outset. It's not *exactly* what I envisioned, but it comes closer than my earlier books did. I'm very happy about that.

What do you plan to write next? Could you imagine a day when you might retire from the craft?

Asking me that right now is like asking a woman who's just had a baby when she plans to get pregnant again. I can't believe I'll ever write another book. And daily I imagine retiring from the craft. But I've been saying that for years.

 JESSICA STRAWSER is the editor of *Writer's Digest*.

CHAPTER 68

A CONVERSATION WITH STEPHEN KING & JERRY JENKINS

BY JESSICA STRAWSER

One is arguably the best-known writer of our time. The other made his name writing the end of the world as we know it in the Left Behind series. If this unique pairing seems unlikely, look closer. A conversation with the two yields both parallels and polarity—and candid insights as well as mutual respect.

How did the two of you meet?

JENKINS: We happened to have the same audio reader, a brilliant voice actor named Frank Muller. In November 2001 Frank was in a horrible motorcycle accident that left him brain damaged, incapacitated, and barely able to speak. One of Frank's brothers started a foundation to assist with the obscene expenses, and Stephen became aware that I was helping out.

Stephen was carrying the lion's share, undoubtedly contributing more than half of the total the foundation raised, but he called me one day to thank me for my part and to suggest other ways we might be able to help Frank. Needless to say, when my assistant told me Stephen King was on the phone, I quickly ran through my list of practical joking friends to decide how to greet whoever was claiming to be him. But, just in case, I said my usual, "This is Jerry."

I had to squelch a laugh when he said, "Steve King."

The Complete Handbook of Novel Writing

Who calls Stephen King "Steve"? Well, Stephen King does. We learned that we read each other's stuff and laughed about being strange bedfellows. Then we agreed to [meet to] visit Frank at a rehabilitation facility.

Your works are in some ways polar opposites, but in other ways parallels can be drawn. What do you think of each other's books? Do you imagine you share an audience?

KING: I got to know [Jerry] through the Left Behind series, which has a lot in common with *The Stand*—both are stories about the end of the world, with Christian overtones (mine has more four-letter words). While I'm not a big believer in the Biblical apocalypse and end-times, I was raised in a Christian home, went to church a lot, attended MYF (Methodist Youth Fellowship—lots of Bible drills, which every writer could use, Christian or not), and so I knew the story. The Left Behinds were like meeting an old friend in modern dress. I very much enjoyed *The Youngest Hero*, which is a crackerjack baseball story written by a man who must be a serious stat freak. Jerry writes sturdy prose and plots well. He's also warm and compassionate. Understands families inside and out. There's a lot there to like.

JENKINS: Much of my audience tells me they read Stephen's works. Others, of course, find horror horrifying, and some of his stuff pushes the envelope of comfort for them. Even for me, I lean more toward *The Green Mile* than, say, *Carrie*, but regardless of what one thinks of the genre, Stephen's talent is no longer up for debate.

What compels you to write?

JENKINS: I write because I can't do anything else. I like to say I don't sing or dance or preach; this is all I do. But I [also] have a passion for my subject matter. I was a sportswriter as a teenager (after being injured playing sports), but felt called to full-time Christian work. I thought that would mean I'd have to give up writing and become a pastor or a missionary. I was thrilled to find out I could use my budding writing gift and accomplish the same thing.

KING: Jerry's direct and correct: I can't do anything else. And every day I marvel that I can get money for doing something I enjoy so much.

What do you need to consider in writing about belief systems and other themes that are intensely personal to your audience?

JENKINS: It's one thing to preach to the choir, as we often say. It's quite another to try to make a particular faith understandable, palatable and hopefully even attractive to the uninitiated or the patently hostile. I'd had some experience writing to a crossover audience (the general market) because I had done many sports personality books (Hank Aaron, Walter Payton, Orel Hershiser, Nolan Ryan, et al.), but when Left Behind crossed over in a big way, I quickly realized the spot I was in.

Here I was, writing fiction with an overtly Christian theme (the Rapture of the church at the end of time) to an audience that suddenly seemed to include everybody. I tried to remember always where my readers were coming from and to be sure to stay away from insider language.

Of course, the singular challenge I had was to allow the message to come through without letting it overwhelm the fiction. The story has to be paramount. Readers must fall in love with the characters and want to keep turning the pages. The minute your novel starts to read like a sermon, end of story.

KING: The old Robert (*Psycho*) Bloch witticism applies here: "Thou shalt not sell thy book for a plot of message." Jerry said it, and I'll double down: Story comes first. *But*—and I think Jerry will agree with this, too—what you write ought to be about *something* you care about. Why else would you spend all that time and expend all that effort?

What are your secrets for making readers suspend their disbelief and immerse themselves in your imagined worlds?

KING: Making people believe the unbelievable is no trick; it's *work*. And I think Jerry would agree that belief and reader absorption come in the details: An overturned tricycle in the gutter of an abandoned neighborhood can stand for everything. Or a broken billboard. Or weeds growing in the cracks of a library's steps. Of course, none of this means a lot without characters the reader cares about (and sometimes characters—"bad guys"—the reader is rooting against), but the details are always the starting place in speculative or fantasy fiction. They must be clear and textured. The writer must have a good imagination to begin with, but the imagination has to be muscular, which means it must be exercised in a disciplined way, day in and day out, by writing, failing, succeeding, and revising.

JENKINS: Ironically, the definitions of nonfiction and fiction have flip-flopped these days. Nonfiction has to be unbelievable, and fiction has to be believable.

So, to my mind, the task (and I agree with Stephen that it's no trick) of getting readers to buy your premise and temporarily suspend disbelief is to *yourself* believe your premise with all your heart.

For me that meant that for the Left Behind series, I believed the biblical prophecies are true and will happen some day. Then I went about trying to show what it might look like, all the while owning it. When Stephen writes about what Edgar Allan Poe referred to as the phantasmagorical, I imagine him pecking away in the dark, all the while telling himself, "This could happen."

As to why people like to escape into other worlds, that has to do with this world. People are longing for something beyond themselves and their current circumstances. They want either hope or escape—or both.

What do you think it is about your books—and each other's books—that keeps people up at night? While writing, do you ever frighten yourself?

JENKINS: From my perspective, Stephen's gift is this incredible ability to recognize and exploit details of life and squeeze from them every ounce of meaning. I'm reading his *N.* right now and find myself constantly saying, "That's how I would feel! That's how I would say it!" (I'm speaking of identifying with the characters, not with the author. If I could say it the way Stephen says it, the Left Behind series would be just one of a string of megahits, rather than an anomaly in my career.)

As for frightening myself, it happens that by, in at least this sense, being part of the Stephen King school of fiction (trying to put interesting characters in difficult situations and writing to find out what happens) allows me to have the same emotions the reader will have. Since I write as a process of discovery—even though I know this is all coming from my subconscious—I am often surprised, delighted, scared, disappointed, saddened, etc., by what happens. If it's serendipitous to me, it certainly should be to the reader, too.

At least it gives me an out when readers demand to know why I killed off their favorite character. I can say, "I didn't kill him off; I found him dead."

KING: I usually feel in charge. But not always. You know how Jerry says, "I didn't kill him, I found him dead"? That *does* happen. It happened to me in *Cujo* when the little boy died. I never expected that. I wasn't frightened, but I was sad when that happened. Because it seemed outside my control.

Why do you think the battle between good and evil never ceases to fascinate readers? In what ways does it continue to fascinate you?

KING: The battle between good and evil is endlessly fascinating because we are participants every day. Sometimes we see it on TV, as in the Mumbai terrorist attacks, and sometimes we see it on the street, as when a big kid pushes a smaller one or some maladjusted individual indulges in a little drive-by harassment. We feel it when we're tempted to skim a little money or do a little running around outside the relationship or participate in some deal we know damn well is skeevy. When evil is vanquished in a book, most of us feel cathartic triumph.

I think we're also looking for strategies to use in our daily battle. And, let's face it, we enjoy the conflict. That's what makes pro football such a ratings wow, not to mention [pro] wrestling. And—rule of thumb—those of us who root for the "good guys" are probably well adjusted. But writers must be fair and remember even bad guys (most of them, anyway) see themselves as good—they are the heroes of their own lives. Giving them a fair chance as characters can create some interesting shades of gray—and shades of gray are also a part of life.

What are the challenges of writing for "constant readers," as Stephen calls them? What's fun about having a devoted fan base?

JENKINS: Readers come to respect you, believe in you, and set certain expectations for you. I always want each book to be better than the last, and sometimes readers want to stay where they're comfortable. People still ask for more Left Behind books. Sixteen was plenty. I'd be surprised if people didn't occasionally ask Stephen for sequels to some of his classics. But writers need to grow, too, and try new things.

Stephen, am I right? Do your fans obsess over the old stuff and want more of the same?

KING: They just want a good story, and I think they come to crave your *voice* even more than the story itself. It's like having a visit with an old friend. As for revisiting old stories ... I remember a very young fan in Houston (it was my first book tour) telling me that he loved *'Salem's Lot* and thought I should write "a squeal in that jenner." After a moment of frantic cranial cogitation, I realized he was saying "a sequel in that genre." I *have* thought of writing a "squeal" to one of my early books, mostly because I've never done it before.

Jerry, do you write from a place of uncommon spiritual insight?

JENKINS: I wouldn't say it's uncommon spiritual insight, but it does come from a lifetime of belief. In many ways writing Left Behind, a story I had been telling since I was a teenager, felt right because I grew up in a tradition that believed it. I am neither theologian nor scholar, but I understand the story and am fascinated by it. When I assisted Billy Graham with his memoir *Just As I Am*, again, it felt right, as if I had been prepared for it by a lifetime of passion for the same tradition.

When writers "outside" the faith attempt to write about these same things, the base audience senses their disconnect and their discomfort.

Stephen, a lot of your constant readers seem to think that, on some level, you must be channeling some sort of other world entirely. Is there any truth to that?

KING: I have no particular spiritual insights, but I think every writer who does this on a daily basis has a "back channel" to the subconscious that can be accessed pretty easily. Mine is wide and deep. I never write with an ax to grind, but I sense strongly that this world is a thin place indeed, simply a veil over a brighter and more amazing truth. To me, every ant, cloud, and star seems to proclaim that there is more to existence than we know. I suppose that sounds like naturism and pantheism, and to some degree it is, but I also believe in a power greater than myself. If I die and that turns out to be wrong, there's this advantage: I'll never know.

How has your writing evolved over time? In what ways do you feel your audience has evolved with you?

KING: For sure my audience has grown older with me, and to a greater or lesser degree, wiser. Certainly more sophisticated. I think I have a greater grasp on my narrative powers than I used to have (*that'll* start to degrade in another ten years or so, as the gray cells begin dying at a faster and faster rate), but I still refuse to recognize any limits to my gift. I think it's important to keep on pushing the envelope. I also like to think that I'm being "discovered" by younger readers, but who really knows? Certainly I haven't evolved as a writer by consciously trying to evolve; I just keep writing and hoping to find good new stories. In truth, I hardly ever consider the audience at all. And I don't think it's wise to. I have a built-in desire to please; that should be enough. Beyond that, I'm just trying to amuse myself. Usually that amuses others, too. Which makes me a lucky man. True for Jerry as well, I'd guess.

JENKINS: I hope my writing has become more spare and direct over the years. The longer I write, the less patient I am with needless words. That's fortunate, because my audience has kept pace with the culture, in which technology has reduced us all to short attention spans and sound bites.

That said, a good book can't be long enough for my taste. And a bad book can't be short enough.

You've both written with co-authors and seen your work interpreted into film. What is most satisfying about such collaborations? What's the worst part?

JENKINS: I don't believe [I] can co-write fiction. At least, I wouldn't want to try. I have such a great working relationship with Dr. Tim LaHaye because he serves as an idea person, a biblical and theological expert, and a great cheerleader. He doesn't try to help with the writing.

KING: I've collaborated with two writers. Stewart O'Nan and I wrote a nonfiction book, *Faithful* (about the Red Sox), and I've written two related novels (*The Talisman* and *Black House*) with Peter Straub. I enjoyed the experience in both cases—enough so that Peter and I will probably write the third and last Talisman book in one or two years. *Faithful* was like a dual diary. With the novels, Peter and I got together and whammed out a "bible." Then we took turns writing the story. The core story for *Talisman* was mine. The core story for *Black House* was Peter's. I tried to write like him, he tried to write like me, and we met somewhere in the middle. Hey, I'm a go-along-to-get-along guy, not a lot of ego, and that made collaboration fairly easy. But I wouldn't want to do it all the time; mostly I like having the playhouse to myself.

JENKINS: As for films, as I'm sure is true with Stephen, some I'm thrilled with, some I don't even acknowledge. I was particularly happy with what Hallmark did with *Though None Go With Me* and what my own son Dallas

(Jenkins Entertainment) did with *Midnight Clear*. Stephen, you're on record for hating a lot of the film treatment of your work. Were there some you were happy with?

KING: Who gave you the idea I hate most of the film adaptations? There are at least eight really good ones, and the only one I can remember hating was [Stanley] Kubrick's cold adaptation of *The Shining*; spending three hours watching an ant farm would be more emotionally uplifting. But the ones that are bad ... I just laugh and then forget them. I'm always interested in what happens, but my expectations are low, which makes life a lot simpler. My favorite adaptation is still Rob Reiner's *Stand by Me*.

JENKINS: Speaking just for me, I think the best film ever made of one of Stephen's works was *The Green Mile*. Usually watching a movie of a favorite book is disappointing, but in that case I kept remarking that it reminded me of what my mind's eye saw as I read.

Stephen, do you consider The Dark Tower series your magnum opus? How do you view it in relation to your complete body of work?

KING: I hope my magnum opus isn't written yet, but by length and ambition, I'm sure most readers would say The Dark Tower is the big one (when they're not naming *The Stand*, that is). Another sign: I don't feel done with it yet. Those seven books feel like the rough draft of one unified novel. I've already rewritten the first one, and I wonder if Jerry sometimes has the urge to revisit Rayford Steele and his buddies and spruce them up. Not saying they're bad as is; just saying sometimes you look back at a completed work and say, "Oh yeah! Now I know what I meant!"

JENKINS: I have made the mistake of saying that my novel *Riven* was indeed my magnum opus. Trouble is, I don't know how to do anything else, so more novels will be coming. And readers will say, "Didn't you retire? How does one follow his own magnum opus?"

So—any thoughts of retirement?

JENKINS: Retire from what? Why would I want to quit doing what I love? Slow down a bit, sure. See the kids and grandkids more, you bet. Retire? Nah. [My wife] Dianna says she's going to put on my tombstone, "Never an unpublished thought."

A Conversation With Stephen King & Jerry Jenkins   451

Stephen, it seems every few years someone breaks the big story that you've announced you're finished. Thankfully it's never proved true. Are you toying with them, or are there times when you feel the tank is empty? (As I've told you, after *Riven* I seriously wondered if I had anything left to say, and your counsel was to not make any rash decisions while recuperating. That proved great advice and I'm back at the keyboard.)

KING: There was a time when I thought I would, because I'd had an accident, I was hooked on pain medication, and everything hurt all the time. Things are better now. When I wonder if I really have any more to say, I pick up a recent novel by John Updike or Elmore Leonard ... which gives me hope of another twenty productive years.

How do you think having written a book for writers helps define your career? Might you pen another?

KING: I think I've said what I have to say about writing, and I'll be interested to see how Jerry answers this question. For me, *On Writing* felt like both a summing-up and an articulation of things I'd been doing almost entirely by instinct. I thought it would be an easy book to write, and it wasn't. I also thought it would be longer than it turned out to be. But you know what we used to say when we were kids, playing Hearts? "If it's laid, it's played"—meaning you can't take back a card once it's on the table. Nor can you invent new cards. I said everything I knew then, and if I added what I know now, it would probably amount to, "Don't write long books, because the critics rip them," and, "Don't end sentences with a preposition." Which I might have said in *On Writing*!

JENKINS: I didn't write *Writing for the Soul* to define my career, but it did give me my only chance to be overtly autobiographical, so in some ways it accomplishes that. Because of my ownership of the Christian Writers Guild, I may have another writing book in my future. This would be more nuts and bolts and less personal, probably.

KING: Last but not least—we're all amateurs at this job, really. It's always new. For me (to quote Foreigner), it always feels like the first time.

 JESSICA STRAWSER is the editor of *Writer's Digest*.

CHAPTER 69

CORY DOCTOROW: ON REVOLUTIONARY ROAD

BY CHRISTINA KATZ

Science fiction novelist, blogger, and technology activist Cory Doctorow is used to being criticized. Some write to the prolific author to say he's foolish for giving away his books online at the same time they come out in print. Others write to say he's foolish for working with traditional publishers in the first place. But thousands of Doctorow's fans write to say they discovered his books through a free download in only a few clicks online. And as long as some of those readers go on to become book buyers, Doctorow says he and his publisher, Tor Books, will keep coming out ahead.

So much for being foolish. The Canadian-born author doesn't shy away from experimenting in new forms: He's authored five novels, including *Down and Out in the Magic Kingdom*, best-seller *Little Brother,* and *For the Win*; as well as two co-written nonfiction books, two short-story collections, and an essay collection—while also co-editing the popular blog Boing Boing (boingboing.net) and writing for publications ranging from *The New York Times* to *Wired* and *Popular Science.*

And Doctorow won't even think about signing a book contract without Creative Commons licensing, which grants a nonexclusive right to create free online versions of his works, even though this stipulation caused a delay in his titles becoming available on shelves in the United Kingdom, where he now lives.

But while he's blazing a trail for the rest of us, can Doctorow take a little heat from the critics?

Not only can he take it, he's not above responding to their skepticism with a few theories of his own.

When you wake up, what are you excited about?

Mornings tend to be motivated by sheer inertia. Maybe slight panic. They are the most ritualized part of the day for me. I have a little tick-list I try to get through before we leave the house around 8 A.M. That's after getting up at 5 A.M. and reading through all the e-mail and the first round of blog posts that have come in overnight, often getting those five hundred words done that I do every day on the novel I'm working on, and doing the household chores. I'm the early riser, so I make the breakfast and then get the baby dressed.

You've said that when you were working full time, you had a similar schedule. Do you write more now that you can?

Each project seems to find its own rhythm and its own daily word count. There was one where I worked very, very long hours, and that was *Little Brother.* That whole book came together in eight weeks for the first draft. And there were days when I was typing so long that my wrists made me stop, where I just couldn't keep working.

Although I was writing really hard, I was working as well, since it was during my Fulbright at the University of Southern California. I was teaching a couple of courses, advising undergrads, I was the faculty adviser for the Students for Free Culture club, and working as an adviser for Electronic Frontier Foundation. I was also traveling; I remember writing a big chunk of *Little Brother* while attending and speaking at the iCommons conference in Rio.

Has becoming a father changed things for you?

One thing fatherhood does is it forces you to be a lot more diligent about how you organize your time. So I'm a lot less apt to take on stuff that is of low value. For example, if I'm going to relax these days, I'll never turn on the television. The books I'm not reading are always more interesting than the shows I'm not watching. When you start to think of your time as packing a knapsack for an adventure in the woods—not wanting to overpack and not wanting to leave anything out, either—and really treat it as a survival kit, you start to get to what matters.

Many of your books have been nominated for—and won—awards. Are literary award events good opportunities to connect with readers?

[What I call] "performative authorship" creates more economic opportunities for writers, but I think that performance isn't always literally standing up in front of a group of people. Blogging is inherently performative. Tweeting is performative. Podcasting is extremely performative. Not only are you performing your work, but there is an immediacy where your voice is right there in your reader's ear. I feel a personal connection with the podcasters I listen to. And that performance makes your readers into people who participate in your economic success not just because they have to in order to consume your work, but because they want to see you succeed.

You've said you learned at the Clarion Science Fiction & Fantasy Writers' Workshop how to sit down at the keyboard and "open a vein." How did that change your writing?

That's a variation on a famous old writing aphorism, something like: "Writing is easy—all you have to do is sit down at your typewriter and open a vein." I was twenty-one when I went to Clarion. Before, when I would sit down at a keyboard, I would feel "the magic"—that feeling that you're putting down words that are entertaining and witty and sometimes very vivid. I would feel the cleverness—that feeling you get if you happen to be the guy who tells the funniest joke in the room at the lull in the conversation. Everybody laughs and for a moment you kind of bask in their adulation.

But what I didn't feel was that kind of heart-tugging feeling—that feeling you get when you're in dangerous territory. The feeling I had before was the feeling of having successfully told a joke; the feeling I try to get now is that feeling you get just before you try the joke, when you don't know if it will succeed. That feeling of trepidation, of being slightly out of control, of taking a risk, of not knowing whether you are going to crash and burn—that feeling.

You've written political thrillers, science fiction, fantasy, nonfiction, and young adult—and in many forms, including books, short stories, and comic scripts. How do you move from genre to genre?

I think of myself as a science fiction writer first and foremost. Partly that's because the job of science fiction writer has always been so politicized and so variegated and so broad. Science fiction writers have historically been polemicists, scientists, technicians, engineers, researchers, public speakers, and agitators.

In terms of the genres, I find it hard to tease them apart. If the science fiction writer's job is to discuss how technology is changing society using fiction, and if the activist's job is to try to influence the way that society changes using technology, then those two jobs seem to me to be pretty closely related. So a blog post might end up being themes in a novel, and the themes in a novel might become part of a speech, and the speech might become part of an op-ed, the op-ed might trigger a short story. And none of those are in a distinct genre.

Genres are useful for marketing; they are a great way to help readers find the material they might want to consume or acquire. But they don't have clean lines you can use to distinguish one type of literature from another. Rather, they describe what kind of audience might be interested in them.

So, which of your own books is your favorite?

It's always the book I'm working on. I wrote *Little Brother* as a break from *Makers*. I started it about a year before I started *Little Brother* and I finished *Makers* a couple of months after I finished *Little Brother*.

But my publisher decided *Little Brother* should come out first because it was so timely. *Makers* happened to be about something that seemed a little implausible at the time: total global economic collapse. My publisher thought, "Oh, well, that's just purely fictional, it's not going to happen anytime soon, so we can put that book out anytime." So they rescheduled it [for November 2009], which turns out to have been a really good time. I don't think writers predict the future, but I think they're pretty good at looking at the present.

All of your books are available for free through a Creative Commons license. Can you explain why the strategy makes good sense to both you and your publisher?

The Internet has lots of stuff that's pretty much as fun to do as reading a book, so you're not really competing with theft; you're competing with being ignored. Given that I hope people will pay attention, I would rather take the attention they want to pay to me and channel it toward telling other people how great my books are than encourage them to slice the binding off one of my books and lay it on a scanner. The books are born digital; they might as well stay digital.

Economically, I might lose some sales, but I will gain more sales than I lose. If more people buy it because they found out about it electronically than [do not buy it] because they got an electronic copy, then I'm up. Since it doesn't cost anything to do free electronic distribution, there's no reason not to do it, provided you believe you're going to end up ahead.

What do you most often tell writers who ask for advice about getting published?

I often get e-mails from writers who say, "I'm working on a novel and I'm really worried that the publisher won't let me have a Creative Commons license and I'm going to have to have this difficult negotiation." And I write back and say, "Well, how's the novel going?" And they write back, "Well, I'm a few chapters in." And I write back and say, "Well, you need to finish the novel first. You can't sell that novel until it's written."

So, there is a lot of potchking—which is a Yiddish word that means fiddling around—that writers do. I think one of the ways you keep on writing is by pausing every once in a while and daydreaming about how nice it will be when the book is finished and published. That's totally legitimate. It's just like daydreaming about what the marathon will be like when you're finished running it. It's one of the things that keeps you running, right?

But it's easy to tip over from daydreaming to making the daydream the main activity. Once you are taking the time you should be spending writing and using it researching technical questions about negotiating the fine details of your contract with your publisher—who as of yet doesn't exist because the book isn't written—you are no longer writing. You are *potchking*.

This is no different than Robert Heinlein's advice to writers: Write, finish what you write, send what you write to an editor. Almost every writer who approaches me for advice is not doing at least one of those three things. And if you are not doing those three things, you are not on a trajectory to publishing work. If you are doing those three things, you may not ever publish your work, but you *need* to do those things, otherwise what you are doing is writing-related activity. You are no longer writing.

So write, finish what you write, and send what you write to an editor. Everything else is gravy.

 CHRISTINA KATZ is the author of *Get Known Before the Book Deal* and *Writer Mama*.

BEST-SELLING ADVICE: Purpose

"[The writer] has to be the kind of man who turns the world upside down and says, lookit, it looks different, doesn't it?" —Morris West

"Indeed, great fiction shows us not how to conduct our behavior but how to feel. Eventually, it may show us how to face our feelings and face our actions and to have new inklings about what they mean. A good novel of any year can initiate us into our own new experience." —Eudora Welty

"I write in a very confessional way, because to me it's so exciting and fun. There's nothing funnier on earth than our humanness and our monkeyness. There's nothing more touching, and it's what I love to come upon when I'm reading; someone who's gotten really down and dirty, and they're taking the dross of life and doing alchemy, turning it into magic, tenderness, and compassion and hilarity. So I tell my students that if they really love something, pay attention to it. Try to write something that they would love to come upon." —Anne Lamott

"The only obligation any artist can have is to himself. His work means nothing, otherwise. It has no meaning." —Truman Capote

"I've always had complete confidence in myself. When I was nothing, I had complete confidence. There were ten guys in my writing class at Williams College who could write better than I. They didn't have what I have, which is guts. I was dedicated to writing, and nothing could stop me." —John Toland

"You need that pride in yourself, as well as a sense, when you are sitting on page 297 of a book, that the book is going to be read, that somebody is going to care. You can't ever be sure about that, but you need the sense that it's important, that it's not typing; it's writing." —Roger Kahn

"The real writer learns nothing from life. He is more like an oyster or a sponge." —Gore Vidal

"I think most writers—and I'm excluding now the adventure and mystery writers—will write about episodes meaningful to them in terms of their own imaginations. Now that would include a great deal of what they experience, but I'm not sure there's an autobiographical intention so much as the use of experience. That's been true in my case: I believe I'm telling the truth when I say that, when I wrote *Catch-22*, I was not particularly interested in war; I was mainly interested in writing a novel, and that was a subject for it. That's been true of all my books. Now what goes into these books does reflect a great deal of my more morbid nature—the fear of dying, a great deal of social awareness and social protest, which is part of my personality. None of that is the objective of writing. Take five writers who have experienced the same thing, and they will be completely different as people, and they'd be completely different in what they do write, what they're able to write." —Joseph Heller

"They have to be given some meaning, the facts. What do they mean? The meaning's going to be influenced by a lot of things in you and your own culture. And some of these things you may be unaware of. But every historian has some kind of philosophy of life and society. ... All kinds of strands and currents and factors are involved. You have to separate and put together and from that we should deduce that there's no situation in the present that's simple, either. No simple answers. And the historian, when he looks over one of these situations, is going to try and consider all these things and try to be objective and fair and balanced, but what he picks out as the meaning will, of course, be what he himself believes." —T. Harry Williams

CHAPTER 70

AUDREY NIFFENEGGER'S ARTISTIC LIBERTIES

BY JESSICA STRAWSER

𝐹𝑒𝓌 𝓉𝒽𝒾𝓃𝑔𝓈 𝓁𝒶𝒷𝑒𝓁𝑒𝒹 an "overnight success" actually are, and Audrey Niffenegger's 2003 debut novel is no exception—if you take into account the four-and-a-half years she spent writing *The Time Traveler's Wife,* or the twenty or so agent rejections she collected when it was finished. But after she signed with Regal Literary and independent publishing house MacAdam/Cage, the term "overnight" wasn't much of an exaggeration. The book quickly became the kind of runaway, worldwide bestseller that writers (and indie publishers) don't dare imagine.

Then came the waiting. As years ticked by, there was the inevitable speculation the book and its author could be relegated to one-hit-wonder status. But those murmurs were muffled when the completed manuscript of Niffenegger's sophomore novel, *Her Fearful Symmetry,* sold at auction to Scribner—for a (widely) reported eyebrow-raising advance of nearly $5 million—and a release date was set. "She really has defied custom and written a spectacular second novel, which is one of the hardest things to do in this universe," Scribner Editor-in-Chief Nan Graham told *The New York Times.* The release of the *Time Traveler* film adaptation only heightened the anticipation.

Niffenegger is known for her creative experimentation in a variety of media. Her artwork is widely exhibited. *The Three Incestuous Sisters* and *The Adventuress,* visual novels she'd created before *Time Traveler,* were commercially published after its success. And she is one of the founders

461

of the Center for Book & Paper Arts at Columbia College Chicago, where she teaches Interdisciplinary Book Arts.

Her Fearful Symmetry is a ghost story set in and around London's famed Highgate Cemetery, where Niffenegger worked as a guide while researching the book. It begins when American mirror-image twins inherit their aunt's flat bordering Highgate. As they adjust to their new lives there, they begin to question their identities, the bonds of sisterhood, and even whether their aunt is really gone after all.

Here the author discusses the writing process, her return to bookshelves, and the artistic bliss that comes with owning your own day.

You've said you set out to teach yourself to write a different kind of book with *Her Fearful Symmetry*. Do you feel you succeeded with that?

On a technical level—the things that I was trying to teach myself to do—the new book is an ensemble where there's a great many point-of-view characters. So I spent quite a lot of time trying to figure out how to pass point of view around in a way that isn't annoying to the reader, but that allows me to get into and out of people's heads so that at any given moment, the reader knows what I want them to know. And that turns out to be surprisingly difficult.

Did you have a process that helped?

The first book was a bit of a continuity nightmare, and so I had all these timelines and charts and things. This one is much simpler because you're not jumping back and forth in time. So what I was essentially trying to do was think about what each character is aware of and what the characters do and don't tell each other, and times when the reader knows more than any one given character—which is most of the time, actually.

How long did the writing take?

I began at the beginning of 2002. I had the idea just as I was finishing *Time Traveler*. Initially in my head I had this apartment and this man who never leaves the apartment but is visited by this young woman. And the apartment was very dark and oppressive, and I knew that there was a cemetery bordering it. I didn't realize at the time that that was essentially a subplot.

Originally I was going to set it in Chicago, and then as I thought about it more I realized that Highgate would be oh so much more—I don't know—crazy, enticing, dramatic.

And also, part of the project as it began to shape up had to do with the idea of writing what is essentially a nineteenth-century novel but to set it in the twenty-first century and to have the people be modern people. But what I'm trying to do is use a lot of the plot devices and ideas that you might find in Wilkie Collins or Henry James.

Did you live in London while researching Highgate?

I've never actually lived in London, but I have spent a lot of time there. My friend Jean Pateman, who the book is dedicated to, [was] the chairman of the Friends of Highgate Cemetery, and for the last several years she's been letting me come and stay in her house.

Just as the city of Chicago was almost a character in *Time Traveler*, Highgate is a strong presence in this book. Is that something you set out to do?

Yes; once I started to really research it, I just was in *love* with it. The characters do get out and about in London somewhat, but London is so massive and so old and so layered that you can't really do a "London" novel that takes in all of London. You have to break it down into bits.

In the book, the twins' neighbor, Robert, is a scholar of the cemetery who has a tendency to get carried away with his research. Was there any of your experience in that?

Totally. That's an inside joke. I have piles and piles and piles of notes. And recently I was thinking I really wish somebody would write that book [about the cemetery's history] that he's writing, because it would be so useful.

Are you thinking about doing that?

I can't; I'm not a historian. But there certainly was a sense that the cemetery itself is much cooler than anything I can write about!

Themes of loss permeate your work. How much do you consciously think about themes as you write?

When you're going to do something that takes as long as a novel takes—this was seven years of work—certain things tend to feel right and to feel more interesting than other things. I just find that I keep being attracted to the same central ideas. I try to do something different and not just make the same thing over and over again. But certainly these are things that affect everyone in our kind of underlying daily life. Even if you don't want to think about death all the time, which we mostly don't, nevertheless it's kind of there, giving daily life more of a sense of beauty.

How significant are your titles to your work?

They have a certain shaping element. When you're constantly thinking of the thing by a certain title, it makes it perhaps seem more cohesive than it is at first, and then after a while the thing kind of grows into the title.

When did you title *Her Fearful Symmetry*?

Somewhere way in the beginning. I had been admiring Philip Pullman's trilogy, *His Dark Materials*, which of course is a quote from Milton, and I suddenly thought, *Oh, I can make a title that kind of chimes like that out of this bit of Blake.*

What influenced your decision to leave MacAdam/Cage and sign with Scribner?

When I first signed with MacAdam/Cage, I believe they had fourteen employees, and by the time [*Her Fearful Symmetry*] was ready they had three. And they just weren't going to be able to do it. They bid on the book, and we offered the book to them. But I just thought, my heavens, how is this going to work? And I *love* MacAdam/Cage. They were fantastic to work with. The problem was that not only were they a different size than they had been, but I am a different size, you know? I'm not even sure that I won't ever work with them again, but it's just a matter of how to go about it. The whole idea of indie publishing is really important to me.

You're probably going to cringe, but I have to ask about the advance.

Cringe cringe!

Did you ever dream it would be so high?

No no no. I was incredulous. Mightily surprised, let's say that.

Do you feel it may lead to heightened scrutiny of the book?

If you wait seven years to put something out, I think there would be scrutiny anyway. I finished the book to my own satisfaction, so if people want to rag on me, that's kind of their business. The only thing I'm actually in control of is what's in the book.

You've said before that you don't have a desire to write full time, but how does that amount of money change your writing life?

I'm also a visual artist—that's kind of my starting point—and back in the 1990s I started going to artist colonies. The one I go to the most is Ragdale. I remember the first time I ever went, I was just like, "I'm going to get up today, and I'm going to do what I want. I'm going to make stuff." And it was such a fantastic feeling to *own your own day.* And I thought, *that's* what to aspire to, just to be in control of your time.

So there was a point a couple of years ago where I suddenly realized that I had achieved control over my day. And that was really exciting. From that point on it's the freedom to make what you want, when you want. I think what we're all looking for is that kind of liberty.

Do you find you do better work in the artist colony environment?

I find it super helpful. I would recommend it to anybody whose daily life feels a little overwhelming. What's great is when you go to these places it's very companionable and it's not like there's some sort of huge pecking order. The younger artists and the more established artists, they just all groove together and it's really kind of idyllic.

Do you think you'll watch the *Time Traveler* film?

No, I don't think so. The movie, it really belongs to the people who made it. It's their work of art.

But sometimes they sent you scripts?

It was a courtesy on their part, and I did read them. But you know, it wasn't really my place. I had no power to do anything whatsoever. So, they made their movie. I was told at the very beginning of being published that of books that get optioned, apparently one in forty gets made. So just the fact that the movie got made is pretty amazing.

Does it pain you to see your visual novels overshadowed by your other fiction?

That the visual things are available at all is amazing, because I [originally] made ten copies of each. And they seem to fall into people's hands almost by accident. Sometimes those people are young art students, who then write and tell me what they thought about it, which is thrilling, because I was an art student once. And so really I'm just delighted that Abrams published them, and they actually have sold fairly respectably for visual novels. I've been pleased with the paths that they take to find an audience.

Do you plan to do any more?

I recently did a comic strip for the London *Guardian* called "The Night Bookmobile." We're going to put that out as a book next year. And I'd like to keep doing that as a series.

What will you write next?

I've started a third novel, which is called *The Chinchilla Girl in Exile*. I'm working off of a short story that I wrote about five years ago that never quite jelled, and the reason it didn't jell was that the idea was bigger than short-story form.

It's about a nine-year-old girl who has hypertrichosis, which basically means she's covered with hair. Originally I was thinking of trying to write a young adult book, but—this happens over and over again—I get going on something, and all of a sudden it's full of darkness and sex and swearing and, you know, so it'll probably end up being unsuitable for children!

The development of e-books is sort of at odds with the book and paper arts you teach and create. Do you think you'll ever reconcile the two mediums?

People seem to have gotten the idea that I'm adamantly opposed to the existence of e-books, which I'm not. There are some very good reasons for e-books to exist. I'm waiting to see how it goes because there's so much uncertainty right now that surrounds e-books. You don't want to come down on the wrong side of some-thing and inadvertently stifle competition or cause a problem for bookstores. It's all in flux, and I think a lot of authors are trepidatious.

And then there's a whole other aspect to it. I trained as a book conservator. So, okay, here you have a digital book. Are we going to be able to read that in one hundred years? Or is it just going to be this weird little piece of code that nobody can unscramble? I mean, people think of books as being problematic. There's been this thing of everybody saying, "They're acidic, and they take up space!" But on the whole, they have endured.

 JESSICA STRAWSER is the editor of *Writer's Digest*.

CHAPTER 71

SHOCK & AWE: CHUCK PALAHNIUK

BY JORDAN E. ROSENFELD

Controversy rides Chuck Palahniuk's back like bad weather, which is exactly how he likes it. When he tried to get his first novel, *Invisible Monsters* (then titled *Manifesto*) published in the early 1990s, some editors secretly loved the dark novel about a model who's shot in the face, but they shied away from acquiring it. Frustrated and rebellious, the Portland native embarked on an even darker book. The result was *Fight Club*, a novel about fist-fighting, anti-corporate power, and identity, which rocketed him from obscurity to success and then fame when the book was adapted into a movie starring Brad Pitt and Edward Norton.

While critics are still uncertain of what to make of Palahniuk's unique blend of dark, irreverent and discomforting fiction—labeling him a "shock writer"—his fans are so passionate, they've organized "The Cult" website (chuckpalahniuk.net), where they act as his unofficial PR team, staunch defenders, and cult of worship.

Though Palahniuk claims he still isn't sure he's made it as a writer, he's written fourteen books (two nonfiction) that have sold millions of copies, and at least three more of his books have been optioned for films. The movie version of *Choke* came out in 2008.

For a man who writes about violence and sex in unabashedly graphic terms, the writer himself is disarmingly soft-spoken, even shy, and extremely private about his personal life. When we spoke, his novel *Rant* had just been published and was garnering harsh reviews from critics. But Palahniuk is a testimony to the aphorism that there's no such thing as bad publicity. Even as critics pan him, his books continue to rise effortlessly on the best-seller charts.

Your path to success didn't follow a straight line. At what point did you feel like you really made it?

I'll let you know when that happens. I don't know if you ever really feel like you've made it. Maybe it was one day when my mom called and said she'd seen a pallet full of my book *Lullaby* at Costco.

Yet you have an incredibly large fan base that even has its own name and website—The Cult. Did they make you feel like a success?

I try to forget about the expectation that's out there and the audience listening for the next thing so that I'm not trying to please them. I've spent a huge amount of time not communicating with those folks and denying that they exist. You realize you have no control over how you're perceived. I want to focus my energy on the thing I can control—which is the next book.

You have such varied and wild new ideas for each novel. When do you know that something has the meat to become a novel?

It's usually a premise that I can present in a short story and bring to my workshop. Hopefully, they can instantly get it and be very excited about it and take it off in different directions. When it gets a response like that, I know the premise is good. When it generates personal stories from other people, when an idea seems to portray an aspect of my experience that's really close to other people's, that's another really good sign that it can go for a few hundred pages.

Is interacting with people a big part of your writing process?

Entirely. My writing has to excite people and depict or include their experiences. That way, every time I go out socially, and people ask, "What are you working on?" and I tell them the premise, I end up illustrating it with anecdotes taken from hundreds of people. That's part of my process—to go out and interact with people. It's very much like an archival process. I understand that the Brothers Grimm would go out and get people talking so they could document folk tales that weren't being documented any other way. I try to offer a little bit of myself—some experience from my life that evokes stories in other people.

That's an interesting point in light of your novel, Rant, which is written as an oral history—a series of interviews about the title character. What made you want to work with this form?

One, I've always found the form just incredibly readable. It's a form that's presented in small nuggets, so whether you enjoy the moment or not, there will always be a payoff at some point. It's such a flexible form that it can be used to make a fairly mundane character much more attractive. For example, the biography of Edith Sedgwick: She really was a spoiled rich girl who did a lot of drugs, but by using this form, her story is more readable, compelling, and dynamic than it actually was.

Second, it's a nonfiction form. You can always tell a more incredible fictional story if you present it with the structure of nonfiction. An example: Orson Welles telling H.G. Wells' *The War of the Worlds* through radio, giving it a credibility or gravitas. And later, doing *Citizen Kane*, a fictional movie using a nonfiction form. Or think of the movie *The Blair Witch Project* that was presented as lost documentary footage that had been recovered. You can tell a more over-the-top incredible story if you use a nonfiction form.

Third, this form allows you to cut things together like a film editor cuts film. You can really experiment with collage and juxtaposing certain elements. Seemingly unrelated things can be placed next to each other, and you don't have to worry about lots of wordy transitional phrases. You can present the best nuggets in whatever order serves it best.

A hallmark of your writing is that you play with form in a way that makes people think differently. why do you like to play with these nontraditional narrative forms?

Laziness. I just hate having to come up with all those transitional establishing shots, all the conventions. You know, the part where the character looks into a shiny mirror or teapot so they can describe themselves—all those hackneyed, obligatory nineteenth-century things. I hate doing that, so I find a nonfiction form that provides me with the structure I need. I've done it with every one of my books.

Let's talk about Rant, the character. He's sort of a pilgrim for authenticity; he's always searching out what's real, even if it's ugly or painful or base. I wonder if you feel like our culture has become sanitized or separate from our humanness? That comes up in a lot of your work.

I'm not sure about the whole culture, but I would be comfortable saying that intellectual culture seems to separate high art from low art. Low art is horror or pornography or anything that has a physical component to it and engages the reader on a visceral level and evokes a strong sympathetic reaction. High art is people driving in Volvos and talking a lot. I just don't want to keep those things separate. I think you can use visceral physical experiences to illustrate larger ideas, whether they're emotional or spiritual. I'm trying to not exclude high and low art or separate them.

I try to provide as many strong experiences as possible so that you're left thinking you experienced or lived through what the characters have. The idea is to try to place the reader in that reality so they really feel like a character.

You often are described as a shock writer and someone who likes to push boundaries and go for the discomfort zone. Are you out to shock or make people uncomfortable?

I'm just trying to record and honor stories that have been told to me because more often than not, everything I write about begins with an anecdote. My first goal is to document an aspect of human experience that won't get documented by any other form of media.

My second goal is to make my workshop laugh on Monday nights and to make my editor laugh.

My third goal is to shock myself—to put something on the page that I never want my mother or nephews to see and that I cannot imagine reading in public. Because if you're always going for the thing you can conceive of, it's boring; you don't force yourself to change. But if you can somehow create something that you can't conceive of at the beginning, you evolve—you discover something that was beyond your capability when you started. That makes more sense to me.

Does it get harder to surprise yourself?

Not really. It's such a harvesting/gathering process. A lot of my discoveries involve other people who bring me stuff that's so outside my own experience. I find myself continually amazed, shocked, and moved by how diverse people's lives are.

What's your writing process like?

My writing process isn't a very organized thing. It seems like I'm always working in some way. Even when people are sending me letters, I'm looking for a really strong anecdote that resonates or doing the research to develop those seeds and illustrate them in different ways. Or I'm talking to people, gathering firsthand experience. The actual writing part is a tiny part of my life. I often write in public. I bring my laptop or write freehand in notebooks. Then, I'll read through them while I exercise or walk the dog. The very last thing I do is the sitting alone at the computer part.

Why do you like to write in public?

Typically, by the time I'm sitting down to write a story draft, I have an idea of the dynamics I'm holding in my head, and I'll know the purpose of the scene. For instance, I often need physical gesture to balance dialogue. If I write in public, every time I need to know what a character is doing with his hand or foot, I can look up and study people and find compelling gestures that I can harvest. Writing in public gives you that access to a junkyard of details all around you.

I read that you haven't had a television in years. Does that influence your writing?

I haven't had television since 1991, and it definitely influences me. As a child of the 1970s, I couldn't hold a narrative in my head; I was lucky if I could hold a joke in my head, because every time you turn on television or radio, it wipes the slate clean—at least in my case. After I gave up television, I found I could carry longer and longer stories or ideas in my head and put them together until I was carrying an entire short story. That's pretty much when I started writing.

Tell us what's next.

I've fallen into a pattern of one kind of acceptable book and one really appalling book—I have to warn you that next year's book, titled *Snuff*, is the appalling book.

When you say "an appalling book," do you actually appall yourself?

I appall my editor. I make myself really, really nervous. Right now, the workshop that I attend on Monday nights is entirely female writers. I'm not sure what kind of material I should present, because I don't want to offend or anger them. With the material for *Snuff*, the women either roared with laughter or told me more experiences that I needed to hear. They ended up egging me on to places I would never have gone. They are an enormous, fantastic resource.

There are a lot of assumptions about what's acceptable to write about, and what's not, but you don't seem to care what people think.

As horrifying as something might be, it's happened to somebody. That's my line of defense. Just because I'm writing about something, it's not so unique or unusual that millions of people aren't already doing it. Sometimes the very best way to deal with unpleasant things is to depict them in ways that allow people to laugh at them and destroy the power of unsayable things, rather than refusing to acknowledge them.

Do you feel you get enough credit for the humor that's in your work?

My workshop laughs a lot. My editor laughs. I have a secret goal with my editor—he has asthma and uses his inhaler, and after I send him a new manuscript, I'll have his assistant phone me and tell me how many times he had to get his inhaler out while reading a draft. It's my secret laugh meter.

Your work causes people to first laugh and then cringe.

That's the idea, the juxtaposition of those opposite states. Tom Spanbauer, who taught me to write, said you have to make them laugh and then, as soon as possible, try to break their hearts.

Do you think you'll ever write a sweet story?

I started to write a children's book about a little boy whose mother dies. After coming home from the funeral, his father leaves him alone in the apartment, and he finds a phone number on a business card that says: "Ladies for all occasions." He phones up and says, "I need a mother," and a jaded escort girl shows up thinking he's a pervert but ends up having this sweet afternoon with this six-year-old boy after he's just buried his mother. As a children's book, it didn't go very far.

I hear that *Choke* is being made into a movie and that a few other books have been optioned. What's it like to undergo a film adaptation of your work? Are you attached to the process?

Once again, I say control the things you can control. As for the rest of it—God bless it all. I know that [the filmmakers'] goal is to do what they do as well as possible.

Did you like the movie version of *Fight Club*?

Yes, I thought they did a fantastic job. But cross your fingers: The *Fight Club* Broadway musical is still alive. I can't say any more than that.

Do you have any advice for budding writers?

I've got so much! One—persevere. I know so many writers who are a hundred times better than me and have longer, greater ideas than mine, but they gave up; they stopped. The biggest talent you can have is determination. Do you use the writing process as your ongoing excuse to keep exploring the world, meeting people and learning things? If you can do that, then the writing itself will be its own payoff and reward.

 JORDAN E. ROSENFELD is a contributing editor to *Writer's Digest* and author of *Write Free* and *Make a Scene*.

CHAPTER 72

DAVID EGGERS:
GOING HIS OWN WAY

BY KRISTIN D. GODSEY

Dave Eggers, poster boy for the Gen X literati, has built a career on writing whatever he feels like, however he wants to, regardless of conventions or genre limitations. On a 90-degree day in May, with the cicadas thrumming loudly through the open windows of Cincinnati's Memorial Hall, he stands before a roomful of writers and acknowledges how he's once again ceded to his own instincts. "I've never worn shorts and a T-shirt to a reading before," he half-apologizes, but no one in the heat-wilted audience could fault him for this choice.

Since his name-making memoir, *A Heartbreaking Work of Staggering Genius*, made waves in 2000 and earned him a Pulitzer Prize nomination, Eggers has had the financial wherewithal—and critical clout—to throw himself into a variety of unusual literary pursuits. In an exclusive sit-down interview following the reading in Cincinnati, Eggers shared his thoughts on self-publishing, his charity work, and why the memoir is the most difficult of all writing forms.

After *A Heartbreaking Work of Staggering Genius*, which was published by Simon & Schuster, you chose to self-publish your first novel through McSweeney's. Why?

It sounds crazy but, first of all, it's more fun to work with your friends than to work with a company in New York. But secondly, we can get a book out in a couple of months, whereas with everyone else you wait thirteen months. And that, to me ... I'm just unusually rankled by that time gap. Because by the time the book comes out, you don't even feel the same way. You're onto something else, but you still have to tour, and you have to pretend you still like the first book.

From the beginning, the object of McSweeney's (or at least one of them) was to try to make some of the best-crafted books possible. So in each case, we try to do something different with the printing process.

With my collection, it's going to be embossed in a way that nobody's really done for a couple of decades. Major publishers, their profit-and-loss needs are very restrictive, so they can't do that. And so they can get a lot more books out there, and they're better at distributing and promoting them than we are, but we feel better with making the book look how we want it to look.

So it's a trade-off. And there's an ongoing myth that we're at war with major publishers, but it's totally blind to the fact that we've always been working with them. The way we've sort of balanced it right now is to do our own hardcovers but do paperbacks with someone else. The paperbacks go through Vintage, and the two Haggis-on-Whey books [the children's books Eggers co-wrote with his brother Toph] will be republished by Simon & Schuster in the fall.

Did you have writing mentors?

Just my teachers. I remember every one of my teachers and every grade and every comment on every paper. I remember my junior year in high school, my English teacher, Mr. Criche, he wrote on a paper I wrote about *Macbeth*: "I sure hope you become a writer." That was actually the beginning, a seed planted in my head.

I try to say the same things to students I know who could do it if they wanted to, you know? It's a heavy thing to lay on somebody, actually. But when they have the talent, I make sure they know it.

Then there was Mr. Ferry, my speech communications teacher, who was really supportive of some incredibly offbeat things I wrote. It's rare to get one of those teachers who'll let you write about, you know, sheep taking over the world. I used to write about that; a friend and I were Sheep Conspiracy Theorists. And Mr. Ferry was cool with that.

I never took a creative writing class in high school, and I took like half of one in college, but it wasn't helpful.

In college, it was my journalism classes that taught the discipline and broke everything down so that you really learned about the preciousness of words. I was taught the economy of words and a sense of responsibility, too.

At the University of Illinois, where I went, they were really into community journalism, and most of the graduates go on to work at small papers, trying to make an impact. So that had a big effect on me.

But stylistically? No, I never really had a style mentor. I guess I just kind of veered around until I settled somewhere. But I'm still settling, I guess.

You've said that you're a relentless self-editor, that you "go through thirty drafts of everything" before you publish it. Did you find that, with a memoir, self-editing becomes a harder process?

Yeah, I'd say that to anybody. It's infinitely harder. You can't treat the words just as words; the sentences, you can't look at them dispassionately. You have to read—especially the more difficult parts you're writing about—you have to read them over and over again. And it's really hard.

There were a lot of passages in that first book that I didn't edit very thoroughly, because I didn't want to go back there. And I just sort of wrote them down and hoped they'd make sense and counted on the editors there to clean them up. So that makes writing anything but a memoir much easier. I wouldn't jump at the chance to do that again.

In terms of structuring and self-editing a memoir, how do you determine what's interesting to the reader vs. what's interesting to just you and the people in the book?

I ended up not cutting anything, if you can believe that. I think that your brain or your subconscious, especially, is a natural storyteller. Chances are, you're going to know what to tell and what not to tell, and what's important.

If you don't have that sense of what's interesting to other people, you might have a harder row to hoe. I guess that's one of the differences between writing that people like to read and writing that's an exercise in your own head. It's the same gene that says, well, this is boring. I'm kind of bored. Everyone goes to parties where people talk endlessly about something that isn't interesting. And you wonder, Man, you're missing that gene, aren't you?

We all suffer from that from time to time, I guess. But I don't know, I guess I'd been thinking about my memoir for a long time so I sort of knew what was going to be important. And beyond that you're filling in, you're saying, "Oh, I need a bridge here between this part and that one, and whatever." The filling-in is the hard part.

Do you think there's any such thing as pure nonfiction? You've said that memoirs can't be 100 percent "real," because you have to reconstruct conversations, etc.

Well, journalism should be pure nonfiction. But I don't think you can make a good, readable book out of pure nonfiction. If you don't do some time compression, you're going to bore the reader to death.

The other thing is, if you want to put anything within quotation marks, then it's not pure nonfiction unless you recorded it. I'm a stickler about that. That's why I explained [in my memoir] how the quotes were done ... because, again, that's my journalism training. You have to tell readers what they're getting, which is a reconstruction as close as you can get it and that's true to the spirit of the people you write about.

And, ideally, you show it to the people who are speaking and say, "Does this reflect how you'd say this?" So that's fidelity to the truth. With my family, we all said, yes, this was the story.

Had you always written fiction, too?

Never. I wrote my first piece of fiction, like, three or four years ago, in a short-story collection edited by Nick Hornby called *Speaking With the Angel*. Before that, I'd only written journalism—features and essays and profiles and all that stuff.

Do you have plans for another novel?

I'm working on two things right now. One is a biography of a Sudanese refugee named Dominic Arou, which has been running in *The Believer*. Three episodes of that have run. The whole thing should be complete in the next year.

And then I've been working on this political novel that's been running on Salon.com for a long time. I don't know when I'll be done with that.

The serialization of your work—you do that a lot. Do you do that by design?

It's a deadline. It keeps you working on a schedule; I recommend it to anyone. I like being out there, rather than being sequestered a year at a time. I always recommend not spending five years alone without any feedback, without finishing portions of what you're working on. But that's me. I need a deadline to eat toast. I'm a procrastinator.

So having eight thousand words a month in *The Believer* for the biography was really helpful to get it started. The Salon piece is the same thing. Some people are much more diligent about working on their own, and that's fine. I really like reading the *Paris Review* interviews about how people go about writing, with Hemingway writing his daily word count on a chalkboard and that kind of thing.So I was like, okay, if you do it that way, you know where you stand.

So if I say I'm going to put three thousand words up on Salon every week as a general goal, it does help. And before you know it, there are probably eighty thousand words done on that so far. I don't think serialization is used as often as it should be.

Was it a big difference shifting gears from a memoir to a novel?

Nah. The first book, even though it was a memoir, I approached it like a novel. So I didn't really feel like it was a stretch to write a novel. I think people who write semi-autobiographical fiction are sort of bridging those two forms, anyway. It's like a memoir where you change the names. So it really wasn't that much of a leap. But it was liberating not to have to worry about your responsibility to the people you're writing about.

So it's incredibly freeing—although, for a while, my fiction was heavily influenced by actual events. Like, I wrote a story about climbing Kilimanjaro that was based on a trip I took, and I had a hard time departing from the real events of my trip. I think that's just a handicap of the journalist. It's hard to use your research and then depart from that when necessary.

So you don't have any interest in writing another memoir?

No. I mean, there's some stuff I'm doing, a collection of stories that are somewhat autobiographical ... but never again that level of revelation. I guess it was cathartic, which is what people always assume, but at the same time, anytime you open up a can of worms like that you're getting into just as much trouble as you would if you'd left it closed. There's no such thing as closure. You open it up and you just get messy again.

 KRISTIN D. GODSEY is a former editor of Writer's Digest.

CHAPTER 73

MASTER OF TRAGICOMEDY: RICHARD RUSSO

BY JANE FRIEDMAN

Validation: That's how Richard Russo describes the impact of winning the 2002 Pulitzer Prize for his fifth novel, *Empire Falls*.

"It gave me permission to continue. It said, 'Keep doing what you're doing.'"

Russo's epic story of a declining New England small town has been hailed by critics as the last great American novel of the twentieth century. It was the inaugural selection of the *USA Today* book club and named 2001's best novel by *Time* magazine.

Empire Falls tells the life story of an unpretentious nice guy, Miles Roby, who's spent all his life managing the town's greasy spoon, Empire Grill. The first chapter opens with Miles waiting at the restaurant for his teenage daughter, Tick, to return from school. She eventually appears hefting a load of books.

"The overarching metaphor is at the book's opening—Tick and her backpack," Russo says. "The larger theme is how kids are carrying too much weight, and what will the weight be in the end. It turns out it's cruelty."

Russo modeled Tick on his own two daughters, who were high-school age when he wrote *Empire Falls*. In some ways, Russo says, the story is a father-daughter love story, but one that ends with a father's worst nightmare: cruelty against his own child.

"I was hoping [the school shooting] wouldn't be the climax. I knew where it was headed, and I didn't want to go there," Russo says. "I used a fair amount of my daughters in the character of Tick—I had grown to love this child. And to turn around and put this fictional child in that kind of mortal jeopardy! But it's a multigenerational book. Everyone's hurt or abused in some way."

As grim as the subject sounds, *Empire Falls* overflows with humorous scenes and characters, for which Russo's earlier novels are well known. *Straight Man* is an academic satire and *Nobody's Fool* is another small-town life novel with tragicomic elements. The latter was made into a motion picture starring Paul Newman; Russo wrote the screenplay.

Whether he's detailing the lives of intellectuals or blue-collars, Russo always builds a vivid setting. Sense of place is crucial in all of Russo's work, particularly so in *Empire Falls*. The dying town envelops Miles' activities, taunting him for never escaping. "Place and its people are intertwined, place is character," Russo says.

Typically, Russo works on a novel for several years, and during that time often returns to the story's beginning to add passages or reshuffle scenes.

"In art, effects often precede the cause. I try to make the novel appear like that's what I was doing all along," he says.

Empire Falls features lengthy flashbacks including a fourteen-page prologue relating the town's history. But Russo says chapter one—set during the present day—was his true start. As he progressed, he saw the need for a backstory, so he started writing about Miles' childhood and the town's history. He later decided to place the flashbacks in italics, as separate sections, to deliver the information.

"I realized how much the past impinged on the present," Russo says. "I have this analogy: If you're building a house and you start digging, and you run into this rock, you have two options. You can either try to dig the rock out, not knowing how big it is or how deep it goes, or you can build around the rock and make it an architectural part of the house, as if it really belongs there. And that's kind of what these flashbacks are like."

Once Russo finishes a novel—which he revises and revises until he can't make it any better—he shows it to his wife.

"She's the first reader, a good reader and generous reader. She tells me when the book loses her attention," he says.

After his wife's read, Russo sends the work to his agents, Nat Sobel and Judith Weber.

"Every single one of my books they've made better, but we don't always agree on what needs to be done. The secret to the relationship is that they're never insistent," he says.

Russo's 2007 book *A Whore's Child* took a different direction. The Whore's Child (Knopf) is a collection of seven short stories—some new, some old.

Although Russo finds that short stories pose a lesser risk ("If short stories fail, it's a month out of your life—damage control"), they are much more difficult for him to write.

"They are all about control, which I've never had a lot of. I'm a creature of digression. You can't allow yourself to be distracted."

Yet distraction is exactly what Russo goes after in his writing environment. He prefers to write in diners or busy places, where his mind can wander and make connections. "You can end up where you didn't mean to go, but it's probably more interesting than where you meant to go in the first place."

Russo's advice to novelists in particular is this: "Whatever you're working on, take small bites. A few pages at a time. Whatever you're working on should be the most exciting thing. The task will not be overwhelming if you can reduce it to its smallest component."

Also: "Don't keep a journal because you'll think what you remembered to write down was important when it's actually not."

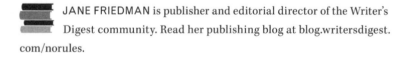 JANE FRIEDMAN is publisher and editorial director of the Writer's Digest community. Read her publishing blog at blog.writersdigest.com/norules.

CHAPTER 74

UNLOCKING THE DOOR: MARGARET ATWOOD

BY KRISTIN D. GODSEY

Like many artists, Canadian writer Margaret Atwood seems uncomfortable with the notion of explaining her craft. She follows no formulas, has no set writing patterns, and brushes off any attempts to dig into how the creative mind works.

But that's not to say that this world-renowned author of such novels as *Cat's Eye, The Handmaid's Tale, Alias Grace,* and *Oryx and Crake,* doesn't have any wisdom to offer her fellow writers. Her nonfiction book *Negotiating With the Dead: A Writer on Writing* is proof of that, and our interview with her revealed some interesting insights that all writers can take to heart.

You're a poet, novelist, short-story writer, and essayist, and always have been, ever since you announced to your friends back in high school that you were going to be a writer. Do you have a soft spot for one genre over the others?

I do when I'm writing it. When I'm in a poetry phase, I think this is the greatest thing and how could I write anything else? When I'm writing a novel, I'm very focused on that, and I can barely read poetry. There's no secret. I've always been a multitasker in all areas of life.

Does that keep you fresh?

It keeps me very busy. But I don't confine myself to writing. Do you want your sewing machine fixed?

You have a distinct voice that shows through in all your published work. There's an intensity, a sense of menace beneath the surface, along with a wry, dark humor. Did you always write this way?

I think everybody goes through an apprenticeship period in which they try different forms. And I certainly did. When we were in high school in the 1950s, in our high school anyway, we didn't read much modern poetry at all. So "The fog comes on little cat feet," and that was about it. Most of the other things we read, if it was prose, it was most likely written before 1900. They taught rhyme, they taught scansion. I knew what the various kinds of sonnets were long before I hit university.

So presumably that's what you started out trying to write?

[Laughing:] I started out sounding sort of like a combination of Lord Byron and Edgar Allan Poe. I wouldn't say that what I was doing back in college was very much like what I sound like now. I'd say that didn't hit until I was twenty-four or twenty-five.

So what changed?

I was writing more formally before. I can't tell you what happened except that it was a very noticeable shift, and it happened all at once. You can't account for anything that happens in the creative mind. It's the eureka experience. The experience comes unbidden.

Is there a particular poem or novel that you think introduces that change?

Yes, it's my first book of poetry, which you can't get in the States, called *The Circle Game*. As for novels, it was the second one I wrote, *The Edible Woman*. My first novel was happily unpublished. I can look at *The Edible Woman*, and I can see where I was going. I can see things in it that I later went on and developed.

So did you see the shift and decide, yes, this is the direction I want to go?

I felt the shift. This is not an intellectual matter.

Was there any conscious effort then to develop it further?

It's not something you develop. It's something you have access to. It's not like scratching away at the architectural drawing board—maybe we need a door-knob here, or we can put this window over here. That may come in the editing process. But the experience you're talking about is more like opening a door, not developing something.

Then you say, I didn't even know that door was there. Shall I go further down this corridor?

Do you ever hesitate in that idea of whether you should go further?

Yes.

But do you generally plod through?

Eventually. But the hesitation can take years. So that's more like, OK, I know the door is there, but I'm not going in there now. I need to get my little vial of magic light or whatever it is we need for these expeditions. Or maybe you say, I'm just not ready to go there yet.

And eventually you're ready.

Eventually, I go through the door. Or so far, that's been true. Let me give you an example: I wrote the first notes and chapters for *Cat's Eye* when I was twenty-five. I didn't write the book itself for another twenty-three years. That's a long hesitation.

Again, is that just an instinctual thing—you know when you're ready to go back?

You know when you're not ready; you may be wrong about being ready, but you're rarely wrong about being not ready. You keep trying, but you may wait a while between the tries.

And in your case, you try something else.

I try something else. That's one of the virtues of being a multitasker. If something's not working, you can go dig up a flower or fix a drape. Or write a different book.

What are your thoughts on the "chick lit" phenomenon?

Well, I wrote the first one: *The Edible Woman*. It was published in 1969.

Do you think that compares with what's being done today?

Have a look! Have a look. It's very *Bridget Jones's Diary* when you come to think of it. She works in an office, it's a shit job—

But your voice doesn't match up with the tone of most of today's chick lit.

Well, some chick-lit books are better than others. I thought *Bridget Jones* was quite a howl. There's good, bad, and mediocre in everything. If you really wanted to, you could say the original chick-lit book is *Pride and Prejudice*. So what is it, if it's about young women we're not supposed to take it seriously? It should be judged on its merits like everything else. A lot of the books we regard as classics today were thought of as cheap junk when they came out. *Dracula* by Bram Stoker is one; so is Mary Shelley's *Frankenstein*. There's a long list.

Let's talk about your writing process. Do you write every day? Can you walk me through a typical writing day for you?

Not every day. I'd like to, but I never did. I've always had either a job or a very busy life. I can't describe my process. It's chaos around here all the time.

So you don't have any sort of weird rituals or anything before you get started?

Oh, I wish. I used to have the pencil-sharpening, pacing-the-floor, anxiety-attack ritual, but things got so I just couldn't afford the time. So I've got that narrowed down to about five minutes of screaming time. [Laughs.]

Sometimes you just come to a stop, and you go do something else. And you do get to a certain age where you realize that the world will actually not stop turning if you don't write anymore.

I guess you don't really suffer from writer's block, then.

I never have, although I've had books that didn't work out. I had to stop writing them. I just abandoned them. It was depressing, but it wasn't the end of the world. When it really isn't working, and you've been bashing yourself against the wall, it's kind of a relief. I mean, sometimes you bash yourself against the wall and you get through it. But sometimes the wall is just a wall. There's nothing to be done but go somewhere else.

That sounds pretty practical.

I'm a very practical person. I grew up in a practical way; I grew up in the north. Make too many mistakes, and you're dead. You usually don't get a whole lot of second chances at certain kinds of mistakes. So let us say I'm cautious but practical.

So how does a Margaret Atwood novel come to be? Do you start with a plot concept? The characters?

I usually start with some voices. Or an image or a place. *The Handmaid's Tale* started with the scene of the bodies hanging from the wall. In the writing, that scene migrated quite far back into the book. But that was the first arresting image that made me feel I really had to go forward with this book.

Do you outline?

No. I did that once. It was a terrible mistake.

So you start with an image—

Yes. It's like overhearing someone talking in the next room. It's like seeing a village a long way off and thinking you have to go there. It's like seeing an object fraught with significance. You wonder why that's there. What is that blood-stained cleaver doing in the middle of the living room floor? I think we'd better look into this!

I'm compelled by something to go and find out more about it. And I've been wrong.

And do you just know when you're wrong?

You know eventually. It may take you two hundred pages. That's unpleasant. But you know when you lose interest.

We all have those "this is drivel" moments. But it would be a "this is drivel" moment that lasts for quite a long time. It's not only drivel on Monday but on Tuesday, Wednesday, Thursday, Friday, and Saturday, too. What am I to make of this? Why did I write that?

You've won the Booker Prize (for *The Blind Assassin*), as well as numerous other prestigious awards for your body of work. Does such recognition change anything in how you approach your work?

I think if I hadn't won them, I'd be a more anxious and ulcer-ridden person.

Really? That's surprising, considering how practical you are.

I know it is. But having had the experience so many times … I'm probably the most short-listed person in the world. To be that short-listed, if I'd never won anything, think how weird it would be.

Can you tell me a little about your writing space?

I don't really have a writing space. I do a lot of writing on airplanes, in airports, in hotel rooms. I do write in my study here, where I have two desks. But I don't use my two desks, because I write on the floor. I lie on the floor—actually, I sort of crouch. I'm more comfortable.

So what are you working on now?

I'm not telling. Never, ever tell. I know that if I told my editors at publishing companies what I was working on, they'd turn green and think I was crazy.

Because of the subject matter?

Yes. That's always been true.

Did you used to tell and then stopped?

I once told the title of a book, and then I changed it and everyone thought I'd written two books. So I never tell anyone anything.

You have to understand, my Western horoscope sign is the scorpion, and we're happiest in the toes of shoes where it's very dark. Nobody knows we're there. And on the Oriental calendar, I'm the rabbit, and we're very happy at the bottoms of burrows. We're very secretive.

 KRISTIN D. GODSEY is the former editor of *Writer's Digest*.

CHAPTER 75

JAMES PATTERSON'S TRADEMARK SUCCESS

BY DIANA PAGE JORDAN

More than 100 million people have read at least one James Patterson book. That's roughly one out of every three U.S. citizens. In 2008, with the publication of *Against Medical Advice*, his first work of narrative nonfiction, Patterson became the first author to have debuted at No. 1 on five *New York Times* best-seller lists: Hardcover Fiction, Hardcover Nonfiction, Mass Market Fiction, Children's Chapter Books and Children's Series. He also holds *New York Times* best-sellers record at 42, according to his publisher.

It all began in 1977 when Patterson's debut novel, *The Thomas Berryman Number*, won an Edgar Award. His breakout hit was *Along Came a Spider*, the first of many novels featuring Deputy Chief of Detectives Alex Cross. Today, his prolific body of work spans multiple genres, including The Women's Murder Club series (a natural, he says, since he grew up surrounded by women), the Detective Michael Bennett books (co-authored with Michael Ledwidge), two young-adult series (Daniel X and Maximum Ride), the occasional historical novel (such as *The Jester*, which he calls "history on adrenalin"), and even romance (including *Suzanne's Diary for Nicholas*, one of his favorites). He maintains this high volume, in part, by working with co-authors—a practice frowned upon by some, but rebutted by Patterson in one word: "teamwork."

His name is so well known that he's even been the subject of a "brand" case study by Harvard Business School students. Yet he says the secret to his success isn't the marketing, though he's a former ad executive who's sold more than 150 million books worldwide. Patterson says his books sell by the millions whatever the genre because they're cinematic, they're fast paced and, well, they're good.

How have you built your name to be such a widely recognized brand?

For me it's always been the same, and this was true when I was in business. I've always concentrated on the product. There are very few cases where people or enterprises or franchises have succeeded unless the product is really good for that audience. [Writers] always want to hear it's the advertising. It isn't—it's the product.

So how do you go about making your material so interesting?

I'm big on having a blistering pace. That's one of the hallmarks of what I do, and that's not easy. I never blow up cars and things like that, so it's something else that keeps the suspense flowing. I try not to write a chapter that isn't going to turn on the movie projector in your head.

My style is colloquial storytelling. It's the way we tell stories to one another—it's not writerly, it's not overdone. In the colloquial style, when you're just telling a story to somebody—and if [you said] some of the stuff that a lot of people put into books—somebody would just say, "Will you please get to the point?" Or, "This story is putting me to sleep." Or, "Could I move to sit next to somebody else at this dinner?" A lot of writers fall in love with their sentences or their construction of sentences, and sometimes that's great, but not everybody is Gabriel García Márquez or James Joyce. A lot of people like to pretend that they are, and they wind up not giving people a good read or enlightening them.

How does your background in advertising play into your success?

What advertising helped me to understand and get into my head very powerfully is that there is an audience out there. People go in and they think they know all the answers, and then they test stuff and find out that nobody paid attention, nobody cared; it was a blip on the screen. So you learn that there is an audience there. I'm always pretending that I'm sitting across from somebody. I'm telling them a story, and I don't want them to get up until it's finished.

I'm very conscious of an audience. I'm very conscious that I'm an entertainer. Something like 73 percent of my readers are college graduates, so you can't condescend to people. You've got to tell them a story that they will be willing to pay money to read.

You're apparently the first author to be a case study for future CEOs at Harvard Business School.

It was a lot of fun and an honor. Once again, the answer to what's happening here is not one that [business students and writers] want to hear. What I have working for me is that I'm very emotional and I'm analytical, and that's not always in the same body.

So I can look at my work and I can write it and try to make it as scary or loving or whatever the scene is supposed to be. And I can step back from it and analyze whether I've come anywhere near creating that.

So what did they teach in that Harvard study?

They were very interested in the notion that I was a brand, in their opinion. And you couldn't talk to a Coca-Cola bottle, but you could talk to me. They wanted to hear what I thought was behind it. I thought a lot of it was the fact that I'm thinking about the reader: I want to create a book that I think people are going to enjoy, that I would enjoy, and I get a kick out of that. Some writers don't. Some serious writers, the last thing in the world they want to do is entertain people, and that's fine, but I do want to entertain people.

On the marketing side, once I've written a book, I want to make sure that the cover is reasonable. And that, within reason, we've stuck our hand up in the air and said, "There's a new book!" which is really all the advertising can do.

You've been working with co-authors. How and why did you begin doing that?

I just have too many stories. I couldn't possibly do them all. People sometimes get wise-assed about the co-writers, but if you saw what happened ... ! For example, with *Sundays at Tiffany's*, I worked with a co-writer, and then I wrote seven drafts. And that happens a lot.

The "factory" comes up occasionally as a phrase. If it's a factory, it's a factory where everything is hand-tooled. If you came here now, you would see just stack upon stack—manuscript, screenplays, etc.—and almost nothing comes out of here that I don't rewrite a lot, in addition to outlining.

How does it work?

With the exception of *The Quickie*, every idea has been mine. I come up with the idea. I write an outline, about which one of my agents says, with this outline I could write the book. Usually, with a co-written book, somebody else will do the first draft and I will do subsequent drafts.

How do you choose your co-authors?

There are some people I've known for a long time. I've known Maxine Paetro for a long time. Peter De Jonge I've known for a long time—he worked with me at J. Walter Thompson [advertising agency]. Michael Ledwidge was a guy who sent me a manuscript. We had both gone undergraduate to Manhattan College, although a long time apart. He was working as a doorman in New York. At the time I was chairman of J. Walter Thompson, and he gave [his manuscript] to my assistant, and my assistant said, "Jim will look at it." Mike went home that night, and he was with his wife and the phone rang in his apartment, and he made a joke to his wife and said, "It's probably James Patterson." And he picked up the phone and it was me.

I said I liked it, and I helped him get an agent. So he sold it, and six or seven years later, he was having a little trouble, and we talked, and I said, "If you'd like, we can try to write a book together," and we wrote *Step on a Crack*. And then we co-wrote the first *Daniel X*. We co-wrote *The Quickie*, which was Mike's idea. We [released] another Michael Bennett [series book] in February, *Run for Your Life*. And the next Michael Bennett is finished, and we're doing another one.

What do you say to those who criticize you for working with co-authors?

Most movie scripts are teams. Television shows are generally written by teams. In the beginning, a lot of series were written with co-authors. Stephen King has written with co-authors. Who cares? It doesn't matter. Read the book. If you don't like the book, you can talk to me about it. It's not an issue of whether it's written by somebody else or not. In America, we get so caught up in individualism and heroes. I'm big on teams. I think teamwork is great. I couldn't possibly do all these stories. I have a file of stories that's four hundred pages thick, and they're stories that I want to tell. Steven Spielberg doesn't go out and do it by himself. I like the co-authored books. I think a lot of them are quite cool.

What would you tell aspiring writers?

If it's commercial fiction that you want to write, it's story, story, story. You've got to get a story where if you tell it to somebody in a paragraph, they'll go, "Tell me more." And then when you start to write it, they continue to want to read more. And if you don't, it won't work.

In terms of literary fiction, that's something different. It should be a point of view on something that's wonderful to read. Too often it's just style. I think style can be fine, but I think it's a little overrated if a book is nothing but style. I'm not as keen on it as some people are.

What are you writing now, and in what genres?

I just finished another historical [novel]. I really like this idea. It's a book that Alex Cross has written based on family stories, so you have your main character actually writing a book, and that's really fun and different. Obviously, [I'm also working on] a lot of crime fiction—The Women's Murder Club series, the Alex Cross series, the Michael Bennett series. We also have the TV series we sold to CBS in which Michael Bennett is the main character. Love stories—*Sundays at Tiffany's* was the most recent. *Suzanne's Diary for Nicholas* was earlier, which I really enjoy. They are most challenging for me because nobody gets killed, so I don't have the cop-out of bringing in that kind of suspense and adventure.

One horror: *You've Been Warned*. *Run for Your Life* will be out. The next Maximum Ride, called *Max*. It's been very successful. I'll go to schools, and you feel like you're a rock star because the whole school has read it and they're just screaming and yelling. In my mind, the best way—or one of the best ways—to get kids reading is to give them books that they love.

I was a very good student, but I didn't particularly like to read when I was younger. I still hate *Silas Marner*. They gave us books that were turnoffs to most of us. And then I worked my way through college at a hospital. I had a lot of free time, and I started reading everything I could find, and it was all serious stuff, but I fell in love. And that passion! You will hear that from a lot of people who do well in things. What's the key? The key is passion, I think. You gotta love it.

It sounds like you've got enough passion to last forever.

I love it! You're lucky if you find something you love to do, and if somebody will pay you to do it. That's my situation. I think I understand what I do well, and what I don't do as well. I tell stories well. I'm not a terrific stylist. *Thomas Berryman*, the first book I wrote, won an Edgar and does have a fair amount of style. I don't think it's a great story, but it does have style, so I have the ability to do it up to a point, but not as much as I'd want to, to write certain kinds of fiction.

What's your secret to success?

I don't think there are a lot of really readable books out there. There are less than people think there are. There's a lot of stuff that you pick it up and you feel like, "I've read this before." It's very hard to grab people. I don't think it's an accident that I'm up there. I don't think it's an accident that John Grisham is up there. John Grisham grabs people. There are a few writers that do it. I don't think it's that easy, and it's not a question of somebody who writes good sentences. It's a question of people being able to tell stories in a way that captivates a lot of readers.

I'm not trying to duck the marketing thing. My advice to most people, in terms of, what should you do after you write your book? Should you invest in some marketing? Should you stand outside a bookstore with flyers? Go write another book. Go write another book! You learned some things writing this book. Make use of them in the next book, and keep your passion going, and get that habit.

DIANA PAGE JORDAN (dianapagejordan.com) interviews writers for radio, television, the Web, and print publications. She's a radio and TV anchor in Portland, Ore.

CHAPTER 76

MEGAN MCCAFFERTY: A CROSSOVER SUCCESS

BY LAUREN MOSKO

After 10 years, five books, and more than 1,500 pages with Jessica "Notso" Darling—the trenchant heroine of *Sloppy Firsts, Second Helpings, Charmed Thirds, Fourth Comings,* and the final installment, *Perfect Fifths*—Megan McCafferty still gets a rush when she thinks about starting her next novel.

It's no wonder. *Sloppy Firsts* enjoyed the grassroots success of debut novelists' dreams. The third and fourth books instantly hit the best-seller lists. But even better than that: Women approach McCafferty at signings and thank her for the teen-angst nostalgia and for giving them a book neither they nor their daughters can put down; teenage girls tell her the series helped them through high school and made them realize they're not alone. Not unlike J.D. Salinger's Holden Caulfield or Kaye Gibbons's Ellen Foster, Jessica Darling is a true crossover success, one whose voice is destined to outlast the "bubblegum bimbos and assembly line meatballers" she's forced to count as her peers.

Though McCafferty assures us the Darling series isn't autobiographical, she certainly drew inspiration from her own adolescent journals, which you can read on her blog (meganmccafferty.com/retroblogger), as well as her roles as a senior editor at *Cosmopolitan* and freelance writer for *Glamour, YM, CosmoGirl!* and other famous glossies. When she realized she truly wanted to be a writer, not an editor, McCafferty lined up enough freelance assignments to keep herself afloat and left publishing to devote herself to books.

Here, she talks about her craft, the path to publication, and the joys and frustrations of series writing.

Tell me about the publication of your first book. How long did it take to sell?

I tell people that it took six months—and ten years. What became *Sloppy Firsts* came out of years and years of my own creative writing. I had all this material—short stories, personal essays, even some dramatic scenes—but it was very unstructured, just a mess of stuff. I'd always been encouraged whenever I took creative writing classes. But at the time, I'd never written anything longer than a twenty-five-page term paper, so the idea of writing a novel was impossible to me.

When I was working at *Cosmo*, my co-worker John Searles sold a two-book deal. I was just blown away by that. I'd always dreamed of writing a book, and here was somebody in my midst who did it. I basically cornered him the way people now corner me and asked, "How did you do it? How can I make this happen for myself?" He said, "Well, you need to get an agent, and in order to get an agent you need to have something to show the agent. Put together the best thirty pages of your future book."

I took thirty pages as law—it was gospel to me. I thought, well, thirty isn't that much more than twenty-five, I probably could do that ... and so I did. I looked through all my old stuff and selected material and used that as my starting point. I rewrote, redrafted and created what ultimately became the first chapter of *Sloppy Firsts*. I showed that to John's agent, who loved it, and she took me on as a client and told me to finish the first half of the book. So then I had an agent and thirty pages—that's all I had—and a dream. Over about a four to six-week period, I wrote like a madwoman. Then we kind of worked it and shaped it, and four months later it was sold to Crown in a two-book deal, based on the first half. We signed the deal in the winter of 2000 and I finished writing it a few months later. It was published in September 2001. The whole thing—from "oh my God how did you get a book deal?" to having my own book deal—was about a year.

When you were writing the first novel, did you imagine it as a series? Did you pitch it as a series?

I played up Jessica Darling's potential as the star of a series, but only in the broadest, most hypothetical sense: "If *Sloppy Firsts* is successful, I'll write three more books about her high school years!" The irony is, that's exactly the type of series I avoided writing. I definitely didn't visualize a series that would take her to college and beyond. Those decisions came gradually, as it became clearer to me with each book that there was great potential in exploring Jessica's development as a person—and a character—over an extended period of time.

Can you talk a little bit about your early relationship with your publisher? What compromises, if any, did you make?

The title really served as a litmus test for potential publishers. I was offered more money by a very famous editor, but one of the first things she said to me was that the title was "depraved," and would have to change. I remember thinking, *If she didn't understand that it's a joke, how do I know that she's going to understand a lot of the other jokes in the books? And what else is she going to ask me to change?* Whereas one of the first things [editor] Kristin Kiser said was, "I love the title. It's hilarious." And so that was it. I was like, "I love you. You're great. You get me."

But she also really understood that I was aiming for this crossover market—that if I wrote the book with enough humor and heart and intelligence, it would appeal not only to girls who are still in high school, but also to those who graduated years ago and have a fondness for teen angst. She absolutely understood that from the very first meeting.

I think that because I chose the right editor, it really made everything else so much easier. She knew exactly how to tell me what I needed to know. She was very direct, and I admire direct. She was right all the time. In the rare cases I did disagree, she respectfully listened to me and said, "Okay, I see your point of view." I really valued her input.

Crown never told me to change my vision for the series or the individual books. Anything Kristin ever asked me to change always made the books better.

You've often said Jessica is the more gutsy high-school girl you wish you could've been. As you began to write, was it difficult to not make the character too wise, hip, or perfect?

Not too perfect—that wasn't a problem because I think perfect characters are boring. Who would want to read about somebody who has it all together?

Sometimes I had to resist the urge to make her too clever for the sake of being clever. I had to jettison jokes that were out of character for her. But overall I think the way Jessica acts and speaks is fitting for someone who's as hyper-intelligent and overanalytical as she is.

Let's talk about the major scenes in the books. Did you spend a lot of time contemplating them before you started to write?

I think about all my scenes. I do so much revising as I go along; I wonder how I could write books if I hadn't grown up in the computer age. I think I'd be a very different writer. I find myself cutting and pasting, changing things around, and deleting whole paragraphs constantly.

I don't necessarily think I put any more thought into [major] scenes than I do to any others. To me, they're all important. Every scene should be essential; there shouldn't be anything in there that doesn't contribute to the plot of the story in some way.

Plotting: Planned or spontaneous? Do you outline much?

Very briefly—not any kind of formal outline that you learn in English class. I have to know how the book ends. If I don't know how the book ends, then I don't know what the point of the book is. I often write the last scene very early in the process, if not first. And then I have very strong ideas for certain plot points along the way. But how I connect those dots to make it to the end is very intuitive and spontaneous.

Often I'll be in the middle of a scene and a character will just kind of walk in as I'm writing and I'll have to figure out, *Why is Sara showing up here? Well, she's clearly going to annoy Jessica. Why is that happening here?* That's kind of the magic of writing, and that's what keeps it exciting for me.

What's thrilling about series writing for you?

The characters have aged ten years between *Sloppy Firsts* and *Perfect Fifths*. So that requires a maturation of tone, content, and format. And by having Jessica and everybody else get older with each book, I've had this unique opportunity to explore how personality traits develop over time. From start to finish, you can see how sixteen-year-old Jessica is the same and how she's different from the twenty-six-year-old Jessica, and how core traits like her intelligence and tendency to over-analyze manifest themselves over time. I didn't intend for it to happen that way, but I'm thrilled that it has because it's not just the "same old, same old" with every book. I couldn't write the same book over and over again.

What are the difficulties? I imagine writing five volumes of Jessica can be a little like becoming roommates with your best friend: You love her dearly, but you start to get a little sick of her.

I never wanted it to get to the point that I was sick of Jessica. I always told myself I'd stop writing about her when I felt her story was finished. And with *Perfect Fifths,* I know I've written an ending that will *hopefully* satisfy my readers. I'm definitely satisfied. I think it's a very fitting conclusion to her story.

That said, I think the most challenging part of writing this untraditional series is making each book stand on its own. It may sound funny, but every time I have a new book coming out, I get e-mail from readers who bought it without knowing there were other books that preceded it. It's challenging to write characters consistently over the course of five books that take place over ten years. Everyone changes, yet there have to be some aspects of their personalities that stay very true and constant from book to book. That's been the most challenging, but in a good way. I think it has pushed me as a writer.

You very deftly summarize everything that happened in previous books as it's pertinent to what's happening in the present of the story. How difficult was that?

So hard. Because I did *not* want it to be like Sweet Valley High, where they just cut and paste paragraphs about the aquamarine eyes and the golden hair ... I didn't want to bore my most devoted readers, who are thinking, *of course we know all this!*

I was always told by my editor that you can't assume. She would say, "Look, I've read all these books very carefully, and I have to be reminded from book to book what's happened before. You can't assume everybody knows everything." So to do that in a clever way—or at least a way that doesn't bore the readers who do remember what's what, or those who are reading the series over the span of a month—is very challenging. I also had to decide on the key points in the story that absolutely needed to be told.

You planned to stop—or at least break from—Jessica after *Second Helpings* and started an entirely different novel, but picked the series up again after a dream. Can you tell us more?

When I was finishing *Second Helpings*, I found out I was pregnant. I thought, *This is good: I'm finishing this book; I'm going to be a mother; I'll take some time off; I'll figure out what I want to do next.*

I think I took off the rest of my pregnancy and about a year after that—the first year of my son's life. It wasn't really by choice; I just couldn't even string two sentences together. I tried writing this book about a singer in a wedding band, but realized I only wanted to write the book so I could have an excuse to sing with a wedding band as research. That's not a good enough reason to write a book. And so the beginning of this novel was terrible; I ended up salvaging it by writing a short story that ended up in an anthology.

I was a year and a half into this break when I had a dream. In the dream, I was telling my agent that I was going to write a third book about Jessica Darling. It was just a very practical conversation I was having: It's going to cover three years instead of one, it's going to cover her college years, it's going to be called *Charmed Thirds* ... and I woke up from the dream and was still suffering from a motherhood lack of sleep. I had to call my agent and ask, "Did I have this conversation with you about this new book I'm writing?" And so I took off. I took notes on it. I thought my subconscious was telling me what I was doing next.

When did you know *Sloppy Firsts* was a big deal? Take me back to those first weeks on the best-seller lists.

I feel it most at my signings, when I hear from readers who tell me how *Sloppy Firsts* got them through high school. And that Jessica Darling made them realize they're not alone. That's when it really hits me; otherwise, I'm very detached, in my office, plugging away at these books.

The first time I had a signing where it was more than just my friends and family who showed up, I thought, *wow, these are strangers. These are just girls who like my books.* That struck me: Not only did I publish a book, but it's a book people actually read and care about, and want to tell their friends about.

I didn't make *New York Times* best-seller list until *Charmed Thirds*, and then again for *Fourth Comings*. It gave me a certain validation, and it certainly helps position me for future books, but it's not something I think about on a daily basis.

Sloppy Firsts was really a very word-of-mouth phenomenon; it's been out for seven years and it still sells as well as when it first came out, if not a little better. It didn't have the benefit of a splashy advertising campaign or extensive media coverage. It didn't have a movie tie-in or anything. And yet it continues to sell well because readers love it enough to tell their friends about it. That kind of grassroots success is something I'm very proud of because I don't know how often it happens.

Do you still get as much of a thrill from it now?

I definitely do. I went to The College of New Jersey last week and spoke to a room full of college-age women. I really get such a high talking to them and answering their questions, and seeing how excited they are about the books, and reading in general. To be a part of that is something I'm just so proud of. I've created this character that's inspired them to come out on a Tuesday night and listen to me talk for an hour, when there's so many more interesting things to do.

Have you ever gotten any backlash from parents, teachers, or librarians because Jessica—as a typical teen—doesn't shy away from crass language and experimentation with drugs or sex?

Not nearly as much as I thought I would. What minimal backlash I've gotten has been far exceeded by the amount of e-mail and face-to-face interactions from parents and librarians, who thank me for writing a book their daughters and students can't put down.

Jessica's had a range of sexual encounters, from romantic and true to cheap and inebriated. How do you approach sex scenes and keep them so honest?

The awkward and icky ones are easier to write than the sincere ones. It's easier to play these scenes for humor than it is real emotional depth. It's very difficult not to resort to softcore clichés. I try to think about the characters and how they would see and feel the experience, and try to express it as they would.

I took a lot of time writing Jessica's de-virginization scene, only because it had been built up so much in the first two books. I knew this was a moment that was going to be important to my readers and to the story. It needed to provide a contrast to all the baser sexual activities that were depicted throughout the books—usually by the other characters, and not Jessica—but it needed to say, "this is real." She's losing her virginity, she's a teenager, and she's the heroine of the novels; I wanted to make sure it was tastefully and respectfully done, but not too precious. It was a very tricky balance.

I've read that the 2006 incident (in which Harvard student Kaavya Viswanathan appeared to plagiarize your material) didn't affect you as a writer. in light of how open you are with the old journals on your blog and the leaking of Stephenie Meyer's manuscript on the Internet, what are your thoughts on intellectual property in the digital age?

Plagiarism has been around far longer than the Internet. In fact, I had a poem published in *Seventeen* magazine when I was fifteen years old. About a year later I was informed that there was a girl who used that same poem to win a statewide poetry competition in Alabama. It took months for people to put together that this had happened. Whereas in 2006, thanks in part to the Internet, the first reader e-mailed me within a week of the same transgression. So in many ways, the Internet makes it easier to break the rules, but it also makes it easier to get caught.

Are you still not talking about what you're working on next?

I'm so focused on finishing *Perfect Fifths*, that's where all my energy is going. But I can say that I have a very intriguing concept—I've been calling it my dystopian high school sex comedy—that I need to nail down.

Right now it's sprawling all over the place. It could possibly be a series. I'm very excited. It's something I'll be working on in early 2009, and I'm hoping it will become public shortly after this article is published.

I thought I was going to take a lot more time after finishing Jessica. I thought I was going to need a year; I've been writing about her for ten years now. But I think part of the reason I'm not so sad is because I'm already very encouraged by this new idea. I have a very long pre-writing process where I'm jotting down ideas in a notebook and ripping out relevant newspaper articles—a long fact-finding mission. I feel like now that I know what [the next book] is, I see stuff all the time. It's like a heightened awareness. I'm now attuned to everything on this particular topic.

 LAUREN MOSKO is a former editor of Writer's Digest Books.

CHAPTER 77

BROCK CLARKE'S DELICIOUS SATIRE

BY MARIA SCHNEIDER

Brock Clarke is friendly, conversational, easy to laugh. He has a boyish face and dresses casually in jeans and well-worn oxford shirts. He looks like a favorite English professor. And in fact, he's the director of a creative writing program. On the hot August day we meet, he's torn himself away from watching the U.S. Open. It's clear he'd be just as happy talking about tennis or baseball as writing, which he says isn't any more useful a profession than, say, plumbing.

In short, this isn't the subversive, fringe-element sort of person you'd imagine had spent the past five years writing a fictional account of torching the homes of famous dead authors. But in fact, that's exactly what he's done. Clarke spent the last five years writing the would-be memoir of Sam Pulsifer, accidental arsonist of Emily Dickinson's house and unlikely icon to literary firebug followers, with his novel *An Arsonist's Guide to Writers' Homes in New England.*

THE AURA OF THE WRITER

An Arsonist's Guide, which was published to wide critical acclaim—and one of the strangest publicity stunts in recent memory—is at once a witty, entertaining read, and a satirical reality check for writers and others entrenched in literary culture. Part literary, part mystery, part memoir, defiantly experimental, it waves an angry fist against the memoir craze as well as the publishing establishment and much of the American literary canon. Clarke's novel seems to delight in the very things he's skewering.

"This book questions what's important about literature," says Chuck Adams, Clarke's Algonquin editor. "Is it the words that are written or the aura of the writer? I think burning down the houses of great writers addresses that."

An Arsonist's Guide makes an unflinching statement about memoirists and their role in the publishing universe. Clarke's earnest, likable, yet bumbling protagonist, Sam Pulsifer, debates the merits of memoirs even as he dubiously plots to write one of his own.

> "I don't understand why you had to steal the story in the first place. Why didn't you go out and do something on your own and then write a book about it?" I'd been in the Book Warehouse, after all, and knew that it could be done. As far as I could tell from the memoir section, if you were a memoirist, you did something—anything—only so that you could write a book about it afterward.

In light of the James Frey and O.J. Simpson publishing messes, this timely criticism of the memoir form strikes an unnerving chord and challenges writers and publishers to stare at some harsh truths. "Brock feels there's an awful lot of truth telling going on—in the form of memoirs—and an awful lot of people who are selling themselves in memoirs," Adams says. "They've so completely blurred the line between fact and fiction."

It seems counterintuitive that the literary establishment powers-that-be would embrace this prodding, and yet, they have. The book has received more glowing reviews than any novel in recent memory.

Adams says when he first read the manuscript of *An Arsonist's Guide*, he realized that it could have that rare bridge potential to be a literary work that also appeals to a wide audience and gains commercial success.

"I just fell in love with the voice," Adams says. "Brock created a character that I immediately fell in love with. I think everyone has a bit of the bumbler inside. I'm always looking for books that have commercial potential and that are really well written. This book is so unusual, and it says something; it really has a point of view."

Adams says readers have had passionate feelings about *An Arsonist's Guide*—they love it or hate it. In fact, he says half the editors at Algonquin Books strongly disliked the book when he acquired it.

"It pushes people's buttons," he says. "I think there's going to be a large young following for this book. It reminded me of Joseph Heller or John Irving. It's an angry, serious book, but it's also funny. I do feel this is an important book, and it will live for a long, long time."

FANNING THE FLAME

So just who is the seemingly mild-mannered author/professor who's setting the literary world aflame? Clarke has been an assistant professor of English at the University of Cincinnati since 2001 and serves as editor of UC's *The Cincinnati Review* literary journal. He contributes to a wide variety of literary journals including *The Virginia Quarterly Review, The Believer, Tin House,* and *The Southern Review.* He's also published two short story collections: *What We Won't Do* and *Carrying the Torch.*

His debut novel, *The Ordinary White Boy,* had the misfortune of being released on September 11, 2001, and fizzled along with nearly every other novel that was released on or around that time.

But even though he's a professor/author, Clarke isn't one to stress over the university professor's imperative to publish. "I've always felt that if I just sat down and did my writing every day, it would take care of itself," he says. He writes at home, nine to noon, six or seven days a week. "I'm always pecking away at something," he says. "After a while, you don't feel right if you don't do your writing every day."

He likes the social interaction and structure that teaching brings and says that being a creative writing teacher informs his own writing. "I find that whatever it is I'm criticizing in my students' work, I often go back to my own writing and find that I'm trying to work through the same problem."

Clarke calls himself a terrible researcher. He set *An Arsonist's Guide* in the decaying industrial New England towns that he already knew well enough to describe vividly. He'd been to Emily Dickinson's house years before, as a student at nearby Dickinson College in Pennsylvania.

While writing *An Arsonist's Guide*, he'd pen a short story when he got stuck. The seed for the novel, in fact, sprung from a short story, "She Loved to Cook but Not Like This," which was published in *The New England Review* in 2000. He felt the theme was underdeveloped and that there was much more territory to explore in his story about a boy who burns down a house. "I couldn't get the story out of my head," he says.

All the while, the memoir craze was simmering and he was thinking about the memoir form and why people read books and love stories and seem to canonize certain authors. He started pulling together these complex themes into what he felt at first was a harshly satirical novel. Clarke didn't much like the way the book was headed in his first draft. "It was too satirical," he says. "It felt dead and bloodless." He turned to his favorite satirists—Mark Twain and Jonathan Swift—writers who were deft at weaving satire into a story. And he went about rewriting the manuscript, creating a more likable, and more sympathetic, character.

You have to keep one important thing in mind when writing satire, Clarke says: "If you're going to make fun of people, you have to be able to make fun of yourself."

A case in point and telling meta-fiction aside is a scene from *An Arsonist's Guide* in which the protagonist picks up *The Ordinary White Boy* (Clarke's first novel) and finds it lacking.

PUBLICITY WILDFIRE

In keeping with *An Arsonist's Guide*'s satiric sensibility and devil-may-care attitude, the novel also launched a shockingly provocative publicity stunt. Last spring, Algonquin Books embarked on a decidedly unconventional publicity campaign for the book.

"Publicists have to get more and more creative, more over-the-top, to promote books now," Clarke says. "Over-the-top" may be an understatement to describe the publicity to launch his book.

At his publicist's request, and in what all concerned felt was undertaken in the spirit of the book, Clarke wrote letters to support the publicity effort. "Brock was game right away," says Michael Taeckens, publicity director for Algonquin Books. "We wanted to do something creative, unique, funny, and slightly askew to resemble the tone of the novel. Letters play a crucial role in *An Arsonist's Guide*, so the campaign seemed like a natural fit."

Reviewers took notice. Ron Charles, for example, began his glowing review in *The Washington Post Book World* with a mention of the campaign.

Charles wrote: "A few months ago, book section editors around the country received a letter on quaint stationery from Beatrice Hutchins. She wanted someone to burn down Edith Wharton's house. Naturally, the good people who care for The Mount, Wharton's stately mansion in Lenox, Mass., contacted the police. But it turned out to be a publicity stunt by Algonquin Books, a small publisher in Chapel Hill, N.C., trying to ignite some interest in Brock Clarke's upcoming novel."

In a remark that aptly sums up the quirky nature of Clarke's novel, Charles wrote: "Some people have no sense of humor when it comes to great literature. Or arson."

 MARIA SCHNEIDER is the former editor of *Writer's Digest.*

PERMISSIONS

Permissions

INDEX

The Complete Handbook of Novel Writing